Praise for Enterprise Services with the .NET Framework

"For anyone involved in the .NET community, it's hard to not have heard of Christian Nagel. Christian is a true heavyweight of .NET in general, and Enterprise Services in particular. By taking a relatively trivial application and architecting it in a way that would allow it to scale without any rework, users will find that using the techniques employed in this book will be of benefit to virtually any company that is running distributed or enterprise applications."

—William G. Ryan, Microsoft MVP, Senior
Software Developer, TiBA Soutions, LLC

"Whether you are a seasoned architect or a new developer, distributed application development can be difficult, since it covers such a wide range of complex technologies. Until now there was precious little in the way of guidance—let alone a consolidated reference. Christian has provided that reference and more—going from the individual technologies to the big picture on how to architect and develop scalable distributed applications. Technical goodness through and through!"

—Clayton Burt, Managing Partner, Onzo, LLC

"Making the transition to distributed application architecture introduces many issues in security and deployment and requires a new way of thinking about events, transactions, and messaging. This book shows developers and architects alike how to use .NET Enterprise Services to create robust, secure, and maintainable applications in a distributed environment. This book is an excellent guide to the sometimes overwhelming field of .NET Enterprise Services."

—Brian Davis, Director of Software Development,
InfoPro Group, Inc., Co-Creator, KnowDotNet.com

Enterprise Services with the .NET Framework

Microsoft .NET Development Series

John Montgomery, Series Advisor
Don Box, Series Advisor
Martin Heller, Series Editor

The Microsoft .NET Development Series   is supported and developed by the leaders and experts of Microsoft development technologies including Microsoft architects and DevelopMentor instructors. The books in this series provide a core resource of information and understanding every developer needs in order to write effective applications and managed code. Learn from the leaders how to maximize your use of the .NET Framework and its programming languages.

Titles in the Series

Brad Abrams, .NET Framework Standard Library Annotated Reference Volume 0-321-15489-4

Keith Ballinger, .NET Web Services: Architecture and Implementation 0-321-11359-4

Bob Beauchemin, Niels Berglund, Dan Sullivan, A First Look at SQL Server 2005 for Developers 0-321-18059-3

Don Box with Chris Sells, Essential.NET, Volume 1: The Common Language Runtime 0-201-73411-7

Keith Brown, The .NET Developer's Guide to Windows Security 0-321-22835-9

Mahesh Chand, Graphics Programming with GDI+, 0-321-16077-0

Anders Hejlsberg, Scott Wiltamuth, Peter Golde, The C# Programming Language 0-321-15491-6

Alex Homer, Dave Sussman, Rob Howard, ASP.NET v. 2.0—The Beta Version, 0-321-25727-8

James S. Miller and Susann Ragsdale, The Common Language Infrastructure Annotated Standard 0-321-15493-2

Fritz Onion, Essential ASP.NET with Examples in C# 0-201-76040-1

Fritz Onion, Essential ASP.NET with Examples in Visual Basic .NET 0-201-76039-8

Ted Pattison and Dr. Joe Hummel, Building Applications and Components with Visual Basic .NET 0-201-73495-8

Dr. Neil Roodyn, eXtreme .NET: Introducing eXtreme Programming Techniques to .NET Developers 0-321-30363-6

Chris Sells, Windows Forms Programming in C#, 0-321-11620-8

Chris Sells and Justin Gehtland, Windows Forms Programming in Visual Basic .NET 0-321-12519-3

Paul Vick, The Visual Basic .NET Programming Language 0-321-16951-4

Damien Watkins, Mark Hammond, Brad Abrams, Programming in the .NET Environment 0-201-77018-0

Shawn Wildermuth, Pragmatic ADO.NET: Data Access for the Internet World 0-201-74568-2

Paul Yao and David Durant, .NET Compact Framework Programming with C#, 0-321-17403-8

Paul Yao and David Durant, .NET Compact Framework Programming with Visual Basic .NET 0-321-17404-6

For more information go to www.awprofessional.com/msdotnetseries/

Enterprise Services with the .NET Framework

Developing Distributed Business Solutions with .NET Enterprise Services

■ Christian Nagel

▼▼ **Addison-Wesley**

Upper Saddle River, NJ • Boston • Indianapolis • San Francisco
New York • Toronto • Montreal • London • Munich • Paris • Madrid
Capetown • Sydney • Tokyo • Singapore • Mexico City

The publisher offers excellent discounts on this book when ordered in quantity for bulk purchases or special sales, which may include electronic versions and/or custom covers and content particular to your business, training goals, marketing focus, and branding interests. For more information, please contact:

U. S. Corporate and Government Sales
(800) 382-3419
corpsales@pearsontechgroup.com

For sales outside the U. S., please contact:

International Sales
international@pearsoned.com

This Book Is Safari Enabled

The Safari® Enabled icon on the cover of your favorite technology book means the book is available through Safari Bookshelf. When you buy this book, you get free access to the online edition for 45 days. Safari Bookshelf is an electronic reference library that lets you easily search thousands of technical books, find code samples, download chapters, and access technical information whenever and wherever you need it.

To gain 45-day Safari Enabled access to this book:
- Go to http://www.awprofessional.com /safarienabled
- Complete the brief registration form
- Enter the coupon code YIMO-T6LM-DV8X-W7MI-AYFB

If you have difficulty registering on Safari Bookshelf or accessing the online edition, please e-mail customer-service@safaribooksonline.com.

Visit us on the Web: www.awprofessional.com

Library of Congress Catalog Number: 2005923698

ISBN 0-321-24673-X
Text printed in the United States on recycled paper at R.R. Donnelley in Crawfordsville, Indiana.
First printing, June 2005

Contents

About the Author

CHRISTIAN NAGEL is a software architect, trainer, consultant, and associate of Thinktecture, offering training and coaching of Microsoft .NET technologies. For his achievements in the developer community he was named Microsoft Regional Director and MVP for Visual C#. He enjoys an excellent reputation as an author of several .NET books, including *Professional C#* (Wrox 2004), *Pro .NET Network Programming* (Apress 2004), and *C# Web Services* (Wrox 2001). He speaks regularly at international industry conferences.

Christian has more than 15 years of experience as a developer and software architect. He started his computing career with PDP 11 and VAX/VMS platforms, covering a variety of languages and platforms. Since 2000 he has been developing and architecting distributed solutions with .NET and C#.

http://www.christiannagel.com
http://www.thinktecture.com

Foreword

CREATING INFRASTRUCTURE-LEVEL CODE TO support complex trans-actional systems (including distributed transactions and even the support for compensating actions instead of simple rollback operations), fine-grained authentication capabilities, a framework for role-based authentication, the transparent support for asynchronous queuing-based interactions, an adaptive threading model, a complete process and control model, and an instrumented hosting environment which supports different levels of indirection (in-process, local, remote) is arguably one of the greatest, most fun, and most challenging things a developer can do. At the same time, it is the very task our customers don't want to see us spending time on. After all, it can hardly be said that developing these features will advance the paying customer's business in any way. One could even say that the manual implementation of all these features would fail a reasonable build-versus-buy analysis. They *should* be a commodity and not something you would have to create manually.

This is where Enterprise Services enters the game. It—especially the underlying COM+ framework—is an integral part of Microsoft's *application server* offering, which provides these features. Yes, Microsoft hasn't been talking too much about their operating system as an application server, but this is essentially what the server editions of Windows have become. We are not talking about file or print servers anymore. Today, Windows systems (and this even includes Windows CE up to a certain point) come with built-in components which would be called—and separately sold as—an *application server* were they developed on other platforms.

On the Windows platform, however, these application server components do not always live on the main stage. As they are essentially *free* modules of Windows systems, no conscious decision of whether or not they should be bought has to be made. They are *just there*. They are the ultimate commodity.

Unfortunately, I have noticed in the past years that only a few developers have spent time looking into these commoditized services as a base for their application's architecture. Most engineers still tend to solve the basic problems outlined above on their own. That would not necessarily be a bad thing, apart from the sad fact that it is usually very easy to get, for example, 80 percent of a transaction management system almost right. In my experience, at least, it's only the final 20 percent which can get incredibly harder. And for transactional systems, only the full 100 percent really counts. (Or would you like to go to your customer and explain that, in certain cases, the accounting system you have built is losing data even though it tells the user that everything is okay? I fear this would certainly not be a pleasant experience.) The same tends to be true for security, scalability, queuing, and instrumentation: Only the full 100 percent counts as these are essential infrastructure services.

But it might not be only selective knowledge—omitting the knowledge about COM+ or Enterprise Services—that leads to the reimplementation of infrastructure code like this. Quite the contrary might be true. If you are similar to me, you might like to approach new technology in a rather hands-down way[1]: Go online, get some samples, run them, change them, learn how the system reacts, dig deeper, learn, and understand. Unfortunately, Enterprise Services doesn't necessarily lead itself to this way of development. When you create your first component marked with [assembly: ApplicationActivation(ActivationOption.Server)], you will immediately notice that there is more going on under the hood than you might have thought in the first place.

Please let me speak a word of caution in this regard: The Enterprise Services framework provides very simple access to implementations of a very

---

[1] This might be the Tim Taylor way of developing: *"Real men don't need instructions."*

complex nature. From time to time, you will therefore need to deal with the complexities of large-scale distributed applications. But that's hardly the fault of the Enterprise Services framework. Instead, it is simply caused by the fact that the creation of large-scale distributed applications itself is a very complex and difficult topic. The combination of Enterprise Service's ease-of-use and its relatively high level of abstraction of a very complex topic leads to a situation in which you will have to know more than you believed you would at first glance. This is why books like this one are so important.

I have known Christian since the early days of .NET. In fact, the days were so early that .NET was still called NGWS (Next Generation of Windows Services) and C# was still codenamed *Cool*. Christian has always been a tremendous author, a remarkable trainer, a smart consultant with real-world experience, a good friend, and a great colleague. There are only a few people in this world who can explain Enterprise Services in reasonable depth—Christian is one of them. It is a true pleasure to see that he found the time to write this book.

Ingo Rammer
Vienna, Austria
http://www.thinktecture.com

Preface

THIS BOOK IS THE RESULT OF MANY years of work. I started developing distributed business solutions on Microsoft platforms when the Microsoft Transaction Server was released in 1996. Since then I have worked on several projects helping customers with the design and implementation of business solutions. I have been asked to do many things—such as integrating existing technologies and creating custom frameworks that can be extended in a flexible way for certain applications.

When Microsoft showed a preview version of .NET at the Professional Developers Conference in 2000 I was really excited about this new technology. Since then I've co-authored many .NET books, including *Professional C#* (Wrox 2004), *Beginning Visual C#* (Wrox 2002), *C# Web Services* (Wrox 2001), and *Prof .NET Network Programming* (Apress 2004).

Many of the things I've learned over the years have been combined to form this book.

Why would you use .NET Enterprise Services? .NET Enterprise Services is the .NET way to use COM+ Services, a technology that is part of the operating system and is used by companies throughout the world. .NET Enterprise Services extends COM+ Services with .NET behavior to make use of this technology. Regardless of whether you use Windows Forms or ASP.NET to create business solutions that have front-end applications, on the server side common features are needed for building scalable and interoperable solutions.

With .NET Enterprise Services you get features such as resource management with object pooling and thread pooling, automatic and distributed transactions, a lose connection between the server and the client for performing callbacks, queued components that can be used as an abstraction layer for message queuing, role-based security, and much more.

Who Should Read this Book?

This book isn't an introduction to .NET programming; there are many other books that fill that role. With this book I assume you already have some knowledge of .NET programming.

Although COM+ is the base of .NET Enterprise Services, COM knowledge is not a requirement for understanding this book or for creating .NET Enterprise Services solutions. However, if you do have COM knowledge and want to integrate existing COM components with .NET applications, this book will provide you with great information.

Organization

This book contains 15 chapters that show the services offered by .NET Enterprise Services. First, this book introduces you to all these services. It then teaches you the fundamentals of Enterprise Services by stepping into the core technologies. Finally, it describes all the services in separate chapters. With each chapter you get an architectural viewpoint of the reasons and usage scenarios of the services and then you dig into the code. After an overview of the technology you will find many code examples, so you not only learn about the features, you also learn how to use them. Throughout the book are tips and tricks that help reveal the best aspects of this technology. The final chapter presents a case study in which different services are combined so you can see them interact in a real-world scenario.

Chapter 1, "Introducing .NET Enterprise Services," provides an overview of the technologies that are related to Enterprise Services. Here you get a clear picture of what technologies you can and should use in your business solutions. A background of the evolution from MTS to COM+ and .NET Enterprise Services helps you better understand these technologies.

Chapter 2, "Object Activation and Context," covers the base technology of COM+ and .NET Enterprise Services. It provides information about how the services are made possible. You also learn about the interception mechanisms. The first serviced components are built in this chapter, and you see contexts and object activation in action.

Chapter 3, "Concurrency," teaches you the basic knowledge of running threads concurrently and how to avoid race conditions and deadlocks. After discussing COM apartment models, the chapter explains COM+ activities. Services Without Components—a new feature with COM+ 1.5— plays an important role in this chapter.

Chapter 4, "COM Interop," is ideal for those who have existing COM components that should be integrated with new .NET serviced components in their business solution. Here you learn the integration of COM and .NET technologies.

Chapter 5, "Networking," provides information about accessing the .NET Enterprise Services application using DCOM, .NET Remoting, and Web services. You will also learn which technologies are preferred based on application context.

Chapter 6, "Data Access," teaches you how to access databases with ADO.NET. This chapter not only provides an introduction to ADO.NET, it also gives you some tips and tricks on how to best use ADO.NET in a distributed environment.

Chapter 7, "Transactions," explains the ACID properties that describe a transaction (Atomicity, Consistency, Isolation, and Durability), shows you how to program transactions with ADO.NET, and describes all the transaction options and settings in .NET Enterprise Services. You'll learn about the functionality of the different features, and how to determine how your components should be configured from a transactional viewpoint.

Chapter 8, "Compensating Resource Manager," demonstrates how you can create your own resource manager that participates with the transactions of the distributed transaction coordinator (DTC).

Chapter 9, "State Management"—should you create stateful or stateless components? Where should you put the state—on the client or on the server? This chapter points out the different options of the state with various application models.

Chapter 10, "Queued Components," is an often overlooked technology with distributed solutions. In this chapter you'll read about the functionality of message queuing, and the abstraction layer Queued Components that makes it possible to invoke methods of components that are automatically converted to messages and thus can be used in a disconnected environment.

Chapter 11, "Loosely Coupled Events," compares COM and .NET event models to the event model that is offered with .NET Enterprise Services. With LCE an interception model is used when the component does not directly interact with the client. You will read about how loosely coupled events can be used in different scenarios, and how filters can be defined.

Chapter 12, "Security," explains authorization, authentication, impersonation, and confidentiality concepts of a distributed solution in regard to Enterprise Services applications. Because many products interact with .NET Enterprise Services in a business solution, this chapter discusses security issues of SQL Server, ASP.NET Web applications, Web services, and .NET Remoting along with the security issues of .NET Enterprise Services itself.

Chapter 13, "Deployment and Configuration," covers how to install and configure server applications and client applications with the proxies that access the serviced components.

Chapter 14, "The Future of Distributed Applications," provides information about upcoming technologies, and how you can prepare for them in your applications today.

Chapter 15, "Case Study" is a roundup of the technologies covered in the previous chapters. It combines their features to build an application that includes technologies from the client side to the database so you can see many .NET Enterprise Services features in collaboration.

Sample Code

The sample code in this book is C#—although in Chapter 4 you can find C++, Visual Basic, and JavaScript code, which demonstrates COM interop. You can download the sample code from the book's website: http://www.christiannagel.com/EnterpriseServices. A Visual Basic .NET version of the code is also available on the website.

Contact

If you have feedback about this book or you want training and/or consulting with .NET Enterprise Services and Web services, you can contact me through my website: http://www.christiannagel.com.

Feedback is always welcome!

Christian Nagel
http://www.christiannagel.com
http://www.thinktecture.com

Acknowledgments

THIS BOOK WOULD HAVE BEEN IMPOSSIBLE for me to complete alone, and so here I want to express my thanks to every single helping hand.

My first special thanks goes to my wife, Elisabeth, for her ongoing support in organizing her "not always easy" husband and for her ability to understand the big picture. She has always made it possible for me to pursue my goals. She helped me organize the startup of my new company, and she was the first to read all the chapters of this book. Although Elisabeth is not familiar with the programming specifics, she did a great job helping with the English grammar. Many times, my thoughts outpaced my ability to write clearly; Elisabeth pointed out areas that needed clarification and provided invaluable input as to the final wording of this text.

Special thanks goes to Dave Sussman, who polished the English for this book. I have read many of Dave and Al's great books, and whenever we meet each other at international conferences, I enjoy every minute of exchanging thoughts and opinions.

Sincere thanks is also given to Don Box, who influenced my work many years ago when I joined his COM presentations. I have always been fascinated by his unique way of presenting technologies and by his ability to hold his audience spellbound.

I am very proud that Addison-Wesley has published this book, and I express my special thanks to the great people in this company, especially to Karen Gettman, Joan Murray, Stephane Thomas, Jessica D'Amico, Ebony Haight, Michael Mullen, Keith Cline, and Michael Thurston.

Without the excellent job of my reviewers—Mario Szpuszta, Christian Weyer, Sam Gentile, Trond Borg, Chris Mitchell, Burt Clayton, Brian Davis, and Brian Geary—this book would not be what it is. Thanks to everybody for all your contributions.

1
Introducing .NET Enterprise Services

APPLICATION DEVELOPMENT HAS CHANGED OVER the past few years, and developers can now concentrate more on the tasks that should be performed rather than technology issues. ASP.NET and Windows Forms offer complex **user interface** (UI) elements that you can use instead of writing them yourself. Likewise, Microsoft .NET Enterprise Services offers a higher level of abstraction. You no longer need to write code to create a custom object pool, to implement an event mechanism, or to create a security infrastructure (all of which had to be done before application servers became available). .NET Enterprise Services offers applications these kind of server features that you can use declaratively by applying attributes to methods, interfaces, classes, and assemblies. This chapter examines when it is useful to apply the functionality offered by .NET Enterprise Services to applications.

Specifically, this chapter covers the following topics:

- Building applications, including an overview of these services (which are discussed in detail throughout the rest of this book) and a comparison of two-tier and multitier applications (which will help you understand the role of .NET Enterprise Services in modern application development)

- The history of application services, showing how COM+ Services has evolved into the .NET Enterprise Services of today (which will help you understand the functionality and interoperability of .NET Enterprise Services)

- .NET Enterprise Services, covering some important terms related to this technology

- Application services, covering the major services the .NET Enterprise Services provides

Building Applications

To enable developers to create data-driven applications easily and quickly, Visual Studio offers (for both Windows and Web applications) controls such as `SqlData-Connection`, `SqlDataAdapter`, `DataView`, and `DataSet`. Not only do these provide great functionality, but they are also easy to use because you can drag and drop them from the toolbox to the forms designer, as shown in Figure 1-1. You can bind datagrids to dataset objects to display and to edit data, which means you can build data-driven applications that allow viewing and editing of data within just a matter of minutes.

Easy and fast development has been possible for some time already using earlier Visual Basic versions. And so, you might be asking yourself what is wrong with this simple way of creating applications. Maybe nothing; it depends. For very simple

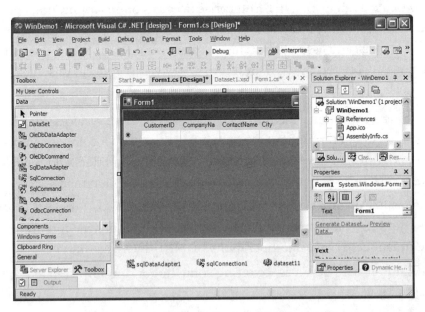

Figure 1-1   Developing a data-driven application with Visual Studio.

applications, with a small number of users, rapid development can be the most productive way to build applications. However, with even just a little more of a complex application, rapid development might not be the most productive way, as you will see soon.

Many Visual Basic 6 applications had a similar application model. The UI, business logic, and data access code were written into the client application, with a direct connection to the database server, as shown in Figure 1-2.

It is very easy to build these two-tier applications. However, problems exist with such application architectures:

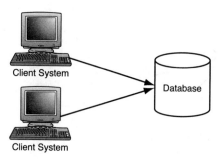

Figure 1-2   Two-tier applications.

- The application does not scale to hundreds or thousands of users. With more and more users, the only option is to replace the database server with a faster system. All users are connected to the database, so a lot of resources are needed.

- If the business logic changes, the application must be redistributed to all client systems. With .NET, redistribution is a lot easier via ClickOnce deployment; however, you must ensure that all client applications are redeployed simultaneously when the business requirements change.

- Database drivers must be installed and maintained on the client systems.

- Database connections cannot be shared among multiple users. Every client needs a separate connection to the database.

- With such client applications, you often need a connection within the **local area network** (LAN). After all, you must consider multination companies.

- A simple two-tier application is not operational if it is on a laptop system that is disconnected from the corporate network.
- It is difficult to split working on the code among multiple developers. For example, the UI programmer might change the business logic quite unintentionally.
- Reusing code among multiple applications is not possible.

Consider a simple business scenario: ordering a course for a customer who is already registered within your course management system. Which possibilities do you have to build a solution for this use case? Figure 1-3 shows the use case diagram of this scenario.

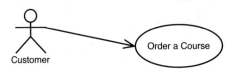

Figure 1-3   Use case.

Under this scenario, you must present a list of courses to the customer, and then the customer can choose one course and register for it. During the registration, not only must the participants entered by the customer be added to the list of attendees, but the customer balance also must be reduced by the course price—and if the customer does not already have a balance available, a receipt has to be prepared. This scenario requires you to add some business logic to the process. You can do so by using custom components. The components are part of a business process, so call them **business components**. Instead of implementing the code accessing the database directly in the UI forms classes, these components are used from the UI, and the data access components serve the role of accessing the database.

Application Layers

In this scenario, for reuse and scalability, you should separate the functionality of the application into the application layers, shown in Figure 1-4.

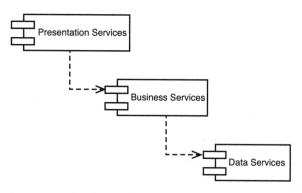

Figure 1-4   Application layers.

Presentation Services

The role of the presentation layer is to offer a UI that displays to the user. With .NET technologies, you can implement presentation services using rich client applications with Windows Forms or thin clients with ASP.NET Web Forms.

Windows Forms offer a rich user experience in which you can use the processing power of the client systems. With rich client applications, many round trips to the server are not required, because you can build a lot of functionality in to the application running on the client system. In contrast to previous technologies where installing such applications was a headache for the system administrators in a big user environment, you can seamlessly install client applications with .NET; only the .NET runtime is required on the client system.

You just have to include a link inside an HTML page referencing a Windows Forms application on the Web server to install the application on the client system. This technology is known as **ClickOnce deployment** (formerly known as **no-touch deployment**). When the user opens the page with Internet Explorer[1] and clicks the link that references the Windows Forms application, the application is automatically installed on the client system. While the application is running, it can check for updates on the server to download new assemblies dynamically.

With ClickOnce deployment, you just have to think about the security configuration. By default, what can be done on the client system—if the assembly is installed from the Internet—is very restrictive. Applications do not have permissions to harm your computer.

Rich clients can also install applications in the usual way via Windows Installer on the client system but use an automatic update by receiving new assemblies from a Web service.

Business Services

Instead of mixing the business logic directly with the code of the UI, you can separate the business logic into its own classes. Putting these classes into separate assemblies makes it easy to reuse the business logic from multiple parts of the application and in other applications.

In the previously described scenario, you can first separate the UI from a business component that is responsible for ordering courses. The course order requires a combination of activities: creating a receipt and adding the attendees to the course list. You can split these activities into multiple components, `CourseControl` and `ReceiptControl`, as shown in Figure 1-5. These components can also be used from other parts of the application or from other applications.

Business components can make use of Enterprise Services. As you learn in this chapter about the various services this technology offers, you can decide whether you can improve your application via these services.

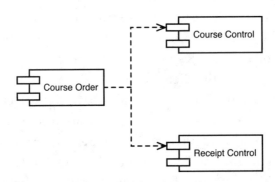

Figure 1-5 Business components.

Data Services

Data service components written with .NET can use ADO.NET to access relational databases and hierarchical data such as XML. Similar to business components, data access components can be reused from different parts of the application and with other applications. Data access components can also get great use out of Enterprise Services (for example, automatic transactions). In the example scenario, multiple components that should participate within a single transaction are used. Instead of passing the transaction as an argument to the method calls, automatic transactions pay attention to the fact that either all components succeed with their work, or none of that happens.

Advantages of Multiple Tiers

Getting back to the list presented earlier about the disadvantages of using business and data access logic from within the UI classes, what about the same items with an application design using multiple tiers? Consider the following:

- With components separated into UI, business, and data components, the application can scale to hundreds or thousands of users. You have the option to use all these components on a single system with a small number of users, but you can also distribute the components among multiple systems. The following scenarios assume that the business components are running on a middle-tier server.

- If the business logic changes, you do not have to redistribute the application to all clients when the business components are running on server systems. You only have to update the server systems.

- You do not have to install and maintain database drivers on the client systems, because the database access happens from the data components (which may run on a middle-tier server).

- Database connections can be shared among multiple users, because the connections are not done directly from the client system, but from a middle-tier server.

- You can partition the application in such a way that clients can run on slow networks in different countries (while others use a LAN, for example).

- If you use message queuing technologies, the application can be operated in a disconnected environment (for example, on a laptop system or on a Pocket PC).

- By separating the application into multiple components, you can facilitate the division of the work among multiple developers.
- You can reuse code among multiple applications.

The preceding list seems to indicate only advantages to multitier applications, but this is not the case. Unlike a simple application, you expend more effort needed building a multitier application. Multitier applications do require less effort in the long term, however, allowing reuse of the components and easier maintenance and deployment.

Logical Tiers and Physical Systems

Separating the application into multiple logical tiers does not require the use of multiple systems. Logical tiers can be seen completely independent of the physical deployment of the solution. In a small environment with a few users, for example, the .NET Enterprise Services applications together with the databases can run on a single system, as shown in Figure 1-6.

With more and more users, it is not only possible to **scale up** with a system that has more and faster CPUs and a lot of memory, but it is also easy to **scale out** by adding multiple machines. Not only is it possible to separate the database from the system running the .NET Enterprise Services application, but you can also split the .NET Enterprise Services application among multiple servers, as shown in Figure 1-7.

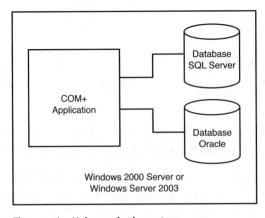

Figure 1-6   Using a single system.

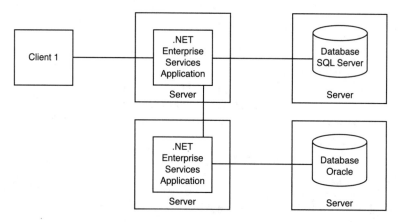

Figure 1-7 Scale out with multiple systems.

Clustering Solutions

.NET Enterprise Services is scalable to really big solutions. With an ASP.NET Web application, you can use multiple Web servers for **network load balancing** (NLB). Contrary to its predecessor, ASP, ASP.NET has special support for such a scenario in which sessions are supported across multiple Web sites with a session server. The ASP.NET application can use business components that are distributed across multiple systems or **component load balancing** (CLB). From these components, the SQL Server database can be accessed. With SQL Server, you can use the feature of **cluster services** for automatic failover in case one of the database systems fails. To avoid disk errors, you can use a RAID system for redundancy in case of disk failures. The **Microsoft Application Center** enables you to manage such a solution. Microsoft Application Center is a deployment and management tool from Microsoft to manage groups of servers as if they were a single server. Figure 1-8 illustrates such a solution.

Service-Oriented Architecture

Today it is impossible to discuss application architectures without talking about **service-oriented architecture** (SOA). SOA is a natural evolution of application architectures.

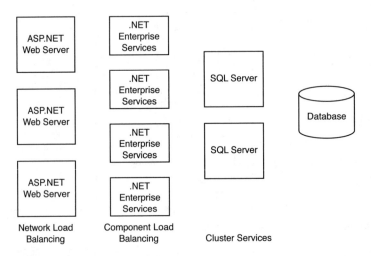

Figure 1-8   Clustering solutions.

In the past, programs were written using functional decomposition. Using functions in the programs made it possible to reuse code and made it easier to read (in contrast to just a single large code block). However, programs began to become more and more complex. With functional decomposition, it was not easy to find out what functions changed what data. To deal with these issues, **object-oriented programming** was invented. In object-oriented programming, objects contain functions in addition to data. Object-oriented programming relies on the concepts of **abstraction**, **encapsulation**, and **inheritance**. Abstraction means that only the relevant parts of an object are looked at, and all attributes not important for the solution are ignored. Encapsulation means that data and methods are coupled inside a class, and that data is hidden from outside access. With inheritance, classes can be reused and extended.

Programs are still getting more and more complex, and reuse is still not as easy as originally thought. New applications do not run on a single system but require information from different systems that may be spread across different organizations. SOA adds another level of abstraction.

The heart of SOA is a Web service. With SOA, a service layer is added between the client (consumer) and the business objects. The service layer is a **boundary** that decouples the consumer from the business objects; it defines a **contract** that is used by the consumer to get functionality from the service (see Figure 1-9). The service completely controls its data and denies the outside world direct access.

The only way to access the services is by sending **messages**. Messages are sent in the **SOAP**[2] **format**. This makes the message independent of the platform. Messages arriving at the service are validated against security policies and business rules. Using messages rather than method calls makes this architecture independent of the technology and versioning issues of the business logic.

The consumer can use an agent that makes it easier to access the service (because the agent knows the business rules of the service, and so it can cache data, keep session state, and so on).

With SOA, object-oriented programming is not dead: When creating object-oriented applications, developers still often use functional decomposition within objects. The same can be said of SOA: Within services, developers use objects.

Along with Web services, using .NET Enterprise Services for business objects is a good option.

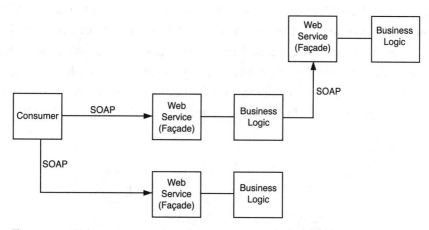

Figure 1-9 Web services as a boundary.

Smart Clients

Now it is time to consider the client application. A special version of a rich client application is a smart client application. When using a smart client, you can work independently of a server application (for example, using a laptop that is disconnected from the network). Microsoft Outlook 2003 is a good example of a smart client application. With Outlook 2003, all data is stored on the client system and is synchronized with the Exchange Server when the server is available. The user does not have to manually connect to and disconnect from the server; the connect/disconnect occurs automatically behind the scenes. Outlook 2003 caches all e-mail from the user on the client. If the user searches for an e-mail, writes new e-mail, or adds calendar information, it is all done locally. As soon as the Exchange Server is available, all the data is synchronized. The synchronization happens in both directions: Newly arrived e-mail is synchronized from the server to the client, while user edits are synchronized from the client to the server.

A smart client is "smart" to its users insofar as the user can work seamlessly in a disconnected distributed environment. To make this possible, the client application itself needs a data layer to write information to a local data store. The local data store can consist of simple XML files up to a local database, where the **Microsoft Data Engine** (MSDE) might be a good choice.

Figure 1-10 shows the layers that are needed on the client system with a smart client application. A smart client usually needs presentation, business, and data layers on the client system. These layers are used to cache data and synchronize it with the server system where the business and data layers are available, too. The business and data services can have a different implementation on the client and server systems; for example, the data layer on the client can use XML files or the MSDE to store

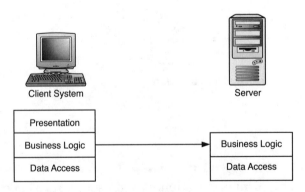

Figure 1-10 **Smart client layers.**

data, whereas the server system uses the features of a full-blown database such as Microsoft SQL Server. Serviced components can be used on both the client and the server.

The History of Application Services

To understand the concepts and functionality of .NET Enterprise Services, you need to know something about the history of this technology, which has its roots in the **Microsoft Transaction Server** (MTS). With both MTS and the follow-on product, **COM+ Services**, COM objects have been used that take advantage of the COM+ Services functionality. Nowadays, COM objects can be used together with .NET components that use these services. .NET Enterprise Services offers some features for coexistence of COM and .NET to make a smooth transition possible. Because of the origins of .NET Enterprise Services, a lot of characteristics of .NET Enterprise Services are based on the COM technology. Some knowledge of COM knowledge will not only help you integrate .NET components in a COM solution, but it will also give you an understanding of the roots of this technology.

COM and .NET

In November 1997, a *Microsoft Systems Journal* article discussed potential COM enhancements. These ideas never made it into COM, but instead they appeared with .NET. Although .NET originated from COM, some problems surfaced either because of historical extensions or because of some system deficiencies, so a lot of things were changed. The following sections examine COM and .NET similarities and differences.

Language Support

You can write COM components in a lot of different languages. One of the goals of COM was to have support for and coexistence of multiple languages. This goal was reached by using interfaces, and the COM specification defined the memory layout of the methods in the interfaces.

With COM, you can write objects with languages such as Visual Basic, C++, J++, Delphi, and many more. A language different from the one used to write the COM object can instantiate it and invoke methods and properties. If you write a COM object with C++, however, you have no guarantee that the object can be used from Visual Basic or VBScript. For such a guarantee, you must design the interface in such a way that it can be used from the target client language. To write COM components for a Visual Basic client, you must restrict the interfaces to automation-compatible data types, the data types that Visual Basic clients can understand. And doing so does not guarantee that a VBScript client can use such an object. A scripting client may have different restrictions: VBScript can only use one IDispatch[3] interface, for example. A scripting client cannot use multiple interfaces, and it cannot use other interfaces.

When writing a COM component, you must be aware of every client language that will be used to access the component. Supporting both scripting and compiled client languages in an optimal way requires significant programming effort. Whole books have been written dealing just with this subject.

As with COM, you can use many programming languages to write and access .NET components. However, there is a big difference: .NET has a **Common Language Specification** (CLS) that defines the minimum requirements a language must support. If you restrict the public and protected methods and properties of a class to the data types defined in this specification, it is guaranteed that every .NET-supported language can use the component.

The assembly attribute [CLSCompliant(true)][4] marks the assembly as CLS compliant, and the compiler can check whether the methods and properties are indeed compliant. With Visual Studio .NET 2003, both the Visual Basic .NET and C# compilers check whether the public and protected access of the class are CLS compliant if the attribute [CLSCompliant()] is applied, but the C++ compiler does not.

Object Lifetime Management

In the COM world, the lifetime of objects is managed with a reference count for every interface. The COM object must be aware of every variable that is used with the interface. If an interface is referenced, you must increment the reference count. If the variable referencing the interface is not needed anymore, you have to decrement the reference count. As soon as the reference count of all interfaces goes to zero, the object can destroy itself. Memory leaks are produced if you forget to release references to COM objects.

COM not only causes troubles if you forget to release references: You also face the problem of circular references. If two or more objects reference themselves but cannot be accessed from outside, they are released only when the process ends.

With .NET, a garbage collector handles memory management (in contrast to the COM reference count principle). For this reason, memory under .NET is often referred to as managed—you do not have to worry as much about memory leaks[5] because the garbage collector ensures that unused objects are destroyed.

Metadata

Metadata describes an assembly and all types within it. When building a .NET assembly, the description of all classes, methods, and parameters is written as metadata into the assembly. The predecessor of the .NET metadata is the COM type library. Similar to the .NET metadata, the type library describes the interfaces, methods, and parameters. The difference is that the .NET metadata is extensible. When you are building COM objects with C++, not all required information might make it into the type library, because the type library syntax does not accept all ways in which interfaces can be described for a C++ component. With COM, the type library is optional, and with C++ clients, it is not always used. With .NET, the metadata is required.

Inheritance

In COM, interfaces can derive from other interfaces. However, inheriting from COM objects is not possible—that is, you cannot have implementation inheritance. When writing COM objects with C++, you can use inheritance with the C++ classes, inheriting the interfaces, but not with the implementation of those classes. C++ inheritance requires that the base and derived classes all be written in C++.

.NET makes it possible to derive .NET classes from other .NET classes, irrespective of the language. .NET supports implementation inheritance. The base class can be written with C#, whereas the derived class can be written with Visual Basic .NET. .NET also allows implementation inheritance, which is when deriving from classes in the Framework.

Late Binding

COM has different interface types to be implemented by COM objects and used by clients. With a `vtable` interface, the client has to know in advance the methods and properties offered by the interface. With a `vtable` interface, **early binding** is always used—the client must know the methods at compile time. With `IDispatch` interfaces, you can find out a reference to the implementation at runtime. The client just needs a method name and passes the method name to the `IDispatch` interface to find out a reference to the implementation at runtime; this is known as **late binding**.

With .NET, you can do late binding with the reflection mechanism. With reflection, you can create objects and invoke methods dynamically by reading the metadata from the assembly.

Threading

COM offers automatic synchronization for COM objects, achieved with the help of so-called apartments. An **apartment** is a logical context that maps threads and COM objects. A thread creates an apartment or enters an existing apartment, and a COM object marks the apartment type it wants to live in with the COM configuration in the registry.

The different apartment names and configuration information used with COM apartments are not easy to understand. This confusion has arisen as new features and operating system versions have emerged:

- In Windows NT 3.1, all COM objects of one process were accessed only by a single thread. Synchronization was done using Windows message queues. Programmatic synchronization was not necessary. At that time, the term *apartment* did not exist for COM objects; instead, the term *context* was used. Today, objects with such a behavior are running only in the first **single-threaded apartment** (STA). In the registry, such objects don't have an entry for the apartment type.

- Windows NT 3.51 added the single-threaded apartment (STA) type for synchronized access. Similar to the behavior of Windows NT 3.1, synchronization is not needed for instance methods and properties, because only one thread can access the object. With this change, multiple apartments can coexist inside one process. Therefore, multiple COM object can live in the same apartment. Different objects can be accessed concurrently, so access to static members and global variables must be synchronized. This behavior increased COM scalability. The necessary registry configuration entry is `ThreadingModel = Apartment` to get such a behavior.

- **Multithreaded apartments** (MTAs) were added with Windows NT 4. Here multiple threads can access the COM object by living in such an apartment concurrently. This model is the most scalable, but it requires programmatic synchronization. A COM object that wants to live in such an apartment defines the registry entry `ThreadingModel = Free`.

  Crossing apartments incurs some overhead because a thread switch is needed. If the thread accessing the COM object just enlists within an STA, and the COM object defines an MTA, the MTA is created automatically. However, performance degradation happens when crossing apartments. To be best prepared for such scenarios, the object can be marked with the registry entry `ThreadingModel = Both`, which means the object is completely happy either with an STA or an MTA.

- Windows 2000 added another apartment type: **thread-neutral apartments** (TNAs). This apartment type is only available for COM objects that are configured with COM+. The synchronization issue that was the major idea with COM apartments moved out from this model to a COM+ service. Instead of having the synchronization within the apartment, COM+ **activities**[6] are used.

  You can have automatic synchronization by using activities with TNAs. In contrast to STAs, the object accessing the TNA object can be on a different thread. (With STAs, the same thread is used to access the object.) This has a big advantage over STA because TNA objects do have a lot more scalability, but without the additional programming work that needs to be done with MTAs.

  The registry entry for TNA objects is `ThreadingModel = Neutral`, or `ThreadingModel = Both` for objects that are happy with STA, MTA, and TNA.

With pure .NET applications, the apartment concept is not used; instead, multi-threading is the default.

You can read a lot more about synchronization and apartments in Chapter 3, "Concurrency."

Configuration

COM components must be configured in the registry. With .NET, component registration is not necessary. All information needed about the component can be found within the assembly—in the metadata. With a .NET component, installation can occur with a simple XCOPY deployment.

When you're using .NET components with .NET Enterprise Services, XCOPY deployment is still possible—but the client application needs to run with administrative privileges. Therefore, you do not have this option for production systems. You learn how to deal with this issue in Chapter 2, "Object Activation and Contexts," and in Chapter 13, "Deployment and Configuration."

Error Handling

In COM, error handling was defined so that every COM method must return a value of type HRESULT. With an HRESULT, one bit defines a success or failure. The other bits define more information about success or failure.

Instead of a return type for errors, .NET uses exceptions. An exception can be generated by throwing an object of a type that is derived from the class Exception.

Handling exceptions is much more flexible because exception handlers can be nested, multiple exception types can be dealt with depending on their class hierarchy, and the place to handle the exception can be near the failing methods or in a common place.

Now that you know the similarities and differences between COM and .NET, it is time to turn your focus to the predecessors of .NET Enterprise Services.

Microsoft Transaction Server

An **application server** allows hosting and managing of business components and offers services that can be used declaratively. The first application server was the

Microsoft Transaction Server (MTS). Version 2 of MTS was published in 1997 with the Windows NT 4.0 Option Pack.

The big idea behind this product was to make it easy for developers to use services that are offered from the operating system, such as transaction management. With only declarative attributes, it is possible to get some intercepting code so that you do not have to write it yourself.

Figure 1-11 shows an example of components configured with MTS. Object A has the declaration `Transaction=Not Supported`, and object B is marked with `Transaction=Required`. Because of these different requirements, object A needs a different context[7] than object B. With objects that require a different context, a proxy is used for the interaction. If object A invokes a method in object B, a proxy is used, and this proxy can invoke some intercepting code that is offered by a service. With object C that has the same requirements as object A, no proxy is used; object C is called directly.

Because COM was the Microsoft object model of that time, MTS was based on COM and extended it. COM already had, like MTS, some interception concepts (as you have seen with apartments). Depending on the configuration of the object, a different apartment was chosen for synchronization purposes. The problem with COM was that it was not extensible enough. So if you installed a COM object with MTS, the MTS configuration changed the COM registry in a way that the executable of MTS was registered rather than the **dynamic link library** (DLL) of the COM server. This extension of COM not only had the problem that the MTS configuration was

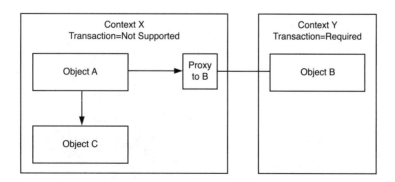

Figure 1-11   Configured components crossing contexts.

overwritten when the COM object was re-registered, but it also influenced programming the object. If a COM object that runs inside MTS creates another COM object that is also configured for using MTS, you cannot use the normal COM activation method `CoCreateInstance`. Instead, MTS offers its own method for creating COM objects, which enables passing the context between the affected objects.

One of the most important services offered by MTS was automatic transactions. By just configuring a COM object to require a transaction, the transaction was automatically enlisted with the distributed transaction coordinator. Such transactions can also be distributed across machines and across different databases as long as these databases support a standard two-phase commit protocol, such as SQL Server and Oracle.

As you can understand from this discussion, MTS offered a lot of help, but it also had some issues that required special attention. With Windows 2000, MTS was replaced by COM+.

COM+ 1.0

COM+ was the successor of MTS. With Windows 2000, the base services of MTS moved together with the COM functionality into COM+ base services. The MTS services are now known as **COM+ Services** (see Figure 1-12).

With Windows 2000, COM+ had the version number 1.0, and COM+ 1.0 was an evolution of MTS. Microsoft changed the name MTS to show that this application

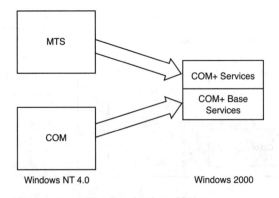

Figure 1-12   MTS migrating into COM+.

server is not only useful when transactions are needed but that it offers a lot more functionality that can be used by applications that do not use transactions; Microsoft named this product COM+ Services.

COM+ Services uses COM+ base services as its foundation, which in turn is an improvement over COM. COM+ not only knows about the context, but it also provides enough extensibility points to integrate other services without the need to deal with such objects differently. So the MTS **application programming interface** (API) calls that had been used with Windows NT 4.0 to create new objects and to return a reference to an interface are no longer needed.

Some services, such as loosely coupled events and queued components, were added with Windows 2000. In addition, the COM interfaces to write the configuration data of the components programmatically to the COM+ metabase changed.

Now that you know the predecessors of .NET Enterprise Services, you can learn about the current state of .NET Enterprise Services and how Enterprise Services relates to COM+.

.NET Enterprise Services

.NET Enterprise Services is the new name used to access the COM+ Services with managed .NET components. It is not just a new name for COM+ Services; many .NET features are integrated into this application service technology. .NET makes it a lot easier to use these services (when compared to creating COM components as had to be done earlier). Contrary to some assumptions, with .NET Enterprise Services, no COM wrappers are used to interact with the .NET component from a .NET caller inside a single process; instead, .NET features have been added to the service architecture to make it as smooth as possible to use these services from .NET components. .NET remoting is used behind the scenes to create a context for .NET components.

Figure 1-13 shows how COM+ Services can be used from COM components and from .NET components.

Applications and Components

It is important that you understand some terms that relate to this technology. Figure 1-14 shows the relation of the terms *applications*, *components*, *interfaces*, and

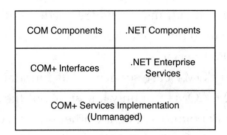

Figure 1-13   COM+ and .NET Enterprise Services.

methods. A serviced **component** is running within a .NET Enterprise Services **application**. Contrary to a Windows application or a console application, such an application is not necessarily related to a single process. An application can be configured as a server or a library application. A server application has its own process named dllhost.exe. For a server application, it is also possible to start multiple processes. A library application runs in the process of the client. If the serviced component is used within an ASP.NET page, the client process is the process that hosts the ASP.NET runtime (aspnet_wp.exe with Windows 2000 or Web Server Worker Process w3wp.exe on Windows Server 2003).

You can configure multiple components to run within a single application. With .NET, a component is represented by a class that derives directly or indirectly from the base class System.EnterpriseServices.ServicedComponent. With such a component, you can declare the runtime services to use. A component implements **interfaces**, and an interface groups **methods** together.

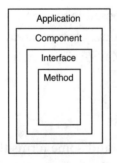

Figure 1-14   Applications and components.

Declarative Programming

You use runtime services by declaring requirements of the component or method with attributes. Functionality commonly used with business applications, such as transactions, can be found with the services offered, and you just have to apply an attribute to a class to use a runtime service. For example, to use automatic transactions within your component, you just add the attribute [Transaction (TransactionOption.Required)]. When the component is instantiated, the .NET Services automatically start a transaction for you and either commit the transaction when the component is disposed of or roll back the transaction if exceptions occur.

Catalog

Serviced components must be configured in the .NET Enterprise Services metabase. With COM, the components had been configured within the registry, and COM+ invented another configuration database with the metabase. All the information, such as whether a component takes part in a transaction, supports just-in-time activation, uses queued components, and so on, is written in the metabase. A component that is configured in the metabase is known as a **configured component**.

Configuration of a .NET component inside Enterprise Services can happen dynamically when the client is started or manually by using a registration tool.

Chapter 13 covers the different ways a serviced component can be registered with this database.

Administration

.NET Enterprise Services applications and components can be configured and maintained with the MMC admin tool Component Services, as shown Figure 1-15. You can find this tool by going to the Start menu (Administrative Tools, Component Services). Here you can see all configured applications and components. This tool enables you to change the configuration and to see the running instances of the configured components.

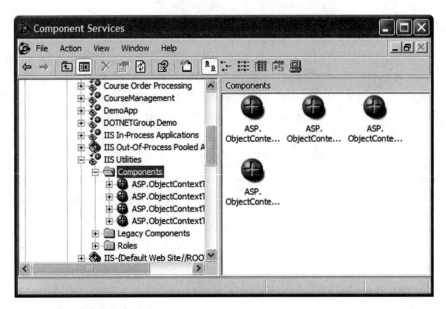

Figure 1-15   Component Services Explorer.

Application Services

Generally, .NET Enterprise Services is used because of the services this technology offers, including the following:

- Automatic transactions
- Queued components
- Loosely coupled events
- Role-based security

The following sections explain what these major services are and where you can use them.

Automatic Transactions

One of the most-used features of .NET Enterprise Services is automatic transaction management. Instead of dealing with transactions programmatically, which implies starting and committing or aborting a transaction, you can use the attribute [Transaction] to mark a class requiring automatic transactions. With this attribute, a transaction is automatically created and enlisted with the **distributed transaction coordinator** (DTC). The DTC is a distributed service that is part of the operating system. If the method completes successfully, the transaction is committed; otherwise, it is aborted.

This has the advantage of reducing the code by a few methods. However, there is a far bigger advantage with larger applications that use multiple components: Using attributes, you can specify whether a component should take part in an existing transaction and influence its outcome or start a new transaction. Only if all objects participating in the transaction are successful is transaction committed. If one of these objects fails in task completion, the transaction is rolled back for all objects involved in it (even objects that succeeded but participated in the same transaction). Without these automatic transactions, the client would have to deal with partial outcomes, or it would be necessary to pass the transaction from one method to another. Transaction management is a lot easier with automatic transactions.

The DTC also enables you to distribute transactions across different systems. Figure 1-16 shows two .NET Enterprise Services applications that access multiple databases. A single transaction can span multiple databases from different vendors. The

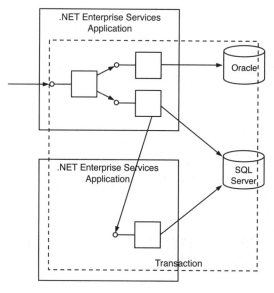

Figure 1-16   Transactions spanning multiple databases.

database just has to support OLE transactions or an XA-compliant (a two-phase commit) protocol.

Distributed transactions are covered in Chapter 7, "Transaction Services," and in Chapter 8, "Compensating Resource Management."

Queued Components

Usually, methods are called in the serviced component synchronously. With **queued components** (QCs), you can invoke methods asynchronously. QCs also work in a disconnected environment. The client can run on a laptop that is disconnected from the network while the application invokes methods that are defined with a QC in a recorder.

The overall QC architecture is shown in Figure 1-17. The recorder writes the method calls as messages in a message queue. As soon as the laptop connects to the network, the message is forwarded to the target queue. With the .NET Enterprise Services application, a listener reads the message from the queue, and the player invokes the method in the QC.

QCs are discussed in Chapter 10, "Queued Components."

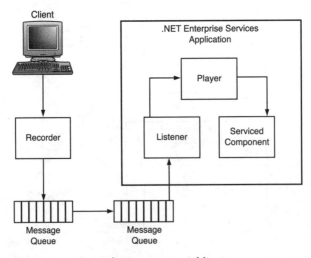

Figure 1-17   Queued components architecture.

Loosely Coupled Events

The term *event* is used when a server component invokes a method in the client. With COM applications, for the server to invoke methods in the clients, connection points are used. In this case, the client registers an event sink with the server, and when the event happens, the server invokes a specified method in the sink object. This is very similar to .NET remoting events. Both with COM and with .NET, remoting clients and servers are **tightly connected**.

COM+ Services uses a **loosely coupled events** (LCEs) facility. With a COM+ application, the COM+ facility is inserted between client and server (see Figure 1-18). The publisher (the component) registers the events it will offer by defining an event class. Instead of sending the events directly to the client, the publisher sends events to the event class that is registered with the LCE service. The LCE service forwards the events to the subscribers, which are the client applications that registered a subscription for the event.

If you use the LCE facility, the server does not have to deal with all the clients because this is done by the LCE service.

LCEs are discussed in Chapter 11, "Loosely Coupled Events."

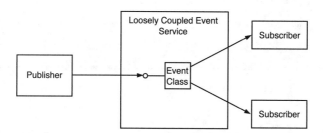

Figure 1-18   Loosely coupled events.

Role-Based Security

Instead of dealing with users and user groups that are created by the system administrator, and the need to create complex programming code for using the system access control lists, you can use simple strings that represent user roles. These strings are defined with a .NET Enterprise Services application by the developer and just need to be unique within the application. The system administrator then assigns users and user groups that belong to these roles; thereafter, the programming code only has to deal with roles.

In Figure 1-19, the administrative tool Component Services Explorer shows a view of three roles defined with the application `CourseManagement`: Managers, Normal Users, and Power Users. Just by specifying configuration entries with .NET attributes, you can define what user roles may access which components/interfaces/methods.

Role-based security is discussed in Chapter 12, "Security."

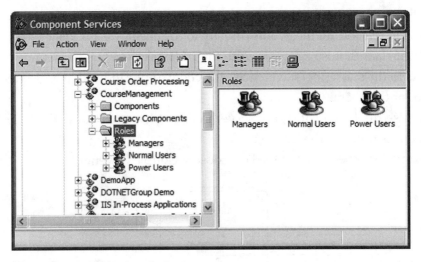

Figure 1-19   Configuration of roles.

New Features with COM+ 1.5

Windows XP and Windows Server 2003 both ship with COM+ 1.5, which offers some new features. You can use these features with version 1.0 and 1.1 of the Microsoft .NET Framework.

The following list summarizes these features:

- **SOAP services**—Using SOAP services, you can access components by using .NET remoting and the SOAP formatter. Both stateless and stateful components are supported.

- **Windows services**—If you configure the COM+ application as a Windows service, it will start automatically when you boot the system. You can also interact with the service by sending specific service commands.

- **Transaction isolation level**—The isolation level defines the degree to which one transaction must be isolated from another one. As of Windows 2000, all declarative transactions use the isolation level serializable. This is the safest isolation level, because it prevents updates and inserts outside of the transaction. This isolation level guarantees that the data is correct, but it can affect concurrency negatively. With many transactions, this high isolation level is not needed. Starting with Windows XP, you can specify lower isolation levels, such as read uncommitted, read committed, or repeatable read.

- **Private components**—A private component can only be activated from within a COM+ application in which the component resides. Such a component is not accessible to the client application.

- **Application pooling**—To increase scalability for single-threaded processes, multiple processes can be started with the same COM+ application.

- **Application recycling**—As a stability enhancement, application recycling is a new feature. If a problem with the COM+ application is detected, the process is restarted. You can configure recycling options in terms of the number of times the application is started, how much memory is used, the number of methods that are called, or the number of objects that are activated.

- **Services without components**—You can use services such as transactions and activities without creating serviced components. Therefore, a simple .NET application can benefit from services without going through the configuration of an Enterprise Services application. To use this feature with Windows XP, Service Pack 2 is required.

- **Partitions**—If you need multiple configurations for the same COM+ application, you can use partitions. Examples of when this can prove useful include offering multiple versions of the same application and using the same application with different configurations. If you offer one application to multiple customers, you might need different configurations. Partitions are only available with Windows Server 2003.

As you can understand, Windows Server 2003 offers a lot of features to enhance enterprise application stability, scalability, and maintainability. Enterprise Services now is a mature platform for enterprise-level applications.

Summary

This chapter opened with a discussion about building applications and specifically compared two-tier and multitier applications to help you understand the role of .NET Enterprise Services in modern application development (including the ability to scale up and scale out). The focus then turned to the history of application services, showing how COM+ Services has evolved into the .NET Enterprise Services of today.

You then learned a number of terms related to .NET Enterprise Services and should now understand the terms *applications*, *components*, *interfaces*, and *methods* (among others) in the context of .NET Enterprise Services.

The last part of this chapter provided an overview of the services offered with this application server technology: automatic transactions, queued components, loosely coupled events, role-based security, and new features that are available with Windows XP and Windows Server 2003.

1 ClickOnce deployment is only possible with Internet Explorer.

2 SOAP is an XML format that is defined here: `http://www.w3.org/TR/soap12-part1`.

3 The IDispatch interface is used by COM clients for late binding. This interface is described in more detail in Chapter 3, "Concurrency."

4 With attributes, the metadata of .NET assemblies can be extended. When the compiler detects an attribute, an attribute instance is created and stored with the metadata in the assembly.

5 If you are doing interop with native code, you still have to worry about memory leaks.

6 Activities are discussed in Chapter 3.

7 In this scenario, with this context, suppose for a moment that a runtime environment is defined by the configuration of the Object class. Chapter 2 discusses contexts in more detail.

2
Object Activation and Contexts

THE PRECEDING CHAPTER PROVIDED AN OVERVIEW of distributed applications and the services that are offered with .NET Enterprise Services. In this chapter, you learn about the base technology for serviced components.

This chapter opens by discussion contexts, from both a .NET and a COM+ perspective, and then the focus shifts to creating and using a serviced component. The chapter then discusses object and application activation, with an emphasis on just-in-time activation and object pooling.

Specifically, this chapter covers the following topics:

- .NET and COM+ contexts
- Creating a serviced component with the base class `ServicedComponent` and using the required attributes
- Object activation features with construction strings, just-in-time activation, object pooling, and private components
- Application activation features to compare library and server applications, Windows services, application pooling, and application recycling

Contexts

All code executes in some platform-provided runtime environment. In traditional operating systems, the primary form of the runtime environment is a process. An operating system process not only provides resources to your code such as virtual memory, threads, and kernel objects, but it also introduces an isolation boundary between your code and everyone else's code. This isolation not only provides some degree of protection from other people's faults, but it also provides your code with distinct characteristics such as a unique security principal or current directory.

Isolating code is not only useful with the process, but also within the process. COM, COM+, and the **Common Language Runtime** (CLR) have all found it necessary to replicate this model to give code finer-grained isolation within a single operating system process. In both COM+ and the CLR, the finest-grained unit of isolation is called a **context**.

COM+ contexts are a subdivision of a COM apartment,[1] which itself is a subdivision of an operating system process used to group objects to threads. CLR contexts are a subdivision of a CLR application domain, which itself is a subdivision of an operating system process used to group objects that share a common security and version policy. Contexts are the heart of the COM+ and .NET Enterprise Services programming model and architecture. Each component that is configured in the COM+ catalog is automatically associated with a context. This context enables interception and thus all the services discussed in Chapter 1, "Introducing .NET Enterprise Services."

With COM+, a configured object is always running inside a context. The context needed by the object is defined by context attributes that are specified with the serviced component class. The context attributes define the runtime requirements of a component. If an object is called from a client object that is already running inside a context (because it is a configured object, too), it is checked whether this context is compatible with the context that is required by the object. If it is, the object runs inside the same context as the calling object.

If the context is not compatible with the requirements defined by the component, a new object context is created. Both the CLR and COM+ rely on proxies to enforce context boundaries between objects. A **proxy** is an object that acts as a stand-in for the real object that resides in a distinct context. The proxy is responsible for switching contexts before and after a method call.

As a context is defined by a set of properties that state the runtime needs of an object, defining a context for an object means that the object can only be accessed directly from within this context. If a client object accessing this object has a different context associated, it cannot invoke methods of the context-bound object directly, and needs a proxy instead.

Figure 2-1 shows an example of such a scenario. Object A defines that it needs a context with the property `Synchronization=Not Supported`, whereas object B has the need for `Synchronization=Required`. If object A wants to invoke methods with object B, it cannot do so directly; it must use a proxy instead. The proxy invokes intermediate code to fulfill the requirement of object B that is running in context Y (for example, by placing a lock).

Object C has the same requirements for the context as object A. If object A invokes a method with object C, object C is accessed directly without use of a proxy.

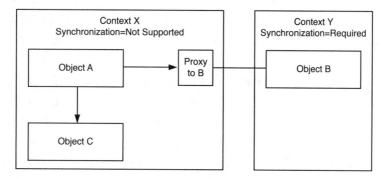

Figure 2-1 Accessing objects across contexts.

Comparing Agile Objects with Context-Bound Objects

An agile object is the opposite of a context-bound object. A context-bound object is bound to a context, whereas an agile object is independent of the context.

TIP: Reality Check—Agile Objects

COM objects are always bound to a context. Normal .NET objects are agile. Agile objects have the great advantage in that they can participate in the context of the caller. With COM, for a component to participate in a COM+ context, it must be configured with COM+. This is not necessary with .NET. A simple .NET class that is used by a configured component is running within the same context.

> Agile objects make it possible to write the business and data access logic in simple .NET classes, and the serviced component acts as a simple wrapper that uses the .NET classes.

.NET Remoting Contexts

A .NET object is bound to a context if its class derives from the base class `ContextBoundObject`. To define the context for the derived class, attributes are used, and these attributes must derive (directly or indirectly) from `Context-Attribute`. With .NET 1.1, there is one documented attribute class in the .NET Framework that has a base class `ContextAttribute: SynchronizationAttribute`.

The technology that is used with .NET objects crossing contexts is **.NET remoting**. So the classes `ContextBoundObject` and `SynchronizationAttribute` can be found in the namespace `System.Runtime.Remoting.Contexts`. Do not be afraid of performance issues within one application domain. For cross-context communication inside one application domain, TCP or HTTP channels are not used; .NET remoting uses an inter-application-domain channel instead, with which it is not necessary to leave the process.

> **NOTE: The .NET Framework Has Two Synchronization Attributes**
>
> Do not mix up the classes `SynchronizationAttribute` with the namespaces `System.Runtime.Remoting.Contexts` and `System.EnterpriseServices`. The attribute class from the first mentioned namespace will be used now, whereas the second one is discussed in Chapter 3, "Concurrency."

What Is an Application Domain?

With Win32 applications, the application boundary is the process. Each process has its own virtual memory, so that different processes cannot influence the outcome of each other. .NET has another security boundary: the application domain. A single process can host multiple application domains, where objects from one domain cannot interact with objects from another domain directly. For communication between objects in different application domains, .NET remoting is used. In such a scenario, an inter-application-domain channel is used for object communication across multiple application domains.

Application domains can be used as a security boundary between multiple applications inside the same process, but it is also a useful feature to dynamically load code that can be explicitly removed after use by unloading the application domain.

Application domains can be created programmatically, and there are also some .NET hosting environments that create application domains by themselves. One example is the ASP.NET runtime, which uses multiple application domains to separate Web applications.

You can also use a .NET context to get **synchronized access** to objects. In the Console application sample shown in Listing 2-1, class A derives from the class ContextBoundObject and is marked with the attribute [Synchronization], so that access to it is synchronized. To demonstrate that access to an object of class A is synchronized, two threads are used to access the method Method1. In the Main method of class Test, a new object of type Test is instantiated, where an instance of the class A is created as a field. Next, a new thread is started that invokes Method1 of the contained object, and from the main thread Method1 is called a second time. Using t1.Join, the main thread waits until thread t1 is completed. So you can see easily what thread is doing the method; the threads are given names.

Listing 2-1 Synchronization Using .NET Contexts

```
using System;
using System.Threading;
using System.Runtime.Remoting.Contexts;

[Synchronization()]
class A : ContextBoundObject
{
    public void Method1()
```

```
        {
            string threadName = Thread.CurrentThread.Name;
            Console.WriteLine(threadName + ": Method1 started");
            Thread.Sleep(3000);
            Console.WriteLine(threadName + ": Method1 finished");
        }
    }
    class Test
    {
        A obj = new A();

        public void ThreadMethod()
        {
            obj.Method1();
        }

        static void Main(string[] args)
        {
            Test test = new Test();

            // create and start a thread
            Thread t1 = new Thread(new ThreadStart(test.ThreadMethod));
            t1.Name = "Thread 2";
            t1.Start();

            // invoke Method1 with the main thread
            Thread.CurrentThread.Name = "Thread 1";
            test.obj.Method1();
            t1.Join();
        }
    }
```

Next you can see the output of running the application. Method1 is started and finished before it is started a second time from the second thread. The order of the threads invoked might be different. All access to the object is synchronized.

```
Thread 1: Method1 started
Thread 1: Method1 finished
Thread 2: Method1 started
Thread 2: Method1 finished
```

If the attribute [Synchronization] is removed from class A, the two threads run concurrently, as shown here:

```
Thread 1: Method1 started
Thread 2: Method1 started
Thread 2: Method1 finished
Thread 1: Method1 finished
```

Using Synchronization Mechanisms

Using the attribute [Synchronization] looks like an easy way to synchronize access to all instance members of a class. Instead of using lock statements, a lot less code is required. However, in many cases, the lock statements should be preferred because synchronization added to every method reduces scalability. With the attribute [Synchronization], locking happens with every method instead of the methods that share the same data.

TIP: Reality Check: .NET Remoting Synchronization Attribute

Do not use the [Synchronization] attribute with real applications. Instead, use lock statements where more fine-grained synchronization requirements can be defined.

Contexts with Serviced Components

The base class for all serviced components is ServicedComponent in the namespace System.EnterpriseServices. This class derives from the class System.ContextBoundObject, so all serviced components do have a .NET remoting context. Unlike the example before, with serviced components, there are a lot more attributes to specify the context.

Consider one more example using contexts. Figure 2-2 shows object A, which defines the attributes Transaction=Required and Synchronization=Required. With the creation of object A, a transaction is automatically created because the Transaction attribute indicates that this is required. In the figure, the transaction is shown with the Transaction ID 0815. In addition to the transaction, the object has a synchronization requirement, as stated by the `Synchronization` attribute. To synchronize access to objects, COM+ uses **activities**. The newly created activity has the ID 4711. Object A invokes a method with object B. Object B defines the attributes `Transaction=Required` and `Synchronization=Requires New`. Because of the different requirements to the context regarding synchronization, a new context is needed for object B, and a proxy is used to intercept the method call from object A to object B. This proxy just forwards the transaction to the context of object B, because the transaction alone does not lead to different requirements. However, synchronization is dealt with in a different way: Object B needs a new activity, so a new one with the ID 5123 is created.

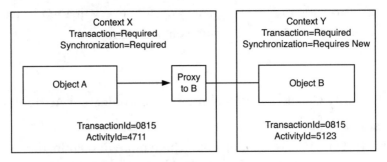

Figure 2-2   Enterprise Services contexts.

This example shows that different context requirements lead to the use of a proxy that enables the runtime to intercept method calls. This interception can happen at object creation time and during a method call.

Object Activation Interception

When a configured object is created, the creation is intercepted by the COM+ runtime. This interception makes it possible so that instead of creating a new object, an object that is ready to use and waiting in a pool can be taken out of the pool to do some work for the client. The interception also makes it possible to pass an initialization string, which is configured with the serviced component, to a newly created object.

Method Call Interception

When a method is called and the context between the calling object and the called object is different, method call interception occurs. Examples are transactions and **just-in-time activation** (JITA) and **deactivation**. (An object is activated and deactivated with every method call.)

With COM+ 1.5, the interception is implemented with native code. On the other hand, .NET components use managed code. Often I hear discussions that this can be a performance problem because of COM interop. In fact, most times this is not an issue because COM interop is not used with one .NET component calling another .NET component inside the same Enterprise Services application. Actually, the process is shown in Figure 2-3. If both the calling and the called object are written with managed code, the method call happens directly in managed code. Of course, the service functionality is implemented by using unmanaged code. Here the change from managed to unmanaged code occurs, but this is independent of the parameters that are passed with the method call from object A to object B. That's why marshaling of the data to unmanaged code, and unmarshaling to managed code, is not necessary.

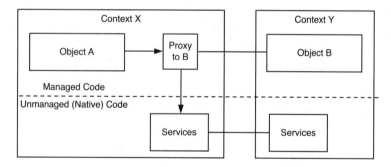

Figure 2-3   Method call interception.

Accessing Context Information

You can access information about the context with the utility class ContextUtil, which has only static properties and methods. The static properties of this class are shown in Table 2-1.

Table 2-1   Properties of the Class ContextUtil

Property	Description
ContextId	Every context has a unique identifier. This unique identifier is returned from the property `ContextId`.
ActivityId	Activities are used for synchronization. A single activity can cross multiple contexts. The property `ActivityId` returns the unique identifier of the activity.
ApplicationId	A .NET Enterprise Services application has a unique identifier, the application ID. This identifier can be specified with an assembly attribute and can be read with the property `ApplicationId`.
ApplicationInstanceId	Every time the application is started, a new ID for the application instance is created. You can read such an ID with the property `ApplicationInstanceId`.
PartitionId	With Windows Server 2003, the same application can be offered using multiple configurations. This is done with partitions; the property `PartitionId` returns the ID of the partition.
DeactivateOnReturn	Setting `DeactivateOnReturn` to true means that the done bit of the object should be set, so that the object can be deactivated when the method call returns.
IsInTransaction	If the object runs inside a transaction, `IsInTransaction` returns true.
TransactionId	The unique identifier of the transaction is returned with the property `TransactionId`.
Transaction	The `Transaction` property returns an object that represents the DTC transaction. This object implements the interface `ITransaction`.
MyTransactionVote	With the property `MyTransactionVote`, you can influence the outcome of the transaction. The vote can be set using a value defined with the enumeration `TransactionVote: Abort` or `Commit`.
IsSecurityEnabled	With the read-only property `IsSecurityEnabled`, you can check whether security is enabled with the COM+ application.

Mixing .NET and COM+ Contexts

Contexts have also been available with COM objects running in a COM+ application. We discussed earlier that .NET components do use .NET contexts running in a .NET Enterprise Services application. What if a .NET component is using a COM object that is running within the same application? What happens if both objects should participate within the same transaction? There is some good news! It can be done, and interoperability plays an important role.

COM objects do not know about the .NET context; only the COM+ context can be used instead. To make this possible with .NET components, you must take note of the following behavior: When a .NET component is created, there is not only a .NET remoting context created, but a COM+ context as well. This is done with the nondocumented attribute, [ServicedComponentProxy], which is associated with the class ServicedComponent. The attribute class ServicedComponentProxyAttribute derives from the class ProxyAttribute. With the [Proxy] attribute, you can associate a custom proxy class with your .NET remoting class that will be used by .NET remoting instead of the default proxy. .NET Enterprise Services makes use of this feature where the class ServicedComponentProxy takes the role of the proxy to call a .NET component running in .NET Enterprise Services. This proxy makes it possible to introduce both a .NET context and a COM+ context.

The following two subsections examine scenarios where a COM object is called from a .NET component, and vice versa.

A .NET Component Calling a COM Object

If a .NET serviced component is created, not only is a .NET context created, but also a COM+ context, which is connected to the .NET context. If the .NET component now creates a COM object that is configured with COM+ Services, the COM object is running in the same context if the requirements of the COM object are similar to the requirements of the .NET component.

The COM object is used by the .NET component with the help of a runtime callable wrapper (RCW) class so that the COM object looks like a .NET object (see Figure 2-4).

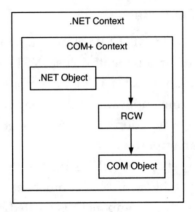

Figure 2-4   .NET calling a COM object.

A COM Object Calling a .NET Component

Figure 2-5 reflects a scenario the other way around, where a COM object invokes methods in a .NET component. COM does not know about a .NET context, so when the COM object gets instantiated, only a COM+ context is created. If this COM object creates a .NET object, a .NET context will be created. The .NET context will be associated with the COM context to make it possible for the same transaction to be shared.

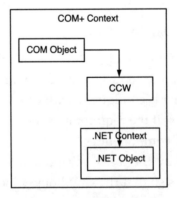

Figure 2-5   COM calling a .NET component.

To make this .NET object look like a COM object for the calling COM object, a COM callable wrapper (CCW) is used.

Now you have enough information about contexts to start with the first serviced component. The first component is a very simple example with the main purpose of demonstrating the basic steps for using .NET Enterprise Services.

Creating a Serviced Component

To create a serviced component, you always have to create a class library project, no matter if the application should run inside the client process or if it uses its own process. With the class library project, you have to reference the assembly `System.EnterpriseServices` in the file `System.Enter-priseServices.dll` to access the types needed, and you should import the namespace `System.EnterpriseServices`.

In addition, you have to do the following:

1. Define configuration information for the application with assembly attributes.

2. Sign the assembly using a strong name. Optionally, you can install the assembly in the global assembly cache.

3. Create an interface to define the methods that should be offered by the component. Although the usage of an interface is not a strict requirement, it is necessary if you want to use some specific services.

4. Create a class that derives from `ServicedComponent`, and implement the interface that has been defined in Step 3.

5. Add attributes to the class to specify the services needed.

6. Configure the application.

Now it is time to consider the details. In the first example, a serviced component will be created that receives course orders in an XML format and writes the orders in a comma-separated format to a unique file for further processing by other applications.

Assembly Attributes

With assembly attributes, you can define application configuration options. Assembly attributes just have to be defined globally; the projects created with Visual Studio always have the file assemblyinfo.cs where you can add these attributes.

The attributes [ApplicationName], [Description], [ApplicationActivation], and [ApplicationAccessControl] are defined within the file assemblyinfo.cs, as shown in Listing 2-2.

Listing 2-2   Assembly Attributes

```
using System.EnterpriseServices;

[assembly: ApplicationName("Course Order Processing")]
[assembly: Description("Sample Application for Enterprise Services")]
[assembly: ApplicationActivation(ActivationOption.Library)]
[assembly: ApplicationAccessControl(false)]
```

The attribute [ApplicationName] defines the name of the Enterprise Services application. After registration of the serviced component, you can see this name in the Component Services Explorer. The [Description] attribute enables you to add a description of the application, which also shows up in the Component Services Explorer.

With [ApplicationActivation], you specify whether the application should use its own process or the process of the client application. Setting the option ActivationOption.Library means that the COM+ application should run in the process of the client. ActivationOption.Server specifies that the COM+ application should run in its own process. In this case, an instance of dllhost.exe will be used.

With a library application, there is no support for object pooling and queued components. However, with library applications, you have the advantage that invoking method calls is faster because no cross-process communication is necessary. Server applications have fault isolation for unsafe and unmanaged code. The process of the client application is not affected by a breaking component.

The attribute [ApplicationAccessControl] specifies whether role-based security should be enforced when the component is accessed.

> **NOTE: Default Access Control Configuration**
>
> If the attribute [ApplicationAccessControl] is not specified, there is no access check with .NET Framework 1.0. This changed with version 1.1. Here an access check is enabled if this attribute is not applied. So it is best to always specify this attribute.

All the attributes that can be specified at the assembly level are listed in Table 2-2.

Table 2-2   Assembly Attributes

Attribute	Description
ApplicationId	[ApplicationID] defines a unique identifier of the application. If this attribute is not specified, a unique identifier is created automatically.
ApplicationActivation	This attribute defines whether the application should be configured as server or library application. The possible options are ApplicationOption. Library and ApplicationOption.Server. A library application is running in the process of the client, whereas a server application has its own hosting process dllhost.exe.
ApplicationNameDescription	[ApplicationName] and [Description] show up in the Component Services Explorer. [Description] can be used with applications, classes, methods, and interfaces.
ApplicationAccessControl	The attribute [ApplicationAccessControl] is used to enable/disable access checking, authentication, and impersonation. You will use this attribute in Chapter 12, "Security."
SecurityRole	With [SecurityRole], you can define a user role that can be used to allow a user group access to methods. This is also discussed in Chapter 12.
ApplicationQueuing	The attribute [ApplicationQueuing] is used for queued components, which are dealt with in Chapter 10, "Queued Components."

Signing the Assembly

Assemblies of serviced components must have **a strong name** for unique identification. A strong name consists of the name of the assembly, the version number, the culture, and a public key. You can create a public/private key pair using the strong name utility `sn.exe` that ships with the .NET Framework and Visual Studio. `sn -k mykey.snk` creates the file `mykey.snk`, which contains both a public and a private key. The generated file will then be specified using the assembly attribute `[AssemblyKeyFile]`, as shown in Listing 2-3.

Listing 2-3   KeyFile Attributes

```
[assembly: AssemblyDelaySign(false)]
[assembly: AssemblyKeyFile("../../../mykey.snk")]
[assembly: AssemblyKeyName("")]
```

Referencing Strongly Named Assemblies

When referencing other assemblies from a signed assembly, the referenced assemblies must be signed, too. The reason is that the strong name is used to guarantee that the assembly has not been changed after the signature was applied. If referenced assemblies are not signed, this guarantee would be useless.

Strongly Named Assemblies

To uniquely identify assemblies, a simple name is not enough—a strong name is needed. A strong name consists of the assembly name itself, the version number, the culture, and a public key.

Besides providing a unique identification of the assembly with the strong name, a signature is added to the assembly with the private key. This signature guarantees that the assembly cannot be replaced by a different vendor with a different key.

Global Assembly Cache

For many services, it is optional to put the assembly in the global assembly cache. With the registration of the component, the complete path to the assembly is written to the registry. You can find information about the assembly, path, and runtime version with the registry key `HKCR\CLSID\<CLSID of the component>\ InprocServer32`, as shown in Figure 2-6.

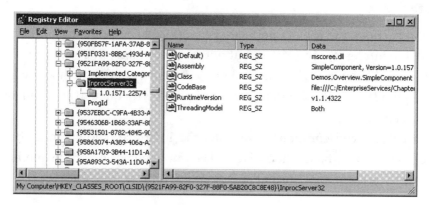

Figure 2-6   Registry configuration.

The `CodeBase` configuration information shows the path to the assembly. This registry configuration is only used with COM interop. .NET clients invoking the serviced components use standard .NET behavior to find the assembly—either in the directory of the client application or in the global assembly cache. With a server assembly, the CodeBase is used by the `dllhost.exe` process that activates the serviced components through COM interop.

What Is the Global Assembly Cache?

Assemblies can be private or shared. Private assemblies are always in the same directory as the application using these assemblies, or in a subdirectory of the application. If an assembly is used by multiple applications and is not copied with every application, it is a **shared assembly**. Shared assemblies can be either in a common directory on the local system or on a server, or they can be installed in the global assembly cache. Shared assemblies must have a strong name.

The **global assembly cache** (GAC) allows installation of multiple versions of the same assembly. By default, the client application uses the same version with which it was built. It is also possible to configure the version that should be used by an application.

Using Interfaces

Some services require the use of interfaces. For serviced components, it is not a strict requirement to implement interfaces, but without interfaces, there are some restrictions. For example, if you want to use role-based security at the method level, interfaces are required. In addition, interfaces are required with queued components and loosely coupled events.

In the first serviced component sample, the interface (shown in Listing 2-4) `ICourseOrder` defines the method `Order`. The implementation of this method will accept a course order in XML format and store it within unique files.

Listing 2-4　ICourseOrder Interface

```
public interface ICourseOrder
{
    void Order(string xmlOrder);
}
```

In some small sample applications in this book, for the sake of simplicity, interfaces are not used. With applications that will go into production, you should *always* use interfaces as a contract, because this is a clearly defined boundary for the clients to use.

Use Interfaces as Contracts

Define a clear contract for the serviced components by defining interfaces.

ServicedComponent Class

A serviced component must derive from the class `ServicedComponent`. The class `ServicedComponent` itself derives from `ContextBoundObject`, giving it a .NET context. `ContextBoundObject` itself derives from `MarshalByRefObject`, which is the base class for all objects that can be called remotely; so calling it across the network is not only possible but also a necessity with serviced components.

The class `CoursesComponent` is shown in Listing 2-5. `CoursesComponent` derives from the base class `ServicedComponent` and implements the interface `ICourseOrder`. The only attribute that is applied to this class is `[EventTrackingEnabled]` so that the component can be monitored with the Component Services Explorer (and offer other more useful tracking data). It is disabled by default to get maximum performance.

Because the method `Order` will be quite fast, you can add a `Thread.Sleep` for testing purposes with monitoring.

The methods `CreateFile`, `CloseFile`, and `GetText` are helper methods that are discussed later together with the implementation of the method `Order`.

Listing 2-5 CourseComponent Class

```
using System;
using System.EnterpriseServices;
using System.Xml;
using System.Globalization;
using System.IO;

namespace Demos.Introduction
{
    [EventTrackingEnabled]
    public class CourseComponent : ServicedComponent, ICourseOrder
    {
        public CourseComponent()
        {
        }

        public void Order(string xmlOrder)
        {
```

```
        // Implementation of Order
    }

    private StreamWriter writer = null;

    private void CreateFile()
    {
        // Implementation of CreateFile
    }

    private void CloseFile()
    {
        // Implementation of CloseFile
    }

    private string[] GetText(XmlElement xmlCourse, string tagName)
    {
        // Implementation of GetText
    }

  }
}
```

Why Monitoring Is Disabled by Default

Monitoring events with serviced components is disabled by
default, because it causes some overhead. With event tracking
enabled, every method call to the component is intercepted to inject
the event handling service functionality. To make interception possible, every component is running within a different context.

On the positive side, however, this option is an easy way to monitor the application.

ServicedComponent Methods

The class ServicedComponent has some protected methods (Table 2-3) that can be
overridden for use with some of the services that were discussed in Chapter 1. All
these methods are used in this chapter.

Table 2-3   ServicedComponent Methods

Protected Method	Description
Construct	The method `Construct` can be overridden to get an object initialization string at object creation. The default construction string can be specified with the attribute `[Construction-Enabled]`.
ActivateDeactivateCanBePooled	The methods `Activate`, `Deactivate`, and `CanBePooled` are used for pooled objects.
Dispose	Calling `Dispose` releases the unmanaged resources held by the serviced component. With the exception of JITA-configured serviced components, you should invoke `Dispose` to release resources early. With JITA, there is not a 100 percent rule, as discussed later in this chapter.

Class Attributes

With the class, you can specify many attributes to influence the use of services. All the attributes that can be specified at the class level are listed in Table 2-4.

Now consider the implementation of the methods of the `CourseComponent` class. An example of XML data that the class deals with is shown in Listing 2-6. The course list that is passed to the component for course ordering consists of a course number, a title, the start date of the course, and a list of attendees.

Listing 2-6   XML CourseOrder Example

```xml
<Courses xmlns="http://thinktecture.com/2005/06/CourseOrder.xsd">
   <Course Number="MS-2349">
      <Title>.NET Framework</Title>
      <StartDate>2005-10-08</StartDate>
      <Attendee>Nelson Piquet</Attendee>
      <Attendee>Ayrton Senna</Attendee>
   </Course>
</Courses>
```

Table 2-4   ServicedComponent Class Attributes

Attribute	Description
Description	This attribute was already discussed with assembly attributes. Not only can it be used to describe the application, but it also can be used to describe the component.
MustRunInClientContext	The attribute [MustRunInClientContext] means that if the context of the caller is not compatible with the required context of the component, an exception is thrown.
EventTrackingEnabled	Applying the attribute [EventTrackingEnabled] allows monitoring of the serviced component.
ConstructionEnabled	With the attribute [ConstructionEnabled], the system administrator can define a string that is passed to the component at initialization time.
JustInTimeActivation	The attribute [JustInTimeActivation] is used to decrease the load with the server, because the component itself can decide when it should be deactivated.
ObjectPooling	If the initialization time is longer than the method execution time, you can think about creating an object pool. This is done with the attribute [ObjectPooling].
PrivateComponent	If a component should only be used within the application, it can be marked as a private component. This option is only available with COM+ 1.5.
Synchronization	To get synchronized access to the component from the .NET Enterprise Services runtime, the [Synchronization] attribute is used.
Transaction	With the [Transaction] attribute, we can specify transactional requirements of the component.
SecurityRole	This attribute defines roles that can be used with the application. Applying this attribute to the class has a different meaning; here it means that users of this role are allowed to access the component.
COMTIIntrinsics	With this attribute, a transaction from the COM Transaction Integrator can be passed from the outside to the context of the class. This can be used to integrate IBM Customer Information Control System (CICS) and IBM Information Management System (IMS).

Table 2-4   (continued)

Attribute	Description
Eventclass	The attribute [EventClass] is needed for loosely coupled events.
InterfaceQueuing	The attribute [InterfaceQueuing] can be applied to both the classes and the interfaces. Calls on methods of the class/interface are queued with the help of queued components.
ExceptionClass	For queued components, this attribute marks a class to handle errors.
LoadBalancingSupported	If the load-balancing service is installed, this attribute allows the component to make use of this service.

When the serviced component receives the XML data (Listing 2-6) in the argument of the Order method, the XML data is read to write course orders to a comma-separated file. Listing 2-7 shows some helper methods that are implemented with the CoursesComponent class.

CreateFile creates a new file with a unique name, which is created with help of the method Guid.NewGuid (which returns a 128-bit unique identifier). The constructor of the StreamWriter class is used to create a new file in the C:\temp directory.

The method CloseFile does nothing more than to close the stream that was opened with CreateFile.

WriteToFile accepts the course number, the course title, the start date of the course, and the name of the attendee and writes this data to the comma-separated file. To make the date that is written to the file independent of the language of the user and the system, the invariant culture that is returned from CultureInfo.InvariantCulture is used to format the date.

The method GetText is a helper method that parses XML data of a single course that is sent as the first argument and returns the inner text of the elements that is defined with the second argument tagName.

The method `Order` was defined with the `ICourseOrder` interface in Listing 2-4. This method will be called from the client; it makes use of all other methods discussed earlier. Here all courses that are passed as XML are split into single course elements that are processed further by the method `GetText`, so that finally each attendee can be written to the new file format with the method `WriteToFile`.

Listing 2-7   Methods for the CoursesComponent Class

```
private StreamWriter writer = null;

// Creates and opens a unique file
private void CreateFile()
{
    string uniqueName = Guid.NewGuid().ToString();
    writer = new StreamWriter(@"C:\temp\Courses " +
                             uniqueName + ".txt");
}

private void CloseFile()
{
    writer.Close();
}

// Write course information to the comma-separated file
private void WriteToFile(string courseNumber, string title,
                         DateTime startDate, string attendee)
{
    writer.WriteLine("{0};{1};{2};{3}", courseNumber, title,
        startDate.ToString("d", CultureInfo.InvariantCulture),
        attendee);
}

// Parses the XML data of a single course for the XML element
// tagName to return the inner text elements
private string[] GetText(XmlElement xmlCourse, string tagName)
{
    string[] text = null;

    XmlNodeList nodeList =
        xmlCourse.GetElementsByTagName(tagName);
    if (nodeList.Count < 1)
        throw new CourseException("No elements of type <" +
                             tagName + "> available");

    text = new string[nodeList.Count];
    for (int i = 0; i < nodeList.Count; i++)
```

```
      {
        XmlElement element = nodeList[i] as XmlElement;
        if (element != null)
        {
          text[i] = element.InnerText;
        }
      }

      return text;
    }

    public void Order(string xmlOrder)
    {
      CreateFile();

      XmlDocument doc = new XmlDocument();
      doc.LoadXml(xmlOrder);
      XmlNodeList courses = doc.GetElementsByTagName("Course");
      foreach (XmlNode nodeCourse in courses)
      {
        XmlElement xmlCourse = nodeCourse as XmlElement;
        if (xmlCourse != null)
        {
          string courseNumber = xmlCourse.GetAttribute("Number");
          string title = GetText(xmlCourse, "Title")[0];
          DateTime date = DateTime.Parse(
            GetText(xmlCourse, "StartDate")[0]);
          string[] attendees = GetText(xmlCourse, "Attendee");
          for (int i = 0; i < attendees.Length; i++)
          {
            // Write data to course file
            WriteToFile(courseNumber, title, date, attendees[i]);
          }
        }
      }
      CloseFile();
    }
```

All code needed to create a simple Enterprise Services application with a simple component has now been written. Next, the application must be configured.

Component Registration

Unlike simple .NET applications, deployment with .NET Enterprise Services is different, because these applications must be configured with the COM+ catalog. There is also a way to register these components dynamically without starting an installation program. However, the preferred way for deployment is using manual registration.

Dynamic Registration

Dynamic registration (also known as lazy registration) happens automatically as soon as a .NET client application is started using the .NET component. Because of the metadata information that is added to the assembly using the assembly attributes, the .NET Enterprise Service application is created automatically.

However, dynamic registration has some important restrictions:

- The client application must be a .NET application. With a COM client, dynamic registration is not possible.

- The client application must have administrative privileges. If the client application is ASP.NET, the default account used to run the process of the ASP.NET runtime is ASP.NET. This account does not have administrative rights. To avoid security problems, do not give administrative permissions to this account. If the Web application has security leaks from which users could break into the system, they only have the rights of the ASP.NET account.

- It is not possible to install the assembly in the global assembly cache using dynamic registration.

Therefore, dynamic registration is only useful during development time. However, during development time, it has a big advantage insofar as it is not necessary to do manual configuration with every build.

Component Services Registration Rule

With a production system, you should use manual registration.

Manual Registration

You can register the application manually by using the command-line tool regsvcs.exe, or a custom application using the class RegistrationHelper.[2]
The options of regsvcs.exe are listed in Table 2-5.

Table 2-5   Regsvcs.exe Options

Option	Description
/fc	This option is set by default. If the application does not exist, it is created; if it already exists, the existing application is used, and the new components are configured.
/c	With the option /c, the application is created. If the application already exists, an error is returned.
/exapp	If you specify /exapp, the application must already exist. If it doesn't exist, an error is returned.
/tlb:<type lib>	regsvcs creates a type library to be used by COM clients. With /tlb, the name of the type library file can be specified.
/reconfig/noreconfig	/reconfig reconfigures the application configuration from the attributes in the assembly, whereas /noreconfig leaves the current configuration intact. /reconfig is the default option.
/componly	With /componly, only the component is configured, but not interfaces and methods.
/appdir:<path>	With Windows XP and Windows Server 2003, an application directory can be specified. This directory can be used to place application-specific files in that directory (e.g., configuration files).
/u	With /u, you can uninstall the application.

Starting regsvcs.exe with the default options to register the DLL MyServiced-Component.dll, you can see here that the assembly is installed, and a type library describing the components is created.

```
> regsvcs MyServicedComponent.dll

Microsoft (R) .NET Framework Services Installation Utility Version
1.1.4322.535
Copyright (C) Microsoft Corporation 1998-2002. All rights reserved.
```

```
Installed Assembly:
    Assembly: C:\Chapter 2\CourseOrder\bin\Debug\CourseOrder.dll
    Application: Chapter 2 Demo
    TypeLib: G:\Chapter 2\CourseOrder\bin\Debug\CourseOrder.tlb
```

Administrative Tool

After the application is registered, you can use the Component Services Explorer to view and configure the component. This tool can be found by selecting Administrative Tools, Component Services. Starting the tool, it shows the application Course Order Processing, which was named with the assembly attribute [ApplicationName], in the tree view on the left side of the component Demos.Introduction.CoursesComponent with the interface ICourseOrder (see Figure 2-7).

Selecting the Properties of the Course Order Processing enables you to configure the application properties.

Within the General tab, as shown in Figure 2-8, you configure the name of the application and the description and see the application ID. These values have been configured with the values in the assembly attributes.

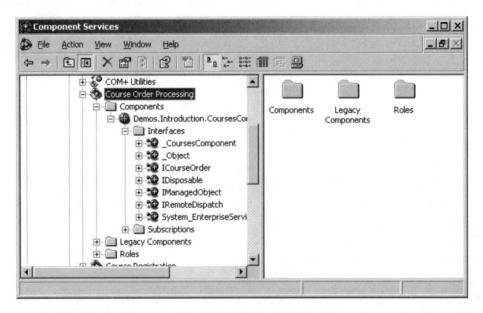

Figure 2-7 Component Services Explorer opening the registered component.

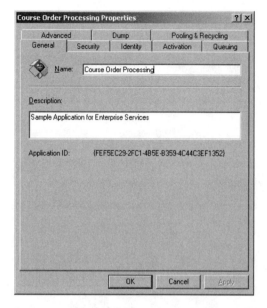

Figure 2-8   General properties of the application.

You can configure the serviced component itself with the Component Services application. Just click the serviced component in the left tree view, and choose the menu options Action, Properties. The dialog box shown in Figure 2-9 will display. On the General tab, you can see the name of the component, the CLSID, and the APPID for unique identification; the description that is configured with an assembly attribute; and the hosting DLL. With all serviced components that have been written with .NET code, the hosting DLL is `mscoree.dll`, which offers access to the component by using COM interoperability.

Throughout this book, you will learn about the other options to configure applications and components. By now, you already know how to create a simple component; the options for object activation are discussed next.

Client Applications

Creating a client application by using a serviced component is as simple as creating a normal client application. Creating instances and invoking methods of serviced components is similar to using normal .NET classes. Besides referencing your own

Figure 2-9 General properties of the component.

assembly, you also have to reference the assembly `System.EnterpriseServices` in the file `System.EnterpriseServices.dll`, because the class `CoursesComponent` derives from the class `ServicedComponent` (see Listing 2-5) that is defined in that assembly.

The code for the client application is very simple, as shown in Listing 2-8. Here a console application is used, and in the `Main` method, an object of the class `CoursesComponent` is created with the `new` operator. In the sample, the `using` statement is used so that `Dispose` will be called automatically to release the unmanaged resources at the end of the `using` scope.

Listing 2-8   Client Application

```
using System;
using Demos.Introduction;

class Client
{
    [STAThread]
    static void Main(string[] args)
```

```
    {
        using (CoursesComponent courseOrder = new CoursesComponent())
        {
            courseOrder.Order(
                "<Courses>" +
                    "<Course Number=\"MS-2349\">" +
                        "<Title>.NET Framework</Title>" +
                        "<StartDate>2005-10-10</StartDate>" +
                        "<Attendee>Nelson Piquet</Attendee>" +
                        "<Attendee>Ayrton Senna</Attendee>" +
                    "</Course>" +
                    "<Course Number=\"MS-2124\">" +
                        "<Title>Programming with C#</Title>" +
                        "<StartDate>2005-10-24</StartDate>" +
                        "<Attendee>Niki Lauda</Attendee>" +
                    "</Course>" +
                "</Courses>");
        }
    }
}
```

If the serviced component is not already registered, it will be registered the first time when a new instance is created. Starting the client application is all that is needed for dynamic registration. However, the scenario described only works if the client is running on the same machine. Using a client from a different system requires more work, as is discussed in Chapter 5, "Networking."

As you have seen, creating and using a serviced component is very easy with .NET. Indeed, it is a lot easier compared to preceding technologies with Visual Basic 6 or C++. Until now, no services offered by .NET Enterprise Services have been used. The first service functionality demonstrated is object activation, after a short introduction on how to debug Enterprise Services applications.

Debugging

An important task that you need to understand is how Enterprise Service applications can be debugged. With library applications, this should be easy; but how about server applications? It is impossible to configure every Enterprise Services application for debugging purpose as a library application, so take a look at how debugging can be done.

Library Applications

Debugging library applications with Visual Studio is easy. With Visual Studio, you can create a single solution that includes two projects: one project for the client, and one project for the server application. Just define breakpoints in the class library and start the client application with debugging; the program will halt with the breakpoints.

Server Applications

Debugging server applications is a bit different. Because the server application is a component library, it cannot be started directly from Visual Studio. Each application configured as a server application is running in a process dllhost.exe. Therefore, you must start the server application first. You can do this either by using the Component Services Explorer or by starting the client application, which in turn starts the server application by instantiating a serviced component.

With the Component Services Explorer, you can start the application with the menu entry Action, Start after clicking the application in the tree view.

The other option is to start the client application with Visual Studio. If you have the project of the client application and the project of the serviced component in the same solution, you can start multiple debugging sessions with one running instance of Visual Studio.

After starting the server application, you can see the process dllhost.exe in the Processes dialog box from Visual Studio. You can open this dialog by selecting Debug, Processes within Visual Studio, as shown in Figure 2-10.

There is one important issue with the process dllhost.exe when debugging. In case the Type column of this process only shows Win32 (but not .NET), the .NET runtime is not loaded. To debug .NET code, the .NET runtime must be loaded *before* the debugger is attached. To load the runtime, you have to start the client application. With the first instantiation of a serviced component, the .NET runtime is loaded in the server process.

Figure 2-10 shows the dllhost.exe process with the .NET runtime loaded (you know this because the type of the process shows .NET and Win32). Clicking the Attach button opens the dialog box shown in Figure 2-11. By default, the check box with the Common Language Runtime is selected when the runtime is loaded. You can also select Microsoft T-SQL if you want to debug into stored procedures.

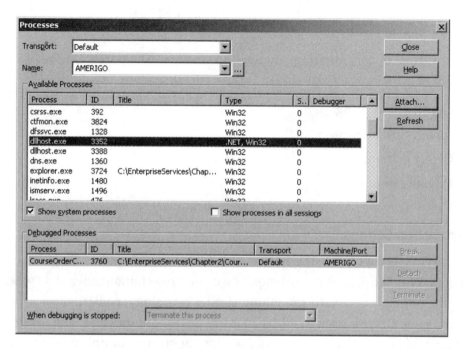

Figure 2-10   Attaching the debugger to dllhost.exe.

Figure 2-11   Selecting program types for debugging.

Object Activation

Now it is time to consider object activation features. The parts that are of interest with object activation are as follows:

- Construction strings
- Just-in-time activation
- Object pooling
- Private components

Construction Strings

With serviced components, it is not possible to use anything other than default constructors. With the default constructor, you cannot pass initialization data when creating the object. You can do something similar by using a construction string, but here the same string is used to initialize every instance of the class. The construction string can be changed by the system administrator, so one example where this is useful is to configure a connection string to connect to a database.

You can add the construction string that will be added to the configuration metabase with the attribute [ConstructionEnabled] and the named property Default. In the class, you have to override the method Construct that is defined in the base class ServicedComponent. This method will be called by the COM+ infrastructure with every newly created object.

Listing 2-9 shows changes to the CoursesComponent class created earlier, where the path to the created files is no longer fixed with the code, but instead is set as the default construction string with the attribute [ConstructionEnabled]. The overridden method Construct receives the construction string as its argument and uses it to initialize the member variable, path, that will be used in the method CreateFile to set the course order data file path.

Listing 2-9   Using Construction Strings

```
[ConstructionEnabled(Default=@"C:\temp")]
[EventTrackingEnabled]
```

```
public class CoursesComponent : ServicedComponent
{
    private string path;

    public CoursesComponent()
    {
    }

    protected override void Construct(string s)
    {
        path = s;
    }

    private void CreateFile()
    {
        string uniqueName = Guid.NewGuid().ToString();
        writer = new StreamWriter(path + @"\Courses " +
                                  uniqueName + ".txt");
    }

//...
```

The construction string can be changed by the system administrator with the Component Services Explorer by selecting the Activation tab with the component configuration, as shown in Figure 2-12. In this dialog box, you can see the informal message not to store security-sensitive information here. Where security-sensitive information can be stored is discussed in Chapter 12.

Instead of using this tool, you can create a custom application to maintain the application. Creating admin components for such a task is shown in Chapter 13, "Development and Configuration."

Just-in-Time Activation (JITA)

JITA is a feature to reduce the load of the server. With a JITA-enabled component, the object lifetime is independent of the client using the object. The server component itself decides when the object should be deactivated by setting a done bit. If a client invokes a method with an object that was already deactivated, a new object is created and activated. The object is deactivated on choice of the server component, and a new instance is automatically activated when the client invokes the next method using the same reference to the server component.

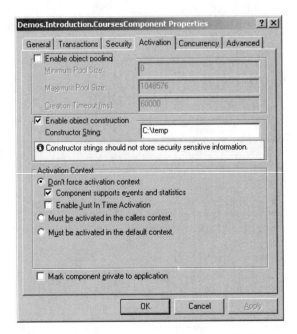

Figure 2-12   Object construction string enabled.

With JITA components, it is important to pay attention to the state of the object. After deactivation, the state is lost. With the next method call using the same reference by the client, a newly initialized object is used. The sample component shown in Listing 2-10 demonstrates exactly this issue: how state can be kept with JITA objects, and when state will be lost.

Listing 2-10 shows the class CoursesComponent, which has been changed to use JITA. JITA is enabled by applying the attribute [JustInTimeActivation] to the class. The class JustInTimeActivationAttribute also has a constructor with a Boolean argument where JITA can be enabled or disabled, but the default is to enable JITA.

For JITA, two methods from the base class ServicedComponent should be overridden: Activate and Deactivate. Activate is called by the runtime after the object is instantiated. In this example, the member variable writer is initialized to write to a newly created file. Deactivate is called by the runtime before the object is destroyed. Here the stream is closed. The calls to the methods CreateFile and CloseFile have been removed from the Order method, because the invocation of these methods is now put into the overridden methods Activate and Deactivate.

With the method `Order`, the attribute `[AutoComplete]` method is added. By applying this attribute, the done bit of the object will be set, and the object will be deactivated after the method call completes.

Listing 2-10 Serviced Component Class with Just-In-Time Activation

```
[JustInTimeActivation()]
[ConstructionEnabled(Default=@"C:\temp")]
[EventTrackingEnabled]
public class CoursesComponent : ServicedComponent, ICourseOrder
{
    private StreamWriter writer = null;
    private string path;

    public JitaDemo()
    {
    }

    // Creates and opens a unique file
    private void CreateFile()
    {
        string uniqueName = Guid.NewGuid().ToString();
        writer = new StreamWriter(path + @"\Courses " +
                                uniqueName + ".txt");
    }

    private void CloseFile()
    {
        writer.Close();
    }

    protected override void Activate()
    {
        // init object
        CreateFile();
    }

    protected override void Deactivate()
    {
        CloseFile();
    }

    [AutoComplete]
    public void Order(string xmlOrder)
    {
        XmlDocument doc = new XmlDocument();
```

```
    doc.LoadXml(xmlOrder);
    XmlNodeList courses = doc.GetElementsByTagName("Course");
    foreach (XmlNode nodeCourse in courses)
    {
        XmlElement xmlCourse = nodeCourse as XmlElement;
        if (xmlCourse != null)
        {
            string courseNumber = xmlCourse.GetAttribute("Number");
            string title = GetText(xmlCourse, "Title")[0];
            DateTime date = DateTime.Parse(
                GetText(xmlCourse, "StartDate")[0]);
            string[] attendees = GetText(xmlCourse, "Attendee");
            for (int i = 0; i < attendees.Length; i++)
            {
                WriteToFile(courseNumber, title, date, attendees[i]);
            }
        }
    }
}

//...


}
```

You can set the done bit of the component in two ways: by applying the attribute [AutoComplete] as you have seen, or programmatically by using the utility class ContextUtil to set the property DeactivateOnReturn to true. Both ways for object deactivation are shown in Listing 2-11. If both the attribute and the property DeactivateOnReturn are used inside a method, DeactivateOnReturn overrides the setting defined by the attribute.

Listing 2-11 Two Ways to Deactivate Objects

```
[AutoComplete]
public void Method1()
{
    // state will not be available after the method completes
}

public void Method2()
{
    // state will not be available after the method completes
    ContextUtil.DeactivateOnReturn = true;
}
```

Use DeactivateOnReturn Only with JITA Components

Setting the property `ContextUtil.DeactivateOnReturn` to true is only allowed with JITA-configured components. If this is not the case, an exception of type `COMException` is generated with the message "The requested operation requires that JITA be in the current context and it is not."Conversely, the attribute `[AutoComplete]` is ignored if the component is not JITA enabled.

After the component is registered, you can see the JITA configuration on the Activation tab of the serviced component tool, as shown in Figure 2-13.

NOTE: Registration Message with [AutoComplete] Methods

If the application is registered with `regsvcs.exe`, with `[AutoComplete]` methods, you will see this message: "The class 'Courses.Demos.CoursesComponent' has no class interface, which means that unmanaged late bound calls cannot take advantage of AutoComplete methods." This is not a problem with managed .NET clients, just with COM clients. You learn how this issue can be resolved with COM clients in Chapter 4, "COM Interop."

With JITA components, you have to be aware of state. With every method where the done bit is set—either by applying the attribute `[AutoComplete]` or by setting the done bit with `ContextUtil.DeactivateOnReturn`—the state is lost after the method is completed. If you need state to be kept intact, you can set the done bit to false. Keeping state in different ways is discussed in Chapter 9, "State Management."

Why Enable JITA?

JITA should be enabled to support scalability by making the lifetime of the object independent of the client. No resources in the server will be held if the client is still holding a reference to the object. Transactional objects, which are discussed in Chapter 7, "Transaction Services," require JITA.

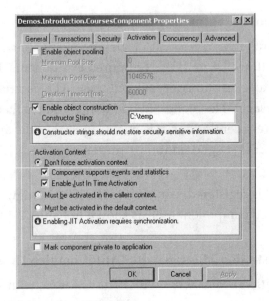

Figure 2-13 JITA activation.

JITA and Object Disposing

Should the client call `Dispose` with JITA-enabled objects? If the object is deactivated with the method call applying the attribute `[AutoComplete]` or with the property `DeactivateMethodOnReturn`, the object itself is deactivated after the method call. However, the client still keeps a proxy to the component that stays active for the next method calls. If the client would disconnect by invoking the `Dispose` method, a higher overhead would be the result of this action. When the client disposes of the serviced component, the proxy is released.

> **TIP: Reality Check—JITA**
>
> JITA is a very useful option with serviced components. With JITA, the object defines the lifetime of the object; the object defines when the state is lost and the object is deactivated rather than the client application.

Object Pooling

Object pooling is a useful service for objects that have a long initialization sequence (for example, if it is necessary to connect to a legacy server, or to create a complex matrix for mathematical calculations). If the time needed for the method invocation is shorter than the time needed for the initialization sequence, you should think about using object pooling.

With object pooling, the initialization sequence happens before the first client needs an object: At application startup, the objects that are specified with the minimum pool are created and initialized.

Similar to JITA, object pooling is configured with an attribute; here the attribute is named `[ObjectPooling]`. Table 2-6 lists the named properties of this attribute.

With the exception of the `CreationTimeout` property, it is also possible to specify the property values with the constructor. The default value for the `CreationTimeout` is 60 seconds.

Listing 2-9 shows the class `CourseComponent` changed to use object pooling. The class `CourseComponent` has the new attribute `[ObjectPooling(true, 100, 1000)]` applied. The values define that the minimum pool size is 100 objects, and the maximum pool size is set to 1,000 objects. Using the attribute `[JustInTimeActivation]` with pooled objects has the advantage that the object itself can decide when it should be put back into the pool. Without this attribute, the client would decide when the object should be deactivated with a call to `Dispose`, as shown earlier with JITA.

Table 2-6   Properties of the ObjectPooling Attribute

Named Property	Description
`CreationTimeout`	The `CreationTimeout` specifies the number of milliseconds a client will wait until it gets an object from the pool. If the time elapses, an exception is thrown.
`MinPoolSize` `MaxPoolSize`	With `MinPoolSize` and `MaxPoolSize`, you can specify the minimum and maximum number of objects to put into the pool.

The overridden method `Activate` is called by the runtime when the object is taken from the pool before it is used. Here you can initialize the object to a call-specific state. Compared to the implementation earlier, the overridden method `Activate` has been changed, so that a new file is created only if the variable `writer` is set to `null`. This way one object will not change the file to write the order data to; in addition, the initialization time needed is reduced.

In the implementation of the method `Deactivate`, the object state can be reset to its initial state—to a state before the method `Activate` was called—so that it can be put back into the pool. `Deactivate` is called after the done bit is set of the object; this is when a method with the attribute `[AutoComplete]` completes the method, or if the client invokes `Dispose` for stateful objects. Before the object is put back into the pool, the runtime invokes the method `CanBePooled`. The object is being put back into the pool only if this method returns true. If `CanBePooled` returns false, the object is destroyed instead of putting it back into the pool. This is useful for objects with one-time use. With one-time-use objects, the object is initialized before it is needed, but after use it is destroyed, and a newly created object is put into the pool.

The method `Dispose` is overridden to close the file stream after the object is either disposed by the client or when the garbage collector releases the object by calling the `Finalize` method of the base class, which in turn invokes the `Dispose` method.

With the sample in Listing 2-12, multiple course orders should be written to one file, but after ten course orders, a new file should be created. This behavior is implemented with help of the `usageCount` variable that is incremented every time the object is taken from the pool. With the `Deactivate` method, the file is closed if the `usageCount` variable has a value higher than ten. In the method `CanBePooled`, the object returns information about whether it should be returned to the pool or not, depending on the value of the `usageCount` variable.

Listing 2-12 Serviced Component Class Using Object Pooling

```
[EventTrackingEnabled]
[ObjectPooling(true, 100, 1000)]
[JustInTimeActivation]
[ConstructionEnabled(Default=@"C:\temp")]
public class CourseComponent : ServicedComponent, ICourseOrder
{
    private StreamWriter writer = null;
```

```csharp
private int usageCount;

public CourseComponent()
{
}

protected override void Activate()
{
    if (writer == null)
    {
        // the object is used for the first time
        // create a new StreamWriter to write course
        // information to a file
        string uniqueName = Guid.NewGuid().ToString();
        writer = new StreamWriter(path + @"\Courses " +
                                  uniqueName + ".txt");
        usageCount = 1;

    }
    else
    {
        usageCount++;
    }
}

protected override void Deactivate()
{
    writer.Flush();

    // close the file if the object has been used
    // for 10 times
    if (usageCount > 10)
    {
        writer.Close();
        writer = null;
    }
}

protected override bool CanBePooled()
{
    if (usageCount > 10)
    {
        // the object should not be put back into the pool
        return false;
    }
    else
    {
```

```
            // returning the object into the pool is OK
            return true;
        }
    }

    protected override void Dispose(bool disposing)
    {
        if (disposing && writer != null)
        {
            writer.Close();
            writer = null;
        }
        base.Dispose(disposing);
    }

    // Object will be put back into the pool
    // after this method completes
    [AutoComplete]
    public void Order(string xmlOrder)
    {
        // Implementation is the same as before
    }
}
```

Where to Put Initialization Code

Do not put initialization code where the context is needed to the constructor of the class. The first time the context is available is in the method `Activate`.

Dispose Pattern

Freeing resources is also an issue with managed code, especially if native code is involved. Resources can be freed either by the garbage collector or by the programmer. The dispose pattern deals with both variants.

For freeing resources by the garbage collector, you can implement a C# destructor. The C# compiler generates a `Finalize` method that is overridden from the `Object` class. This method is called by the garbage collector before the object is destroyed.

To make freeing resources possible by the programmer himself, the interface `IDisposable`, which defines the `Dispose` method, can be implemented.

Both the `Dispose` and the `Finalize` methods should release resources. However, the work you can do in either method differs because if the programmer disposes the object himself, you can do a lot more compared to the work that should be done by the garbage collector. With the garbage collector, the order of objects destroyed and the thread calling `Finalize` are not defined.

To deal with these issues, the dispose pattern defines a `Dispose` method with a Boolean argument, as follows:

```
public class Resource : IDisposable
{
   public Resource()
   {
      // allocate resource
   }
   ~Resource()
   {
      // this is called by the garbage collector
      Dispose(false);
   }
   public void Dispose()
   {
      // this is called by the programmer
      Dispose(true)
   }
   protected virtual void Dispose(bool disposing)
   {
      if (disposing)
      {
         // free embedded resources
         GC.SuppressFinalize(this);
      }

      // embedded resources are freed by the garbage collector
      // don't access embedded references here
   }
}
```

With the configuration tool, you can see object-pooling configuration values on the Activation tab of the component configuration, as shown in Figure 2-14.

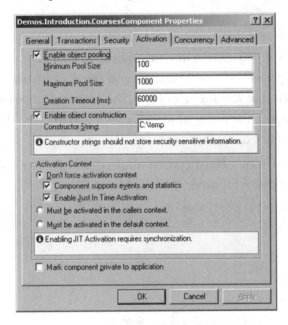

Figure 2-14   Object pooling configuration.

Client Application Using Multiple Threads

With the client application, multiple threads can be started to show using a lot of objects concurrently, as demonstrated in Listing 2-13. The main method of a thread is `CourseOrder`. Here a component is instantiated, and the method `Order` is called repeatedly. Threads are created and started in the `Main` method of the `Test` class. The property `Background` of the threads is set to false, so that the threads keep running when the thread of the `Main` method finishes. This way, it is not necessary to keep the main thread waiting until all subthreads have completed.

Listing 2-13   Client Application Using Multiple Threads

```
using System;
using Demos.Introduction;
using System.EnterpriseServices;
using System.Threading;

class Test
```

```csharp
{
   private const int threadCount = 50;
   private const int iterations = 100;

   public Test()
   {
      courseOrder = new CoursesComponent();
   }

   // thread method
   private void CourseOrder()
   {
      CoursesComponent courseOrder = new CoursesComponent();
      for (int i = 0; i < iterations; i++)
      {
         courseOrder.Order(
               "<Courses>" +
                 "<Course Number=\"MS-2349\">" +
                   "<Title>.NET Framework</Title>" +
                   "<StartDate>2005-10-10</StartDate>" +
                   "<Attendee>Emmerson Fittipaldi</Attendee>" +
                   "<Attendee>Mika Hakkinen</Attendee>" +
                 "</Course>" +
                 "<Course Number=\"MS-2124\">" +
                   "<Title>Programming with C#</Title>" +
                   "<StartDate>2005-10-24</StartDate>" +
                   "<Attendee>Michael Schumacher</Attendee>" +
                 "</Course>" +
               "</Courses>");
      }
      courseOrder.Dispose();
   }

   [STAThread]
   static void Main(string[] args)
   {
      Test t = new Test();
      Thread[] threads = new Thread[threadCount];
      for (int i = 0; i < threadCount; i++)
      {
         threads[i] = new Thread(new ThreadStart(t.CourseOrder));
         threads[i].IsBackground = false;
         threads[i].Start();
      }
   }
}
```

Monitoring Object Pooling

If the application is configured as a server application, you can see an actual object count. The view from Figure 2-15 shows the Component Services Explorer when the Components entry is selected in the tree view and the view is set to the menu option View, Status. The titles describing the numbers are a little bit misleading. With the column Pooled, you don't see the number of objects in the pool; instead, the complete object count is shown. These objects currently are in and out of the pool. The number of client connections is shown with the title Objects. The column with the title Activated shows the number of activated objects that are associated with clients.

The counts shown here are not available with library applications, because multiple client processes would use different pools, and a summarized count for all client applications would not give a useful meaning.

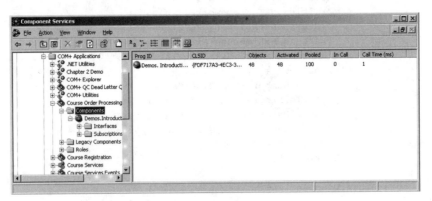

Figure 2-15 Monitoring objects with the Component Services Explorer.

Disposing of Pooled Objects

If pooled objects are also JITA enabled, the component itself decides when it should be deactivated. If pooled objects are not JITA activated, the client has to dispose of the object either using the `Dispose` method or the `using` statement (which calls `Dispose` automatically). Otherwise, the object stays allocated for the client, and you not only waste server resources, but you can also easily reach the maximum number of pooled objects before the garbage collector cleans up.

> **TIP: Reality Check: Object Pooling**
>
> You should consider pooled objects when the activation of components takes more time than calling a method. An example scenario where object pooling proves useful is when the component connects to a legacy server, and the connection takes more time.
>
> Object pooling is also a useful option if you have just a specific number of resources. Here the maximum pool size can specify the resource count available.

Private Components

A new feature with COM+ 1.5 is the support for private components. Components marked with the attribute [PrivateComponent] can only be activated within the application, but not with a client of the application. Figure 2-16 shows such a scenario. Here component A is used by the client application. Component A itself can activate objects B and C, which are marked with the attribute [PrivateComponent], because component A is running inside the same application as components B and C. Components D and E are running within another application. Because component E is also marked as a private component, it may not be accessed by A, B, or C.

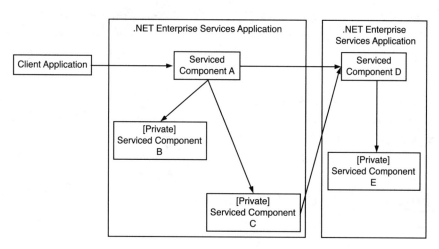

Figure 2-16   Use of private components.

Private components are a very useful feature to hide components that should be used only from within the application, but not from the outside. This is something similar to the C# `internal` keyword to allow access only from within the same assembly. `[PrivateComponent]` is independent of the assembly scope because components A, B, and C may be defined within different assemblies. It would also be possible to implement components A and D within the same assembly.

If there is an attempt to create a private component from outside of the COM+ application, a `COMException` with the message "Access is denied because the component is private" is returned.

Application Activation

Now that you know how objects can be activated, we can discuss configurations for library and server applications. This section covers the advantages/disadvantages of library and server applications, and some more options with application configuration.

As discussed earlier, a library application is running in the process of the client; a server application is running in its own process.

Library applications have a big performance advantage. With a client accessing the components, there is no need for a process switch, which has overhead, and no COM interop is needed with a .NET client—the components can be accessed directly. The disadvantage with library applications is that you cannot share some objects between multiple clients, and the application will be stopped with the client. If an ASP.NET application is a client of an Enterprise Services component that is configured as a client application, the component is running in the ASP.NET runtime process `aspnet_wp.exe` (IIS5) or `w3_wp.exe` (IIS6). This means that if this process is recycled, the application instance is recycled, too. All objects running in this application would be lost. This should not be a problem with stateless components, but it is with stateful components.

Server applications run in their own process, `dllhost.exe`, so interprocess communication is always necessary. This interprocess communication is done either by using DCOM with COM interop, or with the help of .NET remoting. In Chapter 5, the advantages and disadvantages of these options are discussed.

You can configure the following options only with server applications:

- **Identity**—The identity defines the user account that is associated with the process of the application. The application will have the privileges of this user.

- **Windows services**—Starting with Windows XP and Windows Server 2003, an Enterprise Services application can be offered as a Windows service. This way, the application can be started automatically at boot time of the system, and you can control the application with service control commands.

- **Application pooling and recycling**—In addition to Windows services, another new feature with Windows XP and Windows Server 2003 is application pooling and recycling. Figure 2-17 shows these configuration options. With application pooling, multiple instances of the application are started. This helps with scalability, because each client request with stateless components is dispatched to the next process. Application recycling helps with stability by offering a quick fix, particularly for native components that need a lot of memory. With application recycling, the application can be restarted depending on a lifetime, the memory used, an expiration timeout, or the number of calls.

> **TIP: Reality Check: Application Recycling**
>
> By configuring application recycling, you can get great reliability for your application. No matter if there is a memory leak or the application hangs because of a different reason, with application recycling, the process is restarted automatically without affecting actual clients.

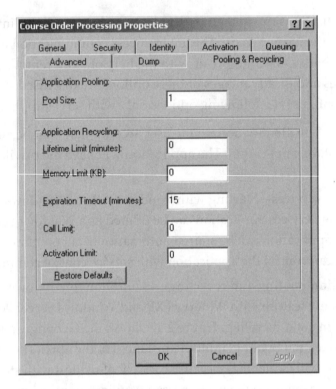

Figure 2-17   Application pooling configuration.

Summary

This chapter discussed the foundation of all .NET Enterprise Services: the context. You have seen that .NET Enterprise Services is more than just a renaming of COM+ Services, because .NET Enterprise Services already makes inside use of the .NET remoting context.

You created your first Enterprise Services application with a serviced component by deriving a class from the class `ServicedComponent`, used assembly and class attributes to define the Enterprise Services configuration, and configured this application with manual and dynamic registration.

This chapter also discussed object activation options, such as JITA and object pooling, and application activation options as a library or server application.

1 You can read more about COM apartments in Chapter 3, "Concurrency."

2 The class `RegistrationHelper` is discussed in Chapter 13, "Deployment and Configuration."

3
Concurrency

THIS CHAPTER COVERS THE SYNCHRONIZATION FEATURES offered by .NET
Enterprise Services. Synchronization has a big history with COM components,
where the need to lock some data for multithreaded access was initially hidden from
the programmer. With later COM versions, Microsoft added more and more options
to make it possible to build scalable components, but these features often removed
the simplicity of the first ideas and made this technology quite complex, mainly
because of the different terms used.

This chapter presents a clear picture of the concepts used with COM synchronization for interoperability with COM and .NET components. It also shows you
how you can now use synchronization with .NET Enterprise Services.

Specifically, this chapter covers the following topics:

- Why and when synchronization is needed
- Apartments for synchronization in the COM world
- Activities for synchronization with Enterprise Services
- Using the [Synchronization] attribute
- How causalities help with reentrancy
- Activities without using serviced components

Synchronization Overview

If multiple threads are used to access an object, you must make sure that two threads do not change the same data simultaneously—you have to be aware of concurrency issues. Concurrency problems can happen with a simple scenario as shown in Listing 3-1. In this example, the method `Foo` checks the member variable `val` to see whether it is set to 5. If this is the case, some code will be executed because of this condition.

The problem with this scenario is how thread scheduling is done. If one thread starts executing the method `Foo`, it can be interrupted by the operating system any time (for example, after the `if` statement returns true). The Windows operating system schedules threads and can interrupt any thread executing to give the control of the CPU to another thread. Now another thread is selected to continue its operation, and the second thread that is running in the same process is possibly also executing the method `Foo`. Because `val` still has a value of 5, the second thread also enters the `if` statement and increments `val` to 6. Now the first thread may be selected again, which increments the variable `val` to 7. The result is some unexpected behavior. What happens here is commonly known as **race condition**. It is assumed that one thread wins the race, but this is not always the case because of unpredictable CPU allocation behavior.

The particular pity with this issue is that this behavior only appears at random. The program can run thousands of times without a problem, because the thread is not interrupted during that operation, whereas at rare times the problem occurs just because of the scheduling behavior of the operating system. Also, the program will behave differently with debug and release builds. Having multiple CPUs in the system might increase the chance of having threading problems, because the operating system might schedule threads of the same process on multiple CPUs. Multiple CPUs can increase the application performance, but only with well-designed applications.

To avoid the described problem, you have to synchronize threads within the application. You can do so with the C# `lock` keyword, as shown next.

Listing 3-1   Method with Race Conditions

```
public void Foo()
{
    if (val == 5)
    {
        val++;
        // Do something because of val == 6
        //...
    }
}
```

Using Locks

The `Foo` method that was shown in the previous section is changed to use the `lock` statement[1] in Listing 3-2. Here the `lock` statement is used to lock the current instance of the class. Only one thread may lock access to this object. Therefore, the first thread executing the `lock` statement succeeds, whereas the second thread has to wait on the `lock` statement until the lock to the object is released by the first thread. The lock is released as soon as the closing bracket of the lock is reached.

Listing 3-2   Synchronized Method Using the lock Statement

```
public void Foo()
{
    lock (this)
    {
        if (val == 5)
        {
            val++;
            // Do something because of val == 6
            //...
        }
    }
}
```

Behind the scenes, the C# `lock` statement uses the `Monitor` class and generates `Monitor.Enter` and `Monitor.Exit` statements to lock the object.

> **NOTE: Synchronization Within .NET Framework Classes**
>
> With the classes of the Microsoft .NET Framework, usually all static methods are synchronized and thus thread-safe, whereas all instance methods are not synchronized. To be on the safe side, you always have to check the MSDN documentation. Thread safety is documented with every class. With classes that may be accessed from multiple threads, you have to be aware of the locking issue, and you have to synchronize access to the methods of the class where state of the object is accessed.

Implementing locking is not the only issue that you must pay attention to; you also have to concentrate on how to do locking correctly. Too many unnecessary locks will decrease the performance of the application, because threads would wait longer than necessary. Using locking the wrong way can also lead to deadlocks.

Figure 3-1 shows a deadlock scenario. If thread 1 issues a lock to object A that is accepted, and while it has the lock for object A it issues a lock for object B, another thread might do it the other way around: first locking B, and then locking A. Now a deadly situation can happen: The lock to A from the first thread is accepted, and then the next thread gets a chance to get the CPU and issues a lock to B. Now thread 1 waits for object B, while thread 2 waits for object A. This is a typical **deadlock situation**, which can happen at random depending on the thread scheduling of the operating system. A deadlock will occur if two threads wait for each other to give up a lock.

This might look obvious in a simple method, but the locks can be hidden far into the call stack. To resolve such an issue, you should always do the locks in the same order.

> **TIP: Reality Check—Multithreading Issues**
>
> With multithreaded applications, you must carefully pay attention to threading issues. If you do not pay attention from the beginning, threading issues are hard to fix because problems occur only once in a while. If you are using a multi-CPU system, threading problems happen more often because multiple threads of a single process run concurrently.

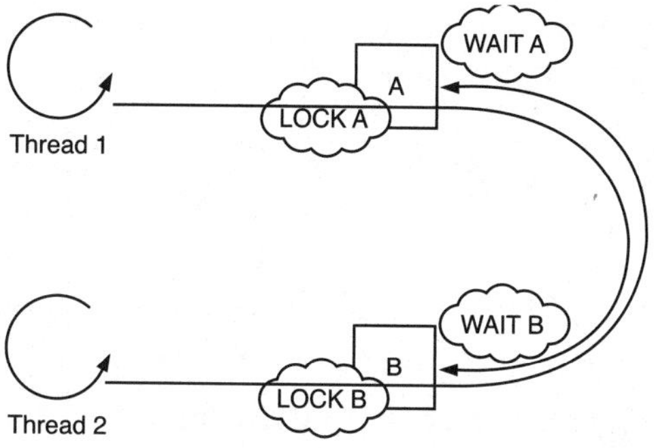

Figure 3-1   Deadlock situation.

Interlocked Class

The simple increment operation `val++` is not thread-safe! If the variable `val` is accessed by multiple threads, the access to it must be synchronized.

With simple increment and decrement operations, it is not necessary to place a lock on an object. You can use the utility class `Interlocked` instead. This class offers the static methods `Increment`, `Decrement`, `Exchange`, and `CompareExchange`. These methods are thread-safe. Instead of writing `val++`, you can do this:

```
System.Threading.Interlocked.Increment(ref val);
```

Using the `Interlocked` class would not help in the previous example with the method `Foo` where the code was dependent on the value returned from the increment operation, because the lock is already given up as soon as the `Increment` method completes.

More Synchronization Options

Instead of the `lock` statement, you can also use the `[Synchronization]` attribute from the namespace `System.Runtime.Remoting.Contexts`, as discussed in Chapter 2, "Object Activation and Contexts." But now you need to be aware of the features offered by Enterprise Services that lead you to the `[Synchronization]` attribute in the namespace `System.EnterpriseServices`. With COM components, Microsoft invented apartments as a synchronization boundary, and they still play an important role with serviced components. Even more important are activities, which are discussed after apartments in this chapter.

Apartments

One Microsoft goal with COM technologies was that Visual Basic developers should not have to deal with synchronization issues; programming should be easier. This was the major reason why **apartments** were invented.

The reason why apartments are introduced here is because you have to know the concepts and issues when integrating with COM objects. With a pure .NET solution, just the COM+ 1.5 concept of activities is important.

> **NOTE: Apartments and .NET**
>
> If you write pure .NET applications and you do not interact with existing COM objects, you can skip the next few sections and continue to read at the section ".NET Enterprise Services Interaction." If you are interested in what the apartment options in the serviced component configuration are about, you should read the next sections anyway.

With the first release of COM, all COM objects running inside one process were accessed by just a single thread. Accessing the object from a different thread automatically meant calling the object by using a proxy that switched to the thread that allowed accessing the object. Soon this led to scalability problem; therefore, with Windows NT 3.51, apartments were invented.

An apartment is used to intercept a method call by the COM runtime to synchronize access to an object. A COM component describes the apartment it wants to live in by using a registry configuration entry. Depending on the apartment, access to the object may or may not be synchronized.

Do you detect similar ideas with the contexts discussed in Chapter 2? Indeed, you can compare apartments with contexts: Similar to contexts, with apartments, interception happens by invoking some services code before the method call is started. The similarities go even further: Before the term *apartment* was used, the name was *context*.

With COM, three different apartment types are available:

- Single-threaded apartments
- Multithreaded apartments
- Thread-neutral apartments

Within a .NET application, the apartment where the thread is running can be read with the `ApartmentState` property of the `Thread` class. The `ApartmentState` property returns an `ApartmentState` enumeration that can have the values `STA`, `MTA`, and `Unknown`.

Single-Threaded Apartments

The **single-threaded apartment** (STA) was created with Windows NT 3.51. Only a single thread may run inside an STA, so in many cases, writing of locking code for synchronized access is not necessary. However, inside a single process, multiple apartments can coexist; so if objects running inside different apartments access some shared state, it is necessary to synchronize access to this shared state.

Figure 3-2 shows a process with two STAs. Objects A and B are running in the first STA and may only be accessed from thread 1. Objects C and D are running in the second STA and may only be accessed from thread 2. If object A is used within a method of object C, a proxy must be used to access object A from STA 2. This proxy forwards the method call to thread 1 so that thread 1 can do synchronized access to object A.

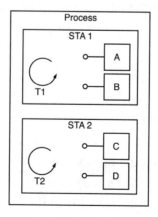

Figure 3-2   Single-threaded apartments.

If an object is used from a different apartment from the calling object, in general you do not have to take care that a proxy is used for accessing the object. If the object is accessed by using COM interfaces, crossing apartments is automatically done by the COM runtime.

A thread creates an STA apartment by invoking the COM API call `CoInitialize`. With .NET, a thread can also create an STA apartment by using the attribute `[STAThread]`. If you use Visual Studio .NET 2003 to create your applications, the attribute `[STAThread]`[2] is applied by default to all `Main` methods, so the main thread of the application will create an STA. COM objects that are created by this thread and that want to live in an STA can be accessed without crossing the apartment. A COM object defines that it wants to live in an STA with the registry entry `Threading-Model=Apartment`.

Instead of using the attribute `[STAThread]` with the new thread, you can associate the thread to an apartment by setting the `Thread` property `ApartmentState` to `ApartmentState.STA` before starting the thread.

By crossing the apartment with a method, you always lose some performance, because leaving and entering an STA always invokes a thread switch.

> **Visual Basic 6 Components**
>
> Visual Basic 6 and earlier versions could only create components bound to the single-threaded apartment. If you are accessing VB6 components in your application, you always have to pay attention to this issue because you might have scalability problems.

STA Thread Pool

With an Enterprise Services application, a pool for STA-bound objects is created. Using STA-bound objects, you have to be aware of this issue: The number of threads in this pool is seven times the number of CPUs when the first STA object is created, and it can grow up to ten times the number of CPUs with a higher load.

Let's look at an example with ten objects instantiated. How many threads are used here? With an assumption of one CPU in the system and the initial number of seven threads per CPU, object 8 is using the same thread as object 1, and object 9 is using the same thread as object 2. Of course, this can lead to scalability problems.

What Is a Thread Pool?

Creating threads takes some time. If you have some jobs to do by multiple threads, you can create threads in advance, so there is no wait necessary until a thread is created. The threads just wait until they get some information about a method to run. After the method is completed, the thread moves back into the wait state.

Multiple threads that are waiting for a job to be done comprise a thread pool. The thread pool can be resized dynamically so that demands for threads can be fulfilled.

With .NET, you can create a thread pool with the help of the Thread-Pool class. This class is in the namespace System.Threading. You can pass a method that should run by a thread from the thread pool to the static method QueueUserWorkItem. This method accepts a WaitCallback delegate where you can pass the method; in the example, this is Method1. After the call to QueueUserWorkItem, the method Method1 is invoked by a thread from the thread pool as soon as one of the threads is free to do some work.

```
using System.Threading;

public class Test
{
    public void Method1(object state)
    {
        // ...
    }

    static void Main(string[] args)
    {
        Test obj = new Test();
        ThreadPool.QueueUserWorkItem(
            new WaitCallback(obj.Method1));

        //...
    }
```

> **TIP: Reality Check—Single-Threaded Apartments**
>
> If you have old Visual Basic components that you want to use within your solution, these components only support STA. With such components, you can reduce scalability problems by using stateless implementations; however, there is still the restriction with the STA thread pool that can be an issue with a large solution. If you have a pure .NET solution, however, there is no need to think about STA issues.

Multithreaded Apartments

Windows NT 4 saw the introduction of the **multithreaded apartment** (MTA). Within such an apartment, multiple threads may run simultaneously. COM objects that are configured to run within an MTA must be written in a thread-safe manner.

Figure 3-3 shows a process with an MTA. Three threads are running within the MTA to access two COM objects.

Inside a single process, only one MTA can exist. All threads that use the COM API call `CoIntitializeEx` with the option `COINIT_MULTITHREADED` will enter the single MTA of the process. With .NET applications, a thread is associated to the MTA by using the attribute `[MTAThread]` or by setting the `Thread` property `ApartmentState` to `ApartmentState.MTA` before starting the thread.

A COM object defines that it wants to live in an MTA by specifying the registry entry `ThreadingModel=Free`. If the client thread uses a different apartment from the one that is configured with the COM object, a new apartment that fulfills the requirements of the object is created automatically.

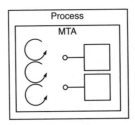

Figure 3-3   Multithreaded apartment.

Although it is not possible to have more than one MTA in a single process, it is quite normal to have multiple STAs and one MTA inside a process, as Figure 3-4 demonstrates.

A thread switch always occurs when crossing an STA or an MTA. A thread switch also means some overhead with invoking methods of objects that live in a different apartment. To reduce this overhead, a COM object can also specify the registry entry `ThreadingModel=Both`, which means the object can live either in an STA or an MTA. The apartment will be selected on the thread that is creating the object—the apartment will be the same apartment the thread is running in.

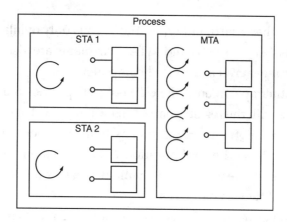

Figure 3-4   STAs and MTA inside one process.

MTA Thread Pool

Enterprise Services applications also have a pool of MTA threads. Unlike the STA pool, the MTA pool has no boundary and can grow dynamically when more MTA threads are needed.

There is just one MTA inside a process, but in this MTA, the number of threads can grow as needed.

Thread-Neutral Apartments

Starting with Windows 2000, a new apartment type was introduced: the **thread-neutral apartment** (TNA).

> **NOTE: Different Names for the TNA**
>
> For some time, the apartment was called neutral threaded apartment (NTA), but being so different from the other apartments, it was renamed to thread-neutral apartment (TNA). To make the naming more complex, it is sometimes referred to as neutral apartment (NA). You will find all three terms in the MSDN documentation; but NTA, TNA, and NA concerning multithreading and apartments all mean the same. In this book, I am sticking to the term *TNA*.

Contrary to the other apartment types, the TNA is only available for objects configured with COM+ Services. STA and MTA apartments are also available for COM objects that are not registered as serviced components.

Similar to the other apartments, the COM object specifies that it wants to live in a TNA. This is done with the registry entry `ThreadingModel=Neutral`. The registry configuration `ThreadingModel=Both` means that the object can live either in an STA, MTA, or TNA. Now the configuration `Both` means one of three. This might sound silly; however, the reason for this name derives from the history when `Both` was really just one of two: STA or MTA.

The main difference from the TNA to the other apartments is that a thread never specifies to enter a TNA. Instead, the thread enters the apartment during the method call and leaves it when the method call is finished. This has a big performance advantage, because a thread switch does not occur for entering a TNA; just some variables for the apartment context are changed. Saying that a thread lives either in an STA or an MTA, it is valid to say that a thread just visits a TNA.

What about thread-safe access to COM objects living in a TNA? This is an important aspect with this apartment type: The synchronization feature moved out from the apartment to the COM+ **activity**. With the help of an activity, it can be guaranteed that only one thread accesses an object within a TNA at the same time. The difference from STA is that with single-threaded apartments, it is always the same thread accessing the object, but with TNA, it can be a different one.

> **Why Are STAs Still in Use Today?**
>
> Nowadays, the STA model is only needed for objects that have a thread-affinity (for example, if a user interface element is accessed; window handles do have thread affinity). With COM+ Services or .NET Enterprise Services, the preferred apartment type is TNA.
>
> In case you are using serviced components directly on the client system as a library application where user interface elements are accessed, STA is the option to use.

Now you have learned quite a lot about the history of COM apartments and are ready to step into the .NET Enterprise Services-specific features.

.NET Enterprise Services Synchronization

In the preceding section, the apartment types STA and MTA were used for synchronized access. STA does not allow concurrent access to objects, whereas MTA does.

The preferred apartment type with COM+ is TNA, and with TNA the synchronization is not an issue of the apartment; we get an activity instead. It is important for you to understand the following terms used with Enterprise Services synchronization before delving into the details:

- An activity defines a **synchronization domain** where only one logical thread is allowed to execute at a time. A logical thread can consist of multiple physical threads, but it consists of one task that is forwarded by one thread to the next.

- The second important term with synchronization is **causality**. The causality is a chain of physical threads that spans a logical thread.

Later in this chapter, you get your hands on some code and examples to help you understand these terms.

Activity

An activity defines a synchronization domain where only one logical thread is allowed to execute at the same time. This synchronization domain can span multiple applications and even multiple processes. That is why the thread is called a **logical thread**—different processes do have different physical threads. A different name used for the logical thread in this regard is a causality. Instead of using locks with threads, causality locks are used with activities.

A graphic will help you understand activities. Figure 3-5 shows two activities and how a single activity can flow across multiple processes and applications. In the figure, you can see two activities where the activity boundaries are illustrated with broken lines. One activity crosses multiple contexts, applications, and processes. The first thread starts the activity by calling a method with object A. Object A invokes a method with object B; this continues to objects C and D. The activity spans all the method calls from objects A to D. If another thread tries to invoke a method with object A, B, C, or D while this activity is running, the thread has to wait until the activity is finished. In the figure, at the same time, a different activity is started from a thread invoking a method with object E.

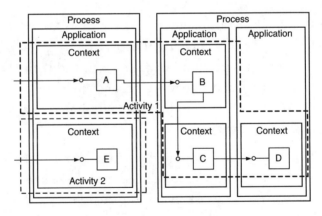

Figure 3-5 Activities.

Using activities, you do not have to lock access to the state of an object programmatically. How does this work? With an activity, the runtime creates a synchronization object (a mutex) that is locked when the activity is entered by a thread. The lock is only done once for a logical thread. As soon as the logical thread has completed its work, the synchronization object is unlocked, and the activity can be used by a different logical thread.

> **Activity Boundaries**
>
> Activities do work across contexts, applications, and processes. Activities are not designed to synchronize access across multiple systems.

Configuring Synchronization

Using .NET Enterprise Services, you can configure synchronization with the attribute class `SynchronizationAttribute` from the namespace `System.EnterpriseServices`. You can apply this attribute to the class that derives from `ServicedComponent`. The default constructor of the attribute class `SynchronizationAttribute` specifies the option `SynchronizationOption.Required`. The second constructor of this attribute class allows passing a value of the enumeration `SynchronizationOption`.

The possible values for the `SynchronizationOption` are `Disabled`, `NotSupported`, `Required`, `RequiresNew`, and `Supported`. Consider what these options mean:

- `Disabled`—The synchronization requirement for the object is not checked when the context of the object is selected/created. The context of the creator might or might not be shared with the creator object. All other properties of the context must be equal with the context requirements of the new object; the synchronization requirements do not just influence the selection of the context. You have to manage multithreaded access by yourself.

- `NotSupported`—The option `NotSupported` means that there is never synchronized access to the object. Similar to the option `Disabled`, you have to manage multithread access yourselves. The difference here is that you can only use the same context as the creator, if the context of the creator does not have synchronization enabled.

- `Required`—With the option `Required`, you always get synchronized access to the object. If the caller already has an activity, the activity of the caller is used. If the caller does not have an activity, a new activity is created.

- `RequiresNew`—The option `RequiresNew` defines that a new activity is always created, regardless of whether the caller already has one.

- `Supported`—The option `Supported` means that the object is happy both with and without an activity. If the caller already has an activity, the object is included with this activity. If the caller does not have an activity, the object does not get one.

The results of selecting a SynchronizationOption are shown in Table 3-1. This table shows what options are needed so that an activity is available for the object and when the activity is shared with the activity of the creator.

Transactional Options and Synchronization

For transactional and JITA objects, synchronization is automatically adjusted to SynchronizationOption.Required. With objects using these services, the only two options allowed are Required and RequiresNew; an activity is always required with these services.

Synchronization Example

Let's create one simple example using synchronization. In this example, you will also see when it is useful to use the option RequiresNew rather than Required.

The first scenario is described in Figure 3-6. Here we have the components A and B, both with the synchronization option Required. Object A is created from the main thread, which in turn creates object B. Object B will be returned to the client application, and the client application uses a second thread to access object B. While the first thread accesses object A, the second thread must wait before it can access object B.

Table 3-1 Synchronization Options

SynchronizationOption Value	Running in Activity	Shares Creator Activity
Disabled	If the creator has an activity, and the context is shared	If the creator has an activity, and the context is shared
NotSupported	Never	Never
Required	Always	If the creator has an activity
RequiresNew	Always	Never
Supported	If the creator has an activity	If the creator has an activity

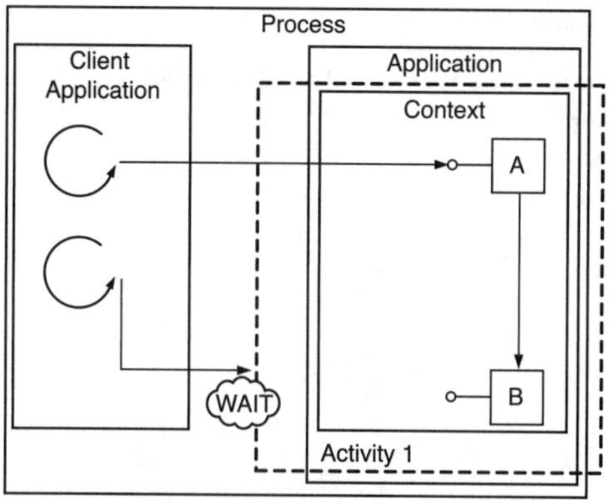

Figure 3-6   Synchronization with an activity.

With the assembly attributes of the component library, the application configuration values and the key file for the assembly are defined as shown in Listing 3-3.

Listing 3-3   Assembly Attributes

```
[assembly: AssemblyDelaySign(false)]
[assembly: AssemblyKeyFile("../../../../mykey.snk")]
[assembly: AssemblyKeyName("")]

[assembly: ApplicationName("Synchronization Demo")]
[assembly: Description("Sample Application for Enterprise Services")]
[assembly: ApplicationActivation(ActivationOption.Library)]
[assembly: ApplicationAccessControl(false)]
```

Class A is the entry point to the application. The option we use with the attribute [Synchronization] is SynchronizationOption.Required, so an activity will always be available. The method GetB creates and returns an object of type B to the caller. The methods Sleep and GetActivityId are used to demonstrate synchronization issues. Sleep just does a Thread.Sleep and writes informal messages to the console. Because the application is configured as a library application, these messages can be seen in the console of the client. GetActivityId returns the unique ID of the activity by using the class ContextUtil.

Listing 3-4   Synchronized Class A

```
[Synchronization(SynchronizationOption.Required)]
[EventTrackingEnabled]
public class A : ServicedComponent
{
    public A()
    {
    }

    public B GetB()
    {
        return new B();
    }

    public void Sleep()
    {
        Console.WriteLine("A.Sleep started");
        Thread.Sleep(2000);
        Console.WriteLine("A.Sleep finished");
    }

    public Guid GetActivityId()
    {
        return ContextUtil.ActivityId;
    }
}
```

Class B offers Sleep and GetActivityId methods similar to class A. Because class B is not instantiated from the client application, this class can be marked as a private component.[3]

Listing 3-5   Synchronized Class B

```
[Synchronization(SynchronizationOption.Required)]
[EventTrackingEnabled]
[PrivateComponent]
public class B : ServicedComponent
{
    public void Sleep()
    {
        Console.WriteLine("B.Sleep started");
        Thread.Sleep(2000);
        Console.WriteLine("B.Sleep finished");
    }
```

```
    public Guid GetActivityId()
    {
        return ContextUtil.ActivityId;
    }
}
```

The client application is just a simple console application. The class `Client` has two member variables `aObj` and `bObj` that are used to reference the serviced components. In the `Main` method, these variables are initialized after an object of type `Client` is created. The variable `bObj` is initialized by a call to the method `GetB` of the class A. Then a new thread with the `Main` method `ThreadMethod` is started immediately. In the main thread, the activity ID of the `aObj` is written to the console before the `Sleep` method is called. Finally, a new activity is started by creating a new object of type A where the activity ID is also written to the console.

In the `Main` method of the thread, we just write the activity ID of the activity where `bObj` resides to the console, and invoke the `Sleep` method to evaluate synchronized access.

Listing 3-6   Client Application Accessing Synchronized Objects

```
using System;
using System.Threading;
using Demos.Synchronization;

class Client
{
    private A aObj;
    private B bObj;

    static void Main(string[] args)
    {
        Client client = new Client();
        client.aObj = new A();
        client.bObj = client.aObj.GetB();

        new Thread(new ThreadStart(client.ThreadMethod)).Start();

        Console.WriteLine("aObj: {0}",
                    client.aObj.GetActivityId().ToString());
        client.aObj.Sleep();
```

```
    A a = new A();
    Console.WriteLine("a: {0}", a.GetActivityId().ToString());

    client.aObj.Dispose();
    a.Dispose();
}

public void ThreadMethod()
{
    Console.WriteLine("bObj: {0}",
                        bObj.GetActivityId().ToString());
    bObj.Sleep();
    bObj.Dispose();
}
}
```

Starting the client application registers the .NET Enterprise Services application automatically. After the application is registered, you can see the concurrency configuration with the component properties in the Component Services Explorer, as shown in Figure 3-7. With the Synchronization Support option, Required is selected because of the serviced component configuration with the value SynchronizationOption.Required.

In addition to the synchronization support configuration demonstrated in Figure 3-6, you can see that the Threading Model shows Any Apartment. The reason for that is because the default option for .NET components configured with .NET Enterprise Services is ThreadingModel = Both within the registry. This is an especially important issue if the application is configured as a library application, which will be shown soon.

Starting the client application, you will get output that looks similar to that shown with the following console output. The activity ID of aObj and bObj is the same, because bObj was created from within the activity of aObj, and with the configuration SynchronizationOption.Required, the same activity is used. In addition to that, you can see that B.Sleep is only started after A.Sleep was completed. Although different client threads are used here, the second thread is blocked until the activity is available. Object A, which was created from a different client task, has a new activity, as you can see from a different activity ID.

```
aObj: 3568a216-710a-47ab-8b39-81f9a002ae7d
A.Sleep started
bObj: 3568a216-710a-47ab-8b39-81f9a002ae7d
A.Sleep finished
B.Sleep started
a: 391c3f11-fd7c-4408-8c0a-627f4f994318
B.Sleep finished
```

Changing the configuration of component B also changes the behavior completely. If the synchronization configuration for class B is set to the option `SynchronizationOption.RequiresNew`, there is a different behavior, as shown in Figure 3-8. Here again, as in the previous scenario, the client application creates

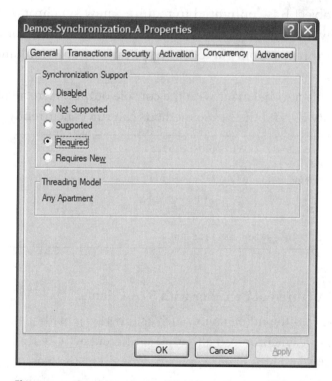

Figure 3-7   Concurrency properties.

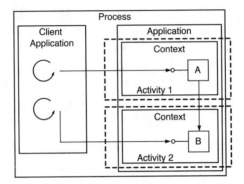

Figure 3-8 Two activities used in the same logical thread.

object A, and object A creates object B and returns a reference to B. The only difference is that object B is configured to require a new synchronization, so object B will get a new activity that is independent from the activity of object A. As a result, the two threads from the client application can simultaneously access objects A and B.

You can see this new behavior with the console output. Here all objects do have a different activity ID, and the `Sleep` methods can run concurrently.

```
aObj: 01e55a3e-ddd6-4917-afc7-4e98cc3a8e74
A.Sleep started
bObj: 318e887e-6067-4f32-a32b-7346fbe4cde1
B.Sleep started
A.Sleep finished
B.Sleep finished
a: 1f6df1b6-6291-4b95-82da-a83530f62e04
```

NOTE: A Different Behavior with STA Clients

If you see a different behavior, such as the `Sleep` methods still seem to run synchronized although a different activity ID is shown, the apartment of the client application might be the reason.

If the `Main` method of the client application has the attribute `[STAThread]` applied, the client thread automatically creates a single-threaded apartment; and because in the sample a library application is used, and the components accept all apartments by the registry configuration, the STA client apartment will be the one used by the components. Earlier in this chapter, we discussed the synchronization features of STA, and these apply here, too. To change the behavior to the one seen here, you just have to remove the attribute [STAThread]; by default, .NET creates an MTA thread.

Of course, the client influences the apartment of the component only if the Enterprise Services application is configured as a library application.

Reentrancy

Another important aspect with synchronization is **reentrancy**. Reentrancy refers to when a single object is invoked multiple times by the same call flow. Reentrancy is made possible by a **causality-based lock**.

An activity uses a causality-based lock. Contrary to other Win32 API synchronization mechanisms, the causality lock does not use a physical thread, but a logical thread. Causality locks have the advantage that synchronization with Enterprise Services does not hinder reentrancy. Consider the scenario in Figure 3-9.

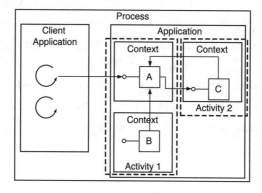

Figure 3-9   Activities and reentrancy.

This figure shows two objects with a callback. Object A invokes methods in object C, and object C does a callback in object A. Although it is not allowed for a second client thread to invoke a method in object A when the activity is running, the callback from object C is working without a problem because this call flow has the same **causality ID**.

Selecting the Synchronization Option

So, what apartment and what activity should be selected for .NET components?

The default apartment configuration with .NET serviced component is Both, as shown and configured in the registry. The configuration value Both means that any apartment (STA, MTA, or TNA) is accepted. Usually this is an option you can live with. If the application of the serviced component is configured as a server application, the component will run inside an MTA and can be accessed from different threads. If the application is configured as a library application, the client defines the apartment to use. The default apartment with ASP.NET applications is the MTA. With console or Windows applications, the apartment is defined by the attribute [STAThread] or [MTAThread], which is applied to the Main method. If an STA is used, you have to pay special attention to synchronization in case you are using multiple threads. The STA hinders the multiple threads that are using the serviced component, no matter how the activity is configured. Using an STA for the serviced component is only a requirement if the component uses state that is bound to a single thread—e.g., thread local storage, or window handles.

What about the activity configuration? For most cases, the option SynchronizationOption.Required is the best choice. This way you get synchronized access to the component. If multiple threads should access the component concurrently, you should change this option to SynchronizationOption.NotSupported. If you want synchronized access to the components, but the second component should be accessed concurrently with the first component that was used to create the second one, SynchronizationOption.RequiresNew might be the best option—as demonstrated in the synchronization example shown earlier.

> **TIP: Reality Check: Activities and Stateful Components**
>
> If you pass object references for stateful components across method calls, you must pay attention to activities and reentrancy issues. With stateless components, you do not have a reentrancy issue because a new object is used with every method call. Stateless[4] components should be the preferred option because this increases scalability, and not passing around object references makes the move to the follow-up technology Indigo[5] easier.

Services Without Components

Windows Server 2003 and Windows XP SP2 have a new feature with Enterprise Services: services without components. This enables the use of activities and transactions directly inside a method without deriving the class from `ServicedComponent`. Using this new feature, you can bind activities to a thread or create new contexts within a method.

To explain how activities without serviced components work, this section covers the following topics:

- `ServiceDomain` class
- `ServiceConfig` class
- `Activity` class
- Using a new activity
- Starting a new context

ServiceDomain Class

With the `ServiceDomain` class, a code block can run in its own context. `ServiceDomain` makes it possible to create a context that is independent of the context that it is currently run in.

ServiceDomain has just two static methods: Enter and Leave. If Enter is used, a context is created that is defined by the ServiceConfig object, which is passed to the method. With Leave, the context is exited to return to the previous context.

ServiceConfig Class

With the ServiceConfig class, you can define the context attributes for the context that should be created with the ServiceDomain or Activity classes. The properties of the class ServiceConfig are listed in Table 3-2.

Activity Class

With the Activity class, you can create a new activity. The constructor of this class accepts a ServiceConfig object, so with the ServiceConfig, you can define the attributes of the activity. After creating the activity, you can either invoke a method synchronously or asynchronously that will use the activity, or bind a thread to the activity. The methods of the Activity class are listed in Table 3-3.

Table 3-2   ServiceConfig Property

Properties	Description
Binding	If you use resources that are bound to a thread (e.g., thread local storage) or window handles, it can be defined that only one thread of the STA pool is used by setting the Binding property to Binding Option.BindingToPoolThread. By default, the context is not bound to a thread; the default setting is BindingOption.NoBinding.
IISIntrinsicsEnabled	If the class is used within an ASP.NET application, by setting this option to true, you can access ASP.NET objects, such as the application and session objects, and user information.
Inheritance	If you set the property Inheritance to InheritanceOption.Inherit, all properties of an already existing context are used for creating the new context. With IneritanceOption.Ignore, the existing context is ignored and a completely new context is created.

`SxsDirectory`
`SxsName`
`SxsOption`
	The `Sxs{}` properties are for side-by-side support of native DLLs. These options make it possible for different versions of native DLLs, now called Win32 assemblies, to coexist. Such a behavior that is normal to .NET assemblies is now possible with Win32 DLLs.

`PartitionId` `PartitionOption`	This option is only useful with serviced components running within an Enterprise Services application. Here you can get and set the partition that should be used for the application. You can use multiple partitions for an application to support different application configurations.
`Synchronization`	With the `Synchronization` property, you can define one of the `SynchronizationOption` values previously discussed to define the synchronization needs of the activity.
`ThreadPool`	This property defines the thread pool that should be used for the activity. The thread pool can be either the STA or the MTA thread pool with the options `Thread-PoolOption.STA` and `ThreadPoolOption.MTA`. Setting the property to `ThreadPoolOption.Inherit` ensures that the same thread pool as the parent context is used. The value `ThreadPoolOption.None` is not allowed with activities.

`TrackingEnabled`
`TrackingAppName`
`TrackingComponentName`
	With serviced components, the attribute `[EventTrackingEnabled]` is used to enable monitoring the component. Contexts, activities, and transactions can also be monitored without using serviced components. Setting the option `TrackingEnabled` to true allows you to use a COM+ spy program to monitor serviced components.

`COMTIIntrinsicsEnabled`	With `COMTIIntrinsicsEnabled`, you can define whether the COM Transaction Integrator should be used.
`BringYourOwnTransaction`	You can set `BringYourOwnTransaction` to an existing transaction object so that the new context will participate in the existing transaction.

`Transaction`
`TransactionDescription`
`TransactionTimeout`
`IsolationLevel`
`TipUrl`
	These properties are used to define the transaction behavior of the context. How to use these options is shown in Chapter 7, "Transaction Services."

Table 3-3   Methods of the Activity Class

Method	Description
SynchronousCall	With the SynchronousCall method, an object that implements the interface IServiceCall can be passed. IServiceCall defines the method OnCall that will be invoked when calling the method SynchronousCall.
AsynchronousCall	As with the SynchronousCall method, you can pass an object that implements IServiceCall with AsynchronousCall. Contrary to the first method, here the method call is started asynchronously.
BindToCurrentThread UnbindFromThread	Instead of defining a method that should be invoked with the activity, you can bind the activity to the current thread with the method BindToCurrentThread, so that from now on all methods of this thread run in the activity. UnbindFromThread removes the activity from the thread.

Using a New Activity

Now take a look at a small example using these classes. In the example shown in Figure 3-7, the class SyncDemo implements the interface IServiceCall. You can use classes with these interfaces with the methods SynchronousCall and AsynchronousCall of the class Activity. The interface just defines a single method OnCall, where you can implement the work that needs to be done and that requires an activity.

Listing 3-7   Implementing the Interface IServiceCall

```
class SyncDemo : IServiceCall
{
    public void OnCall()
    {
        Console.WriteLine("OnCall started");
        Console.WriteLine("running in the activity: {0}",
                ContextUtil.ActivityId);
        Console.WriteLine("running in an {0} thread",
                Thread.CurrentThread.ApartmentState.ToString());
        System.Threading.Thread.Sleep(3000);
```

```
        Console.WriteLine("OnCall finished");
    }
}
```

Listing 3-8 shows a client application using this class. The Main method of the application is marked with the attribute [STAThread], so that the main thread joins a single-threaded apartment. You can change this to [MTAThread]; as soon as you join one apartment type, however, you have to stay within it. In the Main method, an object of type ServiceConfig is created to set the context requirements for the activity. To use an MTA thread for the SyncDemo object, you set the ThreadPool property to ThreadPoolOption.MTA. The Synchronization property is set to SynchronizationOption.Required, so this is a request to use the synchronization service. Now you can create a new activity by passing the config object to the constructor of the Activity class. The work to be done inside the activity is passed to the methods AsynchronousCall and SynchronousCall of the activity object. Because of the required synchronization, these methods will not overlap, although they do run on different MTA threads of the pool.

Listing 3-8   Client Application Using Services Without Components

```
class Test
{
    [STAThread]
    static void Main(string[] args)
    {
        ServiceConfig config = new ServiceConfig();
        config.ThreadPool = ThreadPoolOption.MTA;
        config.Synchronization = SynchronizationOption.Required;

        Activity activity = new Activity(config);

        SyncDemo serviceCall = new SyncDemo();
        Console.WriteLine("starting the first async call");
        activity.AsynchronousCall(serviceCall);

        Console.WriteLine("starting the second async call");
        activity.AsynchronousCall(serviceCall);

        Console.WriteLine("starting the synchronous call");
        activity.SynchronousCall(serviceCall);
    }
}
```

The console output of the application demonstrates that the three method calls do not overlap, and the activity ID shown for all these methods is the same.

```
starting the first async call
starting the second async call
starting the synchronous call
OnCall started
running in the activity: 2c383439-0b79-44e0-8ccc-acb214f3d904
running in an MTA thread

OnCall finished
OnCall started
running in the activity: 2c383439-0b79-44e0-8ccc-acb214f3d904
running in an MTA thread

OnCall finished
OnCall started
running in the activity: 2c383439-0b79-44e0-8ccc-acb214f3d904
running in an MTA thread

OnCall finished
```

Changing the `Synchronization` property to the value `Synchronization-Option.NotSupported`, you can see that the methods run concurrently, and there is no activity.

```
starting the first async call
example, shown in figure starting the second async call
starting the synchronous call
OnCall started
running in the activity: 00000000-0000-0000-0000-000000000000
running in an MTA thread

OnCall started
running in the activity: 00000000-0000-0000-0000-000000000000
running in an MTA thread

OnCall started
running in the activity: 00000000-0000-0000-0000-000000000000
running in an MTA thread

OnCall finished
OnCall finished
OnCall finished
```

Starting a New Context

Creating and using a new context with the ServiceDomain class is demonstrated in Listing 3-9. Here the required context properties are defined with the Service-Config class, where the Synchronization property is set to Synchronization-Option.Required. The context is created by using ServiceDomain.Enter, and the ID of the activity is accessed with the ContextUtil class. Inside this context, a new context is created with ServiceDomain.Enter. Because the same properties for the context are passed, no new activity will be created. Before a third context is entered, the Synchronization property of the newly to be created context is changed to SynchronizationOption.RequiresNew, which will create a new activity. Finally, for every call to ServiceDomain.Enter, a call to ServiceDomain.Leave must be done.

Listing 3-9   Using the ServiceDomain Class

```
[STAThread]
static void Main(string[] args)
{
    ServiceConfig config = new ServiceConfig();
    config.Synchronization = SynchronizationOption.Required;

    ServiceDomain.Enter(config);
        Console.WriteLine("Outer  - activity: {0}",
                        ContextUtil.ActivityId);

        ServiceDomain.Enter(config);
            Console.WriteLine("Middle - activity: {0}",
                            ContextUtil.ActivityId);

            config.Synchronization = SynchronizationOption.RequiresNew;
            ServiceDomain.Enter(config);
                Console.WriteLine("Inner  - activity: {0}",
                                ContextUtil.ActivityId);

            ServiceDomain.Leave();
        ServiceDomain.Leave();
    ServiceDomain.Leave();
}
```

The output to the console is as expected. For the first two contexts, we have the same activity, but the third context shows a different activity.

```
Outer  - activity: 694b63ca-2596-4461-8ab9-db76afab4928
Middle - activity: 694b63ca-2596-4461-8ab9-db76afab4928
Inner  - activity: 522dfb6d-cf0f-4759-8d19-5ab5f4d7739d
```

The result of the context of a context that was created with the `ServiceDomain` class can be influenced with the class `ContextUtil`, as shown in Chapter 2. In Chapter 7, you can read about using the `ServiceDomain` class with transactions.

> **TIP: Reality Check: Services Without Components**
>
> Services without components is a great feature because the application can be installed easily with copy and paste. You do not have to write registry keys.

> **TIP: Reality Check: Using Services Without Components Within Serviced Components**
>
> Activities without serviced components are not only an interesting feature without serviced components, but they are also of great use within serviced components. Within serviced components, you can create new contexts within methods because it is not necessary to define context properties at the component level; you can change the context within methods.

Summary

This chapter discussed synchronization features with .NET Enterprise Services. In this chapter, you learned why synchronization is needed and what problems can occur without synchronized access.

Apartments played a big role with COM. They are not that important anymore, but some problems can occur because of a wrong apartment configuration. Therefore, this chapter covered the architecture of the different apartment models: STA, MTA, and TNA.

As discussed in this chapter, with .NET Enterprise Services, you get activities and causalities. An activity is a synchronization domain that can cross context and process boundaries. Only one logical thread may access an activity at the same time. A causality is a chain of physical threads that make up a logical thread. Causalities make it possible to allow reentrancy into an object.

Because Windows Server 2003 offers a new way to get synchronized access without serviced components, this chapter examined the new `Activity` class.

1 With Visual Basic .NET, you can use the `SyncLock` statement similar to the C# `lock` statement.

2 The attribute `[STAThread]` has no meaning for .NET components. It is only used when COM objects are accessed. However, you must be aware that a COM component might be wrapped by a .NET component.

3 Private components are discussed in Chapter 2.

4 Chapter 9, "State Management," covers the different options where you can put the state.

5 Indigo is discussed in Chapter 14, "The Future of Distributed Applications."

4

COM Interop

COM WAS VERY POPULAR, AND THERE are billions of lines of existing COM code. When using .NET Enterprise Services from your applications, there is a good chance that you will not port all your components and all your applications to this new technology. You want to integrate your existing components and applications with .NET instead.

This chapter covers interoperability with different COM clients, and using COM components from .NET objects within the same call flow.

Until now, the samples in this book only used simple .NET clients to access .NET components configured with .NET Enterprise Services. With .NET Enterprise Services, it is not only possible to use .NET clients, but also COM clients. Depending on the client type, COM has different requirements.

In Chapter 1, "Introducing .NET Enterprise Services," some major differences between COM and .NET were discussed. This chapter examines how .NET components can integrate with COM.

Specifically, this chapter covers the following topics:

- Default interop settings
- Interfaces
- Applications
- Metadata
- COM client types
- Integration with COM components

.NET Clients Without COM Interop

Until now in this book, just .NET clients have been used to access serviced components. Let's review and summarize what has been done so far using .NET clients. There is hardly a difference between accessing serviced components and accessing normal .NET components.

But what is special about accessing serviced components from a .NET client application is defined in a few steps: After registration of the serviced component, you just have to do the following:

1. Reference the assembly `System.EnterpriseServices`.

2. Reference the assembly of our serviced component library.

3. Use the serviced component like an ordinary .NET class.

For development of the client application, these steps are always fine, regardless of whether the client application is running on the same system as the server or on a different system. If the client application is running on a different system, you must take some more actions before deployment. The communication protocol between two systems is DCOM or .NET remoting.[1] With DCOM, COM interop plays an important role.

Side-by-Side Support

.NET enables you to use multiple versions of the same assembly in a single process. The same is true for an Enterprise Services application. Configuring different versions of the assembly with the default options of `regsvcs.exe`[2] always creates new serviced component configuration entries with the application.

The client application will use the version that was used while building the client, because this version is listed with the metadata of the client assembly. To use a different version, the same versioning rules as with other .NET applications apply: Application configuration files or publisher policy assemblies can be used.

With multiple versions of the same assembly in one Enterprise Services application, all versions must physically exist. Multiple versions can coexist if you put the assemblies in the **global assembly cache** (GAC).[3] If you don't use the GAC, you must implement a directory structure to manage different assembly versions yourself. If not all assemblies of the different versions are available, several problems will occur. Of course, the client that uses a missing version will fail, but it is also not possible to build an application proxy.

> **NOTE: Application Configuration Files and Publisher Policies[4]**
>
> With shared assemblies, versioning is an important aspect. By default, the client application uses the same version of a shared assembly that was used at compile time. If a different version of a shared assembly should be used, you can define the version with the element `<bindingRedirect>` inside an application configuration file. Instead of redirecting the version of a shared assembly with an application configuration file, the publisher of a shared assembly can define that a new version of the assembly should be used by all applications. This is done by creating a publisher policy assembly. A publisher policy assembly must be installed in the GAC, and it includes nothing more than a configuration file. A publisher policy can be overridden by setting `<publisherPolicy apply="no" />` with an application configuration file.

COM Interoperability

COM clients can be used to access serviced components. In case you already have some configured COM+ components that have been written with COM, you probably want to use them from .NET components. This kind of interoperability is important because it means you don't have to rewrite every component and every client application. A COM component can participate in the same context[5] as a .NET component.

COM interop is not only an issue with a COM client accessing the .NET component, or the .NET component accessing a COM object; it is also used with a .NET client accessing the .NET component in case the serviced application is accessed across processes, or across different systems using the DCOM protocol.

The section examines the COM interoperability with serviced components. Comparing COM with .NET, you might also refer to Chapter 2 when we discussed differences between COM and .NET and evaluated how a COM+ context fits into the picture with .NET contexts. Chapter 3, "Concurrency," was about concurrency, so the COM apartment models played an important part of that chapter.

Working through the previous chapters, you might have already discovered that the tool `regsvcs.exe` not only configures and registers the component for Enterprise Services but also creates the COM type library. The type library holds the metadata of the .NET components for COM clients. The generated metadata and interface types for COM clients can be influenced with many attributes, as you will see in this chapter.

COM Callable Wrappers and Runtime Callable Wrappers

For integration with COM, **COM callable wrappers** (CCWs) are used for COM clients accessing .NET components, whereas **runtime callable wrappers** (RCWs) are used for .NET clients accessing COM objects. Of course, in such scenarios, the .NET client can be a .NET component itself, whereas a COM client can be a COM object.

A CCW behaves like a COM object for a COM client, such as a COM client would expect. As Figure 4-1 demonstrates, a CCW offers interfaces such as `IUnknown` and `IDispatch` for COM clients, although these are not implemented by the .NET component. Also, the CCW can be found in the registry, because COM clients always expect to find their components there. When methods of the CCW are invoked, the CCW invokes methods of the .NET components and deals with the issues of garbage collection by doing COM reference counting.

The CCW also deals with the transformation of data types because the data types are different with .NET and COM. Some data types can be mapped directly because they have the same representation in memory, whereas others must be converted. The data types with the same memory representation are known as **blittable data types** (e.g., `System.Int16`, `System.Int32`, `System.Int64`). The .NET data type `System.String` is converted to a COM `BSTR` data type. `BSTR` is nonblittable.

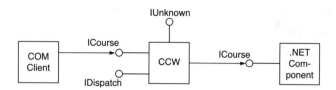

Figure 4-1 A COM callable wrapper (CCW).

If interoperability is used the other way around, an RCW (see Figure 4-2) offers the functionality that a .NET client expects and manages a COM object. The RCW is a good behavioral client to the COM object and offers pure .NET functionality for the .NET client. With .NET, you do not have to pay attention to the release of every reference to every COM interface because this is done by the RCW. However, you still have to pay attention to the behavior of the garbage collector with the undeterministic behavior of freeing memory. Because you are dealing with native resources (COM objects), you must be aware of the dispose pattern.[6] To explicitly release the references to the COM object, you can use the class `Marshal` with the method `ReleaseComObject`. You can find this class in the namespace `System.Runtime.InteropServices`.

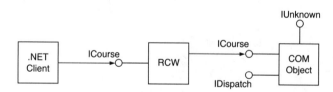

Figure 4-2 A runtime callable wrapper (RCW).

Default COM Configuration

First let's look at a .NET component that is used from a COM client. Here a simple example is shown with no attributes used to configure COM options. In this example, two serviced component classes, and some classes that will be used to pass data to and from the components, are created. The first two classes—shown in Listing 4-1, Customer and CourseInfo—are two simple classes that can be passed as arguments. These classes just have private member variables and public properties to access these variables. To make it possible that these classes can be transferred across the network, you must mark them with the [Serializable] attribute.

Listing 4-1   Serializable Classes

```
[Serializable]
public class Customer
{
    private string name;
    private string company;

    public Customer(string name, string company)
    {
        this.name = name;
        this.company = company;
    }

    public string Name
    {
        get
        {
            return name;
        }
    }

    public string Company
    {
        get
        {
            return company;
        }
    }
}

[Serializable]
public class CourseInfo
{
    private string number;
    private string title;
    private int length;
    private DateTime date;
```

```
    public CourseInfo(string number, string title, int length,
                      DateTime date)
    {
        this.number = number;
        this.title = title;
        this.length = length;
        this.date = date;
    }

    public string Number
    {
        get
        {
            return number;
        }
    }

    public string Title
    {
        get
        {
            return title;
        }
    }

    public int Length
    {
        get
        {
            return length;
        }
    }

    public DateTime Date
    {
        get
        {
            return date;
        }
    }
}
```

Listings 4-2 and 4-3 show the implementation of the serviced component classes. The class CourseManagement implements the interface ICourseManagement, which defines three methods: GetCourse, SetCourse, and GetCourseControl.

GetCourse returns a CourseInfo object to the client. With SetCourse, a Course-Info object is passed to the server. GetCourseControl returns a reference to a CustomerControl object that by itself is a serviced component class. The method SetCourse displays a message box just for testing the component. To use the MessageBox class, you have to reference the assembly System.Windows.Forms and import the namespace System.Windows.Forms.

Listing 4-2   CourseManagement Component

```
public interface ICourseManagement
{
    CourseInfo GetCourse();
    void SetCourse(CourseInfo course);
    CustomerControl GetCustomerControl();
}


[EventTrackingEnabled]
public class CourseManagement : ServicedComponent,
                                ICourseManagement
{
    public CourseManagement()
    {
    }

    public CourseInfo GetCourse()
    {
        CourseInfo course = new CourseInfo(
            "MS-2557",
            "Developing Component-based Applicatons", 5,
            new DateTime(2003, 8, 18));
        return course;
    }

    public void SetCourse(CourseInfo course)
    {
        MessageBox.Show("Course: {0}", course.Title);
    }

    public CustomerControl GetCustomerControl()
    {
        CustomerControl control = new CustomerControl();
        return control;
    }
}
```

> **TIP: Reality Check: Using Dialog Boxes**
>
> With real applications, do not open dialog boxes (for example, message boxes) with serviced components that are running on the server. These dialog boxes are never seen and answered. Error logging and monitoring can be implemented using event logs and performance monitoring. If the serviced component is running on the client, using dialog boxes to communicate with the user is a viable practice.

The class `CustomerControl`, in contrast to the class `CourseManagement`, does not implement an interface, just to show you the differences with the generated code with regard to COM clients. In addition, it is marked with the attribute `[PrivateComponent]` because this class need not be created from the client application; it can only be created inside the Enterprise Services application. With the method `GetCustomer`, a new `Customer` object is returned to the client.

Listing 4-3   CustomerControl Component

```
[EventTrackingEnabled]
[PrivateComponent]
public class CustomerControl : ServicedComponent
{
    public CustomerControl()
    {
    }

    public Customer GetCustomer()
    {
        Customer c = new Customer("Stephane", "Addison Wesley");
        return c;
    }
}
```

Generated Type Library

As previously discussed, building and registering the assembly by using `regsvcs.exe` not only configures the serviced component, but also creates a type library. Now we are going to look into the type library. To read type library information, you can use a tool that can be started from within Visual Studio: Tools, OLE/COM Object Viewer. The OLE/COM Object Viewer enables you to dig into COM objects and even start them. From this tool, you can read type libraries by choosing File, View Typelib.

Figure 4-3 shows the information displayed by the OLE/COM Object Viewer when opening the component. On the left side, you can see coclass and interface definitions for every class in the assembly.

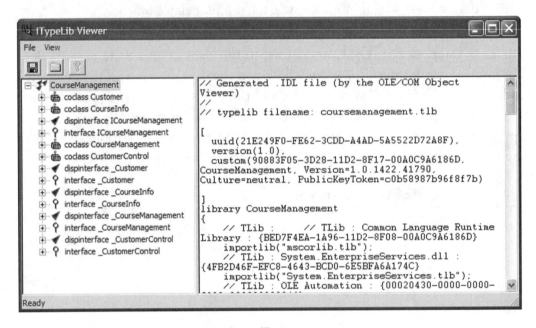

Figure 4-3 OleView opening the generated type library.

Now take a closer look at some details of the generated COM interface definition. For every class that is defined with this source code, a coclass entry was generated. A coclass marks a COM object and lists the COM interfaces that are implemented with the component.

For the serviced component class CourseManagement, the generated output is shown. In the header section, the UUID marks the unique identifier of the component; with COM components, this is also known as CLSID. The custom property with the UUID 0F21F359-AB84-41E8-9A78-36D110E6D2F9 is only useful for .NET clients that will use this metadata. This UUID marks a COM interop feature. (That is, if a .NET class is generated from the type library [a runtime callable wrapper, RCW], it uses the name associated with this UUID to generate a wrapper class.)

```
[
    uuid(4535EEFE-94D3-35FA-943F-057FB4116ED8),
    version(1.0),
    custom(0F21F359-AB84-41E8-9A78-36D110E6D2F9,
           Demos.COMInterop.CourseManagement)
]
coclass CourseManagement {
    [default] interface _CourseManagement;
    interface _Object;
    interface IRemoteDispatch;
    interface IDisposable;
    interface IManagedObject;
    interface IServicedComponentInfo;
    interface ICourseManagement;
};
```

Many of the interfaces that are implemented with a serviced component class are only used internally, so this chapter just briefly mentions `IRemoteDispatch`, `IManagedObject`, and `IServicedComponentInfo`.

`IRemoteDispatch` is necessary for methods declared with the `[AutoComplete]` attribute, which was discussed in Chapter 2, "Object Activation and Contexts." For .NET components, implementing interfaces is not required, but metadata that is needed with methods can only be written to the COM+ catalog by using interfaces. `IRemoteDispatch` is implemented by the runtime to read the `[AutoComplete]` information from the assembly metadata. `IManagedObject` is implemented by the runtime for all managed objects configured with Enterprise Services.

The interface `_Object` defines the methods of the base class `Object`, which allows calling methods from that base class with a client.

The default interface `_CourseManagement` can be used to call the public methods of the class, as is possible with the interface `ICourseManagement`. Because the class `CourseManagement` implements the interface `ICourseManagement`, this interface is also listed here.

The class `CourseInfo` that is also defined within the serviced component assembly is listed with the type information in the type library, too. However, because it does not derive from the class `ServicedComponent`, the type information looks different. In the IDL header section of this coclass, you can see the `noncreatable` property, which does not allow instantiating objects of this class in the client. The other difference you can see is that the only interfaces available with this component are `_CourseInfo` and `_Object`.

```
[
  uuid(BF26C367-4B4F-3017-A5F2-CAF972D2C66F),
  version(1.0),
  noncreatable,
  custom(0F21F359-AB84-41E8-9A78-36D110E6D2F9,
    Demos.COMInterop.CourseInfo)
]
coclass CourseInfo {
    [default] interface _CourseInfo;
    interface _Object;
};
```

The other classes, `Customer` and `CustomerControl`, defined with the sample look similar to the two coclasses already discussed. So let's look at the interface declarations.

The only interface that was defined with the serviced component assembly was `ICourseManagement`. You have seen the interface used in the coclass section of `CourseManagement`. The UUID that is listed here defines the unique identifier for this interface, also known as the **interface ID** (IID). By default, the interface type that is generated is a dual interface, allowing the component to be called from scripting clients. Dual interfaces derive from the COM interface `IDispatch`, as shown here. In addition, you can see all methods that have been defined with the interface, but the method signature has changed so that the return type always is an HRESULT, as is expected with the methods of COM interfaces.

```
[
  odl,
  uuid(11BC9B79-C02C-39D6-A70F-32E83B18DD0E),
  version(1.0),
  dual,
```

```
    oleautomation,
    custom(0F21F359-AB84-41E8-9A78-36D110E6D2F9,
          Demos.COMInterop.ICourseManagement)
]
interface ICourseManagement : IDispatch {
    [id(0x60020000)]
    HRESULT GetCourse([out, retval] _CourseInfo** pRetVal);
    [id(0x60020001)]
    HRESULT SetCourse([in] _CourseInfo* course);
    [id(0x60020002)]
    HRESULT GetCustomerControl([out, retval]
                               _CustomerControl** pRetVal);
};
```

The type-specific interfaces that have not been declared as interfaces with the C#
sources but that have been listed with the coclass sections show up in the generated
IDL definition. However, these interfaces do not list a method. The reason is that the
methods will be resolved only at runtime using .NET reflection.

Many COM servers write their method names and dispatch IDs inside the type
library. This makes it possible to create language-specific type libraries (for example,
with method names that are different in English, German, and French), which makes
it possible to write the program code in a different language by just replacing the
type library. This concept did not succeed because more problems had been introduced[7] (for example, running a system without the correct language-specific type
library).

```
[
    uuid(9DF3A585-8F0A-3648-B291-0C4832871C24),
    hidden,
    dual,
    custom(0F21F359-AB84-41E8-9A78-36D110E6D2F9,
          Demos.COMInterop.CourseInfo)
]
dispinterface _CourseInfo {
    properties:
    methods:
};
```

Now you have learned how the type library is automatically generated without
specifying COM attributes. Dual interfaces are generated by default, but usually this
is not the best option, as you will see soon.

What Is .NET Reflection?

Every .NET assembly contains metadata in addition to the program code. The metadata contains information about the assembly, such as a version number and the information regarding which assemblies are referenced. The metadata also includes information about all types defined with the assembly along with the methods, properties, and fields. Using .NET reflection, you can read this information during run-time and invoke methods dynamically.

Take a look at one example to read and invoke a method dynamically by using .NET reflection. In this example, a component library contains the class Demo with the method Message called dynamically. The class Demo is in the assembly ReflectionLib in the file ReflectionLib.dll.

```
namespace Samples.Reflection
{
    public class Demo
    {
        public void Message(string s)
        {
            System.Console.WriteLine(s);
        }
    }
}
```

With the class Test that is contained in a simple console application, the method Message is called dynamically. First, the assembly is loaded with the Assembly class and the static method LoadFrom. The filename of the assembly is read from the command-line arguments that are passed when starting the application.

With the assembly object that is returned from Assembly.LoadFrom, the metadata of the assembly can be read. The method GetType returns a Type instance representing the type Samples.Reflection.Demo. In case you want to read all types of the assembly, the method GetTypes returns an array of Type objects.

Calling the method `t.GetMethod` returns method information represented in the class `MethodInfo`. With the `MethodInfo` object, you can read the name of the method and get information about the parameters. With the `Invoke` method of the `MethodInfo` class, you can invoke the method dynamically. Because an instance method requires an object when calling the method, an object is created with the `Activator` class. `Activator.CreateInstance` creates an object by passing the `Type` object that is read from the assembly. The `Invoke` method allows you to pass any number of parameters to the target method with an object array. The method `Message` just has one parameter, so an object array with a single object is passed to the `Invoke` method.

As a result, the string `Test` is written to the console in the `Message` method.

```
using System;
using System.Reflection;

class Test
{
    static void Main(string[] args)
    {
        if (args.Length != 1)
        {
            Console.WriteLine("filename needed");
            return;
        }

        string filename = args[0];

        Assembly assembly = Assembly.LoadFrom(filename);
        Type t = assembly.GetType("Samples.Reflection.Demo");
        MethodInfo mi = t.GetMethod("Message");

        object o = Activator.CreateInstance(t);
        object[] parameters = new object[] {"Test"};
        mi.Invoke(o, parameters);
    }
}
```

COM Interface Types

COM makes it possible to define three interface types:

- Custom interfaces
- Dispatch interfaces
- Dual interfaces

The reason for having three interface types can be found in the evolutionary development of COM. The following sections examine these interface types and explain how they can be offered with serviced components.

Custom Interfaces

Using a custom interface, the methods that are exposed with the interface are defined in a **vtable**.[8] With this vtable, just the entry point to this table is needed. The order of the methods is defined with the interface.

Figure 4-4 shows a custom interface. Custom interfaces always derive from the interface IUnknown. IUnknown, the base interface of all COM interfaces, defines three methods: AddRef, Release, and QueryInterface. Following these methods are pointers to the methods defined in the interface ICourseManagement: GetCourse, SetCourse, and GetCustomerControl.

The characteristic of such an interface is that this is the fastest way to invoke a method, but its use is restricted to languages where the interface definition is known at compile time. Scripting clients (for example, VBScript, JavaScript) cannot use these interfaces, whereas Visual Basic 6 clients can.

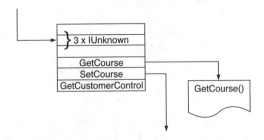

Figure 4-4   Table of a custom interface.

Listing 4-4 shows the interface `ICourseManagement` changed to a custom interface. To declare a custom COM interface with .NET, you can use the attribute `[InterfaceType]` and specify `ComInterfaceType.InterfaceIsIUnknown` with the constructor of the attribute. Using this attribute, you also have to import the namespace `System.Runtime.InteropServices`. All COM interop attributes are defined within this namespace.

Listing 4-4   Defining a Custom Interface

```
[InterfaceType(ComInterfaceType.InterfaceIsIUnknown)]
public interface ICourseManagement
{
    CourseInfo GetCourse();
    void SetCourse(CourseInfo course);
    CustomerControl GetCustomerControl();
}
```

The OLE/COM Object Viewer enables you to look at the IDL code. You can see that the interface `ICourseManagement` now derives from `IUnknown`, and the IDs that had been listed with the methods are removed.

```
[
    odl,
    uuid(11BC9B79-C02C-39D6-A70F-32E83B18DD0E),
    version(1.0),
    oleautomation,
    custom(0F21F359-AB84-41E8-9A78-36D110E6D2F9,
            Demos.COMInterop.ICourseManagement)
]
interface ICourseManagement : IUnknown {
    HRESULT _stdcall GetCourse([out, retval] _CourseInfo** pRetVal);
    HRESULT _stdcall SetCourse([in] _CourseInfo* course);
    HRESULT _stdcall GetCustomerControl([out, retval]
        _CustomerControl** pRetVal);
};
```

Dispatch Interfaces

Scripting clients[9] cannot deal with custom interfaces; they can only use dispatch interfaces. A dispatch interface is an implementation of the `IDispatch` interface, which is known to scripting clients, so there is no need to know the interface layout at compile time.

Figure 4-5 shows the functionality of an `IDispatch` interface. The `IDispatch` interface defines four methods in addition to the `IUnknown` methods. The third and fourth methods are the most interesting ones: `GetIDsOfNames` and `Invoke`. `GetIDsOfNames` is used by a client first to get an ID for a method name. For example, the client passes the method name `GetCourse` to get the ID 0x60020000 returned. This method number or dispatch ID is then used to invoke the method by passing this ID to the `IDispatch` method `Invoke`. `Invoke` then uses another mapping table to get from the dispatch ID to the pointer of the method, so that the method can be invoked.

You might imagine that this is slower than custom interfaces. The mapping mechanism to get the ID from the method name and the invocation of the method by using an ID takes time. There is more than the mapping mechanism; data conversion also happens. `Invoke` accepts a single argument for the parameters that are converted and passed to the target methods.

> **NOTE: Early Binding with Compiled Clients**
>
> Compiled clients that do know the dispatch IDs in advance can reduce the overhead by only calling the `Invoke` method. The mechanism to use only the `Invoke` method is also known as early binding, whereas using both `GetIdsOfNames` and `Invoke` is known as late binding.

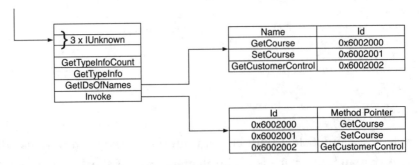

Figure 4-5   Table of a dispatch interface.

To declare a dispatch interface with a .NET interface, you can use the attribute [InterfaceType] and specify ComInterfaceType.InterfaceIsIDispatch in the constructor of the attribute, as shown in Listing 4-5.

Listing 4-5   Defining a Dispatch Interface

```
[InterfaceType(ComInterfaceType.InterfaceIsIDispatch)]
public interface ICourseManagement
{
    CourseInfo GetCourse();
    void SetCourse(CourseInfo course);
    CustomerControl GetCustomerControl();
}
```

Looking at the generated IDL code with the OLE/COM Object Viewer, you can see that ICourseManagement now is a dispinterface. Because the methods defined with a dispinterface are not directly accessed from the COM client (the IDispatch methods are instead), these methods do not return an HRESULT type.

```
[
    uuid(11BC9B79-C02C-39D6-A70F-32E83B18DD0E),
    version(1.0),
    custom(0F21F359-AB84-41E8-9A78-36D110E6D2F9,
           Demos.COMInterop.ICourseManagement)
]
dispinterface ICourseManagement {
    properties:
    methods:
        [id(0x60020000)]
        _CourseInfo* GetCourse();
        [id(0x60020001)]
        void SetCourse([in] _CourseInfo* course);
        [id(0x60020002)]
        _CustomerControl* GetCustomerControl();
};
```

To define a dispatch interface with .NET, you do not have to create a .NET interface at all. Dispatch interfaces can also be defined with a class attribute [ClassInterface] and the value ClassInterfaceType.AutoDispatch, as shown in Listing 4-6 with the class CustomerControl.

Listing 4-6   Defining a Dispatch Interface with a Class Attribute

```
[EventTrackingEnabled]
[PrivateComponent]
[ClassInterface(ClassInterfaceType.AutoDispatch)]
public class CustomerControl : ServicedComponent
{
    public CustomerControl()
    {
    }

    public Customer GetCustomer()
    {
        Customer c = new Customer("Stephane", "Addison Wesley");
        return c;
    }
}
```

Looking at the generated IDL code, you can see that the interface _CustomerControl is declared as a dispinterface, but it does not show methods. The methods do not show up because they are not listed inside tables in the type library as is often the case with normal COM objects; instead, this information will be read by using the reflection mechanism at runtime.

```
[
    uuid(B6DE4A57-F7DC-316D-A383-BF63B97630AA),
    hidden,
    dual,
    custom(0F21F359-AB84-41E8-9A78-36D110E6D2F9,
        Demos.COMInterop.CustomerControl)
]
dispinterface _CustomerControl {
    properties:
    methods:
};
```

If a COM object were developed using C++ and the **Microsoft Foundation Classes** **(MFC)**, dispatch interfaces were usually used, because with the MFC such interfaces could be easily implemented. The MFC was designed in the early COM days.

If the class of the serviced component does not have the attribute [ClassInterface(ClassInterfaceType.AutoDispatch)] applied to it, the dispatch interface is created anyway because this is the default. If you do not

want a dispatch interface created automatically, you can apply the attribute
[ClassInterface(ClassInterfaceType.None)].

Dual Interfaces

Custom interfaces are best for performance; dispatch interfaces can be used by scripting clients. To make the best of both worlds, dual interfaces were designed. A dual interface derives from the interface IDispatch but adds the new methods to the vtable (as shown in Figure 4-6). Clients that only know about the IDispatch can use its GetIDsOfNames and Invoke methods to access the tables to map the name to the IDs and the method pointers, but clients that can access custom interfaces can use them directly.

To declare a dispatch interface with a .NET interface, you can use the attribute [InterfaceType] and specify ComInterfaceType.InterfaceIsDual in the constructor of the attribute, as shown in Listing 4-7. Declaring this attribute is optional, because this is the default for interfaces.

Listing 4-7   Defining a Dual Interface

```
[InterfaceType(ComInterfaceType.InterfaceIsDual)]
public interface ICourseManagement
{
    CourseInfo GetCourse();
    void SetCourse(CourseInfo course);
    CustomerControl GetCustomerControl();
}
```

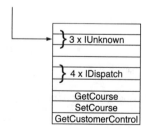

Figure 4-6   Table of a dual interface.

In the IDL declaration, ICourseManagement shows up as a dual interface with methods referenced both in the vtable and with dispatch IDs. Late binding uses the dispatch IDs with the mapping tables.

```
[
  odl,
  uuid(11BC9B79-C02C-39D6-A70F-32E83B18DD0E),
  version(1.0),
  dual,
  oleautomation,
  custom(0F21F359-AB84-41E8-9A78-36D110E6D2F9,
         Demos.COMInterop.ICourseManagement)

]
interface ICourseManagement : IDispatch {
    [id(0x60020000)]
    HRESULT GetCourse([out, retval] _CourseInfo** pRetVal);
    [id(0x60020001)]
    HRESULT SetCourse([in] _CourseInfo* course);
    [id(0x60020002)]
    HRESULT GetCustomerControl([out, retval]
                                  _CustomerControl** pRetVal);
};
```

As with dispatch interfaces, you can declare dual interfaces at the class level, as shown in Listing 4-8.

Listing 4-8   Defining a Dual Interface with a Class Attribute

```
[EventTrackingEnabled]
[PrivateComponent]
[ClassInterface(ClassInterfaceType.AutoDual)]
public class CustomerControl : ServicedComponent
{
    public CustomerControl()
    {
    }

    public Customer GetCustomer()
    {
        Customer c = new Customer("Stephane", "Addison Wesley");
        return c;
    }
}
```

With the declaration ClassInterfaceType.AutoDual added to the class CustomerControl, a dual interface _CustomerControl is created. This interface not only shows up the public methods that have been defined with the class CustomerControl, but also the methods of the base classes of CustomerControl: Object, MarshalByRefObject, and ServicedComponent.

```
[
    odl,
    uuid(D0E44CA4-8D41-3860-8E5F-C36EE7893A59),
    hidden,
    dual,
    nonextensible,
    oleautomation,
    custom(0F21F359-AB84-41E8-9A78-36D110E6D2F9,
           Demos.COMInterop.CustomerControl)
]
interface _CustomerControl : IDispatch {
    [id(00000000), propget,
      custom(54FC8F55-38DE-4703-9C4E-250351302B1C, 1)]
    HRESULT ToString([out, retval] BSTR* pRetVal);
    [id(0x60020001)]
    HRESULT Equals(
                   [in] VARIANT obj,
                   [out, retval] VARIANT_BOOL* pRetVal);
    [id(0x60020002)]
    HRESULT GetHashCode([out, retval] long* pRetVal);
    [id(0x60020003)]
    HRESULT GetType([out, retval] _Type** pRetVal);
    [id(0x60020004)]
    HRESULT GetLifetimeService([out, retval] VARIANT* pRetVal);
    [id(0x60020005)]
    HRESULT InitializeLifetimeService([out, retval] VARIANT* pRetVal);
    [id(0x60020006)]
    HRESULT CreateObjRef(
                   [in] _Type* requestedType,
                   [out, retval] _ObjRef** pRetVal);
    [id(0x60020007)]
    HRESULT Dispose();
    [id(0x60020008)]
    HRESULT GetCustomer([out, retval] _Customer** pRetVal);
};
```

With dual interfaces supporting both dispatch and custom clients, it might seem that dual interfaces are the panacea for COM interface types. However, dual interfaces also introduce new problems. They are restricted to data types that can be packed into a VARIANT, because the Invoke method deals with VARIANTs. This is the same restriction that applies to dispatch interfaces. Another problem is that scripting clients can only use a single interface—it is not good object-oriented design to pack all methods inside a single interface. There have been some patterns to design and to implement multiple interfaces and to offer a scripting client the methods that are available with all interfaces. Before .NET, there was no easy way to implement such a behavior. With .NET, however, you get it automatically: A dispatch interface is created with the class of the serviced component. Because the class implements all methods of the interfaces, you get access to all methods from the scripting client.

Many books describe how to deal with COM interface types and show how to circumvent COM client problems.[10] Nevertheless, in this book, the interfaces are not discussed in more detail, because you already know the most important aspects of using these interfaces with Enterprise Services from a .NET perspective.

> **TIP: Reality Check: What Interface to Use?**
>
> As a summary, for COM clients, you have three different interface types to use: custom, dispatch, and dual interfaces. What interface should you offer with your serviced components? It depends on the type of the client. If the client is a scripting client, the IDispatch interface is a requirement. So, for scripting clients, both the dispatch and dual interface types can be offered. A Visual Basic 6 and C++ client is happy with all interface types, but dispatch interfaces are more difficult to use with C++.
>
> If scripting clients are not needed, the best option to use is custom interfaces.

ComVisible Attribute

By default, all classes and interfaces from our assembly are listed with interfaces and coclasses in the type library to enable access from a COM client. If a class should only be used from within .NET code, you can apply the attribute [ComVisible(false)] to the type. Apply this attribute, and the class/interface will not show up in the type library.

> **NOTE: ComVisible Attribute with Serviced Components**
>
> `[ComVisible(false)]` cannot be applied to classes that derive from the base class `ServicedComponent`. Because COM interop is used to access a serviced component when processes or systems are crossed, interoperability is needed.

Versioning

.NET has a completely different version behavior than COM ever had. The .NET Framework was designed from the ground up to fully support component versioning. Each .NET assembly can contain a four-part version number in the form Major.Minor.Build.Revision that is stored in its manifest. The strong name[11] of the assembly includes this version number. The **Common Language Runtime** (CLR) fully supports multiple versions of the same assembly existing simultaneously in memory. The CLR also supports a full-version policy that can be applied by administrators in XML configuration files, which may be applied on a machine or application basis, binding a client to a specific version of an assembly.

If an assembly is generated by Visual Studio with the assembly attribute `[AssemblyVersion]`, the version is applied automatically as shown:

```
[assembly: AssemblyVersion("1.0.*")]
```

Here the major version number is 1, the minor version number is 0, and the build and revision numbers are generated automatically. With the *, the build number is the number of days since 1-Jan-2000, and the revision number is the number of seconds since midnight divided by two. This guarantees a unique number every time the compiler is started. If you define all four numbers yourself, you have to remember to change the version with every change in the assembly. Otherwise, you can easily have the wrong assembly version number for configured components.

.NET assemblies are uniquely identified with the strong name. As discussed in Chapter 2, "Object Activation and Contexts," the strong name consists of the name of the assembly, the version number, the culture, and the public key, applied to the assembly with the attribute [AssemblyKeyFile].

COM has a completely different concept with versioning and identifying components. With COM, **global unique identifiers** (GUIDS) are used for unique identification of applications, servers, interfaces, and type libraries. A GUID is a unique 128-bit number that is generated from the MAC address of the network card, the time, and a random number. With .NET, you can create such numbers with the static method NewGuid of the Guid class. With Visual Studio, you also get a graphical utility to generate such GUIDs: guidgen.exe, as shown in Figure 4-7. You can also use a command-line tool, uuidgen.exe, to generate unique identifiers.

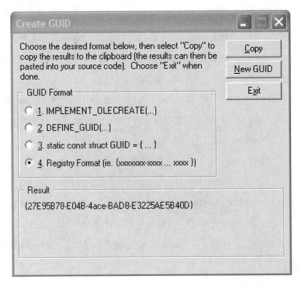

Figure 4-7   Guidgen.exe to create a unique identifier.

With the utility guigen.exe, it is best to set the format to the Registry Format. All other formatters are only of good use if you are developing C++ applications. Every click to the button New GUID creates a new unique identifier. By clicking the button Copy, you copy the GUID to the clipboard, enabling you to paste the GUID anywhere you want.

With COM, a GUID is used to identify applications (APPID), components (CLSID), interfaces (IID), and type libraries (Typelib-Id) with unique IDs. By default, all these IDs are generated automatically, but you can also set the GUID with an attribute.

Applications

COM applications and Enterprise Services applications are identified by the APPID. You can assign a fixed value to the application by defining the assembly attribute `[ApplicationID()]`. If the assembly attribute is not used, a new APPID is created every time the application is registered when the application with the same application name does not already exist. This can be annoying, because with every new APPID, a new client application proxy is needed, too.

The following code shows how the attribute can be used:

```
[assembly: ApplicationID("{C064E108-848D-4ba5-861C-1F20BDDD3FBB}")]
```

With Visual Studio projects, you can add this information to the file `assemblyinfo.cs`.

Components

Components within an application are identified by the class ID (CLSID). The automatically generated CLSID changes with every new version of the assembly. So, by default, this ID changes with every new build when you have defined the * for the build and revision number in the `[AssemblyVersion]` attribute. This default behavior is quite useful, because COM clients use the CLSID to invoke the component, and it must be rebuilt with new assemblies.

Refresh Components with the Component Services Explorer

If you build a new version of the assembly and register it again with Enterprise Services, you have to refresh the components with the Component Services admin tool; otherwise, the new versions might not show up. You can refresh the view by selecting My Computer, choosing Action, Refresh All Components, selecting Components below the application in the tree view, and then selecting Action, Refresh.

If you have multiple components within the assembly and not all of them should get a new CLSID with a new build, you can assign the CLSID with the attribute [Guid()]. The attribute class for this attribute, GuidAttribute, is in the namespace System.Runtime.InteropServices. You can create the GUID needed for this attribute with the utility guidgen.exe.

```
[Guid("49CD1F2F-7A16-4d6e-9D2B-B60E5089CEB2")]
[EventTrackingEnabled]
public class CourseManagement : ServicedComponent,
                                ICourseManagement
```

A COM client can also use a **progid** to create the component. A progid is easier to remember than a CLSID, because it is represented by a pronounceable name. The progid is just an interim step to get to the CLSID. In the registry, all progids are listed directly below the root key HKCR. The progid just maps to the CLSID; with the registry entry of the progid, you can find the CLSID. The value that shows up with the progid is the CLSID of the component. More information about the component can be found with the CLSID, as is discussed soon. The default progid created consists of the class name, including the namespace.

> **NOTE: Max Length of the Progid**
>
> Some COM clients cannot use progids that are longer than 39 characters. If the automatic generated progid is longer than 39 characters, you should assign a progid manually using the attribute [ProgId].

Interfaces

Interfaces have always been the foundation with COM. A mandatory COM rule defines that interfaces may never change—you cannot add or remove methods from interfaces, and you are not allowed to change method parameters. If you want to add new methods or change existing ones, you should design a new interface. However, for COM clients, an interface is not identified by its name, but by its interface ID (IID), and if you change the IID every time a method of an interface is modified, the

COM rules are fulfilled. This requirement is accomplished by the automatic generation of the IID. The IID is automatically generated based on the methods and arguments: the ID stays the same as long as no methods are changed; if one method is changed or added, a new IID is assigned to the interface.

If you want to assign an IID manually, you can do it as with the CLSID with the attribute [Guid()]. This method proves useful when you want to implement an existing COM interface using .NET, allowing legacy COM clients that already know this interface to use the .NET component. You can apply the IID of the previously defined COM interface to the .NET representation of this interface with the same methods and arguments.

COMCompatibleVersion Attribute

Using the automatic behavior to create IIDs, CLSIDs, and APPIDs is normally the best way to deal with these identifiers. But there is a way to influence this automatic ID generation by defining the assembly attribute [assembly: COMCompatibleVersion()]. If you define this attribute, the automatic generated IDs change only if a different version is set with this attribute. This attribute can prove very helpful, but you have to be careful with its use.

Finding Assemblies

One important aspect of using .NET assemblies with Enterprise Services applications is that there must be a way for the .NET assemblies to be loaded by the Enterprise Services runtime. So take a look at how this can be done.

Private and Shared Assemblies

With a .NET application, you have to differentiate between private and shared assemblies.[12] A private assembly is stored in the directory of the executable, or a subdirectory thereof. To find assemblies in a subdirectory, you must configure the <probing> element within the application configuration file. You can install a shared assembly either in the GAC or in a directory that can be shared with other applications. The shared directory cannot only reside on a physical disk, but also on a network share or a Web server. To make the shared directory available, you must configure the <codeBase> element within the application configuration file.

COM Registry Entries

COM uses a different way to find objects—they are found with a registry entry. In the registry hive HKEY_CLASSES_ROOT (HKCR), all COM objects are configured below the key CLSID. For native COM objects, the registry entry HKCR\CLSID\{CLSID}\InProcServer32 shows the full path of the DLL.

With .NET components that can be used as COM objects, there is more information in the registry. The default entry of HKCR\CLSID\{CLSID}\InProcServer references mscoree.dll, as shown in Figure 4-8.

For .NET components below the key InprocServer32, you can find the following configuration values:

- For .NET components, the Default value is mscoree.dll. This DLL is a COM DLL that acts as a wrapper and offers COM interfaces for a .NET component, so that the .NET components can be used as a COM object. mscoree.dll loads and executes .NET assemblies and fulfills the role of the CCW.
- The Assembly value shows the strong name of the assembly (that is, the assembly name, version, culture, and public key token).
- The Class value shows the name of the class, including the namespace.
- The CodeBase is a configuration value for shared assemblies to reference the file of the assembly, including the full path.
- RuntimeVersion is the version number of the .NET runtime.
- The ThreadingModel defines the acceptable apartments of the serviced component. With .NET components, Both is the default setting to allow all COM apartment types.[13]

The functionality of the CodeBase key in the registry has similar functionality to the <codeBase> element in the application configuration file. Like the <CodeBase>

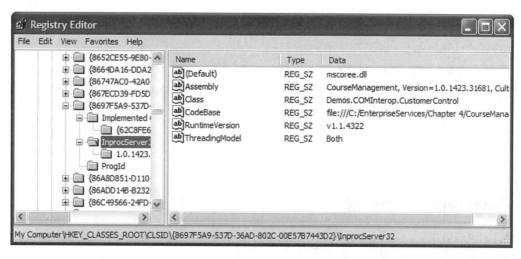

Figure 4-8   COM registry entries.

element, the assemblies referenced with the CodeBase registry entry are also shared. All applications using the same CLSID to reference the COM object use this entry, so it is shared. The problem with this key is that it is not used in every case. Passing a .NET component with DCOM across the network not only invokes COM behavior to find the type with registry entries, but also invokes .NET behavior while serializing and deserializing objects, so both .NET and COM requirements to find the library must be fulfilled.

COM and .NET Requirements

To satisfy the COM requirements, the component must be found by the registry entry. This is needed for activation of serviced components that are activated out-of-process. When serializing .NET objects across the network, the .NET serialization mechanism is active. This is also true if COM clients are used to access the serviced component. For it to work correctly, you must place the assembly holding the serializable class either into the global assembly cache or in a directory that can be found by the application. The current directory of an Enterprise Services application is the system directory <Windows>\System32, so this should not be a real option.

Mixing COM and .NET

Windows Server 2003 does not live fully in a .NET world; we are in an interim state where both .NET and COM rules apply, and COM interoperability is used in many places. The mechanism to find assemblies shows this problem clearly. I think we can expect this behavior to change with future releases.

Visual Basic 6 Clients

Visual Basic 6 is based on COM technologies, so this can be used to demonstrate a COM client accessing our serviced components.

After the serviced component application is registered, you can create a VB6 client. For the demonstration, a simple standard EXE application is suitable. You have to reference the type library `CourseManagement.tlb` that was created by `regsvcs.exe`. `Regsvcs.exe` configures the application in the COM+ catalog and writes the COM registration information to the registry. With VB6, the name of the interface is built up from the type library name and the name of the interface: `CourseManagement.ICourseManagement`. After declaring the variable `oCourse-Management` (Listing 4-9), you can create a new object of type `CourseManagement.CourseManagement`. You can now use the object `oCourseManagement` to get a serialized object to the client with the method `GetCourse`, and a reference to another serviced component running in the Enterprise application with the method `GetCustomerControl`.

Listing 4-9   Visual Basic 6 Client

```
Dim oCourseManagement As COMInteropDemo.ICourseManagement
Set oCourseManagement = New COMInteropDemo.CourseManagement

' get a serialized course object
Dim oCourse As COMInteropDemo.ICourseInfo
Set oCourse = oCourseManagement.GetCourse
MsgBox (oCourse.Number & " " & oCourse.Title)

' get a reference to another serviced component
```

```
Dim oCustomerControl As COMInteropDemo.CustomerControl
Set oCustomerControl = oCourseManagement.GetCustomerControl()

' get a serialized customer
Dim oCustomer As COMInteropDemo.Customer
Set oCustomer = oCustomerControl.GetCustomer()
MsgBox (oCustomer.Name)
```

For the methods where information can be found in the type library, Visual Basic 6 offers Intellisense when writing the application. This is the case with the interface `ICourseManagement` and `ICourseInfo`, but not with `CustomerControl` and `Customer`. The last two types just offer the dispatch interface where the information about methods, properties, and parameters is accessed during runtime with .NET reflection.

So, for Visual Basic 6 clients, the preferred interfaces are custom and dual interfaces. Creating dual interfaces with .NET components is also possible by applying the attribute `[ClassInterface(ClassInterfaceType.AutoDual)]` to the class, as shown earlier.

C++ COM Clients

Visual C++ can use both .NET and COM technologies. With the extensions of Managed C++, this programming environment can be a full .NET client. However, Visual C++ also makes it possible to use C++ as a pure COM client, as demonstrated now. In this C++ example, the serviced component is used from a COM client with the help of C++ smart pointers. Smart pointers make dealing with COM interfaces easier, because you do not have to release the references to the COM objects. This is done by the destructor of the smart pointer.

You can create smart pointer classes with the `#import` statement. This statement references a type library during compile time. Smart pointers are created from the metadata with the information in the type library.

The example in Listing 4-10 shows a C++ client referencing the type library `COMInteropDemo.tlb`. If you compile the program with the `#import` statement, the compiler will create .tlb and .tlh files in the debug directory. Inside these files, you can see wrapper classes and smart pointer definitions that make it easy to use the component.

An extract of the .tlh file where the smart pointers are defined is shown here. The macro _COM_SMARTPTR_TYPEDEF creates a smart pointer with the type of the first argument of this macro (e.g., ICourseManagment) by appending the name Ptr.

```
_COM_SMARTPTR_TYPEDEF(_CourseInfo, __uuidof(_CourseInfo));
_COM_SMARTPTR_TYPEDEF(_CourseManagement,
       __uuidof(_CourseManagement));
_COM_SMARTPTR_TYPEDEF(_Customer, __uuidof(_Customer));
_COM_SMARTPTR_TYPEDEF(_CustomerControl,
       __uuidof(_CustomerControl));
_COM_SMARTPTR_TYPEDEF(ICourseManagement,
       __uuidof(ICourseManagement));
```

Listing 4-10 shows the usage of the smart pointer classes ICourseManagementPtr and ICourseInfoPtr. The smart pointer method CreateInstance instantiates the serviced component, so you can invoke methods such as GetCourse and GetCustomerControl.

There is a separate code block where the smart pointer classes are used. With a separate code block, the object of the smart pointer goes out of scope when the end of the code block is reached. The destructor of the smart pointer releases the COM object by calling the Release method of the IUnknown interface, so you do not have to do this manually.

Listing 4-10   C++ Client Using a Custom Interface

```
// CPPClient.cpp : Defines the entry point for the console
// application.

#include "stdafx.h"
#include <windows.h>
#include <atlconv.h>
#import "COMInteropDemo.tlb"

using namespace COMInteropDemo;

int _tmain(int argc, _TCHAR* argv[])
{
    HRESULT hr;

    hr = CoInitialize(NULL);
```

```
if (FAILED(hr))
{
   return -1;
}


{
   ICourseManagementPtr spCourseManagement;
   hr = spCourseManagement.CreateInstance(
           __uuidof(CourseManagement));

   if (FAILED(hr))
   {
      // error handler
   }

   // get a serialized course object
   ICourseInfoPtr spCourseInfo;
   spCourseInfo = spCourseManagement->GetCourse();

   // get a reference to a serviced component
   _CustomerControlPtr spCustomerControl;
   spCustomerControl =
         spCourseManagement->GetCustomerControl();
```

Using the IDispatch interfaces that are offered with the serviced component class CustomerControl and the Customer class is not as straightforward as the vtable from the previously accessed classes. Listing 4-11 shows the C++ client using the IDispatch interface of the component. With the IDispatch interface, you at first have to invoke the method GetIDsOfNames to get the dispatch ID (dispid) for the method GetCustomer before the method Invoke can be called. With Invoke, the dispatch ID that was returned from GetIDsOfNames is needed.

With C++ clients, custom interfaces are easiest to use.

Listing 4-11   C++ Client Continued Using a Dispatch Interface

```
OLECHAR* szMember = L"GetCustomer";
DISPID dispid;
hr = spCustomerControl->GetIDsOfNames(IID_NULL, &szMember,
   1, LOCALE_SYSTEM_DEFAULT, &dispid);

_variant_t varCustomer;
```

```
        DISPPARAMS params;
        ZeroMemory(&params, sizeof(params));
        hr = spCustomerControl->Invoke(dispid,
            IID_NULL, LOCALE_SYSTEM_DEFAULT, DISPATCH_METHOD,
            &params, &varCustomer, NULL, NULL);


        _CustomerPtr spCustomer = varCustomer;

        szMember = L"Name";
        hr = spCustomer->GetIDsOfNames(IID_NULL, &szMember, 1,
            LOCALE_SYSTEM_DEFAULT, &dispid);

        _variant_t varName;
        hr = spCustomer->Invoke(dispid,
            IID_NULL, LOCALE_SYSTEM_DEFAULT, DISPATCH_PROPERTYGET,
            &params, &varName, NULL, NULL);

        USES_CONVERSION;
        MessageBox(NULL, W2A(varName.bstrVal), "C++ Demo", MB_OK);
    }

    CoUninitialize();

    return 0;
}
```

Scripting Clients

A scripting client can only use the IDispatch interface of the serviced component. With VBScript, the method CreateObject is used to create an instance of the COM object, where the progid of the component is passed as an argument. Behind the scenes, by calling the method courseManagement.GetCourse, the scripting client first invokes the method GetIdsOfNames to pass the method name GetCourse as an argument to receive the dispid. Then it calls the Invoke method where the method of our serviced component is called. What happens here is similar to what you saw earlier with the C++ client—just with a scripting client, this is done by the scripting runtime.

Listing 4-12   VBScript Client

```
' VBScript source code
Dim courseManagement
Set courseManagement =
      CreateObject("Demos.COMInterop.CourseManagement")

Dim course
Set course = courseManagement.GetCourse()
MsgBox course.Number & " " & course.Title

Dim customerControl
Set customerControl = courseManagement.GetCustomerControl()

Dim customer
Set customer = customerControl.GetCustomer()

MsgBox customer.Name
```

A scripting client can only use the IDispatch interface, so only a dispatch and dual interface works for scripting clients.

Calling a COM Object

Similar to using COM clients that access the serviced components that have been written with .NET technology, there is a great integration with serviced components that have been written with COM technology. In such a scenario, you need an RCW that behaves like a .NET component for the .NET client. The RCW itself manages the requirements of the COM object.

The next example shows that a COM object and a .NET component can participate within the same context. As you can see in Figure 4-9, a .NET component implements the interface IContextDemo and will use a COM object that implements the interface ICOMDemo using a RCW. With the sample context, IDs are returned, so you can see that a COM and a .NET component can run inside the same context.

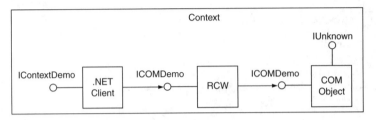

Figure 4-9   .NET and COM components in one context.

C++ Component

The COM example is implemented with C++ and the **Active Template Library** (ATL).[14] The implementation of the method GetContextID that is defined with the interface ICOMDemo is shown in Listing 4-13. Using COM, you can access the object context with the API call GetObjectContext. This method returns a pointer to the interface IObjectContext. The object context implements several interfaces besides IObjectContext. To access the context identifier, you need the interface IObjectContextInfo. This interface defines the method GetContextId, which is called to return the context identifier to the caller.

Listing 4-13   C++ COM Object Method—Returning the Context ID

```
STDMETHODIMP CCOMDemo::GetContextID(GUID* context)
{
    HRESULT hr;

    IObjectContext* pContext;
    hr = GetObjectContext(&pContext);

    if (hr != S_OK)
    {
        return hr;
    }
    if (hr == S_OK)
    {
        IObjectContextInfo* pContextInfo;
        pContext->QueryInterface(&pContextInfo);
        pContext->Release();

        hr = pContextInfo->GetContextId(context);

        pContextInfo->Release();
```

```
    }

    return hr;
}
```

Runtime Callable Wrapper

To use this COM object from a .NET caller, you need an RCW. Using Visual Studio, you can create an RCW by going to Project, Add Reference, and then selecting the COM object from the list of the COM components. However, you cannot use an RCW assembly created in such a way from a serviced component. The problem with such an assembly is that it does not have a strong name.[15] To create a strong-named RCW, you can use the utility `tlbimp.exe`, which utilizes the type definitions from a type library to create an RCW assembly.

In the next example, the type library contained in the file `CPPComponent.dll` is used to create an RCW assembly. The key file for creating the strongly named assembly is referenced with the `/keyfile` option, the namespace of the generated types in the assembly is defined with the `/namespace` option, and the name of the generated assembly is defined with the `/out` option. Using an assembly name such as `Interop.CPPComponentLib.dll` makes clear that this assembly is an RCW assembly.

```
> tlbimp CPPComponent.dll /keyfile:mykey.snk
    /namespace:Demos.COMInterop
    /out: Interop.CPPComponentLib.dll
```

.NET Component

With the .NET component, the RCW assembly must be referenced, using the same method as referencing other .NET assemblies. In Listing 4-14, you can see the only method of the .NET serviced component: `GetContext`. Within this method, the COM serviced component is used to return the context ID of this inner object. Because of the RCW, you can use the COM object just as you would a .NET class. The method `GetContextID` that was implemented in Listing 4-13 returns the context of the inner object and is stored in the variable `innerContext`. The COM object is released by calling `Marshal.ReleaseComObject`. Accessing the context of the .NET component is easily done by using the class `ContextUtil`.[16] The property `ContextId` returns the context identifier. Both context identifiers are returned to the caller as output parameters of the `GetContext` method.

Listing 4-14   Returning the Context ID from a .NET Component

```
public void GetContext(out Guid outerContext,
                       out Guid innerContext)
{
    // Use the COM object
    ICOMDemo innerObject = new COMDemoClass();
    innerContext = innerObject.GetContextID();
    System.Runtime.InteropServices.Marshal.ReleaseComObject(
        innerObject);

    // Access the context id
    outerContext = ContextUtil.ContextId;
}
```

Registration

You can register a .NET serviced component with the COM+ runtime with the utility `regsvcs.exe`. You cannot use this utility with COM DLLs, for which automatic deployment is also impossible. You can register COM DLLs by using drag and drop and selecting the COM DLL and then dropping it into an application in the tool Component Services Explorer. Instead of using drag and drop, you can also install the component by selecting Components in the tree view and by choosing the Action, New Component. This option starts a wizard for installing the component. Just click the button Install New Component(s) and select the COM DLL afterward.

Contrary to .NET, by default COM components have the activation setting Component Supports Event and Statistics selected. You have to deselect this option to allow the COM and .NET components to run within the same context.

Client Application

The client application is a simple console application that creates a new instance of the .NET serviced component `ContextDemo` to invoke the method `GetContext`, as shown with Listing 4-15. The returned context identifiers are written to the console.

Listing 4-15   .NET Client Application

```
static void Main(string[] args)
{
    Demos.COMInterop.IContextDemo obj;
    obj = new Demos.COMInterop.ContextDemo();
    Guid context;
    Guid innerContext;

    obj.GetContext(out context, out innerContext);
    Console.WriteLine("Outer context: {0}",
        context.ToString());
    Console.WriteLine("Inner context: {0}",
        innerContext.ToString());
}
```

Running the application, you will see the context identifiers from the .NET and the COM components. If the configuration of the calling and the called component are similar in that no different contexts are needed, you will see the same context identifiers, as shown here. A COM and .NET component can be running within the same COM+ context.

```
Outer context: 88bbc604-75f5-4a8f-9733-ac6a598c1328
Inner context: 88bbc604-75f5-4a8f-9733-ac6a598c1328
```

Similar to the fact that COM and .NET components can share the same context, both technologies can also be used to share the same transaction, as will be shown in Chapter 7, "Transaction Services."

Summary

Now you have seen COM and .NET integration in the light of .NET Enterprise Services. Serviced components can be called by COM clients, regardless of whether these clients are written with C++, Visual Basic 6, or a scripting client. However, these clients do have different requirements with regard to the COM interface types. To define a specific interface type and to deal with more COM issues regarding application, component, and interface settings, you can use COM interop attributes.

In this chapter, having used different COM clients to access the serviced components, a COM component was used that was accessed by a .NET client. Here a simple runtime callable wrapper with a strong name must be created. COM and .NET components running together can share the same context.

COM interop is not only needed with COM clients accessing the serviced components, but also with .NET clients if the communication with the serviced components happens across different processes, which is discussed in the next chapter.

1 How to use DCOM and SOAP services is discussed in Chapter 5, "Networking."

2 How to use regsvcs.exe to register serviced components is shown in Chapter 2, "Object Activation and Contexts."

3 The global assembly cache is discussed in Chapter 2.

4 You can read more about application configuration files and publisher policy assemblies in the book *Professional C#*, 3rd Edition (Wrox Press), and in *Essential .NET, Volume 1*, by Don Box.

5 .NET remoting and COM+ contexts are discussed in Chapter 3.

6 The dispose pattern is discussed in Chapter 2.

7 One example where this was used was Visual Basic for Applications. Office allowed programming with German and French syntax. The new problem introduced here was using applications in multicultural environments.

8 A vtable is a structure at the beginning of every class that contains memory addresses of the code that is referenced.

9 Visual Basic 4 could only use dispatch interfaces, too. This changed with Visual Basic 5.

10 One book that deals with COM interface design is *Essential IDL: Interface Design for COM*, by Martin Gudgin.

11 Strong names are discussed in Chapter 2.

12 You can read more about private and shared assemblies in the book *Professional C#*, 3rd Edition, in the chapter "Assemblies."

13 COM apartment types are discussed in Chapter 3.

14 The Active Template Library is a C++ class library for development of COM components. You can read more about the ATL in the book *ATL Internals*, by Brent Rector and Chris Sells.

15 This issue with strong names is discussed in Chapter 2.

16 The class `ContextUtil` is shown in Chapter 2.

5
Networking

A .NET CLIENT CAN ACCESS SERVICED components directly only if the client
is running in the same process (i.e., if the Enterprise Services application is configured as a library application). In such a scenario, COM interoperability does not
happen at all. The method parameters are directly passed to the method of the serviced component without the need to marshal and unmarshal them with COM
interop.

This is different when the Enterprise Services application is configured as a server
application, or the application must be accessed from a different system across the
network. In such a case, you can either use DCOM or SOAP services[1] to access the
serviced components. DCOM is the protocol with a long history that was used as a
network protocol between a COM client and a COM server. DCOM is still a good
protocol when it comes to .NET clients accessing serviced components.

With COM+ 1.5, you have another option to access the serviced component
across the network: You can enable SOAP services just by checking a check box.
SOAP services are based on .NET remoting. However, this protocol does not have
as many capabilities as DCOM.

Another way—and for many scenarios the best option—to access serviced components across the network is by adding a façade to the serviced components. Web
services can be a client to the serviced components that acts as the interface to the
client application.

Specifically, this chapter covers the following topics:

- DCOM, which is still a viable option for accessing serviced components
  because it currently offers more features than SOAP services

- SOAP services, which uses the flexibility of .NET remoting as a transport to access serviced components across the network
- Web services (in this chapter implemented with ASP.NET), a very viable option to access the serviced component from a Web server

DCOM

DCOM[2] is the protocol used to access legacy COM objects across process and system boundaries. Although in new applications COM programming is replaced in many areas with .NET technologies, DCOM is still a viable option to access serviced components, because it is very fast and easy to use and the only protocol that flows COM+ context.[3]

However, DCOM is not as flexible as .NET remoting.[4] This section shows how you can use DCOM to access serviced components; but first you need to know about the following:

- DCOM transports
- Creating and using application proxies
- Installing the application proxy

DCOM Transport Protocols

DCOM supports different transport protocols—such as TCP/IP, UDP, and IPX. You can configure the transport protocol that you want to use for DCOM communication, but obviously both the client and the server must have the same protocol configured. For performance reasons, pay attention to the order of configured protocols.

Nowadays the protocol for DCOM is likely an easy choice: TCP/IP. In the early days of DCOM, the Microsoft protocol NetBEUI or Novell IPX would have been important. Although NetBEUI was still available with the DCOM protocol options with Windows 2000, it is no longer available with Windows Server 2003 and Windows XP.

You can configure the DCOM transport protocol to be used with your serviced components with the Component Services Explorer.[5] To open the dialog box shown in Figure 5-1, select My Computer in the tree view, and then choose Action, Properties, Default Protocols. You can see that on my system, Connection-Oriented TCP/IP is the only configured protocol. Other available protocols that you can add are SPX, Datagram UDP/IP, and Tunneling TCP/IP. The order of protocols in this dialog box defines the order in which a connection is tried. If a connection with the first protocol succeeds, the second one is not used. To reduce the connection time, a connection with the first protocol in the list should succeed.

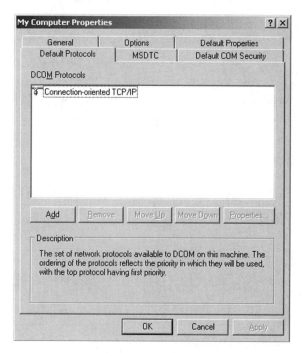

Figure 5-1   DCOM Transport Protocol configuration.

Application Proxies

The clients need the same protocol as the server as well as an application proxy. The application proxy provides the same methods and interfaces that are available with the serviced component, but instead of running the code on the client, the proxy connects to the server and forwards the method call to the serviced component.

Figure 5-2 shows the serviced component implementing the interface `ICourseManagement`. The proxy that is running in the client application implements the same interface.

.NET components can use DCOM with the help of a .NET remoting feature.[6] Every serviced component class derives from the base class `ServicedComponent`, which itself indirectly derives from the class `MarshalByRefObject`. `MarshalByRefObject` is the base class needed for remote objects accessed by .NET remoting. The DCOM functionality is added to the .NET component by .NET remoting attributes: The nondocumented attribute class `ServicedComponentProxyAttribute`[7] is applied to the `ServicedComponent` class. This attribute class derives from the base class `System.Runtime.Remoting.Proxies.ProxyAttribute`. The class `ProxyAttribute` makes it possible to define a custom proxy class in place of the default .NET remoting proxy that is used to connect to the server. With serviced components, the defined proxy class has the name `ServicedComponentProxy`. This proxy class derives from `System.Runtime.Remoting.Proxies.RealProxy` and adds DCOM functionality to the client.

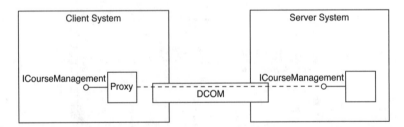

Figure 5-2   Application proxy.

Creating an Application Proxy

You can create an installation program for the client that includes the application proxy, and the target system can be configured with a proxy installation package.

With the installation of the client proxy, the server name will be registered on the client, so that the client will connect to this server using the DCOM protocol. If you are going to create application proxies from a different system than the one intended to be the real server for the client, you can change the name of the system that will be configured with the client in the Component Services Explorer by selecting Options with the properties of My Computer. If you enter a name in the field Application Proxy RSN,[8] this name is used as the name of the server. Figure 5-3 shows this field.

If you do not set the correct server when creating the application proxy, you can also change the server name in the configuration on the client, which is shown later in this chapter.

You can create the installation package for a client proxy by selecting the Enterprise Services application in the tree view and then choosing Action, Export. This menu starts up the Application Export Wizard shown in Figure 5-4.

In the second step, after you click Next, you have to select the option button Export as Application Proxy to create an application proxy, and you have to enter the name of the installation file, as shown in Figure 5-5.

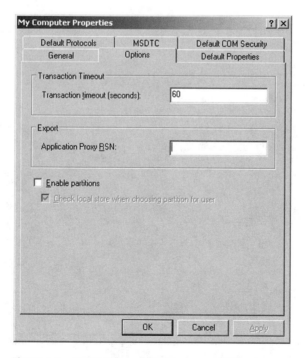

Figure 5-3   Setting the application proxy RSN.

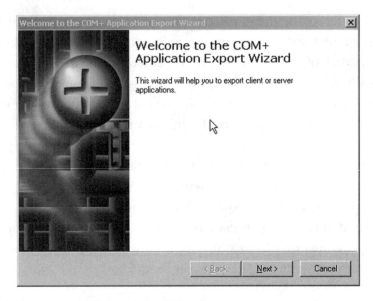

Figure 5-4   Application Export Wizard.

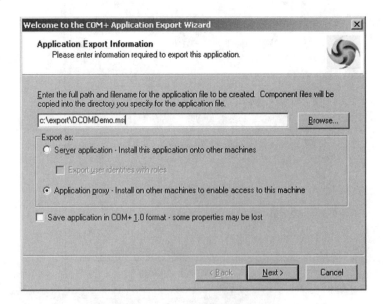

Figure 5-5   Application export information.

If you want to support client applications running on Windows 2000 systems, you must check the check box Save Application in COM+ 1.0 Format. With this setting, some properties that were not available prior to COM+ 1.5 will be lost. COM+ 1.5 on Windows XP and Windows Server 2003 uses a new data format for the configuration, although the old format is still supported, and setting this check box ensures that the old format is used.

Here the filename has been set to DCOMDemo.msi in the directory C:\export.

Clicking the Next button creates an installation package for the client, with both a CAB file and an MSI file. The CAB file just includes the MSI file in a compressed form.

> **Application Proxy on the Server System**
>
> You cannot use an application proxy installation package on the same system where the application is installed. The installation would fail because an Enterprise Services application with the same name is already installed.

Installing the Application Proxy

After copying the installation package to the client, you can install the proxy there. The installation of the package completes these tasks:

- Installation of the client proxy
- Configuration of the client proxy in the registry
- Installation of the serviced component assembly in the global assembly cache

For troubleshooting clients accessing serviced components, it helps to know where the configuration and files can be found; let's look a little closer into these tasks.

The client proxy files are installed in the directory {Program Files}\ComPlus Applications\{APP-ID}. In this directory, you can find the type library and the assembly of the serviced component application. You can find the APPID of the application on the General tab of the application properties in the Component Services Explorer.

The component itself is registered in a similar way on the client as it is on the server. You can verify this with the Registry Editor, as shown in Figure 5-6, selecting the registry key HKCR\CLSID\{CLSID} of the component.

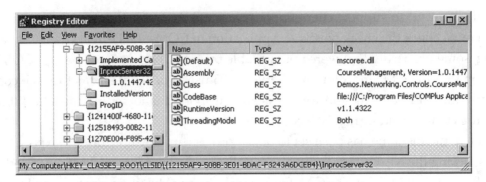

Figure 5-6   Registry configuration of the application proxy.

The configuration difference between the serviced component on the server and the application proxy on the client is that the CodeBase variable references the directory <Program Files>\ComPlusApplications\<APPID>. As discussed before, this configuration is only used for COM interop. To fulfill the .NET requirements when serializing objects across the network, the assembly that holds the serialized classes is also installed into the global assembly cache. This is done during the installation of the application proxy. You can see the assembly in the directory <Windows>\ assembly using Windows Explorer.

The application proxy configuration for the client application will also show up with the Component Services Explorer, where nearly all configuration options are disabled, because it is only useful to configure these options on the server. There is one value you can change with the client proxy: the name of the server. This value can be configured with the Activation tab of the application properties, as shown in Figure 5-7.

Of course, this value is also configured in the registry. You can find the name of the server in the registry at HKCR\AppId\{App-Id}\RemoteServerName.

NOTE: COM Clients and the .NET Runtime on the Client

Using the application proxy on the client system requires the .NET runtime to be installed on the client.[9] This is also the case if the client is a COM client.

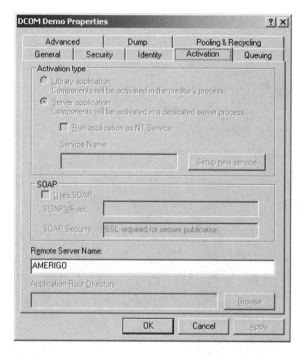

Figure 5-7   Application proxy configuration.

Creating a DCOM Client Application

After installing the application proxy, it is now possible to use one of the clients[10] that
was created earlier, or a .NET client as will be done now, across the network to access
the serviced component.

Here a .NET client is shown that is similar to the COM clients created in Chapter 4, "COM Interop." Listing 5-1 shows a .NET client that uses serviced components.
These are the tasks that you must complete in the client application:

1. Create a serviced component CourseManagement.

2. Get a serialized CourseInfo object from the server to the client.

3. Get a reference to a serviced component object CustomerControl that is running on the server. This is similar to the CourseManagement component,
   except the reference is returned from a method instead of creating a new
   instance.

4. Get a serialized Customer object from the server to the client.

5. Create a new CourseInfo object and pass it to the server.

Listing 5-1   .NET Client Application

```
using System;
using System.EnterpriseServices;

namespace Demos.Networking
{
    class DCOMDemo
    {

        static void Main(string[] args)
        {
            // Create a serviced component across the network
            CourseManagement courseManagement = new CourseManagement();

            // Get a serialized CourseInfo object from the server
            CourseInfo course = courseManagement.GetCourse();

            Console.WriteLine("Course: {0} {1}", course.Title,
                        course.Number);

            // Get a reference to another serviced component
            CustomerControl customerControl =
                courseManagement.GetCustomerControl();

            // Get a serialized Customer object from the server
            Customer c1 = customerControl.GetCustomer();

            Console.WriteLine("Customer: {0} {1}", c1.Name, c1.Company);

            // Create a new CourseInfo object and pass it to the server
            CourseInfo newCourse = new CourseInfo("MS-2524",
                "Developing Web Services", 3, new DateTime(2003, 11, 20));
            courseManagement.SetCourse(newCourse);
        }
    }
}
```

With the serviced component application installed on the server, and the application proxy installed on the client, you can start the client application.

NOTE: SerializationException

If you get a `SerializationException` with the message "Cannot find the assembly" during the method call `SetCourse` where a `CourseInfo` object is passed from the client to the server, there is a good chance that on the server system the assembly is not installed in the global assembly cache. Before or after installing the assembly in the global assembly cache, you also have to stop the Enterprise Services application, if it is still running.

Developing Client Applications

With the installation of the client application proxy, there is a type library available on the client. However, you cannot use this type library to create client applications. If you try to use a **runtime callable wrapper** (RCW) that accesses the serviced component by COM interop, you can't. Using a **COM callable wrapper** (CCW) by using RCW would not make sense. It's just not possible.

To create the client application, you need the assembly of the serviced component.

TIP: Reality Check: DCOM

If distributed transactions are needed, DCOM is the network protocol to use. With DCOM, the COM+ context can be sent across the network, so communication between serviced components can be done using DCOM.

With the client application that accesses serviced components across the network, you should consider using Web services, as shown later in this chapter.

SOAP Services

Besides using DCOM, you can use SOAP services to communicate with Enterprise Services across the network. In Chapter 2, "Object Activation and Contexts," learned that .NET remoting is already built in to .NET Enterprise Services: .NET remoting contexts are used for intercepting .NET components. There is even more support for .NET remoting, however: Serviced components can be invoked via .NET remoting across the network.

You can easily use .NET remoting for serviced components by clicking a check box to turn SOAP services on.

Before writing an example to show how .NET remoting is used to invoke serviced components, the functionality of .NET remoting needs some clarification. If you have not dug into using .NET remoting until now, you will find an overview in the next section, which should be enough to get you started using .NET remoting with serviced components.[11]

.NET Remoting Overview

.NET remoting is an extremely flexible architecture for the communication between .NET applications running in different application domains.[12] The major difference to Web services implemented with ASP.NET is that it offers full object fidelity across the network. ASP.NET Web services uses the .NET XML serializer, which means that only XML-compatible types are supported and only public properties and fields are serialized. In addition to that, ASP.NET only supports stateless components. .NET remoting supports both stateless and stateful components, and with the serialization mechanism of .NET remoting, not only public properties, but also all private data is serialized.

Figure 5-8 gives an overview of this technology. An object that should be accessed across the network using .NET remoting must be represented in a class that derives from `MarshalByRefObject`. Contrary to that, objects that should be transferred across the network must be marked with the attribute `[Serializable]`. The methods of the remote object class that should be available remotely must have a `public` access modifier. The client uses a **proxy** object that offers the same methods as the remote object to invoke methods remotely. The proxy creates **messages** that are passed to **sink objects**. One of the sinks is the **formatter** that is responsible for converting the message to a format that can be transported across the network. The **channel sink** passes the formatted message across a network channel to the server application, the **remoting host**. On the server side, the channel sink receives the message, passes it to the formatter where a message is built again, and the **dispatcher** invokes the methods in the remote object by using the information in the message.

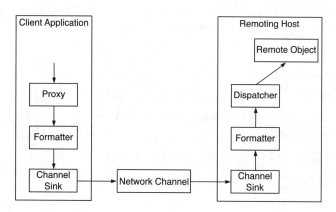

Figure 5-8 .NET remoting architecture.

Having gone through a very broad overview of this technology, let's now concentrate more on the concepts:

- **Remote object**—Using .NET remoting, you have to create a remote object that derives from the class `MarshalByRefObject`. Deriving from this class means that a proxy is used to access the objects from different application domains. The class `ServicedComponent` derives indirectly from `Marshal-ByRefObject`, so the basic needs for serviced components to be called remotely are already fulfilled.

- **Remoting host**—.NET remoting is very flexible regarding the process in which the remote object should be hosted. Any application type can be used to host a remote object. The easiest way to host .NET remoting objects is to use Internet Information Services (IIS), which is the default option for Enterprise Services. However, it is also possible to use a Windows service as a remoting host, or a Windows Forms application. If you use Windows Forms, you can use .NET remoting in a peer-to-peer application scenario.

- **Marshaling**—With .NET remoting, you have to differentiate between objects that will be invoked across the network and objects that are sent across the network. If the class is derived from `MarshalByRefObject`, the object is marshaled by reference, so the object itself is not sent across the network, but a reference to the remote object is. The reference is not just a pointer because this would not be enough to access the object on a different system; instead, the reference includes information such as the host name, port number, and object identifier.

  If an object should be sent across the network, the class must be declared with the attribute `[Serializable]`, and there is no need for the class to be inherited from `MarshalByRefObject`. With serializable objects, all private data is transmitted by default. If private fields should not be serialized, you can mark these fields with the attribute `[NonSerialized]`. To control the serialization mechanism, it is also possible for the class to implement the interface `ISerializable`.

- **Network transports**—For communication across the network, channels are used. With the Microsoft .NET Framework, channels for TCP and HTTP are included. Different channels to communicate across SMTP, Jabber, Message Queuing, and so on have been written by others and are available on the Internet.

- **Data formats**—How the data is formatted with a remoting call depends on the formatter. With .NET 1.1, SOAP and binary formatters are available. The binary formatter can be used as a fast and efficient format with a .NET application on both the client and the server side. The SOAP protocol is a standard for interoperability across different technologies—but contrary to ASP.NET Web services, the SOAP formatter of .NET remoting supports only the SOAP RPC style.[13] SOAP is not primarily a useful formatter with .NET remoting, because .NET remoting needs .NET applications on both ends anyway.

- **Stateful and stateless objects**—.NET remoting offers the functionality of both stateful and stateless objects. A stateful object is known as a **client-activated** object, where the state of the object is kept between method calls. The lifetime of such objects is controlled by a leasing mechanism. Stateless objects are known as **server-activated** or **well-known** `SingleCall` objects (because the

URL to these objects is well known), and are deactivated with every method call. Every method call to the remote object creates a new instance.

Creating a Serviced Component Using .NET Remoting

With Windows XP and Windows Server 2003, you can click a check box to use .NET remoting with Enterprise Services. Either you have to click a check box with the Component Services Explorer, or you can use an attribute to programmatically define that .NET remoting should be used.

With this automatic SOAP configuration, a virtual Web site is configured within IIS, and ASP.NET is used as a hosting process for the remoting objects.

In the next example, .NET remoting with serviced components is demonstrated. As always, for serviced components, a component library with a reference to the assembly `System.EnterpriseServices` must be created. What you have to do with SOAP services is to

* Specify the SOAP service with an assembly attribute with configuration information.

* Create a serviced component class like we have done before.

* Install the generated assembly in the global assembly cache.

* Register the serviced component.

The attribute to turn on SOAP services is `[assembly: ApplicationActivation]` with the named property `SoapVRoot`. `SoapVRoot` defines the name of the virtual directory of the automatic generated Web site, as shown in Listing 5-2.

Listing 5-2   AssemblyInfo.cs to Configure .NET Remoting

```
// AssemblyInfo.cs

[assembly: AssemblyDelaySign(false)]
[assembly: AssemblyKeyFile("../../../../mykey.snk")]
[assembly: AssemblyKeyName("")]

[assembly: ApplicationName("Networking Demo")]
[assembly: Description("Sample Application")]
[assembly: ApplicationActivation(ActivationOption.Server,
                       SoapVRoot="RemotingDemo")]
```

Turning Off Security with the Enterprise Services Application

With the trustworthy computing initiative by Microsoft and Windows Server 2003, there is another important aspect when using .NET Enterprise Services and SOAP services. You have to be aware that .NET remoting does not offer security by itself with .NET version 1.0 or 1.1. Microsoft put a lot of effort into making Windows Server 2003 more secure, and part of the trustworthy computing initiative was to reduce possibilities that the system can be made insecure by wrong administrative decisions: better safe than sorry.

Windows XP has a different behavior with Enterprise Services and SOAP—here security can be turned off unintentionally by turning on .NET remoting with Enterprise Services. With Windows XP, you can configure the serviced component to require security, but this security requirement is just invalidated by turning on SOAP. If you turn on SOAP with Windows XP and use the default settings, any client can access the serviced component by using .NET remoting, regardless of whether client access should be allowed by the security configuration of the component.

Windows Server 2003 makes it easy to use SOAP services across a secure channel.[14] However, this chapter has not yet dealt with security issues, so every client should be given access to the serviced components with SOAP. To make this happen, you have to turn off security for the Enterprise Services application. You do this partly by using attributes in the code, but you also have to configure security relevant items of Web site within IIS.

In the previous examples, with the assembly attribute `ApplicationAccessControl`, access control was already turned off; but now authentication and impersonation should be turned off, which can be done by using the named properties `Authentication` and `ImpersonationLevel`:

```
[assembly: ApplicationAccessControl(false,
           Authentication=AuthenticationOption.None,
           ImpersonationLevel=ImpersonationLevelOption.Anonymous)]
```

Serviced Component Class

Similar to the examples that have been shown earlier in this chapter and in Chapter 4, you will create a few classes to look at how data can be passed with .NET remoting. The class `RemotingDemo` is the implementation of the serviced component; `CourseInfo` is a class that is serialized across the network. Both of these classes are shown in Listing 5-3.

Listing 5-3   Serviced Component Application to Be Used with .NET Remoting

```
using System;
using System.EnterpriseServices;
using System.Windows.Forms;

namespace Demos.Networking
{
    [Serializable]
    public class CourseInfo
    {
        public CourseInfo(string number, string title, int length,
            DateTime date)
        {
            this.number = number;
            this.title = title;
            this.length = length;
            this.date = date;
        }

        private string number;
        public string Number
        {
            get
            {
                return number;
            }
        }

        private string title;
        public string Title
        {
            get
            {
                return title;
            }
        }

        private int length;
        public int Length
        {
            get
```

```
    {
        return length;
    }
}

private DateTime date;
public DateTime Date
{
    get
    {
        return date;
    }
}
}


[EventTrackingEnabled]
public class RemotingDemo : ServicedComponent
{
    public RemotingDemo()
    {
    }

    private CourseInfo course;

    public CourseInfo GetCourse()
    {
        if (course == null)
        {
            course = new CourseInfo(
                "MS-2557",
                "Developing Component-based Applicatons", 5,
                new DateTime(2003, 8, 18));
        }
        return course;
    }

    public void SetCourse(CourseInfo course)
    {
        this.course = course;
        MessageBox.Show("Course: {0}", course.Title);
    }
}
```

In addition to the stateful class `RemotingDemo`, another serviced component is shown in Listing 5-4. The second serviced component does not keep state. When using .NET remoting well-known objects, it is important that you do not keep state with the serviced component. For well-known objects, you have to use **object pooling** and **just-in-time activation** (JITA).[15] If object pooling were not used, new resources on the server would be allocated with every method call—and you would have to wait until the garbage collector cleaned up.

The class `StatelessComponent` has the attribute `[JustInTimeActivation]` applied to it so that it can be automatically deactivated by the server after a method call. Automatic deactivation is done here with the `[AutoComplete]` attribute applied to the method `GetValue`. The attribute `[ObjectPooling]` defines the pool size. To return the object to the pool after its use, you also have to override the method `CanBePooled` to return true. This method will just demonstrate that state is indeed not kept, and every time this method is called, 1 will be returned.

For COM clients, you cannot use the `[AutoComplete]` attribute without using interfaces, or creating a dual interface with the class. The registration utility complains if this is the case, so the attribute `[ClassInterface]` is applied to the class `StatelessComponent`.

Listing 5-4 Stateless Serviced Component for .NET Remoting Access

```
[JustInTimeActivation()]
[ObjectPooling(MinPoolSize=10, MaxPoolSize=300)]
[ClassInterface(ClassInterfaceType.AutoDual)]
[EventTrackingEnabled()]
public class StatelessComponent : ServicedComponent
{
    private int state = 0;

    [AutoComplete]
    public int GetValue()
    {
        return ++state;
    }

    protected override bool CanBePooled()
    {
        return true;
    }
}
```

Configuring the Server Application

Contrary to what you have seen in previous chapters, to use SOAP services you *must* install the serviced component assembly in the global assembly cache. Otherwise, the registration will fail with an error message that is not very helpful: "An unknown error occurred while configuring components." With an assembly installed in the global assembly cache, it is possible to register the assembly manually using `regsvcs.exe`. The registration process does not allow registration of an assembly that uses the SOAP option if you have not first put it into the global assembly cache, because otherwise IIS cannot find the assembly.

Therefore, the next tools to use after building the assembly are `gacutil -i` to install the assembly in the global assembly cache and `regsvsc` to register the application. After a successful configuration, you can use the Component Services Explorer to verify that Uses SOAP is selected with the Application Activation options, and RemotingDemo is the name of SOAP VRoot, as shown in Figure 5-9.

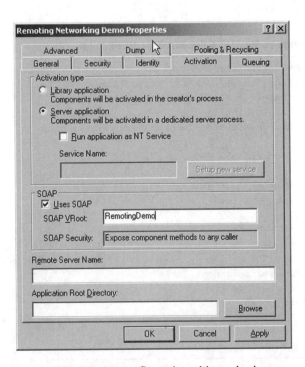

Figure 5-9 .NET remoting configuration with serviced components.

NOTE: Configuring SOAP with Windows Server 2003

If you cannot select the SOAP configuration with the Component Services Explorer, you have to turn security completely off (no authorization, authentication for calls must be set to none, and the impersonation level must be anonymous). With security turned off, the activation dialog box in Windows Server 2003 shows the SOAP security information: "Expose component methods to any caller."

Chapter 12, "Security," explains how you can use .NET remoting in a secure manner with the HTTPS protocol. With production systems, you should always use the HTTPS protocol with .NET remoting.

Configuring Internet Information Server

As previously discussed, using the SOAP option also creates a virtual Web within IIS, which you can see with the Internet Information Services Manager. The .NET remoting configuration is done in the `web.config` file. The content of this file is discussed soon, but first you need to understand IIS configuration. In Figure 5-10, you can also see the files `default.aspx` and `default.disco`. With Windows Server 2003, these files are created only if you define a JITA component with the application. On a Windows XP system, these files are created anyway but are only useful with JITA components. The directory where all these files are put is not the usual IIS directory, but the directory <Windows>\System32\com\SoapVRoots\<SOAPVRoot> instead.

The ASP.NET page `Default.aspx` has some code to show links to all **WSDL** (Web Services Description Language) documents[16] that describe the services of the serviced components. The .NET remoting runtime automatically creates WSDL documents for all remoting objects that are accessible with the SOAP formatter.

NOTE: SOAP Services and WSDL

Don't forget that SOAP services does not give you platform independence—this does not change as WSDL is offered. The

WSDL that is created by .NET remoting is an object-oriented view of Web services that only supports the old RPC style. As you will see later in this chapter, with ASP.NET Web services you can get a document-centric approach that is platform independent and allows better versioning.

You can try to access the file `Default.aspx` from a browser, but if accessing this file fails, you might need to check your security settings with Windows Server 2003. The ASP.NET account needs access permissions to the temporary ASP.NET files. With Windows Server 2003, the Network Service account is used by default by the ASP.NET runtime. (The account name is ASPNET on Windows XP and Windows Server 2000.) The directory where temporary ASP.NET files are created is <Windows>\Microsoft.NET\Framework\<version>\Temporary ASP.NET Files.

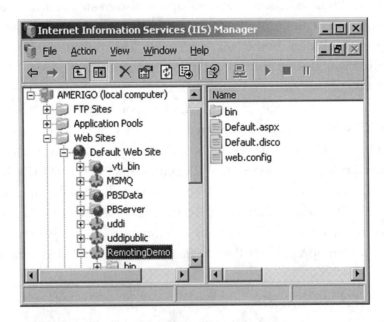

Figure 5-10   IIS Configuration for .NET remoting.

You can use the file `Default.disco` for automatic discovery of Web services on a system. This uses the DISCO protocol (defined by Microsoft) to discover Web services on a server if the server name is already known. As time goes on, DISCO will be replaced by the WS-Inspection standard that was defined by Microsoft and IBM.

As previously mentioned, Windows Server 2003 has default configurations to help you avoid wrong system administrator decisions. If you want to provide access to everyone, you have to do this explicitly. This is also true for the Web site configuration that was created by selecting the SOAP option. If you select the Web site from the IIS Manager, you have to enable anonymous access in the Properties dialog box via Directory Security, Authentication and Access Control, as shown in Figure 5-11.

In addition, you have to deselect Require Secure Channel (SSL) via the Directory Security, Secure Communications dialog box, as shown in Figure 5-12.

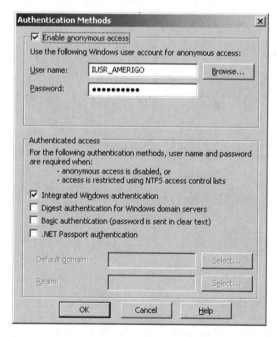

Figure 5-11 Enable anonymous access with the IIS configuration.

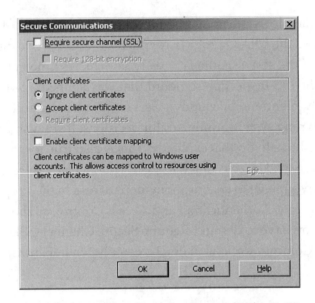

Figure 5-12   Disable Require Secure Channel (SSL) with IIS.

Configuring .NET Remoting

As discussed previously, the SOAP option creates a file web.config that is put into the directory of the new Web site. This file holds the .NET remoting configuration to access the serviced components. Listing 5-5 contains the source of this configuration file.

Listing 5-5   .NET Remoting Configuration File

```
<?xml version="1.0" encoding="utf-8"?>
<configuration>
  <system.runtime.remoting>
    <application>
      <channels>
        <channel ref="http server" />
      </channels>
      <service>
        <wellknown mode="SingleCall"
            type="Demos.Networking.RemotingDemo,
            CourseManagement, Version="1.2.1.0, Culture=neutral,
            PublicKeyToken=44567e4f551838af"
            objectUri="Demos.Networking.RemotingDemo.soap" />
        <activated
```

```
            type="Demos.Networking.RemotingDemo, CourseManagement" />
        <wellknown mode="SingleCall"
            type="Demos.Networking.StatelessComponent,
            CourseManagement, Version="1.2.1.0, Culture=neutral,
            PublicKeyToken=44567e4f551838af"
            objectUri="Demos.Networking.StatelessComponent.soap" />


        <activated
            type="Demos.Networking.StatelessComponent,
                CourseManagement" />
      </service>
    </application>
  </system.runtime.remoting>
  <system.web>
    <identity impersonate="true" />
    <authentication mode="Windows" />
  </system.web>
</configuration>
```

The remoting configuration is inside the element `<system.runtime.remoting>`. The child element `<channels>` defines all channels that are used with this application. `<channel ref="http server" />` references the channel class `System.Runtime.Remoting.Channels.Http.HttpServerChannel` that is configured within the machine configuration file `machine.config`.

Inside the `<service>` element, all offered serviced components are defined. The `<activated>` element defines a client-activated remoting object that keeps state. This element just requires a type attribute where the name of the class (including its namespace) and the assembly name must be specified.

```
<activated
    type="Demos.Networking.RemotingDemo, CourseManagement" />
```

The `<wellknown>` element is used to access stateless components. The `mode` attribute allows `SingleCall` and `Singleton`[17] configurations. With Enterprise Services, `SingleCall` is the only option that is useful.[18] In contrast to the `<activated>` element, with the `<wellknown>` element, the complete strong name of the assembly must be specified, which includes the name of the assembly, the version number, the culture, and the public key token. The term *well known* is applied to these object types because the URI to this object type is well known by the client. You must define the

URI with the attribute `objectUri`. The default URI created is the name of the class appended with `soap`. For .NET remoting components that are hosted by IIS, as is the case in the sample scenario, the extension must be `soap` or `rem`, depending on whether the SOAP or the binary formatters are used. You configure these extensions with the ASP.NET runtime ISAPI[19] extension in IIS.

```
<wellknown mode="SingleCall"
           type="Demos.Networking.RemotingDemo,
           CourseManagement, Version="1.2.1.0, Culture=neutral,
           PublicKeyToken=44567e4f551838af"
           objectUri="Demos.Networking.RemotingDemo.soap" />
```

The identity and authentication configuration values are used by the ASP.NET runtime to forward the user information to the serviced component.

Manually Changing the Configuration

The automatically generated configuration file `web.config` just serves as a starting point for SOAP services. Always check the entries and modify them accordingly to your needs. Every time the application is re-registered, new entries are added to the file. You have to delete the old ones manually.

Creating a .NET Remoting Client

With SOAP services, it is not necessary to create an application proxy to add registry configuration entries. You also don't need to put the serviced component assembly into the global assembly cache. On the client system, just the serviced component assembly is needed, which is used to access the metadata. A simple ClickOnce deployment is possible with these .NET clients.

The client shown in Listing 5-6 is a simple console application that is used to access the serviced component. With this application, you just have to reference the assembly of the serviced component and the assemblies `System.EnterpriseServices` and `System.Runtime.Remoting`.

Before you can instantiate the serviced component, you have to configure .NET remoting. First, a new HTTP channel is created and set up with the remoting runtime using `ChannelServices.RegisterChannel`. After that, the client-activated remote object is configured with `RemotingConfiguration.RegisterActivatedClient-Type`. The well-known object is configured with `RemotingConfiguration.RegisterWellknownClientType`.

Listing 5-6   Client Using .NET Remoting

```
using System;
using System.Runtime.Remoting;
using System.Runtime.Remoting.Channels;
using System.Runtime.Remoting.Channels.Http;
using Demos.Networking;

class RemotingClient
{
    static void Main()
    {
        ChannelServices.RegisterChannel(new HttpChannel());

        RemotingConfiguration.RegisterActivatedClientType(
               typeof(RemotingDemo),
               "http://amerigo/RemotingDemo");

        RemotingConfiguration.RegisterWellKnownClientType(
               typeof(StatelessComponent),
               "http://amerigo/RemotingDemo." +
               "Demos.Networking.StatlessComponent.soap");
    }
}
```

A different way to set up the remoting infrastructure is by using a configuration file that looks similar to the `web.config` file seen on the server. Listing 5-7 shows the .NET remoting configuration values in a client application configuration file. The channel used here is an HTTP client channel, and instead of having the `<service>` element that was created in the `web.config` file, you have to use the `<client>` element for the client. The `<client>` element has the associated attribute `url`, where you have to define a URL to specify the Web site. The type of the serviced component class is defined with the `<activated>` element, similar to the `web.config` file.

You can choose the filename of the remoting configuration file as you want. However, if you put the .NET remoting configuration inside the application configuration file,[20] you will find it easier to maintain configuration changes.

Listing 5-7 Configuring .NET Remoting for the Client

```xml
<?xml version="1.0" encoding="utf-8" ?>
<configuration>
  <system.runtime.remoting>
    <application>
      <channels>
        <channel ref="http client" />
      </channels>
      <client url="http://amerigo/RemotingDemo">
        <activated
            type="Demos.Networking.RemotingDemo,
               CourseManagement" />
        <wellknown
type="Demos.Networking.StatelessComponent, CourseManagement"
url="http://amerigo/RemotingDemo/Demos.Networking.StatelessComponent.soap" />
      </client>
    </application>
  </system.runtime.remoting>
</configuration>
```

This configuration file is used by calling `RemotingConfiguration.Configure`, which is the only method you need to set up .NET remoting.

After setting up .NET remoting, you can create and use the serviced component. With stateful components, do not forget to invoke the `Dispose` method, as done here with the `using` statement. The client code using a configuration file is shown in Listing 5-8.

Listing 5-8 .NET Remoting Client Using a Configuration File

```csharp
static void Main()
{
    RemotingConfiguration.Configure("RemotingClient.exe.config");

    using (RemotingDemo obj = new RemotingDemo())
    {
        CourseInfo course = obj.GetCourse();
        Console.WriteLine(course.Title);

        CourseInfo newCourse = new CourseInfo(
            "MS-2524", "ASP.NET Web Services", 3,
            new DateTime(2003, 11, 1));
        obj.SetCourse(newCourse);
    }
}
```

With the configuration as it is now, everything works up to the last method `obj.SetCourse`. To pass anything other than simple data types from the client to the server, as is done with `SetCourse`, you also have to change the configuration of .NET remoting on the server. .NET remoting changed the behavior of passing a serialized object with version 1.1 of the Microsoft .NET Framework. You can configure the deserialization behavior with the option `typeFilterLevel` of the formatter, which has two allowed values: `Low` and `Full`. `Low` is the default, and has some restrictions (e.g., it does not allow deserialization of types that implement the `ISerialize` interface, or types that live in an assembly with a strong name without the attribute `[AllowPartiallyTrustedCallers]`). Setting the `typeFilterLevel` to `Full` allows deserialization of these objects. Thus, to send custom types to the server where they are deserialized, you have to change the configuration within `web.config`, as shown in Listing 5-9.

Listing 5-9 Server-Side Configuration File That Allows Passing Objects to the Server

```xml
<?xml version="1.0" encoding="utf-8"?>
<configuration>
  <system.runtime.remoting>
    <application>
      <channels>
        <channel ref="http server">
          <serverProviders>
            <formatter ref="soap" typeFilterLevel="Full" />
          </serverProviders>
        </channel>
      </channels>
      <service>
        <wellknown mode="SingleCall"
            type="Demos.Networking.RemotingDemo,
            CourseManagement, Version="1.2.1.0, Culture=neutral,
            PublicKeyToken=44567e4f551838af"
            objectUri="Demos.Networking.RemotingDemo.soap" />
        <activated
            type="Demos.Networking.RemotingDemo, CourseManagement" />
        <wellknown mode="SingleCall"
            type="Demos.Networking.StatelessComponent,
            CourseManagement, Version="1.2.1.0, Culture=neutral,
            PublicKeyToken=44567e4f551838af"
```

```
              objectUri="Demos.Networking.StatelessComponent.soap" />
          <activated
              type="Demos.Networking.StatelessComponent,
                    CourseManagement" />
        </service>
      </application>
    </system.runtime.remoting>
    <system.web>
      <identity impersonate="true" />
      <authentication mode="Windows" />
    </system.web>
  </configuration>
```

With this small change in the configuration file, the application is running as expected. Now it is possible to send a serialized object from the client to the server.

If you add the code shown in Listing 5-10 to the `Main` method of the client application, you will see that the stateless component is indeed stateless. The method `GetValue` always returns 1. In the Component Services Explorer, you can also monitor the objects, and you can see that they *are* reused.

Listing 5-10   **Calling the Stateless Component**

```
StatelessComponent obj = new StatelessComponent();
for (int i=0; i < 1000; i++)
    Console.WriteLine(obj.GetValue());
```

Disadvantages of SOAP Services

So the question to ask is which networking option should be used, DCOM or SOAP services? You have seen that with SOAP services, it is not necessary to install an application proxy on the client. You can use ClickOnce deployment instead, where just a .NET assembly and a configuration file are needed. As you will learn in Chapter 12, when using the HTTPS protocol with SOAP services, the application proxy is required.

SOAP services has some disadvantages that you should not forget. If you use DCOM, you can send a COM+ context from the client to the server; this is not possible with .NET remoting. For example, if the client has already created a distributed transaction, to use the same transaction on the server, your only networking option is to use DCOM. If the client does not create a COM+ context, .NET remoting is a viable option.

.NET Remoting and Performance

With .NET remoting, two channels, TCP and HTTP, are available, of which the TCP channel is usually faster than the HTTP channel. If you want to use the TCP channel with serviced components, you can create a custom host that can be implemented in a Windows service. However, the .NET remoting TCP channel can have a scalability problem if multiple clients are accessing the server simultaneously. You can avoid this problem by using IIS as the remoting host, as in the example. With IIS, the HTTP channel of IIS is used, which does not have scalability problems.

To get more performance out of the HTTP channel, you can use the binary formatter rather than the SOAP formatter. However, the best option with regard to performance is to use DCOM.

.NET Remoting and Application Proxies

Similar to the DCOM configuration discussed earlier, you can create an application proxy if SOAP services is configured. You can use the application proxy in the same way as before. However, if SOAP services is configured, the application proxy connects to the server by using .NET remoting.

TIP: Reality Check: SOAP Services

The name SOAP services is misleading with serviced components. Because .NET remoting is used behind the scenes, and .NET remoting does not offer the current SOAP version, you should not consider using .NET remoting for platform-independent clients accessing serviced components. You should use Web services instead, as discussed in the next section.

If you consider using .NET remoting with a binary formatter for performance reasons, you will find DCOM faster than .NET remoting. The only advantage of .NET remoting compared to DCOM is that with .NET remoting, you do not have to install an application proxy on the client system, and you can use ClickOnce deployment for the client applications. However, this advantage is invalidated if security is needed. With a secure communication, an application proxy is still required, as discussed in Chapter 12.

Web Services

Plenty of other books[21] focus on Web services as their topic, but because Web services play an important part of Enterprise Services applications, they have a place here, too. As shown in Figure 5-13, Web services can act as a client to .NET Enterprise Services and as a server part to a rich or smart client application and other server applications (potentially running on different machines or even in different companies). The background processing is done by .NET Enterprise Services, and Web services can act as a façade. With the technology used that way, Web services can access the serviced components with the DCOM protocol, and Web services can offer the platform-independent SOAP protocol to Windows and Web clients.

Figure 5-13   The role of Web services with .NET Enterprise Services.

Overview

Contrary to the networking options that were discussed earlier in this chapter, Web services are platform independent, whereas DCOM and .NET remoting are Microsoft-specific technologies. Although .NET remoting offers SOAP as a protocol, with .NET remoting, .NET applications are required on both the client and the server. In contrast, if you create a Web service, you can use a different platform to write the client application.

Web services are based on standards such as SOAP, WSDL, and UDDI:

- **SOAP**[22]—SOAP is the definition of XML-based information that can be used to exchange documents between different systems. A client sends a SOAP message to the server, and the server replies with a SOAP message to the client. The SOAP message consists of a SOAP envelope that contains an optional header and a body. Inside the header, context information may be passed. The body usually contains information about the methods that are to be invoked with the service together with the data that is passed.

- **WSDL (Web Services Description Language)**—WSDL defines a contract for Web services. Contrary to interfaces, which are method-based contracts, WSDL is a message- and interface-based contract. WSDL does not define all contracts for Web services; there can be more, such as policy contracts.[23] WSDL consists of message definitions or links to message definitions based on XML schemas. Those message definitions form the business documents that will be exchanged using SOAP.

  The contract that is used with COM components is the type library. It lists the interfaces and methods of a COM component. This is very similar to the metadata of a .NET assembly. Both of these contracts are object oriented, whereas the WSDL contract is a message-based contract in an XML format.

- **UDDI (Universal Description, Discovery, and Integration)**—A UDDI server can be used to search for Web services that implement some specific functionality. Web services that are publicly available are listed at `http://www.uddi.org`, which is a public UDDI server. You can also set up your own UDDI server if the Web services should only be available within the enterprise, or for partners. Windows Server 2003 includes a UDDI server that just needs to be configured. You can use the UDDI server to search for a specific functionality that is implemented by a Web service, but you can also use it for failover. The client can ask the UDDI server for the binding information to a specific Web service. When the Web service is not available anymore, the client queries the UDDI server again for alternative binding information.

Implementing a Web Service with ASP.NET

Looking into the generated source file, you can see one thing immediately: If you create an ASP.NET Web service project using Visual Studio, you can easily implement Web services by applying the attribute [WebMethod] to public methods. This attribute is used by the ASP.NET runtime to offer the method via the SOAP protocol, and a description of the Web service in the form of a WSDL document is created.

In the next example, the serviced component CourseManagement is slightly modified so that you can see how an array of custom objects can be returned from the serviced component, and then this information is passed from the Web service to the client application. To make this happen, the method GetCourses is added to the class CourseManagement (see Listing 5-11). This method just creates an array of CourseInfo objects and returns it to the caller. In the sample implementation, the argument categoryId is ignored and three courses are returned anyway.

Listing 5-11   GetCourses Method

```
public CourseInfo[] GetCourses(string categoryId)
{
    CourseInfo[] courses = new CourseInfo[3];
    courses[0] = new CourseInfo(
        "MS-2524", "ASP.NET Web Services",
        5, new DateTime(2005, 8, 8));
    courses[1] = new CourseInfo(
        "MS-2555", "Windows Forms",
        5, new DateTime(2005, 9, 5));
    courses[2] = new CourseInfo(
        "MS-2557", "Enterprise Services",
        5, new DateTime(2005, 10, 3));
    return courses;
}
```

The client application of the serviced component now is a Web service. You can create a Web service by using the ASP.NET Web Service Project Wizard. With the samples, the Web service has the name CourseServices.

With Web services, be aware that the types defined with XML schemas are not the same types used with the serviced components. With the serviced components, some entity classes such as CourseInfo were created. With .NET remoting, these classes were used both on the client and on the server systems, because with .NET remoting, you usually have the same assemblies on the client and on server systems. This also requires that both the client and the server must be written with .NET technologies. With Web services, however, you are technology independent. Web services are also a better boundary to decouple the client from the back-end infrastructure and thus add an additional trust boundary. To use such a behavior, you should also have special classes that define the messages passed from the Web service to the client, and vice versa.

To demonstrate a Web service method that is invoked by the client application and returns an array of courses back to the client, you must create classes that represent the messages. You can see the classes `Course` and `CourseDate` in Listing 5-12, which includes public fields that represent the data that is sent. An internal constructor is used to convert an instance from the entity classes to the classes that represent the messages.

Furthermore, note that with this class, XML attributes are used to influence the generated XML schema. You can use attribute classes such as `XmlElement-Attribute` and `XmlAttributeAttribute` to define XML elements and XML attributes and specify different names that should be used within XML. You can also change the XML namespace that is used within the schema, which you can set with the attribute `[XmlType]`. With this XML namespace, I always include a year, and possibly a month, so that newer versions can be easily differentiated.

To plan for the future, the attribute `[XmlAnyElement]` is used to define any optional types. If new fields are added with future versions of this class, the current contract is fine because any XML element is allowed.

The XML attribute classes are defined within the namespace `System.Xml.Serialization`.

The classes `GetCoursesRequest` and `GetCoursesResponse` directly define the messages sent from and to the client. `GetCoursesRequest` has just one field, `CategoryId`. `GetCoursesResponse` includes an array of `Course` elements. To define the XML representation of arrays, use the attributes `[XmlArray]` and `[XmlArrayItem]`. You can also use these attributes to convert an `ArrayList` to a normal array with XML serialization.

Listing 5-12   Course Class for the Web Service

```
[XmlType(Namespace=
    "http://thinktecture.com/webservices/2005/CourseManagement")]
public class Course
{
```

```csharp
    public Course()
    {
    }

    internal Course(Entitities.CourseInfo course)
    {
       Number = course.Number;
       CourseDates = new CourseDate[course.CourseDates.Count];
       for (int i = 0; i < course.CourseDates.Count; i++)
       {
          CourseDates[i] = new CourseDate(
                (Entities.CourseDate)course.CourseDates[i]);
       }
    }

    [XmlAttribute()] public string Number;
    public string Title;
    public CourseDate[] CourseDates;

    [XmlAnyElement] public XmlNode[] Any;
}

[XmlType(Namespace=
   "http://thinktecture.com/webservices/2005/CourseManagement")]
public class CourseDate
{
    public CourseDate()
    {
    }

    internal CourseDate(Entities.CourseDate courseDate)
    {
       CourseDateId = courseDate.Id;
       Length = courseDate.Length;
       Location = courseDate.Location;
       Price = courseDate.Price;
       StartDate = courseDate.StartDate;
    }

    public Guid CourseDateId;
    public int Length;
    public string Location;
    public decimal Price;
    public DateTime StartDate;

    [XmlAnyElement] public XmlNode[] Any;
}
```

```
[XmlType(Namespace=
    "http://thinktecture.com/webservices/2005/CourseManagement")]
public class GetCoursesRequest
{
    public string CategoryId;

    [XmlAnyElement] public XmlNode[] Any;
}

[XmlType(Namespace=
    "http://thinktecture.com/webservices/2005/CourseManagement")]
public class GetCoursesResponse
{
    [XmlArray("CoursesList")]
    [XmlArrayItem("Course")]
    public Course[] Courses;

    [XmlAnyElement] public XmlNode[] Any;
}
```

> **NOTE: Differentiate Web Services and Entity Classes**
>
> To differentiate classes that are used with Web services from business classes used with serviced components, I always use different .NET namespaces (for example, `Thinktecture.Entities` and `Thinktecture.Services`).

The `WebMethod` itself is shown in Listing 5-13. The method `GetCourses` requires a `GetCoursesRequest` input message and returns a `GetCoursesResponse` message. The method `GetCourses` from the serviced component returns an array of `CourseInfo` entity objects. This array is converted to the courses array that was defined earlier to represent the message. Finally, a `GetCourseResponse` object is returned that contains the course information.

Listing 5-13   Implementation of a Web Method

```
[WebMethod]
[SoapDocumentMethod(ParameterStyle=SoapParameterStyle.Bare)]
public GetCoursesResponse GetCourses(GetCoursesRequest Request)
{
    Controls.ICourseManagement cm =
```

```
        new Controls.CourseManagement();
Entities.CourseInfo[] courseInfos =
        cm.GetCourses(Request.CategoryId);

Course courses = new Course[courseInfos.Length];
for (int i = 0; i < courseInfos.Length; i++)
{
    courses[i] = new Course(courseInfos[i]);
}

GetCoursesResponse resp = new GetCoursesResponse();
resp.Courses = courses;
return resp;
}
```

Creating a Proxy

For the client application, you can create a proxy class with the `wsdl.exe` utility. The proxy class allows the client application to call simple methods and creates SOAP requests to send the SOAP messages to the Web service.

You can see a part of the generated proxy class in Listing 5-13. This class is created by passing the WSDL document to the `wsdl.exe` utility. The proxy class `CourseServices` derives from the base class `SoapHttpClientProtocol`. This base class is responsible for creating a SOAP request and sending this request to the Web service. Within the method `GetCourses`, you can see a call to `this.Invoke`. This is a method of the base class `SoapHttpClientProtocol`, and it's the actual method that creates the SOAP request from its parameters. The client application can create an instance of the `CourseServices` class and invoke the `GetCourses` method, which calls the Web service.

Instead of using the command-line utility `wsdl.exe`, you can use Add Web Reference within Visual Studio. This Visual Studio option and `wsdl.exe` make use of the same .NET classes in the namespace `System.Web.Services.Description`.

Listing 5-13   Wsdl.exe-Generated Proxy Class

```
[System.Web.Services.WebServiceBindingAttribute(
    Name="CourseServicesSoap",
    Namespace=
```

```
        "http://thinktecture.com/2005/CourseManagement/Services")]
[System.Xml.Serialization.XmlIncludeAttribute(typeof(object[]))]
public class CourseServices :
        System.Web.Services.Protocols.SoapHttpClientProtocol
{
    public CourseServices() {
        this.Url =
            "http://localhost/CourseServices/CourseServices.asmx";
    }

    [System.Web.Services.Protocols.SoapDocumentMethodAttribute(
    "http://thinktecture.com/2005/CourseManagement/Services" +
        "GetCourses",
    Use=System.Web.Services.Description.SoapBindingUse.Literal,
    ParameterStyle=
        System.Web.Services.Protocols.SoapParameterStyle.Bare)]
    [return: XmlElement(Namespace=
            "http://thinktecture.com/2005/CourseManagement/Services")]
    public GetCoursesResponse GetCourses(
            [XmlElement(Namespace=
                "http://thinktecture.com/2005/CourseManagment/Services")]
        GetCoursesRequest Request)
    {
        object[] results = this.Invoke("GetCourses", new object[] {
            Request});
        return ((GetCoursesResponse)(results[0]));
    }
}
```

TIP: Reality Check: Web Services

You gain many advantages by using Web services to access serviced components. With Web services, you get a platform-independent abstraction layer (perhaps not needed), and you get a layer that can be independent of the version of the serviced components. If the serviced components change, you do not have to update the client applications as long as the Web service contract does not change.

Web services with ASP.NET also ease the move to the next technology, codenamed Indigo (see Chapter 14, "The Future of Distributed Applications").

Summary

This chapter discussed some different options to access Enterprise Services applications. You can access serviced components directly by using the DCOM protocol or .NET remoting. DCOM is the fastest option. It allows passing contexts across the network, but DCOM needs an application proxy on the client that is configured in the registry. This is where .NET remoting shows its advantage: When using .NET remoting, you can deploy the client application as with other rich .NET client applications: with ClickOnce deployment. However, .NET remoting has the disadvantage that contexts cannot be passed across the network, and it is slower than DCOM.

This chapter also discussed Web services. Although Web services do not interact directly with the serviced components, this technology plays an important role insofar as it is a very useful façade to serviced components. With ASP.NET Web services, you get a platform-independent way to access the serviced components, and you add another layer to support the smart client principles. Web services are discussed in more detail throughout the remainder of this book.

1   The name SOAP services is very misleading. The name suggests that you get platform independence. However, this is not true with SOAP services as it is offered by the Enterprise Services technology. Instead, .NET remoting is used behind the scenes and does not offer platform independence (as discussed in this chapter).

2   DCOM is the short name for Distributed COM.

3   If DCOM is used without COM+ Services, it is difficult to configure. With COM+ Services and .NET Enterprise Services, DCOM is easy to use.

4   .NET remoting has a documented way for changing channels, formatters, and adding sinks that intercept the message flow.

5   The Component Services Explorer is part of the Administrative Tools.

6   Chapter 2, "Object Activation and Contexts," shows the integration of the .NET remoting context with the COM+ context.

7   The classes discussed in this section are not documented. These classes may change with future editions, and you should not rely on their presence. This section should just help you understand how DCOM functionality is added to serviced components.

8   RSN stands for remote server name.

9 Of course, this requirement only exists for serviced components written with .NET code. Because you are reading this book, you would not create new COM+ components with VB6 or C++ ATL, would you?

10 COM clients are discussed in Chapter 4.

11 .NET remoting cannot be covered in detail in this book. You will find more information about .NET remoting in the book *Advanced .NET Remoting*, by Ingo Rammer.

12 Application domains are discussed in Chapter 2.

13 The difference between DOC and RPC styles is discussed in Chapter 14, " The Future of Distributed Applications."

14 Security and using secure channels with .NET Remoting is discussed in Chapter 12.

15 Object pooling and just-in-time activation are discussed in Chapter 2.

16 WSDL is an XML format to describe operations and parameters of Web services. Later in this chapter, WSDL is discussed in more detail.

17 With a singleton, just a single object is created that is shared among all clients.

18 If you want to create singletons with Serviced Component applications, you can create an object pool and define a pool count of 1.

19 ISAPI is the Internet Server Application Programming Interface, which is used to extend the functionality of IIS.

20 With .NET applications, the application configuration file has the same name as the executable, appended with .config.

21 See Keith Ballinger's book *.NET Web Services—Architecture and Implementation*.

22 SOAP once was the name for Simple Object Access Protocol. However, this protocol was developed further, and now it is just known as SOAP.

23 Policies with Web services are discussed in Chapter 14.

6

Data Access

T HE FOCUS IN THIS CHAPTER IS on reading and writing data from a database, using ADO.NET as the data access technology. This chapter takes a closer look at querying data, adding data, and updating records, all using ADO.NET.

In this chapter, you also learn how to separate data access classes into different assemblies, which is considered good practice. This chapter is not meant to explain the ADO.NET classes in detail,[1] but it does focus on features that are interesting to use from serviced components.

Specifically, this chapter covers the following topics:

- ADO.NET overview
- .NET data providers
- A sample database
- Entity classes
- Database access with the `DataReader`
- Using datasets

ADO.NET Overview

ADO.NET is the technology to read and update databases and read and write XML data. The major elements of ADO.NET are the .NET data provider, the dataset, and XML classes, as shown in Figure 6-1.

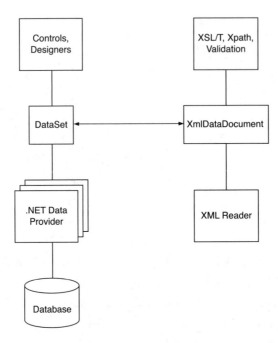

Figure 6-1   ADO.NET overview.

The .NET data provider consists of classes and interfaces used to access databases. .NET 1.1 includes native data providers for SQL Server and Oracle, and data providers for OLE DB and ODBC, so that you can use any OLE DB provider or ODBC driver. For access to other databases, you can find native data providers on the Internet.

The dataset is a memory-based data store that contains tables with data, including their relations and constraints, such as primary keys. The dataset is designed for disconnected behavior, so it is possible to send the dataset to a client without holding resources on the server.

One great feature of the dataset is built-in XML support. Datasets can be accessed by using XML features such as DOM, XPath, and XSLT with the help of the XmlDataDocument class, which derives from the base class XmlDocument. Although the class XmlDocument is used to access XML data with the DOM model, the XmlDataDocument class adds dataset integration so that a dataset can be converted to an XML document and vice versa.

Let's look into a .NET data provider in more detail. A data provider consists of connection, command, data reader, and parameters (see Figure 6-2). The connection object is used to open and close connections to the database. For reading records, the data reader allows for fast retrieval of data; it is a forward-only, read-only view of the data. The data reader uses the associated command object to specify the SQL statement.

The dataset is independent of the data provider; a single dataset object can be filled from different data providers. The connection of the dataset with a data provider is done by a data adapter, an object that encapsulates the commands to fetch data from the provider (using the `Fill` method) and flush changes back to the provider (using the `Update` method).

In this book, the SQL Server data provider (found in the namespace `System.Data.SqlClient`) will be used to access Microsoft SQL Server. You can use this data provider to access SQL Server 7.0 and later. You can access earlier versions of SQL Server by using the .NET data provider for OLE DB.

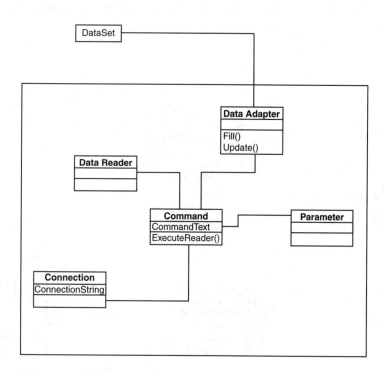

Figure 6-2   .NET data provider.

The .NET data provider for SQL Server consists of the main classes `SqlConnection`, `SqlCommand`, and `SqlDataReader`. The class `SqlConnection` is used to connect to a database and to begin and commit transactions.[2] With the `SqlCommand` class, you can specify SQL commands to query for records or to insert, to update, and to delete records, or if using the `SqlDataReader`, to walk through all records.

Sample Database

The database used in this chapter (and in the following ones) is shown in Figure 6-3. The database consists of a `CourseInfo` table that contains information about courses, a `CourseDates` table that is associated with courses and includes specific course dates and the course length (because the length can differ with different course dates), an `Attendees` table with information about course attendees, and the association table `CourseAttendees` that maps the attendees to their courses.

The tables have a `uniqueidentifier` as primary key field, a `timestamp` to verify row changes, and an `active` field that enables you to set courses and attendees inactive without deleting the row entries.

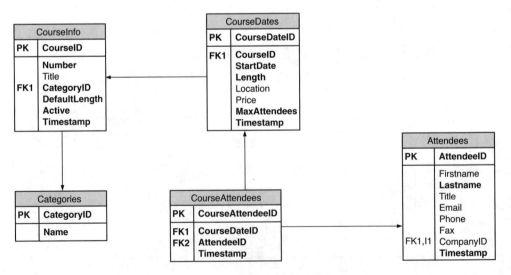

Figure 6-3 Database diagram for the CourseManagement database.

Identifiers and Timestamps

What is notable about the tables in this database is that a `unique-identifier` for the identifier column is used. SQL Server uses a GUID with the `uniqueidentifier` data type. A GUID, when compared to an integer as an identifier, has the disadvantage that it needs more data space; a GUID has a length of 16 bytes. However, GUIDs do have a big advantage in distributed scenarios: Using integer values as row identifiers, the identifier must be created on the SQL Server system to get a unique value. GUIDs can be created on any system; there is no need to do a separate round trip to the server to get the identifier.

The tables also use a `Timestamp` column. If you add a `Timestamp` column to a table, this column is automatically updated if the record is changed. This behavior is very useful when data is updated. If two users change the same record simultaneously, only the timestamp value needs to be compared with the current value in the database to find out that the record was already updated.

Entity Classes

For the entity classes that can be sent across different tiers and for the classes that are used to access the database, it is a good practice to use separate assemblies. By doing so, it is easy to define a clear dependency of the assemblies: The entity classes will be needed in multiple tiers and so referenced from many projects, whereas the database classes just need to be referenced from some serviced component assemblies. In the sample, you will find the entity classes in the assembly `SamplesCourse-Management.Entities`.

Figure 6-4 shows the assemblies used in this chapter. `Samples.CourseManagement.Entities` contains all entity classes, such as `Course` and `CourseDate-Collection`, and the dataset classes that will be created; the assembly `Samples.CourseManagement.Data` contains all classes with direct access to the database.

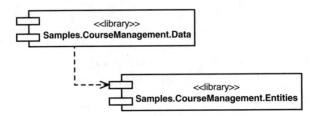

Figure 6-4 Assemblies.

In Listing 6-1, you can see the class Course that acts as a data holder to encapsulate the course identifier, number, title, and timestamp. The class Course is marked with the attribute [Serializable] so that it can be serialized across .NET remoting or DCOM boundaries.[3]

In the database, the column CourseId is of type uniqueidentifier, and the column Timestamp is of type timestamp. With .NET, the uniqueidentifier maps to a System.Guid type, and the timestamp maps to a byte array of eight elements. The course number and title, which are nchar(10) and nvarchar(50), in the database both map to the String type in the Course class. All the fields can be accessed through properties.

The fields courseId and timestamp only provide read-only access, because these fields may not be changed after the Course object is instantiated. The values for these fields are set in the constructors. You can use the default constructor to create a new course and initialize the course identifier with the NewGuid method of the Guid class. The timestamp is not needed for newly initialized objects, so it is set to null. If course data is read from the database, you can use the constructor to pass a course identifier and a timestamp.

Listing 6-1 Course Entity Class

```
using System;

namespace Samples.CourseManagement.Entities
{
    [Serializable]
    public class Course
    {
        public Course()
```

```
{
   courseId = Guid.NewGuid();
   timestamp = null;
}

public Course(Guid courseId, byte[] timestamp)
{
   this.courseId = courseId;
   this.timestamp = timestamp;
}

readonly private Guid courseId;
public Guid CourseId
{
   get
   {
      return courseId;
   }
}

private string courseNumber;
public string CourseNumber
{
   get
   {
      return courseNumber;
   }
   set
   {
      courseNumber = value;
   }
}

private string title;
public string Title
{
   get
   {
      return title;
   }
   set
   {
      title = value;
   }
}

readonly private CourseDateCollection courseDates =
      new CourseDateCollection();
```

```
public CourseDateCollection CourseDates
{
   get
   {
      return courseDates;
   }
}

private bool active;
public bool Active
{
   get
   {
      return active;
   }
   set
   {
      active = value;
   }
}

readonly private byte[] timestamp;
public byte[] Timestamp
{
   get
   {
      return timestamp;
   }
}
   }
}
```

With the database tables, you have seen that the CourseInfo table is associated with the CourseDates table. The same association exists with the Course class, which has a private field courseDates of type CourseDateCollection and a read-only property to expose the course dates.

CourseDateCollection is a type-safe custom collection class, as you can see in Listing 6-2. With object-based collection classes such as the class ArrayList, it is possible to put the wrong object types into the collection, leading to runtime errors. Using type-safe collection classes, you will get compile errors when wrong object types are put into the collection. A type-safe collection class can easily be implemented by deriving from the base class CollectionBase, which implements the interfaces IList, ICollection, and IEnumerable. When deriving from this base class, you just have to add the methods to provide type-safe access to the objects in the collection. With the CourseDateCollection class, the method Add is overloaded with a parameter of type CourseDate, an entity class that is very similar to the Course class; it just holds the data for course dates. Also, an indexer of type CourseDate is implemented in the CourseDateCollection class, to provide index access to the collection. Within the implementations of the Add method and the indexer, the List property of the base class is used. With the List property, you can access the ArrayList object that is used inside the CollectionBase class.

Listing 6-2   Custom Collection Class CourseDateCollection

```
public class CourseDateCollection : CollectionBase
{
    public CourseDateCollection()
    {
    }

    public void Add(CourseDate courseDate)
    {
        List.Add(courseDate);
    }

    public CourseDate this[int index]
    {
        get
        {
            return (CourseDate)List[index];
        }
        set
        {
            List[index] = value;
        }
    }
}
```

Instead of using a custom type-safe collection class such as CourseDateCollection, you can use ArrayList directly. ArrayList has the disadvantage that it can hold objects of any type (derived from Object), so you can detect errors only at runtime. With type-safe-collections, you get errors at compile time. You can also use normal arrays for collections. Normal arrays are type-safe; however, you cannot resize such arrays.

Generics

With .NET 2.0, it is no longer necessary to create custom type-safe collection classes. Instead, .NET 2.0 has support for generics and includes the generic collection class `List` in the namespace `System.Collections.Generic`. The field `courseDates` can be of type `List<CourseDate>`:

```
readonly private List<CourseDate> courseDates =
    new List<CourseDate>();
public List<CourseDate> CourseDates
{
    get
    {
        return courseDates;
    }
}
```

With `List<CourseDate>`, a collection type is defined that may only include `CourseDate` objects. With the `ArrayList` class, it is possible to add any data type to the collection, whereas with a generic collection class, the only type that is allowed is specified within the angle brackets. If you use generics, the compiler can check for wrong object types, whereas if you use an object-based collection class such as `ArrayList`, an exception occurs while running the program.

Database Access

To access the database, the assembly `Samples.CourseManagement.Data` is created. In this assembly, the class `CoursesData` is used to access the `CourseInfo` table in the database. Because the `Course` class is needed here, the assembly `Samples.CourseManagement.Entities` must be referenced. For the database classes, the namespaces `System.Data` and `System.Data.SqlClient` are needed.

You can see the first part of the class `CoursesData` in Listing 6-3. In the constructor of the class `CoursesData`, the connection string is set. This makes it possible to set the connection string dynamically (for example, with the construction string[4] of serviced components).

Listing 6-3   CoursesData Class

```
using System;
using System.Data;
using System.Data.SqlClient;
using System.Collections;
using Samples.CourseManagement.Entities;

namespace Samples.CourseManagement.Data
{
    public class CoursesData
    {
        private string dsn;

        public CoursesData(string dsn)
        {
            this.dsn = dsn;
        }

        //...
```

Database Query

Getting the data from the database is demonstrated with the GetCourses method, shown in Listing 6-4. This method returns an array of Course objects. Instead of returning an untyped ArrayList, you can create a custom type-safe collection class or (with .NET 2.0) use generics, as previously discussed.

Within the implementation, a SqlConnection object is created and initialized with the connection string that has been set earlier in the constructor. The method CreateCommand returns a SqlCommand object that is associated with the connection, and the SQL SELECT statement is set with the CommandText property. The SQL statement SELECT CourseId, Number, Title, Active, [Timestamp] FROM Courses queries all columns from the CourseInfo table.

The connection.Open method either creates a new connection to access the database or gets a connection from the connection pool. The command.ExecuteReader method returns a SqlDataReader object that you can use to read record by record. The parameter CommandBehavior.CloseConnection is passed to the ExecuteReader method to ensure the connection is closed as soon as the DataReader is closed.

Calling the Read method of the DataReader object enables you to walk through all records, and it returns false if there are no more records. A record can be accessed by using the indexer of the DataReader and either passing the index of the selected column (you can count the selected column from the SELECT statement, so this is independent of the database[5]) or by passing the column name. Instead of using the indexer, you can use Get{Type} methods such as GetString or GetBoolean. The methods, including the type name, are faster because unboxing is not done with value types; however, these methods do have the disadvantage that you cannot pass the column name as argument.

> **NOTE: Boxing and Unboxing**
>
> *Boxing* in this context is a term that means to convert a value type variable (e.g., int, short) to a reference type (objects). Unboxing is used for a conversion the other way around: to convert a reference type to a value type. Because boxing and unboxing are done automatically when converting value and reference types, usability is increased. However, boxing and unboxing also impact performance, particularly if used inside a loop and thus done several times.

The column values that are read are set with a new Course object, and this course object is added to the ArrayList that is returned by the method.

Listing 6-4 Querying Data with the CoursesData Class

```
public ArrayList GetCourses()
{
    ArrayList courses = new ArrayList();

    SqlConnection connection = new SqlConnection(dsn);
    SqlCommand command = connection.CreateCommand();
    command.CommandText = "SELECT CourseId, Number, " +
        "Title, Active, [Timestamp] FROM CourseInfo";
    connection.Open();
    SqlDataReader reader = command.ExecuteReader(
        CommandBehavior.CloseConnection);
    try
    {
        while (reader.Read())
```

```
    {
        Course course = new Course(
                (Guid)reader[0], (byte[])reader[4]);
        course.CourseNumber = reader.GetString(1);
        course.Title = reader.GetString(2);
        course.Active = reader.GetBoolean(3);
        courses.Add(course);
    }
}
finally
{
    reader.Close();
}

return courses;
}
```

Connection Pools

Two-tier applications often just used a single connection for the lifetime of a process. With distributed applications, connections should be opened just before they are needed and released immediately after. This latter method has the advantage that the number of connections needed matches the number of users concurrently accessing the database. One reason why connections had been held open by an application was that opening the connection is resource-intensive and time-consuming; keeping the connection open saved time. This is different with connection pools.

If a connection pool is used, the Open method of the Connection class does not create a new connection, but gets an existing connection from the connection pool instead. If there is no matching connection (that is, connection string details, user identity, etc.), a new connection is created. When a connection is closed, it is not physically closed, but returned to the connection pool where it becomes available for the next user. Avoiding repetitive connection opening and closing can save a large amount of time. With the .NET data provider for SQL Server, you can set the Pool-ing property of the connection string to define whether a connection pool should be used. By default, the Pooling property is set to true. How many connections should be put into the connection pool can be set with the `Min Pool Size` and `Max Pool Size` properties. By default, the minimum pool size is set to 0, and the maximum pool size is set to 100.

Together with the data from the `CourseInfo` table, data from the `CourseDates` table is also needed to get the course dates. The method `GetCourseDatesByCourse` is implemented in the class `CourseDatesData`. This class is very similar to `Course-Data`; it just reads and writes data from the table `CourseDates` rather than the table `Courses`. Comparing the method `GetCourseDatesByCourse` to `GetCourses` results in the difference that the first one requires a parameter to read only the course dates for a specific course. Here the SQL `SELECT` statement includes a `WHERE` clause: `WHERE CourseId = @CourseId`, and the parameter `@CourseId` is set using the `Parameters` property of the `SqlCommand` object. The method `command.Parameters.Add("@CourseId", SqlDbType.UniqueIdentifier)` adds a parameter named `@CourseId` of type `SqlDbType.UniqueIdentifier` to the parameters collection of the command object; accessing the property `command.Parameters["@CourseId"].Value` sets this parameter value to the `courseId` that was received by the method with the `course` object.

Listing 6-5 Querying Data with a Parameter

```
public CourseDateCollection GetCourseDatesByCourse(
    Course course)
{
    CourseDateCollection courseDates =
        new CourseDateCollection();

    SqlConnection connection = new SqlConnection(dsn);

    SqlCommand command = connection.CreateCommand();
    command.CommandText = "SELECT CourseDatesId, " +
        "StartDate, Length, Location, Price, MaxAttendees, " +
        "[Timestamp] FROM CourseDates WHERE " +
        "CourseId = @CourseId";
    command.Parameters.Add("@CourseId",
        SqlDbType.UniqueIdentifier);
    command.Parameters["@CourseId"].Value =
        course.courseId;

    connection.Open();
```

```
SqlDataReader reader = command.ExecuteReader(
        CommandBehavior.CloseConnection);

try
{
    while (reader.Read())
    {
        CourseDate courseDate =
            new CourseDate(course,
                           reader.GetGuid(0),
                           (byte[])reader[6]);

        courseDate.StartDate = reader.GetDateTime(1);
        courseDate.Length = reader.GetInt32(2);
        courseDate.Location = reader.GetString(3);
        courseDate.Price = reader.GetDecimal(4);
        courseDate.MaxAttendees = reader.GetInt32(5);
        courseDates.Add(courseDate);
    }
}
finally
{
    reader.Close();
}

return courseDates;
}
```

Building SQL Strings

Do not build SQL strings that include a WHERE clause by using string concatenation because this can leave you open to SQL injection attacks. These allow misbehaving SQL statements to be added to your SQL statement. Using named parameters to build up SQL strings ensures you are safe from the problem of possible SQL injection.

Insert

Adding newly created courses to the database is done by calling the AddCourse method that you can see in Listing 6-6. The INSERT SQL statement uses some named parameters that are set using the Parameters property of the SqlCommand object.

Similar to the database access methods you have seen before, within `AddCourse`, connection and command objects are created and the `CommandText` property is set. Because parameters are needed with the `INSERT` statement, the parameters are also set, and to invoke the SQL statement, the `ExecuteNonQuery` method is called. `ExecuteNonQuery` just returns an integer value that returns the number of rows modified. With the `INSERT` statement, a value of 1 should be returned.

Listing 6-6   Adding New Data with the CoursesData Class

```
public void AddCourse(Course course)
{
    SqlConnection connection = new SqlConnection(dsn);
    SqlCommand command = connection.CreateCommand();

    command.CommandText = "INSERT INTO CourseInfo (CourseId, " +
        "Number, Title) VALUES (@CourseId, @Number, " +
        "@Title";
    command.Parameters.Add("@CourseId",
        SqlDbType.UniqueIdentifier);
    command.Parameters.Add("@Number", SqlDbType.NChar, 10);
    command.Parameters.Add("@Title", SqlDbType.NVarChar, 50);
    command.Parameters.Add("@Active", SqlDbType.Bit);

    command.Parameters["@CourseId"].Value = course.CourseId;
    command.Parameters["@Number"].Value = course.CourseNumber;
    command.Parameters["@Title"].Value = course.Title;
    command.Parameters["@Active"].Value = course.Active;

    connection.Open();
    try
    {
        if (command.ExecuteNonQuery() != 1)
        {
            throw new CourseDataException("Course insert failed");
        }
    }
    finally
    {
        connection.Close();
    }
}
```

Update

If you use the Visual Studio wizard-generated code to update records, all modified columns are checked to determine whether they have been changed. An exception is thrown if any of the columns has been modified after the data has been read. By using Timestamp columns, as done here, it is not necessary to verify all columns, as shown in Listing 6-7 where the UPDATE SQL statement only compares the Timestamp column.

As with the methods before, connection and command objects are created, the CommandText property is set (now with the UPDATE statement), parameters are set, and the statement is executed by calling the ExecuteNonQuery method.

Listing 6-7   Updating Data with the CoursesData Class

```
public void UpdateCourse(Course course)
{
    SqlConnection connection = new SqlConnection(dsn);
    SqlCommand command = connection.CreateCommand();

    command.CommandText = "UPDATE CourseInfo " +
        "SET Number = @Number, Title = @Title, " +
        "Active = @Active WHERE " +
        "(CourseId = @CourseId) AND " +
        "(Timestamp = @Timestamp)";

    // Define parameters for the command
    command.Parameters.Add("@CourseId",
        SqlDbType.UniqueIdentifier);
    command.Parameters.Add("@Number", SqlDbType.NChar, 10);
    command.Parameters.Add("@Title", SqlDbType.NVarChar, 50);
    command.Parameters.Add("@Active", SqlDbType.Bit);
    command.Parameters.Add("@Timestamp", SqlDbType.Timestamp);

    // Set parameter values
    command.Parameters["@CourseId"].Value = course.CourseId;
    command.Parameters["@Number"].Value = course.CourseNumber;
    command.Parameters["@Title"].Value = course.Title;
    command.Parameters["@Active"].Value = course.Active;
    command.Parameters["@Timestamp"].Value =
        course.Timestamp;

    connection.Open();
    try
    {
```

```
        command.ExecuteNonQuery();
    }
    finally
    {
        connection.Close();
    }
}
```

Calling Stored Procedures

Instead of using dynamic queries with the SELECT, INSERT, and UPDATE statements, you can invoke stored procedures. A stored procedure to update a course is shown in Listing 6-8.

Listing 6-8   Stored Procedure UpdateCourseInfo

```
CREATE PROCEDURE UpdateCourseInfo
(
    @CourseId uniqueidentifier,
    @Number nchar(10),
    @Title nvarchar(50),
    @DefaultLength int,
    @Active bit,
    @Timestamp timestamp
)
AS
    UPDATE CourseInfo
    SET Number = @Number, Title = @Title,
        DefaultLength = @DefaultLength, Active = @Active
    WHERE (CourseId = @CourseId) AND (Timestamp = @Timestamp)
    RETURN
```

If calling the stored procedure (Listing 6-9), the method UpdateCourseInfo can be changed to have the CommandText property of the SqlCommand object changed to the name of the stored procedure and the CommandType property set to Command-Type.StoredProcedure. The parameters that are needed by the stored procedure are similar to the parameters that were used in the UPDATE statement in Listing 6-7.

Listing 6-9   Calling a Stored Procedure

```
public void UpdateCourse(Course course)
{
```

```
SqlConnection connection = new SqlConnection(dsn);
SqlCommand command = connection.CreateCommand();

command.CommandText = "UpdateCourseInfo";
command.CommandType = CommandType.StoredProcedure;

// Define parameters for the command
command.Parameters.Add("@CourseId",
    SqlDbType.UniqueIdentifier);
command.Parameters.Add("@Number", SqlDbType.NChar, 10);
command.Parameters.Add("@Title", SqlDbType.NVarChar, 50);
command.Parameters.Add("@Active", SqlDbType.Bit);
command.Parameters.Add("@Timestamp", SqlDbType.Timestamp);

// Set parameter values
command.Parameters["@CourseId"].Value = course.CourseId;
command.Parameters["@Number"].Value = course.Number;
command.Parameters["@Title"].Value = course.Title;
command.Parameters["@Active"].Value = course.Active;
command.Parameters["@Timestamp"].Value = course.Timestamp;
connection.Open();
try
{
    command.ExecuteNonQuery();
}
finally
{
    connection.Close();
}
}
```

Stored Procedures or Dynamic Queries?

Stored procedures do have some advantages and disadvantages when compared to dynamic queries. The disadvantage of stored procedures is that using them, you are bound to a specific database. The syntax of stored procedures is different from database to database. However, with stored procedures, you have the advantage that you can get better security by not allowing users access to tables. You can define the security in such a way that the user who is configured with the serviced component application[6] is only allowed to access stored procedures.

Datasets

A major feature of ADO.NET is independent of a .NET data provider: the **dataset**. A dataset is a memory-resident representation of data that offers a relational programming model: It includes tables, relations, and constraints. Within a dataset, you can navigate through parent and child rows. The `DataSet` class is defined in the namespace `System.Data`—as you can see, this class is not inside the namespace of a .NET data provider. The `DataSet` class is independent of the provider; one `DataSet` instance can be filled with multiple .NET data providers and with XML data. Another feature of the dataset is that it is disconnected from the data source, so it is possible to use it in a distributed solution; the dataset can be passed around. The dataset also retains changed data, allowing not only the current data to be accessed, but also the original data, which proves useful when handling concurrency conflicts with optimistic concurrency updates.

Figure 6-5 shows the `DataSet` class with associated classes. The class `DataSet` can contain multiple tables in the form of the `DataTable` class. Similar to a database, relationships can be defined between these tables using the `DataRelation` class. The `DataTable` class consists of collections containing columns, constraints, and rows. A column is defined with a `DataColumn` class, which has properties to define the name, data type, a default value, and the maximum length. The `Expression` property allows the value of the column to be created dynamically. The constraints of the table are defined with classes that derive from the `Constraint` class: `UniqueConstraint` and `ForeignConstraint`. Every row in a `DataTable` collection is defined by a `DataRow` object, and the `Item` property of a `DataRow` allows single columns of the row to be accessed. To indicate the status of the row, the `RowState` property is used. This is a value of the enumeration `DataRowState`, which defines the values `Added`, `Deleted`, `Detached`, `Modified`, and `Unchanged`. For concurrency checking, values of the `DataRowVersion` enumeration (`Current`, `Default`, `Original`, and `Proposed`) can be used when accessing a column.

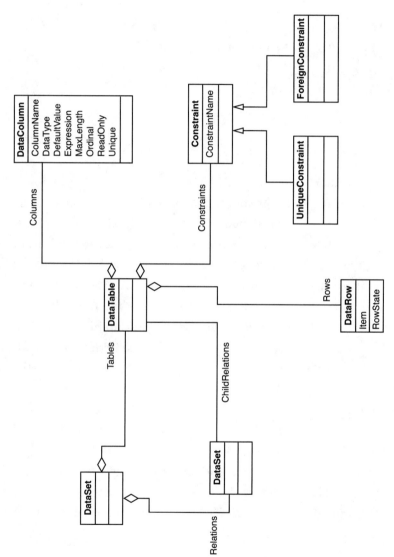

Figure 6-5   Dataset associations.

> **Tables in a Dataset**
>
> There is not necessarily a one-to-one mapping for a table in a database and a table in the `DataSet` class. One table in the dataset can map to multiple tables in the database and vice versa. A dataset table can also be made up programmatically with columns that are created dynamically, or can be read from an XML file.

Filling Datasets

Listing 6-10 shows how you can create a dataset. Here the method `GetCourses` is changed so that a dataset is returned. In the method, a `DataSet` object is created by passing the name of the dataset to the constructor. Then a `SqlDataAdapter` is created. The `SqlDataAdapter` (in the namespace `System.Data.SqlClient`) is part of the .NET data provider for SQL Server and acts as a bridge from the dataset to the .NET data provider. Data is fetched from the database using the `Fill` method, and changed data is written back to the database using the `Update` method. Here the `Fill` method is used to create the table `Course` in the dataset and to fill it with data from the database `CourseInfo` table. The command that is passed to the constructor of the `SqlDataAdapter` defines the SQL `SELECT` statement that is used to read the data from the database.

After the data from the `CourseInfo` table is filled in the dataset, a new `SqlDataAdapter` object is created to fill the `CourseDate` table in the dataset. As discussed before, the dataset can contain multiple tables.

A relation named `Courses_CourseDates` is added to the dataset by calling the method `ds.Relations.Add`. The parent and child column of the relation are defined with the second and the third argument. The fourth argument `true` defines that a constraint for the relation should be added to the dataset.

Listing 6-10   Returning a Dataset

```
public DataSet GetCourses()
{
    DataSet ds = new DataSet("Courses");
```

```
SqlConnection connection = new SqlConnection(dsn);

// Fill the Course table in the DataSet
string command = "SELECT CourseID, Number, " +
    "Title, Active, [Timestamp] FROM CourseInfo";
SqlDataAdapter adapter = new SqlDataAdapter(command,
    connection);
adapter.Fill(ds, "Course");

// Fill the CourseDate table in the DataSet
command = "SELECT CourseDateId, CourseId, StartDate " +
    "Length, Location, Price, MaxAttendees, " +
    "[Timestamp] FROM CourseDates";
adapter = new SqlDataAdapter(command, connection);
adapter.Fill(ds, "CourseDate");

// Define a relation from the Course to the
// CourseData table
ds.Relations.Add("Courses_CourseDates",
    ds.Tables["Course"].Columns["CourseId"],
    ds.Tables["CourseDate"].Columns["CourseId"],
    true);

return ds;
}
```

Listing 6-11 shows how you can use an untyped dataset. The dataset is returned from the `GetCourses` method shown in Listing 6-10. The `Tables` property of the dataset returns a `DataTableCollection` where an indexer with the name of the table is used to get a `DataTable`. The `DataTable` object has a property `Rows` that returns a `DataRowCollection`. With a `foreach` statement, you can loop through all `DataRow` objects. In the `foreach` block, the columns `Number` and `Title` are accessed by using indexers.

Listing 6-11 Using an Untyped Dataset

```
using Samples.CourseManagement.Data;
using System.Data;

public class Test
{
    static void Main()
    {
```

```
        string dsn = "server=localhost;database=Courses;" +
            "trusted_connection=true";
        CoursesData db = new CoursesData(dsn);

        DataSet ds = db.GetCourses();
        foreach (DataRow row in ds.Tables["Course"].Rows)
        {
            Console.WriteLine("{0} {1}", row["Number"], row["Title"]);
        }
    }
}
```

With Visual Studio, you can also create typed datasets. A typed dataset is a class that derives from the class `DataSet` and adds properties for tables and columns in addition to inner classes that represent the tables. You can create a typed dataset with the Dataset XML schema editor, as shown in Figure 6-6. Using this editor, you can drag and drop tables or stored procedures from the server explorer to the designer surface. Visual Studio 2005 automatically adds relations to the schema. With Visual Studio .NET 2003, you have to add relations yourself. In the class view, you can see the Dataset XML schema editor with the classes `Course` and `CourseDate`.

Listing 6-12 shows the same method `GetCourses` that was shown in Listing 6-10, but here a typed dataset is returned rather than an untyped dataset. The variable `ds` is now a reference to an object of type `CoursesDataset` rather than `DataSet`. With the `Fill` method of the adapter, the parameter passed is the table inside the dataset that can be accessed with a property—in the example, the properties `Course` and `CourseDate` map to the tables `Courses` and `CourseDates`. Because the relation of the dataset tables is already defined with the XML schema, there is no need to define the relation programmatically, so the code to create the relation from Listing 6-10 is removed here.[7]

Listing 6-12 Returning a Typed Dataset

```
public CoursesDataset GetCourses()
{
    CoursesDataset ds = new CoursesDataset();

    SqlConnection connection = new SqlConnection(dsn);

    // Fill the Course table in the DataSet
    string command = "SELECT CourseID, Number, " +
        "Title, Active, [Timestamp] FROM CourseInfo";
```

```
SqlDataAdapter adapter = new SqlDataAdapter(command,
      connection);
adapter.Fill(ds.Course);

// Fill the CourseDate table in the DataSet
command = "SELECT CourseDateId, CourseId, StartDate " +
      "Length, Location, Price, MaxAttendees, " +
      "[Timestamp] FROM CourseDates";
adapter = new SqlDataAdapter(command, connection);
adapter.Fill(ds.CourseDate);

// With the schema, the programmatic creation of
// the relation is no longer needed
return ds;
}
```

Listing 6-13 shows how you can use a typed dataset. You can compare this with the code in Listing 6-11 with the untyped dataset. With the typed dataset, to access a table you can use a property with the name of the table instead of an indexer, as used earlier. The property `Course` of the typed dataset returns a typed representation of the `Course` table, the `CourseDataTable` class. Every row is represented with the `CourseRow` class, which has properties such as `Number` and `Title` to access the

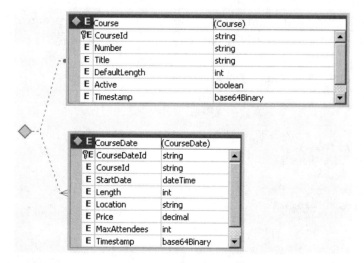

Figure 6-6   Dataset editor.

columns. The `CourseRow` and `CourseDataTable` classes are defined as inner classes in the class `CoursesDataset`.

Listing 6-13   Using a Typed Dataset

```
CoursesDataset ds = db.GetCourses();
foreach (CourseRow row in ds.Course.Rows)
{
    Console.WriteLine("{0} {1}", row.Number, row.Title);
}
```

Updating Datasets

The `SqlDataAdapter` is the interface to the database not only for filling the dataset with data, but also to update changes from the dataset to the database. As you saw earlier, reading data from the database is done with the `SelectCommand` that is associated with the data adapter. To write changes back to the database, you must define multiple commands: `UpdateCommand`, `InsertCommand`, and `DeleteCommand`. The `InsertCommand` is used on new rows added to the dataset to insert the new row into the database, the `DeleteCommand` deletes database records, and the `UpdateCommand` updates existing database records.

For updating the `CourseInfo` table, you use the stored procedure `Update-CourseInfo` (Listing 6-14). When the data is updated with the SQL UPDATE statement, the timestamp value changes. The new value for the timestamp is needed in the dataset, so the changes are returned with the SELECT statement after the update.

Listing 6-14   Stored Procedure UpdateCourseInfo

```
CREATE PROCEDURE UpdateCourseInfo
    (
        @CourseId uniqueidentifier,
        @Number nchar(10),
        @Title nvarchar(50),
        @DefaultLength int,
        @Active bit,
        @Timestamp timestamp
    )
AS
    UPDATE CourseInfo
    SET Number = @Number, Title = @Title,
```

```
        DefaultLength = @DefaultLength, Active = @Active
WHERE (CourseId = @CourseId AND [Timestamp]=@Timestamp)

SELECT CourseId, Number, Title, DefaultLength, Active
FROM CourseInfo WHERE CourseId = @CourseId
RETURN
```

Listing 6-15 shows the helper method `CreateCommandsForUpdate`. This method returns three `SqlCommand` objects as output parameters to insert, update, and delete records from the `CourseInfo` table. With the implementation, `SqlCommand` objects are instantiated, and the respective stored procedure and the parameters are assigned. With all the parameters, the `SourceColumn` is set to the column of the dataset table. The `SourceVersion` property defines whether the original or the current data that is stored in the dataset should be used.

To have the updated records returned to the caller, the stored procedures `AddCourseInfo` and `UpateCourseInfo` return the updated records, as shown in Listing 6-14. To get these changes back to the dataset, the `SqlCommand` property `UpdatedRowSource` is set to the value `UpdateRowSource.FirstReturnedRecord`. With this setting, the first record that is returned from the stored procedure is set to the current row in the dataset that is updated.

Listing 6-15 Create Command Objects for Dataset Updates

```
private void CreateCommandsForUpdate(
     out SqlCommand insertCommand,
     out SqlCommand updateCommand,
     out SqlCommand deleteCommand)
{
   SqlConnection connection = new SqlConnection(dsn);

   // define the insert command
   SqlCommand insertCommand = new SqlCommand(
        "AddCourseInfo", connection);
   insertCommand.CommandType = CommandType.StoredProcedure;
   insertCommand.Parameters.Add("@CourseId",
        SqlDbType.UniqueIdentifier);
   insertCommand.Parameters.Add("@Number", SqlDbType.NChar,
        10);
   insertCommand.Parameters.Add("@Title", SqlDbType.NVarChar,
        50);
   insertCommand.Parameters.Add("@DefaultLength",
        SqlDbType.Int);
```

```
insertCommand.Parameters["@CourseId"].SourceVersion =
     DataRowVersion.Current;
insertCommand.Parameters["@Number"].SourceVersion =
     DataRowVersion.Current;
insertCommand.Parameters["@Title"].SourceVersion =
     DataRowVersion.Current;
insertCommand.Parameters["@DefaultLength"].SourceVersion =
     DataRowVersion.Current;
insertCommand.Parameters["@CourseId"].SourceColumn =
     "CourseId";
insertCommand.Parameters["@Number"].SourceColumn = "Number";
insertCommand.Parameters["@Title"].SourceColumn = "Title";
insertCommand.Parameters["@DefaultLength"].SourceColumn =
     "DefaultLength";

// the inserted row is returned from the stored procedure
insertCommand.UpdatedRowSource =
     UpdateRowSource.FirstReturnedRecord;

// define the update command
SqlCommand updateCommand = new SqlCommand(
     "UpdateCourseInfo", connection);
updateCommand.CommandType = CommandType.StoredProcedure;
updateCommand.Parameters.Add("@CourseId",
     SqlDbType.UniqueIdentifier);
updateCommand.Parameters.Add("@Number", SqlDbType.NChar,
     10);
updateCommand.Parameters.Add("@Title", SqlDbType.NVarChar,
     50);
updateCommand.Parameters.Add("@DefaultLength",
     SqlDbType.Int);
updateCommand.Parameters.Add("@Active", SqlDbType.Bit);
updateCommand.Parameters.Add("@Timestamp",
     SqlDbType.Timestamp);
updateCommand.Parameters["@CourseId"].SourceVersion =
     DataRowVersion.Original;
updateCommand.Parameters["@Number"].SourceVersion =
     DataRowVersion.Current;
updateCommand.Parameters["@Title"].SourceVersion =
     DataRowVersion.Current;
updateCommand.Parameters["@DefaultLength"].SourceVersion =
     DataRowVersion.Current;
updateCommand.Parameters["@Active"].SourceVersion =
     DataRowVersion.Current;
updateCommand.Parameters["@Timestamp"].SourceVersion =
```

```
        DataRowVersion.Original;
updateCommand.Parameters["@CourseId"].SourceColumn =
        "CourseId";
updateCommand.Parameters["@Number"].SourceColumn =
        "Number";
updateCommand.Parameters["@Title"].SourceColumn =
        "Title";
updateCommand.Parameters["@DefaultLength"].SourceColumn =
        "DefaultLength";
updateCommand.Parameters["@Active"].SourceColumn =
        "Active";
updateCommand.Parameters["@Timestamp"].SourceColumn =
        "Timestamp";

// the updated row is returned from the stored procedure
updateCommand.UpdatedRowSource =
        UpdateRowSource.FirstReturnedRecord;

// define the delete command
SqlCommand deleteCommand = new SqlCommand(
        "DeleteCourseInfo", connection);
deleteCommand.CommandType = CommandType.StoredProcedure;
deleteCommand.Parameters.Add("@CourseId",
        SqlDbType.UniqueIdentifier);
deleteCommand.Parameters.Add("@Timestamp",
        SqlDbType.Timestamp);
deleteCommand.Parameters["@CourseId"].SourceVersion =
        DataRowVersion.Original;
deleteCommand.Parameters["@CourseId"].SourceColumn =
        "CourseId";
deleteCommand.Parameters["@Timestamp"].SourceVersion =
        DataRowVersion.Original;
deleteCommand.Parameters["@Timestamp"].SourceColumn =
        "Timestamp";
}
```

Listing 6-16 shows the method UpdateCourses, which accepts a CoursesDataset as a parameter. Within this method, the command objects that are returned from the helper method CreateCommandsForUpdate are assigned with the InsertCommand, UpdateCommand, and DeleteCommand properties of the SqlDataAdapter. The Update method uses the corresponding commands to write all changes of the Course table to the database.

Listing 6-16   Updating the Dataset

```
public void UpdateCourses(CoursesDataset ds)
{
    SqlCommand insertCommand;
    SqlCommand updateCommand;
    SqlCommand deleteCommand;
    CreateCommandsForUpdate(out insertCommand,
            out updateCommand, out deleteCommand);

    SqlDataAdapter adapter = new SqlDataAdapter();
    adapter.InsertCommand = insertCommand;
    adapter.UpdateCommand = updateCommand;
    adapter.DeleteCommand = deleteCommand;

    adapter.Update(ds.Course);
}
```

If both courses and course dates must be updated, you must be aware of the order when updating the database tables `CourseInfo` and `CourseDates`. Because of the dependency between these tables, when adding new records, you must add the `CourseInfo` records before `CourseDates`. With deleting records, `CourseDates` records must be deleted before `CourseInfo` records.

To get such a scenario, you must split up the call of a simple `Update` as used in Listing 6-16 to multiple updates, where only records are deleted or updated. Listing 6-17 shows how you can split the update.

Both the `DataSet` and a `DataTable` objects have a method `GetChanges` that enables you to define whether inserted, updated, or deleted rows are needed. Calling the method `GetChanges` with the parameter value `DataRowState.Modified` returns all rows that have been modified, whereas the parameter value `DataRow-State.Added` only returns the added rows. The returned `CourseDataTable` is passed to the `SqlDataAdapter` object to write the changes to the database. The data that is updated must be written back into the dataset, which you can do by using the `Merge` method.

Now it is possible to add code to write changes to the course dates in a similar way. Deletion of course dates must be done before deletion of courses, whereas inserting course dates must be done after inserting courses.

Listing 6-17   Updating the Dataset with Multiple Tables

```
public void UpdateCourses(CoursesDataset ds)
{
    SqlCommand insertCommand;
    SqlCommand updateCommand;
    SqlCommand deleteCommand;
    CreateCommandsForUpdate(out insertCommand,
            out updateCommand, out deleteCommand);

    SqlDataAdapter adapter = new SqlDataAdapter();
    adapter.InsertCommand = insertCommand;
    adapter.UpdateCommand = updateCommand;
    adapter.DeleteCommand = deleteCommand;

    // 1. update modified courses
    CoursesDataset.CourseDataTable modifiedCourses =
            (CoursesDataset.CourseDataTable)ds.Course.GetChanges(
                DataRowState.Modified);
    if (modifiedCourses != null)
    {
        adapter.Update(modifiedCourses);
        ds.Merge(modifiedCourses);
    }

    // 2. insert new courses
    CoursesDataset.CourseDataTable insertedCourses =
            (CoursesDataset.CourseDataTable)ds.Course.GetChanges(
                DataRowState.Added);
    if (insertedCourses != null)
    {
        adapter.Update(insertedCourses);
        ds.Merge(insertedCourses);
    }

    // 3. delete courses
    CoursesDataset.CourseDataTable deletedCourses =
            (CoursesDataset.CourseDataTable)ds.Course.GetChanges(
                DataRowState.Deleted);
    if (deletedCourses != null)
    {
        adapter.Update(deletedCourses);
        ds.Merge(deletedCourses);
    }
}
```

Business Objects or Datasets

The typed dataset is very helpful insofar as tables and columns are available as property names. This is a big advantage when compared to untyped datasets, where only indexers can be used to access columns and rows. However, the typed dataset still has disadvantages if you compare this technology to entity classes. With a typed dataset, all the members of the base class `DataSet` are available, which you sometimes want to avoid. For example, you can use indexers to access column values because the indexers are implemented in the base class `DataSet`. The use of entity classes enables you to avoid such a behavior.

Also, datasets do have a relational representation of data. Using business objects, you can have better reuse of your business components and design the objects based on completely different approaches and design principles.

However, a dataset does have a big advantage because it knows about original data in addition to current data. This knowledge can be used to resolve optimistic concurrency conflicts. With entity classes, you have to implement such a behavior yourself. Datasets also allow sorting and filtering.

Summary

This chapter discussed using ADO.NET for data access. As you have learned in this chapter, ADO.NET enables you to access relational data by using the .NET data provider for SQL Server with the `SqlConnection` and `SqlCommand` classes and the respective SQL statements. Reading data with the `SqlDataReader` was also discussed, as were datasets.

Transactions have been completely left out of this chapter. They are a primary reason why serviced components are used, and are covered in the next chapter.

1 You can read more about ADO.NET in the book *Pragmatic ADO.NET*, by Shawn Wildermuth.

2 Transactions are covered in Chapter 7, "Transaction Services."

3 Serialization across the network with .NET Remoting and COM is discussed in Chapter 5, "Networking."

4 Using construction strings with serviced components is discussed in Chapter 2, "Object Activation and Contexts."

5 That is why you should not use a query with SELECT *. Using such a query means you are very dependent on database changes.

6 Security is discussed in Chapter 12, "Security."

7 You can also create a relation with an untyped dataset using an XML schema. You can load the XML schema to an untyped dataset programmatically with the ReadXmlSchema method. Loading the schema creates the relations and keys that are defined with the schema.

7

Transaction Services

TRANSACTION SERVICES ARE USUALLY THE MAIN reason why Enterprise Services is used. So that you do not have to deal with transactions programmatically, Enterprise Services offers a way to use transactions by using attributes.

This chapter opens with an overview of transactions, and then examines how you can task transactions programmatically. With this knowledge, you will see the advantages of transaction services offered by .NET Enterprise Services. The focus of this chapter then turns to how you can use Enterprise Services transactions, and how you can access the new features offered with Windows Server 2003.

Specifically, this chapter covers the following topics:

- Transaction overview
- Programmatic transactions
- Automatic transactions
- Transactions with services without components
- Transaction isolation levels

Transaction Overview

So that you can fully understand the transaction support offered by Enterprise Services, it is important for you to have an overall understanding of transactions.

Let's start with an example of a course database and attendees registered for courses. If an attendee who is registered for the Programming ADO.NET course wants to change to the Introduction to .NET course because he does not have the necessary prerequisites for attending the first course, he will be removed from the attendee list of the first course, and added to the attendee list of the second one. If one of these operations fails, the other should not happen either. Here a single transaction is needed. Transactions ensure that data-oriented resources are not permanently updated unless all operations complete successfully.

A transaction is defined by a unit of operations that either all succeed or all fail. If all operations complete successfully inside a transaction, the transaction is **committed**, and the updated data is written permanently. If one operation fails, however, a **rollback** is done; as a result, the data exists as it was before the transaction started.

ACID Properties

Transactions can be defined by four basic properties, easily remembered with the acronym ACID (atomicity, consistency, isolation, durability).

Atomicity

Atomicity ensures that either all updates occur or none at all. Because of the atomicity guaranteed by transactions, you do not have to write code to handle the situation where one update was successful, and another was not.

With the course example just mentioned, if removing the attendee from the first course succeeds, but adding him to the second course fails, the transaction is aborted, and the attendee is not removed from the first course.

Consistency

Consistency means that the result of a transaction leaves the system in a consistent state. Before the transaction was started, the data is in a valid state, as it is after the transaction is finished.

Consistency can be described with the same scenario as discussed with atomicity, to move an attendee from one course to the other. If removing the attendee from the first course fails, but adding him to the second course succeeds, the attendee would be registered for two courses at the same time. This is not a valid scenario; the database would not be consistent. The consistency property says that the transaction must leave the database in a consistent state; so if one part of the transaction fails, all other parts must be undone.

Isolation

Multiple users can access the same database simultaneously. With **isolation**, it is assured that it is not possible outside of a transaction to see data that is being changed inside a transaction before the transaction is committed. It is not possible to access some in-between state that might never happen if the transaction is aborted.

If you do a query to get the list of attendees for all courses, while at the same time a transaction is running to move an attendee from one course to another, the attendee will not be listed on both courses. Isolation guarantees that an interim state of the transaction from outside of the transaction cannot be seen.

Durability

Durability means that a consistent state is guaranteed even in case of a system crash. If the database system crashes, it must be guaranteed that transactions that have been committed are really written to the database.

Distributed Transactions

Enterprise Services supports distributed transactions, where a transaction can cross multiple database systems. These database systems can also be from different vendors.

With distributed transaction resource managers, a transaction manager and a two-phase commit protocol are needed.

Resource managers, as is obvious from the term itself, manage resources. Examples of resources are databases, message queues, or simple files. SQL Server is a resource manager, as is the Oracle database, and the Message Queue server. Resource managers must support the two-phase commit protocol.

The two-phase commit consists of a prepare phase and a commit phase. When updating data, a prepare phase occurs first, during which all participants in the transaction must agree to complete the operations successfully. If one of the participants aborts the transaction, a rollback occurs with all other participants. Agreeing to the prepare phase, the database must also guarantee that the transaction can commit after a system crash. If all participants of a single transaction had a successful prepare phase, the commit phase is started, during which all data is permanently stored in the databases.

A distributed transaction must be coordinated by a transaction manager. For Enterprise Services, the **distributed transaction coordinator** (DTC) is such a transaction manager. The DTC is a transaction manager that supports the X/Open XA Specification for Distributed Transaction, and the OLE Transactions protocol. The X/Open XA protocol is not used natively by the DTC; it must be converted to OLE Transactions by the ODBC driver or OLE DB provider. The X/Open XA Specification is not only supported by Microsoft SQL Server, but also by Oracle. The DTC is a Windows service that is part of the Windows operating system.

The distributed transaction coordinator manages transactions to multiple databases and connections from multiple clients. To coordinate work from different systems in a single transaction, the DTCs of different systems communicate with each other. Connections to resource managers that should participate in a distributed transaction must be enlisted with the DTC. To enlist database connections, the ADO.NET data providers for SQL Server and OLE DB are aware of the DTC, and the connections are enlisted automatically if transactional attributes are used with serviced components.[1]

Figure 7-1 shows a single transaction that is running across multiple systems. Here the transaction is started from component A that is running on server A. Component A has a connection to the database on server C. The connection is enlisted with the DTC on the local system (in this case, the DTC of server A). Component A invokes a method in component B that itself requires a transaction. Component B has a connection to the database on server D. The database connection is enlisted in the DTC of server B. On the database systems C and D, we also have DTCs running that manage the transactional interaction with the resource managers of the dependent systems. Because all four DTCs coordinate the transaction, anyone participating in the transaction can abort it. For example, if the resource manager of server D cannot complete the prepare phase successfully, it will abort the transaction. The DTC of server D will tell all other DTCs participating in the transaction to do a rollback with the transaction. On the other hand, if all members of the transaction are happy with the prepare phase, the DTCs coordinate to commit the transaction.

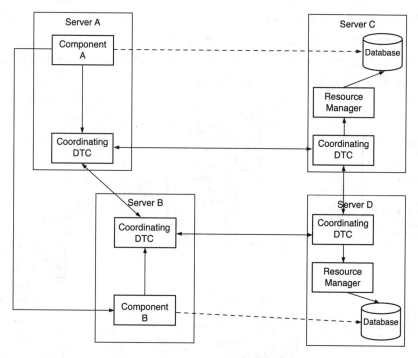

Figure 7-1   Transactions with the distributed transaction coordinator.

Programmatic Transactions

In this chapter, the database that was created earlier is reused. Just as a reminder, the database diagram is shown again in Figure 7-2.

With serviced components, you can do transactions by using attributes. Before looking into these attributes, however, let's take a look at how transactions are done programmatically so that you can easily compare the techniques.

Using the .NET data provider for SQL Server, you can do transactions programmatically with the SqlTransaction class. A new transaction is created with the method BeginTransaction of the SqlConnection class, which returns an object of type `SqlTransaction`. Then the `SqlTransaction` methods `Commit` and `Rollback` can be used to commit or to undo the transaction result.

Let's immediately consider an example, with the class `CourseData`. A connection string is passed into the constructor of this class, as shown in Listing 7-1. The caller of this class can read the connection string from a configuration file if required. To avoid creating a new `SqlCommand` with every method call, a new `SqlCommand` is instantiated in the constructor, and the parameters that are needed to add a new course record are added to the command object.

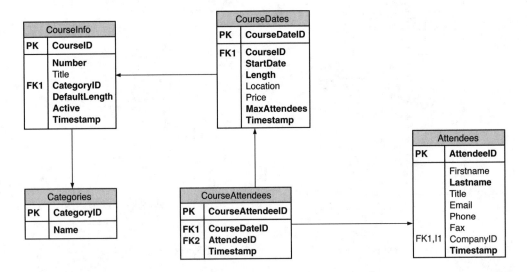

Figure 7-2 Sample database.

Listing 7-1 Programmatic Transactions

```
using System;
using System.Data;
using System.Data.SqlClient;

namespace Samples.Courses.Data
{
    public class CourseData
    {
        private string connectionString;
        private SqlCommand insertCourseCommand;
```

```
public CourseData(string connectionString)
{
    this.connectionString = connectionString;

    insertCourseCommand = new SqlCommand();
    insertCourseCommand.CommandText = "INSERT INTO " +
        "Courses (CourseId, Number, Title, Active) " +
        "VALUES(@CourseId, @Number, @Title, @Active)";

    insertCourseCommand.Parameters.Add("@CourseId",
        SqlDbType.UniqueIdentifier);
    insertCourseCommand.Parameters.Add("@Number",
        SqlDbType.NChar, 10);
    insertCourseCommand.Parameters.Add("@Title",
        SqlDbType.NVarChar, 50);
    insertCourseCommand.Parameters.Add("@Active",
        SqlDbType.Bit);
}
```

In the method `AddCourse` that is shown in Listing 7-2, the connection object is instantiated, the connection is associated with the previously created command object, and the connection is opened. Inside a try block, the `INSERT` statement is executed with the method `ExecuteNonQuery`. Before that, a new transaction is started using the `connection.BeginTransaction` method. The returned transaction object is automatically associated with the connection. If the database insert is successfully, the transaction is committed. If an exception is thrown within `ExecuteNonQuery` because of some error while issuing the database insert, the exception is caught, and a rollback is done in the catch block.

Listing 7-2   AddCourse Method with Programmatic Transactions

```
public void AddCourse(Course course)
{
    int customerId = -1;
    SqlConnection connection =
        new SqlConnection(connectionString);

    insertCourseCommand.Connection = connection;
    insertCourseCommand.Parameters["@CourseId"].Value =
        course.CourseId;
    insertCourseCommand.Parameters["@Number"].Value =
        course.Number;
    insertCourseCommand.Parameters["@Title"].Value =
```

```
                course.Title;
        insertCourseCommand.Parameters["@Active"].Value =
                course.Active;

        connection.Open();
        try
        {
            insertCourseCommand.Transaction =
                connection.BeginTransaction();
            insertCourseCommand.ExecuteNonQuery();
            insertCourseCommand.Transaction.Commit();
        }
        catch
        {
            insertCourseCommand.Transaction.Rollback();
            throw;
        }
        finally
        {
            connection.Close();
        }
    }
```

In the `Test` class of the client application (Figure 7-3), the class `CourseData` is used to create a new course. The connection string passed to the constructor is read from the configuration file using the `ConfigurationSettings` class.

Listing 7-3   Client Test Application

```
using System;
using System.Configuration;
using Samples.Courses.Data;
using Samples.Courses.Entities;

class Test
{

    static void Main()
    {
        // read the connection string from the configuration file
        string connectionString =
            ConfigurationSettings.AppSettings["Database"];

        // write a new course to the database
        CourseData db = new CourseData(connectionString);
```

```
        Course c = new Course();
        c.Number = "MS-2389";
        c.Title = "Programming ADO.NET";
        c.Active = true;

        db.AddCourse(c);
    }
}
```

Listing 7-4 shows the application configuration file that is used by the client application. In the configuration, the database connection string is defined as a child element of <appSettings>.

Listing 7-4 Application Configuration File to Define the Connection String

```
<?xml version="1.0" encoding="utf-8" ?>
<configuration>
  <appSettings>
    <add key="Database"
         value="server=localhost;database=Courses;
         trusted_connection=true" />
  </appSettings>
</configuration>
```

As shown in the previous examples, dealing with transactions programmatically is not a hard task. However, how can the implementation be done if multiple SQL commands should be part of a single transaction? If all these commands are closely related, putting them into a single try block is not a big deal. However, a scenario in which a single transaction should cross multiple components is not so straightforward.

If multiple classes should participate in the same transaction (for example, a customer should be added, and an entry to the course map must also be done), dealing with transactions is not that easy anymore. Take a look at how this can be handled.

Figure 7-3 shows a scenario where a single transaction is useful: If one course attendee wants to change her course schedule, she must be removed from one course list and added to another one. Now it should never happen that the course attendee is added to the new course, but not deleted from the previous one, and it should never happen that the attendee is just removed from a course, but never added to the new course. Both adding and removing the attendee from the course must be part of the same transaction.

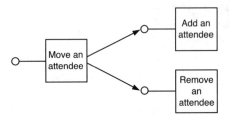

Figure 7-3   Transactions with multiple components.

You can program multiple database actions that are spread across multiple classes, and that should participate in the same transaction, by passing the connection object that is associated with the transaction as an argument to the methods. Inside the methods, the same connection object can be used to participate within the same transaction.

This can get quite complex with many classes and bigger scenarios. You have to decide whether the class should participate in the same transaction, or whether a new transaction should be started. What should happen if an object is called in between that does not use database methods at all? With such a method, it would be necessary to add an additional argument so that the connection object could be passed.

Enterprise Services offers a way to deal with this complexity: **automatic transactions**.

Automatic Transactions

With automatic transactions, you do not have to pass a transaction as an argument of a method; instead, a transaction flows automatically with the context. Using transaction attributes, you can specify whether a transaction is needed.

Using the class attribute [Transaction], you can specify whether objects of the class are aware of transactions, and whether transactions should be created automatically by the Enterprise Services runtime.

The class attribute is applied to the class of the serviced component, as shown in this code segment:

```
[Transaction(TransactionOption.Required)]
public class CustomerDataComponent : ServicedComponent
{
```

Transaction Attributes

The [Transaction] attribute that can be applied to classes that implement serviced components has five different values that you can set with the enumeration TransactionOption. The values of the enumeration TransactionOption are Required, RequiresNew, Supported, NotSupported, and Disabled. Table 7-1 describes what these values mean.

Table 7-1 TransactionOption Enumeration

TransactionOption Value	Description
Required	The value Required marks that the component needs a context with a transaction. If the context of the calling object does not have a transaction, a new transaction is started inside a new context. If the calling object does have a transaction, the same transaction from the calling object is used.
RequiresNew	Similar to the value Required, with RequiresNew the component always gets a context with a transaction; but contrary to Required, a new transaction is always created. The transaction is always independent of a possible transaction of the calling object.
Supported	The value Supported means that the component is happy with or without a transaction. This value is useful if the component does not need a transaction itself, but it may invoke components that do need transactions, and it may be called by components that have already created transactions. Supported makes it possible for a transaction to cross the component, and the calling and called components can participate in the same transaction.
NotSupported	If the component is marked with NotSupported, the component never participates in a transaction. If the calling object does not have a context with a transaction, it can run inside the same context. If the calling object does have a context with a transaction, a new context is created.
Disabled	The option Disabled differs from NotSupported insofar as the transaction in the context of the calling component is ignored.

The meaning of the transaction values you can set with the attribute [Transaction] is greatly influenced by the context of the calling component. Table 7-2 helps make this behavior more clear. In this table, all five transaction values are listed with both variants, whether the calling component is running inside a transaction or not. Column 3 shows whether the component is running in a transaction, and column 4 shows whether the component is running in a new transaction.

Table 7-2   TransactionOption Behaviors

Attribute	Calling Component Running in a Transaction	Running in a Transaction	Running in a New Transaction
Required	Yes No	Always	No Yes
Requires New	Yes No	Always	Always
Supported	Yes No	Yes No	Never
Not Supported	Yes No	Never	Never
Disabled	Yes No	Yes, if calling context is shared No	Never

Supported or NotSupported?

I'm often asked, "Why should a component be marked with Supported to support transactions, although the component does not need transactions itself?"

Figures 7-4 and 7-5 describe why the transactional value Supported is a useful option. In both figures, three objects that call each other are shown. In Figure 7-4, object A has the transactional option Required, and because the client does not have a transaction, a new transaction is created. Object B is marked with the transactional value NotSupported, and object C again has the value Required. Because object B does not support transactions, the context of object B does not have a transaction associated. When object C is called by object B, a new transaction is created. Here the transactions of object A and object C are completely independent. The transaction of object C may commit, whereas the transaction of object A may be aborted.

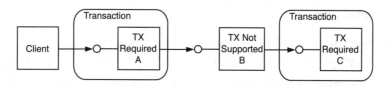

Figure 7-4 Transactional behavior with an interim object transaction NotSupported.

Figure 7-5 shows a similar scenario but with object B marked with the transactional attribute `Supported`. Here the transaction from object A is propagated to B and C. If the database access fails with object C, a rollback with object A occurs, because both objects are running inside the same transaction.

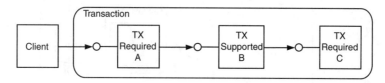

Figure 7-5 Transactional behavior with an interim object transaction Supported.

Required or Requires New?

With the transactional value `Required`, a new transaction is created if a transaction does not already exist in the calling object. If the calling object has a context with a transaction, the same transaction is used. Under some scenarios, a different behavior is required. For example, if object A in Figure 7-6 changes a course map, but object B writes the information to a log database, writing the information to the log should happen independently if the transaction with object A succeeds. To make this possible, object B is marked with the transactional configuration `RequiresNew` (a new transaction is required).

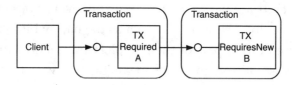

Figure 7-6 Transactional behavior with RequiresNew.

Transaction Streams

A single transaction cannot only be spread across multiple objects; it can also be spread across multiple applications that can run on multiple systems. Inside a transaction stream, all database connections are automatically enlisted in the **distributed transaction coordinator** (DTC).

A transaction stream (Figure 7-7) is started with a root object. A **root object** is the first object in the transaction stream; it starts the transaction. Depending on the configuration of the objects that are called, they will either be part of the same transaction stream, or a new transaction stream will be created.

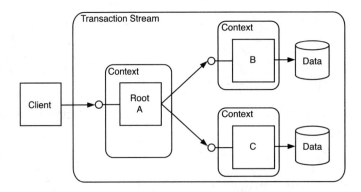

Figure 7-7   Transaction stream.

Transaction Outcomes

Every object, every resource dispenser, and every resource manager participating in a transaction can influence the outcome of a transaction. A transaction is completed as soon as the root object of the transaction deactivates. Whether the transaction should be committed or aborted depends on the done, consistent, and abort bits. The **done** and **consistent** bits are part of every context of every object that participates in the transaction. The done bit is also known as the happy bit. The **abort** bit (also known as the doomed bit) is part of the complete transaction stream. Figure 7-8 shows the done, consistent, and abort bits in conjunction with the serviced components and their contexts.

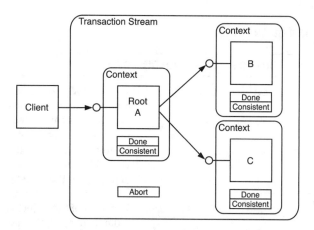

Figure 7-8   Done, consistent, and abort bits.

At object creation time, the done and consistent bits are set to false. With the help of the class ContextUtil, the values of these bits can be changed. Setting the done bit to true means that the work of the object is complete and the object can be deactivated. The consistent bit is responsible for the outcome of the transaction. If the consistent bit is true, the object is happy with the transactional part of its work—the transactional part succeeded.

The abort bit is set to false when the transaction is created. When an object is deactivated, the context of the object is lost, and so are the done and consistent bits. Here the result of the consistent bit is propagated to the abort bit. The object context is deactivated as soon as the done bit is set to true. Now, if the consistent bit is set to false, the abort bit of the transaction stream is set to true, so that the transaction will be aborted. If the consistent bit is set to true, it does not influence the value of the abort bit.

ContextUtil Methods

The ContextUtil class has four methods to influence the values of the done and consistent bits. The methods and their influence of the done and consistent bits are shown in Table 7-3. One thing to keep in mind is that calling these methods only influences the outcome of the method of the serviced component but does not have an immediate result.

Table 7-3 ContextUtil Methods

ContextUtil Method	Done Bit	Consistent Bit	Description
SetComplete	true	true	The method `SetComplete` marks the object as done and consistent. The work of the object is completed, and the transaction can be committed. When the method returns, the object is deactivated, and the vote of the object regarding the transaction is to commit the transaction.
SetAbort	true	false	The work of the object is completed, but it did not succeed; the transaction must be aborted. When the method returns, the object is deactivated, but the transaction vote is to abort the transaction.
EnableCommit	false	true	The work of the object is not completed; it should not be deactivated. However, the first phase of the transactional work was successfully completed. When the method returns, the object will not be deactivated, but the vote for the transaction is to commit the transaction. If the root object of the transaction completes the transaction before the object is called for a second time, the object is deactivated.
DisableCommit	false	false	Similar to `EnableCommit`, with `DisableCommit` the work of the object is not completed. State of the object will be kept, so that it can be invoked another time. However, contrary to the `EnableCommit` method, if the transaction is completed before the object is invoked a second time, the transaction vote is to abort the transaction.

> **The Done Bit Is Ignored If the Transaction Is Finished**
>
> Although the `EnableCommit` and `DisableCommit` methods set the done bit to `false` so that the state of the object can be kept, it can still happen that the object will be deactivated, and the state will be lost. When the transaction is completed (either committed or aborted), all objects participating in the transaction are also deactivated.

Automatic Transaction Example

Figure 7-9 shows the assemblies for the sample application. With the sample application, the assembly `Samples.Courses.Data` includes the class `CourseData` that is doing the database access code with the methods `AddCourse`, `UpdateCourse`, and `DeleteCourse`. The assembly `Samples.Courses.Components` includes the serviced component `CourseDataComponent` that uses the class `CourseData`. The assembly `Samples.Courses.Entities` includes business classes such as `Course`, `CourseData`, and `CourseDataCollection`. These classes are used all over within the application.

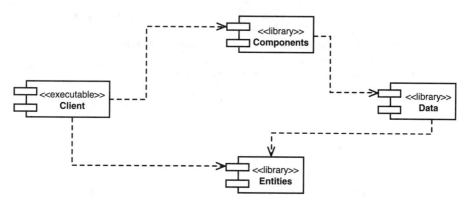

Figure 7-9   Assemblies with the transaction sample.

> **NOTE: Separating Assemblies**
>
> Using automatic transactions, you can use an assembly just for data access that is separated from the serviced component assembly. I always prefer this technique to reduce the code inside the serviced components to a large extent for being flexible with the serviced components technology. With .NET, there is no requirement that the classes accessing the database be configured components. (This was a requirement with COM components.)

Listing 7-5 shows the `AddCourse` method from the `CourseData` class. This method is very similar to the `AddCourse` method that was shown in Listing 7-2. But, contrary to the first implementation of `AddCourse`, here the transactional code has been removed because the transactional support will be added within the serviced component class.

Listing 7-5   AddCourse Method Without Programmatic Transactions

```
public void AddCourse(Course course)
{
    SqlConnection connection =
            new SqlConnection(connectionString);
    insertCourseCommand.Connection = connection;
    insertCourseCommand.Parameters["@CourseId"].Value =
            course.CourseId;
    insertCourseCommand.Parameters["@Number"].Value =
            course.Number;
    insertCourseCommand.Parameters["@Title"].Value =
            course.Title;
    insertCourseCommand.Parameters["@Active"].Value =
            course.Active;

    connection.Open();
    try
    {
        insertCourseCommand.ExecuteNonQuery();
    }
    finally
    {
        connection.Close();
    }
}
```

The implementation of the serviced component class is shown in Listing 7-6. The class `CourseUpdateComponent` derives from the base class `ServicedComponent` and is marked with the attribute `[Transaction(TransactionOption.Required)]`, so that a transaction stream will be created automatically when a new instance is created. The construction string[2] is passed with the method `Construct` that is overridden from the base class. Serviced component construction is enabled with the attribute `[ConstructionEnabled]`. This way the construction string can be changed later by the system administrator.

In the method `AddCourse`, the transaction outcome is influenced with the methods of the class `ContextUtil`: `SetComplete` and `SetAbort`. If the method `db.AddCourse` completes successfully, `ContextUtil.SetComplete` sets the done and consistent bits to mark a successful outcome. If an exception occurs, the exception is caught in the catch block. Here, the consistent bit is set to false by calling the method `ContextUtil.SetAbort`. The exception is rethrown, so that the calling method can get some information about the reason why the method failed. Of course, you can also create a custom exception that is thrown in case of an error.

Listing 7-6 Serviced Component Class CourseUpdateComponent

```
using System;
using System.EnterpriseServices;
using Samples.Courses.Data;
using Samples.Courses.Entities;

namespace Samples.Courses.Components
{
    public interface ICourseUpdate
    {
        void AddCourse(Course c);
        void UpdateCourse(Course c);
        void DeleteCourse(Course c);
    }

    [Transaction(TransactionOption.Required)]
    [ConstructionEnabled(true,
        Default="server=localhost;database=courses;"
        "trusted_connection=true")]
    [EventTrackingEnabled(true)]
    public class CourseUpdateComponent: ServicedComponent,
        ICourseUpdate
    {
```

```
public CourseComponent()
{
}

private string connectionString;

protected override void Construct(string s)
{
    connectionString = s;
}

public void AddCourse(Course c)
{
    CourseData db = new CourseData(connectionString);
    try
    {
        db.AddCourse(c);
        ContextUtil.SetComplete();
    }
    catch
    {
        ContextUtil.SetAbort();
        throw;
    }
}

public void UpdateCourse(Course c)
{
    //...
}
public void DeleteCourse(Course c)
{
    //...
}
    }
}
```

After you have registered the serviced component assembly, you can see the transactional options with the Component Services Explorer. You just have to select the properties of the component and open the Transaction tab (see Figure 7-10). In this dialog box, you can see the transactional option that was defined with the attribute [Transaction].

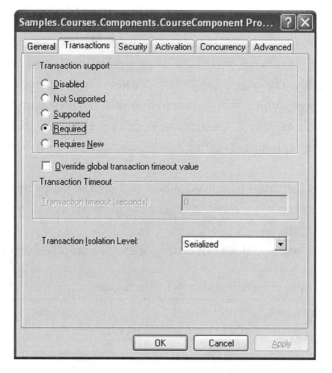

Figure 7-10   Component Services Explorer—transactional options.

If you change the option from Required to Not Supported with the Component Services Explorer, a runtime exception will occur with Windows Server 2003. During runtime, it is checked whether the programmatic configuration corresponds to the manual configuration regarding the transactional behavior.

Transaction Options and JITA

Selecting a transactional option such as Required and Requires-New also requires **just-in-time activation** (JITA)[3] and synchronization. It is not necessary to configure JITA and synchronization explicitly, but these options will be configured automatically.

Setting the Transactional Vote

Instead of setting the transactional vote with the `ContextUtil` class and the methods `SetComplete`, `SetAbort`, `EnableCommit`, and `DisableCommit` indirectly, you can set them directly. The class `ContextUtil` offers the property `MyTransactionVote` for this purpose, which you can set to one value of the enumeration `TransactionVote`: `Commit` or `Abort`. Setting `MyTransactionVote` to `Commit` sets the consistent bit to `true`, whereas setting `MyTransactionVote` to `Abort` sets the consistent bit to `false`.

The done bit is directly influenced when you set the property `DeactivateOnReturn` of the `ContextUtil` class. `ContextUtil.DeactivateOnReturn = true` sets the done bit to true.

The `AddCourse` method does not change a lot, as you can see in Listing 7-7.

Listing 7-7   AddCourse Using the Property MyTransactionVote

```
public void AddCourse(Course c)
{
   ContextUtil.DeactivateOnReturn = true;
   CourseData db = new CourseData(connectionString);
   try
   {
      db.AddCourse(c);
      ContextUtil.MyTransactionVote =
            TransactionVote.Commit;
   }
   catch
   {
      ContextUtil.MyTransactionVote =
            TransactionVote.Abort;
      throw;
   }
}
```

AutoComplete Attribute

Instead of calling `SetComplete` and `SetAbort`, all transaction handling can be done if you apply the attribute `[AutoComplete]` to a method. In this way, the implementation of the method `AddCourse` gets easier, because it is not necessary to catch and to rethrow exceptions. Instead, if the method completes successfully, by applying the attribute [AutoComplete], the done and consistent bits are set to true. On the other hand, if an exception is generated, the consistent bit is set to false at the end of the method. You can see the implementation of AddCourse using the [AutoComplete] attribute in Listing 7-8.

Listing 7-8 AddCourse Using the [AutoComplete] Attribute

```
[AutoComplete]
public void AddCourse(Course c)
{
    CourseData db = new CourseData(connectionString);
    db.AddCourse(c);
}
```

Using the [AutoComplete] attribute, you have to throw exceptions to the caller. The [AutoComplete] attribute sets the consistent bit to false only if an exception is thrown. If you want to handle exceptions in the AddCourse method, you can add a try/catch block where the exception is rethrown (see Figure 7-9). Instead of rethrowing the same exception, you can throw an exception of a custom exception type—it is just important to throw an exception in case of an error.

Listing 7-9 [AutoComplete] Attribute with Exception Handling

```
[AutoComplete]
public void AddCourse(Course c)
{
    try
    {
        CourseData db = new CourseData(connectionString);
        db.AddCourse(c);
    }
    catch (Exception ex)
    {
        // do some event logging
        // re-throw exception
        throw;
    }
}
```

Distributed Transactions

Enterprise Services transactions are enlisted in the DTC, so these transactions can run across multiple systems and across multiple databases. Figure 7-11 demonstrates such a distributed scenario. A single transaction can consist of an update to a SQL Server database, an update to an Oracle database, and writing some messages to a message queue server,[4] all on different systems.

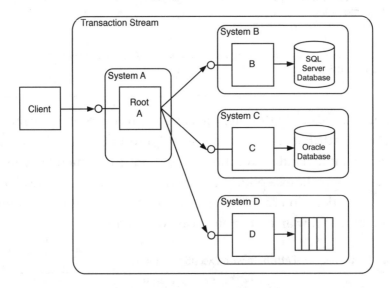

Figure 7-11 Distributed transactions.

Enabling Distributed Transactions with Windows Server 2003

With Windows Server 2003, you explicitly have to enable DTC access over the network. You can do this by selecting the Enable Network DTC Access option (see Figure 7-12) when configuring the application server components.

Transactions with Services Without Components

Starting with Windows Server 2003 and Windows XP SP2, it is possible to create contexts with transactions without defining transactional attributes with serviced

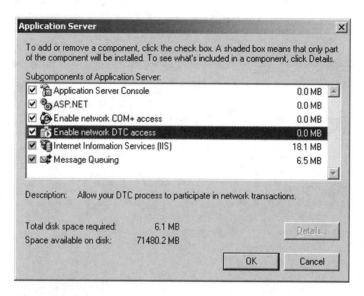

Figure 7-12   Enable DTC with Windows Server 2003.

component classes. You can create transactional contexts with the `ServiceConfig`, the `ServiceDomain`, and the `Activity` classes. This is not only useful without serviced components, but also with serviced components. With serviced components, this feature makes it possible that one method of a class uses a transaction, whereas another does not use it. For example, with the class `CourseData`, it would not be necessary to create a transaction with the method `GetCourses`, where data from the database is read-only, but with the method `AddCourse`, a transaction is necessary.

The code in Listing 7-10 demonstrates using transactions without serviced components. After reading the connection string from the application configuration file and creating a new object of type `CourseData` (`CourseData` is a normal class that does not derive from `ServicedComponent`), a new `ServiceConfig` object is created. With the `ServiceConfig` object, the context can be configured, and the transactional attributes can be set with the `Transaction` property of this class. The values that can be set with the `Transaction` property have already been shown: a value from the enumeration `TransactionOption`. Here `TransactionOption.Required` is used as the value for the `Transaction` property. The context is created as soon as we call `ServiceDomain.Enter`, passing the context configuration information. The next method, `data.AddCourse`, is running inside the context, and the database connection that is used inside this method is enlisted with the DTC. The transaction is committed when the context is left with `ServiceDomain.Leave`, which returns the status of the transaction as a value of the enumeration `TransactionStatus`.

Listing 7-10   Transactions with Services Without Components

```
using System;
using System.EnterpriseServices;
using System.Configuration;
using Samples.Courses.Data;
using Samples.Courses.Entities;

class TransactionsWithoutComponents
{
    [STAThread]
    static void Main()
    {
        Course c = new Course();
        c.Number = "MS-2524";
        c.Title = "ASP.NET Web Services";
        c.Active = true;

        string connectionString =
                ConfigurationSettings.AppSettings["Database"];
        CourseData data = new CourseData(connectionString);

        // create a transactional context
        ServiceConfig context = new ServiceConfig();

        context.Transaction = TransactionOption.Required;

        // enter the transactional context
        ServiceDomain.Enter(context);
        data.AddCourse(c);

        // leave the transactional context
        TransactionStatus status = ServiceDomain.Leave();

        Console.WriteLine("Transaction ended with {0}", status);
    }
}
```

The result of the transaction is returned from the `ServiceDomain.Leave` method. The possible values are listed in Table 7-4.

> **NOTE: Services Without Components Platforms**
>
> If you try running the sample application on Windows XP without SP2, you will get the exception `PlatformNotSupportedException`. Services without components is only supported on Windows Server 2003 and Windows XP SP2.

Some examples of when it is helpful to use transactions without serviced components are as follows:

- Standalone applications.
- With ASP.NET Web services that use serviced components, a root transactional context can be created without serviced component configuration.
- Services without components can also be useful within serviced components: for example, if the serviced component class has one method that requires a transaction, and another method that doesn't require one.

Table 7-4 TransactionStatus Enumeration

TransactionStatus	Description
Aborted	The transaction is aborted. Either the database returned an error, or the method generated an exception, so the transaction is aborted.
Aborting	The transaction is in the process of being aborted.
Committed	The transaction committed successfully. Every member who was participating in the transaction voted the transaction by setting the consistent bit.
LocallyOk	The transaction is neither committed nor aborted. This status can be returned, if the context that is left is running inside another transactional context.
NoTransaction	The context did not have a context, so `NoTransaction` is returned.

Transactions Support with ASP.NET

You can create distributed transactions directly from ASP.NET. Doing so proves useful if the ASP.NET application is a client of the serviced component. With the ASP.NET transactional support, the ASP.NET page can act as the root of the transaction.

The `Page` directive of an ASP.NET page enables you to set the named property `Transaction` to a value you already know from the attribute `[Transaction]`. The allowed values of the `Transaction` property are `Required`, `RequiresNew`, `Supported`, `NotSupported`, and `Disabled`.

```
<%Page language="C#" Transaction="Required" %>
```

When you are calling serviced components from ASP.NET, the transaction can already be created; so multiple components that are called within the same method can participate with the same transaction.

> **Passing Transactions from ASP.NET to Serviced Components**
>
> Passing transactions from the ASP.NET page to the serviced component is only possible with the DCOM protocol, not with .NET remoting.[5]

Transaction Isolation

With Windows 2000, all COM+ transactions used the serialization level for transaction isolation. With Windows XP and Windows Server 2003, you can choose between different isolation levels. The full ACID properties that describe a transaction can only be fulfilled with the serializable transaction isolation level, but sometimes this level is not needed. Using a less-strict transaction isolation level can increase the scalability of the application.

With large numbers of users accessing data, turning knobs on transaction isolation can bring you a lot more performance than you can get out of fine-tuning components. With a data-driven application database, locks can make you lose a lot of performance.

If you want to change transaction isolation levels, you have to be aware of what can happen so that you know when you can change the default values.

Potential Transaction Isolation Problems

Potential problems that can occur during transactions can be grouped into three categories: **dirty reads**, **nonrepeatable reads**, and **phantoms**:

- **Dirty reads**—A dirty read means that you can read data that was changed inside a transaction from outside of the transaction. Suppose that transaction 1 changes some customer data, but this transaction fails, so with a rollback the data is unchanged. If at the same time inside transaction 2 the same customer record is read, the data that is read never really existed, so this is called a dirty read.

- **Nonrepeatable reads**—If the same row is read multiple times, and you get different results with each read, this is called a nonrepeatable read. If you read data in transaction 1, and at the same time transaction 2 changes the data that you have read within transaction 1, and you read the data again within transaction 1, different data will be read inside the same transaction. This is a nonrepeatable read.

- **Phantoms**—A phantom is a row that matches the search criteria, but is not seen in the query. If you do a query based on a condition in transaction 1, while during transaction 2 a new record is inserted that would fit to the query of transaction 1, this row is a phantom. If all rows that match the query in transaction 1 are changed (for example, the salary of all employees that have a salary lower than $1,000 is changed to $1,000), new records that are added with a lower salary level are not updated.

Transaction Isolation Levels

Depending on the serialization level used, one of these described problems can occur, or the isolation level guarantees that the problem cannot occur. With the isolation level, you can specify one of these values: **read uncommitted, read committed, repeatable read**, or **serializable**:

- **Read uncommitted**—With this level, transactions are not isolated from each other. This is the most scalable way for transactions; but with it, all problems described earlier can occur.

- **Read committed**—With a level of read committed, the transaction waits until all write-locked rows that are manipulated by the transaction are unlocked. It is therefore guaranteed that no read of dirty data can occur.

  The transaction holds a read lock for all rows that are read-only, and a write lock for all records that are updated or deleted. The read locks are released with a move to the next record, whereas all write locks are held until the transaction is committed or aborted.

- **Repeatable read**—Repeatable read is functionally similar to read committed. The only difference is that the read locks are held until the transaction is committed or aborted. This way, nonrepeatable reads cannot happen anymore.

- **Serializable**—Similar to read committed and repeatable read, the transaction waits until all write-locked rows that are manipulated by the transaction are unlocked. Similar to repeatable reads, read locks are done for rows that are read-only, and write locks are done for rows that are updated or deleted. What is different with this level is how ranges of data are locked. If a `SELECT * FROM Customers` statement is executed, a table lock is done. This way no new records can be inserted. With the SQL statement `SELECT * FROM Customers WHERE City = 'Vienna'`, all records with the `City` column set to `Vienna` are locked. This way, phantoms are not possible.

Table 7-5 summarizes potential problems that can occur depending on the isolation level.

When to Use Which Isolation Level

Consistency and concurrency have conflicting goals. For consistent data, locking must be done when the data is accessed. For best consistency, the transaction isolation level serializable offers the best support. Locking the data also means that no

Table 7-5   Isolation Level Behavior

Isolation Level	Dirty Reads	Nonrepeatable Reads	Phantoms
Read uncommitted	Yes	Yes	Yes
Read committed	No	Yes	Yes
Repeatable read	No	No	Yes
Serializable	No	No	No

other task may access the data simultaneously. To get better concurrency, you must select a lower isolation level.

Depending on the task to be done, you can select the isolation level accordingly. If only new records are to be inserted, you can set the isolation level to read uncommitted. If data is read once, or multiple times, and if consistency is not required (for example, you are generating a management report), you can set the isolation level to read committed.

Thinking about configuring the isolation level always requires thinking about the complete task that should be protected, what can happen during the time of the task, and how this can influence the task. With this information, you can select the required isolation level.

Specifying the Isolation Level

You can specify the transaction isolation level of a serviced component with the attribute [Transaction] by defining the named property Isolation and setting a value to one of the defined values in the enumeration TransactionIsolation-Level.

```
[Transaction(TransactionOption.Required,
            Isolation = TransactionIsolationLevel.Any)]
[EventTrackingEnabled]
public class CustomerData : ServicedComponent
```

The possible values and their meaning of the enumeration TransactionIsolationLevel are shown in Table 7-6.

Table 7-6 TransactionIsolationLevel Enumeration

TransactionIsolationLevel Value	Description
Any	If you set the isolation level to `Any`, the same isolation level as the calling component is used. If the object is the root object, the isolation level is `Serializable`.
ReadUncommitted	With `ReadUncommitted`, only shared locks are used; exclusive locks are not honored. You should use this option only for read access to generate some results that don't need to be actually up to the second.
ReadCommitted	With this option, shared locks are used while data is being read. After reading the data, the shared lock is released. Before the transaction is finished, the data can be changed.
RepeatableRead	If you set the option to `RepeatableRead`, locks are placed on all data that is used.
Serializable	The level `Serializable` has the best isolation. With this option, updates or inserts that belong to the range of the data that is used are not possible.

If using transactions without components, you can specify the transaction isolation level with the property `IsolationLevel` of the class `ServiceConfig`.

Monitoring the DTC

You can monitor transactions that are enlisted with the DTC by using the Component Services Explorer. Selecting Transaction List in the tree view as a child element of the Distributed Transaction Coordinator shows all current active transactions. Selecting Transaction Statistics opens up the window shown in Figure 7-13. Here you can read the current number of active transactions, the maximum number of transactions that were active concurrently, and the committed and aborted transaction count.

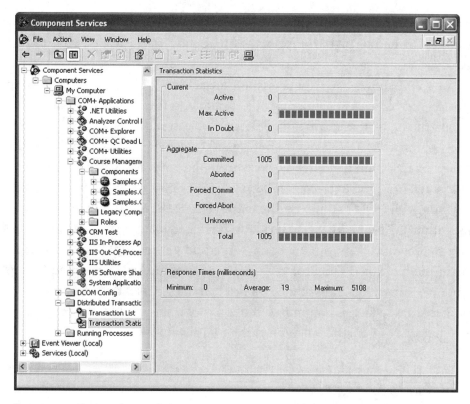

Figure 7-13   Transaction statistics.

Transactions with .NET 2.0

One disadvantage of automatic transactions with serviced components is that these transactions always make use of the DTC, even when local transactions would be enough. Of course, using DTC is more expensive than a local programmatic transaction as was used in Listing 7-2.

With .NET 2.0, a new assembly System.Transactions will be available that includes some new classes dealing with transactions. Particularly worth mentioning are the classes Transaction, TransactionScope, and TransactionManager. These classes are in the namespace System.Transactions. The big advantage of these classes is that the new transaction services know about local and DTC transaction and will support the Web services standard WS-AtomicTransaction[6] in the future. Depending on the scope of the transaction, the fastest possible technology is used.

Listing 7-11 shows one way to create transactions with .NET 2.0.[7] Creating and disposing of a `TransactionScope` object defines a transactional code block. With the constructor of the `TransactionScope` object and the `TransactionScope-Option` enumeration, you can define whether a new transaction is required or whether a transaction that already exists from the outer block should be used. With the parameter of type `EnterpriseSerivcesInteropOption`, you can specify the interaction with COM+ contexts. The method `Complete()` indicates that all operations within the scope of the transaction have been successful. At the end of the `using` statement (where the `Dispose()` method gets called), the transaction outcome of the block is defined. If the `Complete` method was not called because an exception occurred, the transaction is aborted. If the scope of the transaction was successful, the transaction is committed if it is a root transaction. If the scope is not the root of the transaction, the outcome of the transaction is influenced.

Listing 7-11 Programming Transactions with .NET 2.0

```
using System;
using System.Transactions;
using Samples.Courses.Entities;
using Samples.Courses.Data;

class TxDemo
{
    static void Main()
    {
        using (TransactionScope scope = new TransactionScope(
            TransactionScopeOption.Required))
        {
            Course c = new Course();
            c.Number = "MS-2557";
            c.Title = ".NET Enterprise Services";
            c.Active = true;

            CourseData db = new CourseData(connectionString);
            db.AddCourse(c);
```

```
        scope.Complete();
    }
}
```

With Indigo Services, you may declare transactions, as shown in Listing 7-12. This should look similar to the declarative transactions of the serviced components model. The attribute `[OperationContract(TransactionFlowAllowed=true)]` defines that a transaction is created. The attribute `[OperationBehavior(Auto-EnlistTransaction=true)]` defines that the transaction is automatically enlisted with the transaction coordinator.

Listing 7-12   Declaring Transactions with Indigo Services

```
[ServiceContract]
[ServiceBehavior(InstanceMode=InstanceMode.PerCall)]
public interface IDemoService
{
    [OperationContract(TransactionFlowAllowed=true)]
    [OperationBehavior(AutoEnlistTransaction=true)]
    void AddCourse(Course course);
}

[BindingRequirements(
    TransactionFlowRequirements = RequirementsMode.Require,
    QueuedDeliveryRequirements = RequirementsMode.Disallow,
    RequireOrderedDelivery = true
)]
public class DemoService : IDemoService
{
    public void AddCourse(Course course)
    {
        //...
    }
}
```

Summary

This chapter covered the transaction features offered by Enterprise Services. Instead of doing transactions programmatically, you can task transactions automatically by applying the attribute [Transaction] to specify transactional requirements. The transactional options Required, RequiresNew, Supported, NotSupported, and Disabled influence the Enterprise Services interception code so that a new transaction is created, an existing transaction is used, or no transaction is used at all.

The automatic transactions make use of the distributed transaction coordinator, so transactions can also flow across multiple systems.

This chapter also discussed the problems with concurrency and consistency with transaction isolation levels. Changing the isolation level can increase concurrency, whereas consistency is reduced, and vice versa.

Windows Server 2003 also offers the new feature named services without components; transactions are part of this service.

1   The connection string defines whether a connection should be enlisted with the transaction context of the thread. With the .NET data provider for SQL Server, you can define whether the transaction should be enlisted with the Enlist parameter. The Enlist parameter has a default value of true, so that the connection is enlisted with the transaction context. Microsoft .NET data provider for Oracle has the same Enlist parameter.

2   Construction strings are discussed in Chapter 2, "Object Activation and Contexts."

3   JITA is discussed in Chapter 2.

4   Transactions that include Message Queuing are shown in Chapter 10.

5   DCOM and .NET remoting are discussed in Chapter 5, "Networking."

6   WS-AtomicTransaction is discussed in Chapter 14.

7   While writing this book, I am using a Beta version of .NET 2.0. The implementation of .NET 2.0 transactions may change with the release version.

8

Compensating Resource Management

IN THE PRECEDING CHAPTER, YOU LEARNED about transactions and how the resource managers participate in them. The resource managers that have been used so far support transactions for databases with the OLE protocol. Chapter 10, "Queued Components," includes message queuing in the transaction list.

If you want to write your own resource manager to deal with transactions (for example, for transactional file access), .NET Enterprise Services offers an easy way to create resource managers with compensating resource managers (CRMs).[1]

In this chapter, you learn about the architecture of CRMs and how to create your own resource manager.

Specifically, this chapter covers the following topics:

- CRM architecture
- CRM application classes
- CRM application example
- Monitoring

CRM Architecture

If you want to create a resource manager that can participate in a transaction, you must implement the OLE transaction's Two-Phase Commit (2PC) protocol. Microsoft has already done a lot of the work needed to build your own resource manager. An easy way to build your own resource manager is just to build a CRM.

To make use of the CRM architecture, you must implement a **worker** and a **compensator**, and use a clerk object that acts as intermediate to send requests to the compensator. The relationship of these objects is shown in Figure 8-1.

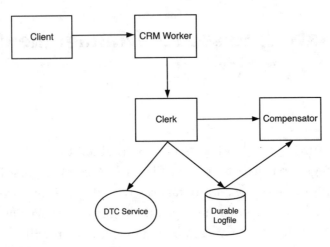

Figure 8-1 Worker, compensator, and clerk.

The worker is a normal serviced component that is called by the client application and does the work you want to get out of the component. For example, the worker can offer methods such as AddCourse and AddAttendeeToCourse, as you have seen in previous chapters. With the worker, you can implement any functionality where you need a transaction, but where there is no existing resource manager that could be used for this functionality. (For example, you can write files to the file system, you can write data to the registry, or you can send e-mail.)

In addition to the usual serviced component implementation, you must implement code to instantiate a **clerk**. Before performing any actions, you must write information about what will be done—with the help of the clerk—to a log file. It is important that the worker logs all changes before doing them so that it is possible to undo the work later if necessary.

The responsibility of the clerk is—besides writing log files initiated by the worker—to communicate with the distributed transaction coordinator (DTC). This communication enables the worker to participate in transactions instantiated by other components. The worker can influence the transaction in similar ways to those you have seen with normal serviced components in the preceding chapter.

You do not have to implement the clerk yourself; this functionality is part of the CRM runtime.

The clerk also instantiates the compensator—this is a component that you must implement to commit and to abort the actions done by the worker. The compensator gets prepare, abort, and commit notifications, in addition to information from the log file that was written by the clerk, so you can approve or undo the operations done by the worker.

CRM Application Classes

Take a look at the classes offered by the assembly System.EnterpriseServices in the namespace System.EnterpriseServices.CompensatingResourceManager. The most important classes you must deal with are Clerk and Compensator.

You can use the Clerk class inside the worker to write log records that can be read later by the compensator. The methods and properties of this class are shown in Table 8-1.

With the clerk, you will write log records that are passed to the compensator, where you will receive objects of type LogRecord. The properties of this class are shown in Table 8-2.

Table 8-1   Clerk Class

Clerk Members	Description
WriteLogRecord	With the method WriteLogRecord, you can pass any serializable[2] object to write information to the log. It is best to declare a custom struct where you can pass all the information you need to approve or to undo the actions with the compensator.
ForceLog	Calling WriteLogRecord does not guarantee that this information is already written to the disk. Before doing any physical changes with the worker, you must force writing it to the disk with the ForceLog method.

Table 8-1   (continued)

Clerk Members	Description
ForceTransactionToAbort	If you call ForceTransactionToAbort, you can abort the transaction immediately.
ForgetLogRecord	Calling ForgetLogRecord removes the last log record.
LogRecordCount	LogRecordCount returns the number of log entries.
TransactionUOW	TransactionUOW returns the unique identifier of the transaction (unit of work).

Table 8-2   LogRecord Class

LogRecord Members	Description
Flags	With the Flags property of the LogRecord class, you can get information about when the log record was written (for example, if the log record was written during prepare, abort, commit, or during a recovery process).
Record	Accessing the Record property enables you to retrieve the record that was written by the clerk with the WriteLogRecord method.
Sequence	The Sequence property returns an integer representing the sequence number of the log record.

The custom compensator must derive from the base class Compensator. The Compensator class has many virtual methods that you can override to react and prepare, commit, and abort messages accordingly.

CRM Application Example

In this section, a simple implementation of a CRM sample application shows you what is necessary to make use of CRM. When using CRMs, you must carefully examine

Table 8-3   Compensator Class

Compensator Methods	Description
BeginPreparePrepare RecordEndPrepare	The method `PrepareRecord` is called for every record that was written in the prepare phase. Before that first record is delivered, the `BeginPrepare` method is called; after the last record, the `EndPrepare` method is called. `Begin`- and `End`-methods are common in the prepare, commit, and abort phases.
BeginCommitCommit RecordEndCommit	In the commit phase, you can override the `CommitRecord` method to receive the log record. This method is called when the transaction is committed, and you can finalize the outcome from the component.
BeginAbortAbort RecordEndAbort	The `AbortRecord` method is called when the transaction is aborted. Here you must undo the actions done by the worker.

transactional behavior because by default CRM does not automatically support the ACID[3] properties; for example, to get isolation, you must implement the worker and the compensator in a way that the changes cannot be accessed from outside. However, you might decide that your solution does not need all ACID properties.

This sample component allows creation of a transaction-oriented file. In this example, the components shown in Figure 8-2 are implemented. The worker is implemented in the class `FileComponent`, which offers the method `CreateFile`; the compensator is the class `FileCompensator`, which derives from the base class `Compensator`.

The component `FileComponent` has the responsibility of creating a file containing a customer ID and a contact name. This file should only be created if the transaction is successful.

Figure 8-3 shows a sequence diagram of the worker and compensator in action. When the client application invokes the method `CreateFile` in the worker component, the worker component in turn informs the clerk about the action to be done and creates a temporary file with the required information. Upon the completion of the transaction (if it is successful), the clerk sends a request to all compensators to complete the transaction by calling `CommitRecord`. With this request, the compensator moves the temporary file to the final destination.

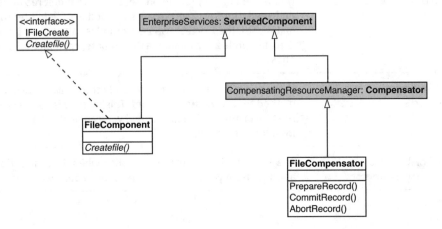

Figure 8-2   CRM application components.

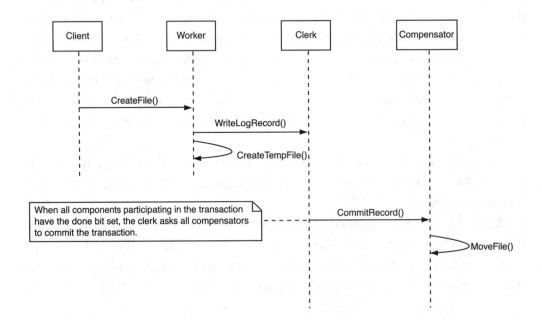

Figure 8-3   Sequence of worker and compensator..

Before you can start implementing CRM worker and compensator components, you must be aware of some facts related to CRM application development, including the following:

- With CRM, the serviced component application must be a server application. Compensator components cannot run within library applications.

- CRM must be enabled with an application attribute. You must mark the assembly with the attribute `[ApplicationCrmEnabled]`.

- The serviced component assembly that includes the compensator must be installed in the global assembly cache. If it is not in the global assembly cache, the `BeginPrepare` method of the compensator class will start, but you will just get an error message that this method failed.

- Contrary to normal serviced components, multiple versions of the compensator class cannot coexist in the same application. Always delete older versions that you have registered before using new versions of the application.

- If you change the format of log entries, you might have to remove old log entries. In Windows XP and Windows Server 2003, you can find the log information in the directory Windows\Registration\CRMLog; in Windows 2000, the directory for the logs is Windows\System32\DTCLog.

- Check the event log when you get errors from the serviced component application. Often, the event log contains more detailed information about the error than the exception message provides.

> **TIP: Reality Check: Check the Event Log**
>
> Check the event log for errors. You should also write information about exceptions that are caught to the event log.

Application Configuration

The application configuration looks like the configuration of other serviced component applications—with the attributes `[ApplicationName]`, `[ApplicationActivation]`, and `[ApplicationAccessControl]` (see Listing 8-1). As discussed earlier, the only option allowed with `[ApplicationActivation]` is `Activa-tionOption.Server`. In addition to normal serviced component applications, you must add the attribute `[ApplicationCrmEnabled]`. The attribute class `ApplicationCrmEnabledAttribute` is defined in the namespace `System.Enterprise-Services.CompensatingResourceManager`, so you must import this namespace.

Listing 8-1 AssemblyInfo.cs—Application Configuration

```
using System.Reflection;
using System.Runtime.CompilerServices;
using System.EnterpriseServices;
using System.EnterpriseServices.CompensatingResourceManager;

//...

[assembly: AssemblyDelaySign(false)]
[assembly: AssemblyKeyFile("../../../../mykey.snk")]
[assembly: AssemblyKeyName("")]

[assembly: ApplicationName("CRM Demo")]
[assembly: ApplicationActivation(ActivationOption.Server)]
[assembly: ApplicationAccessControl(false)]
[assembly: ApplicationCrmEnabled(true)]
```

Because the attribute `[ApplicationCrmEnabled]` is set, after registration of the component, you can see Enable Compensating Resource Managers selected on the Advanced properties of the application configuration (see Figure 8-4).

Helper Classes

Listing 8-2 shows helper classes that the serviced components need. The struct `FileLogRecord` contains the information about the filename that should be created. In the first run, only a temporary file is created; then, only if the transaction is committed does the real filename come into play.

`FileLogRecord` also contains an `Action` enumeration. In the example, the enumeration contains only a single value: `CreateFile`. If you want to extend the example, you can easily extend the enumeration.

The interface `IFileDemo` defines the method `CreateFile` that will be implemented by the worker component.

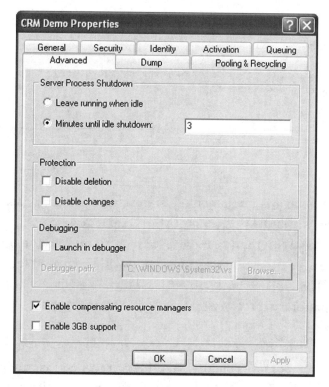

Figure 8-4   Configuration of CRM applications.

Listing 8-2   Helper Classes

```
using System;

namespace Samples.CRM
{
   public enum Action
   {
      CreateFile
   }

   [Serializable]
   public struct FileLogRecord
   {
      public string Tempfilename;
      public string Filename;
      public Action Action;
```

```
    }

public interface IFileDemo
{
    void CreateFile(string filename, string customerId,
        string contactName);
}
}
```

Worker Components

The worker component is implemented in the class `FileComponent`, as shown in Listing 8-3. The attributes `[Transaction]` and `[ConstructionEnabled]` are applied to the class. With the `[Transaction]`[4] attribute and the constructor value `TransactionOption.Required`, a transaction will be created for the component. The attribute `[ConstructionEnabled]`[5] defines, with the named property `Default`, the temporary directory that is used by the component.

The method `CreateFile` is defined by the interface `IFileDemo`. In the implementation of this method, a `FileLogRecord` is created first, it is initialized with the new filename (a temporary filename), and the `Action` enumeration value is set to `Action.CreateFile`. The temporary filename is created with a unique identifier that is returned from `Guid.NewGuid`.

After the log record is created, a `Clerk` object is initialized. The constructor of the `Clerk` class requires the type of the `Compensator` class, a name, and information about the phases when the compensator should be notified. Using the clerk, the method `WriteLogRecord` writes the previously initialized log record. Only calling the method `ForceLog` guarantees that the information is written to disk, which is a requirement before any physical changes are done.

After the log record is written, the real work of the worker component can start. Here just a temporary file containing information that is passed from the caller is written to disk by using the `File` and `StreamWriter` classes.

Listing 8-3　Worker Component

```
using System;
using System.IO;
```

```
using System.EnterpriseServices;
using System.EnterpriseServices.CompensatingResourceManager;

namespace Samples.CRM
{
    [Transaction(TransactionOption.Required)]
    [EventTrackingEnabled(true)]
    [ConstructionEnabled(true, Default="c:/temp")]
    public class FileComponent : ServicedComponent, IFileDemo
    {
        public FileComponent()
        {
        }

        private string tempDir;
        protected override void Construct(string s)
        {
            tempDir = s;
        }

        [AutoComplete]
        public void CreateFile(string filename, string customerId,
                string contactName)
        {
            // Define the log record with information what's done next
            FileLogRecord logRecord;
            logRecord.Filename = filename;
            string tempFilename = Guid.NewGuid() + ".txt";
            logRecord.Tempfilename = Path.Combine(tempDir, tempFilename);
            logRecord.Action = Action.CreateFile;

            // Create a clerk
            Clerk c = new Clerk(typeof(FileCompensator),
                "File Compensator",
                CompensatorOptions.AllPhases);

            // Write a log record before doing a physical action
            c.WriteLogRecord(logRecord);
            c.ForceLog();

            // Create a temporary file containing the data
            StreamWriter writer = File.CreateText(logRecord.Tempfilename);
            writer.WriteLine("{0};{1}", customerId, contactName);
            writer.Close();
        }
    }
}
```

Compensator Components

The compensator for the `FileComponent` is implemented in the class `FileCompensator` (see Listing 8-4). This class derives from the base class `Compensator`, which itself derives from `ServicedComponent`. The only three methods that are overridden from the base class are `PrepareRecord`, `CommitRecord`, and `AbortRecord`.

With `PrepareRecord`, there is no need to do anything special inside this class—just return `false`. Otherwise, the `LogRecord` that is passed by the CRM runtime would not be forwarded to the methods `CommitRecord` or `AbortRecord`.

In the case where the transaction is committed, the CRM runtime calls the `CommitRecord` method. Within the compensator, the actual file that should exist must be created. The filenames that have been passed with the `FileLogRecord` can be accessed by using the `Record` property of the `LogRecord` object. Using the filenames, the `File` class helps rename the temporary file to the real file.

The `AbortRecord` method is very similar to `CommitRecord`, but here only the temporary file is deleted.

Listing 8-4   Compensator Component

```
using System;
using System.IO;
using System.EnterpriseServices;
using System.EnterpriseServices.CompensatingResourceManager;

namespace Samples.CRM
{
    public class FileCompensator : Compensator
    {
        public override bool PrepareRecord(LogRecord rec)
        {
            return false;
        }

        public override bool CommitRecord(LogRecord rec)
        {
            FileLogRecord logRecord = (FileLogRecord)rec.Record;

            switch (logRecord.Action)
            {
                case Action.CreateFile:
```

```
            // create real file
            File.Move(logRecord.Tempfilename,
                logRecord.Filename);
            break;
        }
        return true;
    }

    public override bool AbortRecord(LogRecord rec)
    {
        FileLogRecord logRecord = (FileLogRecord)rec.Record;

        switch (logRecord.Action)
        {
            case Action.CreateFile:
                // delete temp file
                File.Delete(logRecord.Tempfilename);
                break;
        }

        return true;
    }
    }
}
```

After the serviced component application is registered, you can see both the compensator and the worker components with the Component Services Explorer, as shown in Figure 8-5. Remember that with CRM applications, you must not forget to install the assembly in the global assembly cache.

Client Applications

Now you can create a client application to test the serviced component. Client applications are created in the same way you have seen so far, as shown in Listing 8-5. The worker component gets created, and the method `CreateFile` is called. If everything goes well, the file c:/temp/demofile.txt will have the content that was passed with `CreateFile`.

Listing 8-5 Client Application

```
[STAThread]
static void Main(string[] args)
```

```
    {
        try
        {
            Samples.CRM.FileComponent comp =
                new Samples.CRM.FileComponent();
            comp.CreateFile("c:/temp/demofile.txt", "AWL", "Steph");
            comp.Dispose();
        }
        catch (Exception ex)
        {
            Console.WriteLine(ex.Message);
        }
    }
```

You can also try to fail the worker by throwing an exception in the `CreateFile` method—the compensator will deal with the undo mechanism. Alternatively, you can use the worker component from a different serviced component that creates a transaction; in this scenario, you can see whether the worker component participates in the same transaction.

What happens if the machine goes down while a transaction was in process? Because the log information was written before any activity was performed, you have a good chance for recovery. In such a case, when the server application process

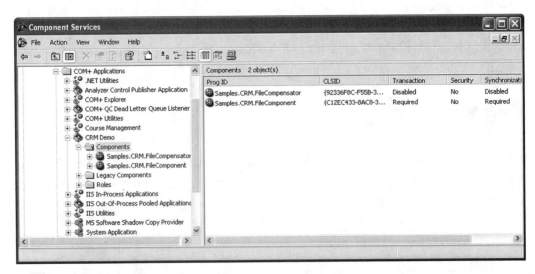

Figure 8-5   Component Services Explorer with registered worker and compensator.

starts up, the CRM runtime finds the log file, talks to the DTC about the outcome of the transaction, and performs the recovery by instantiating the compensator.

Monitoring

You can use the `ClerkMonitor` and `ClerkInfo` classes to monitor the activities of clerks. The `ClerkMonitor` implements the interface `IEnumerable`, so you can enumerate through all running clerks. However, the clerks that are returned are only those running in the same process as the clerk monitor; therefore, you can get to this information only within an "admin" component that is configured in the same application as the worker who instantiates the clerk.

From the enumeration, you will get `ClerkInfo` objects representing every clerk in the process. With `ClerkInfo`, you can access the activity ID, transaction ID, compensator description, and the clerk itself.

Using the COM interface `ICrmMonitorLogRecords` that is implemented by the clerk, you can also access the log records written by the clerk. This interface is not directly available from .NET—you must use COM interop to get to the log file information.

Summary

This chapter has shown how to create a CRM worker and compensator object to create a "lightweight" resource manager that enables you to integrate resources that do not support transactions with the transactional support of serviced components.

The important thing to remember is that all tasks done by the worker must be documented in a log with the help of the clerk. The clerk communicates with the DTC and manages the compensator to commit or abort the tasks performed.

---

1 CRM is an initialism with multiple meanings. Today, CRM usually refers to customer relationship management. In the context of .NET Enterprise Services and COM+, however, CRM refers to compensating resource manager.

2 A serializable object must be declared with the attribute `[Serializable]`.

3 Atomicity, consistency, isolation, and durability (ACID) are discussed in Chapter 7, "Transaction Services."

4 See Chapter 7 for more information about the `[Transaction]` and `[AutoComplete]` attributes.

5 See Chapter 2, "Object Activation and Contexts," for more information about the `[ConstructionEnabled]` attribute.

9
State Management

WITH REGARD TO OBJECT ORIENTATION, YOU have learned that an object has state and behavior. With Enterprise Services applications, however, it is often not useful to keep state with the object. Serviced components can be stateless or stateful. With a completed transaction, as you have seen in Chapter 7, "Transaction Services," state is lost anyway.

When developing Enterprise Services applications, you must think about state, because you have many different options as to where state can be kept. Where you put state can change the scalability of applications.

This chapter covers the alternatives of where to put and how to implement state within Enterprise Services applications, using a Web services façade and a client application.

Specifically, this chapter covers the following topics:

- State characteristics
- Stateful or stateless components
- State with database and files
- The Shared Property Manager
- ASP.NET state management
- Client state management

State Characteristics

Serviced components can be stateful or stateless. Stateful components keep their values in their member variables after multiple calls from the same client. Stateless components are instantiated anew with every method call. Stateless components increase scalability, because no resources are kept on the server in between method calls.

If you are using stateless components, state might still be needed. State is not necessarily kept in member variables of the component; you can put it elsewhere. When writing distributed applications, you must think about where to put state, and with Enterprise Services applications, you can put state in different locations.

Figure 9-1 shows the parts of an Enterprise application where state can be kept. You can put state into the client application or into the serviced component. You can also use shared properties or put the state into a database.

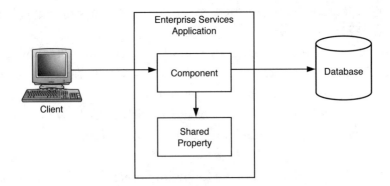

Figure 9-1 State with Enterprise Services applications.

Where you put state is influenced by its characteristics. You can distinguish state according to these categories:

- **Immutable**—Immutable state never changes. Examples of immutable state are my bank statement from November 2003, or a catalog of summer 2003. Although my bank statement changes all the time, the statement of November 2003 does not change anymore.

  The data might be uninteresting, but it never changes. Because of this behavior, you can put immutable data into the cache without worrying about cache inconsistencies.

You can create immutable data with the help of versions and timestamps.

- **Stable data**—Stable data is meaningful across space and time. State data is data that never changes, like immutable data, but it is also meaningful after some time. Compare this with immutable data: The catalog from the year 2004 is usually not of interest in the year 2005. Stable data, for example, is a customer ID that always stays the same.

- **Normalized data**—Normalized data is data that you can easily update. With a normalized database, the same data is not copied across multiple tables, so an update only needs to be done in one place. Sometimes you can access data faster if it is denormalized. With denormalization, there is no need to use joins to get the data.

Some more points regarding state need some attention. With state characteristics, you also have to keep in mind durability, volatility, speed, lifetime, affinity, and size of the data that should be stored.

- **Durability**—Must the state survive system restarts? If yes, the database might be the best option to store the state.

- **Volatility**—How often is the state changed? If state is changed often, it should be changed in the fastest possible way.

- **Speed**—How fast must the state be accessible? Memory access is faster than database access.

- **Lifetime**—How long must the state be available? Some mechanisms allow a very flexible way to control the lifetime of state.

- **Affinity**—Is the state associated with a user, an object, the application, or the complete system (which might consist of multiple applications)?

- **Size**—What is the size of the state? The size is important to know when passing the state across network boundaries. Passing large data repeatedly across the network is inefficient; keeping the data on the server instead might prove more efficient. Be aware that allocating resources on the server increases the load on the server. You also have to keep in mind how often the state is needed, where it is needed, and whether the state should be shared.

In contrast to large data, passing small data across the network is more efficient than allocating resources on the server.

Depending on the answers to these questions, you can decide whether the state should be put in the client, the component, the Shared Property Manager, files, or the database. Taking into account the state location considerations listed here, the following sections cover some of your different options.

Stateful or Stateless Components

Before discussing different options for state, let's start with serviced components. As previously mentioned, serviced components can be stateful or stateless. Stateless offers more scalability, because resources are not allocated with the serviced application.

To create stateless components, you can use the attribute [JustInTimeActivation],[1] and decide within the methods using the attribute [AutoComplete] when the object should be deactivated.

Transactional components are always stateless. Therefore, they can keep state as long as the transaction is running; if the transaction is committed or aborted, however, transactional components are deactivated, and the state is lost.

To create stateful components, you do not have to do anything special; you just do not apply the attribute [JustInTimeActivation].

If you are using .NET remoting[2] to access the serviced component, then whether stateless or stateless components should be used is defined by the .NET remoting configuration. Client-activated objects are stateful, and well-known objects are stateless.

Using stateful components, you have the following characteristics for state:

- Stateful components are not durable. The state is lost as soon as the component is deactivated. Transactional components lose state as soon as the transaction is completed.

- If the state changes often, stateful components can be a good choice. Stateful components allow for extremely fast state changes as long as no process boundaries are crossed—that is, if the caller of the stateful components is running in the same process (for examle, if the serviced component application is configured as a library application, or if the caller is a serviced component). If the caller is on a different system, more time is needed to access the state.

- The lifetime of stateful components is affected by references that are kept. As long as there is a reference to the stateful component available, the state is kept. If you are using .NET remoting to access serviced components, the time of the reference to be available is controlled by a leasing mechanism.

- Stateful components are associated with every caller that has a reference to the component. This can be an association with the client application, or, if the reference is passed along, with multiple client applications. If the reference is shared, attention must be paid to the synchronization. If the component is shared among many clients, it might be best to use custom synchronization by setting the synchronization attribute to the synchronization option [NotSupported].[3] With this option, multiple clients can access the component concurrently. However, a drawback to this option is that you must deal with synchronization issues yourself.

- The size of the state is limited by the size of a process. With a 32-bit operating system, you have 2GB of user space available. The state of all objects inside a process is limited by this boundary; long before reaching this boundary, however, you should think about putting the state into the database.

- An argument against the use of stateful components is when using component load-balancing services. With component load-balancing services, objects are distributed across multiple systems to increase scalability. Because state cannot be shared across systems, when using stateful components, it is necessary to access components on the same system.

Databases and Files

To keep state durable, you can store state in the database, in files, or in the Active Directory.

The database offers a very efficient mechanism for storing state. It is a widely used, hard-tested system with an efficient locking mechanism to support scalable solutions.

> **NOTE: The IMDB Project Was Cancelled**
>
> With the beta of Windows 2000, an in-memory mechanism called IMDB was available that could be used by Enterprise Services applications to access state in memory with a database-style access. For the final release, this product was cancelled because SQL Server itself was much more efficient than IMDB.

Storing durable state in files can be a very attractive mechanism, if the state is stored with the client application. It is also possible to store state inside a database with the client. The Microsoft Data Engine (MSDE) is a free version of the SQL Server that is restricted as to the size and number of concurrent connections (also available with Windows CE). However, you must install the MSDE with an installation program.

If you are using XML files instead to store state with the client application, you do not need a separate installation program. If you are accessing the state stored in XML files, you can use XML technologies such as the XML DOM model, XPath, and XQuery to navigate inside these files. The .NET Framework offers a lot of classes in the namespace `System.Xml` to deal with these technologies.

Isolated Storage

If the client application does not have full trust, you can use isolated storage to store state. You can use isolated storage to access an assembly-specific store to read and write state from assemblies that are loaded from the network—without permissions to write to the normal file system. With isolated storage, you can write data to the system without knowing the actual physical location. The data store is managed by the isolated storage classes.

Listing 9-1 shows an example of how to write data using the classes `Isolated-StorageFileStream` and the `StreamWriter`. For these classes, the namespaces `System.IO.IsolatedStorage` and `System.IO` must be imported. The constructor of the class `IsolatedStorageFileStream` creates a new file with the name `mydata.txt`. With the constructor, you can also specify an `IsolatedStorageFile` object to define whether the data stored should roam with the user. The class `StreamWriter` is used to write the string `data` to the file.

Listing 9-1   Write Data to Isolated Storage

```
static void WriteIsolatedStorageDemo(string data)

    IsolatedStorageFileStream stream =
            new IsolatedStorageFileStream("mydata.txt",
            FileMode.CreateNew);

    StreamWriter writer = new StreamWriter(stream);
    writer.WriteLine(data);
    writer.Close();
    stream.Close();
}
```

Listing 9-2 shows how you can read the data from isolated storage. Under the same filename as before, the file is opened with the IsolatedStorageFileStream and the mode FileMode.Open to open an existing file. With the ReadLine method of the StreamReader class, the line that was written is read again.

Listing 9-2   Read Data from Isolated Storage

```
static string ReadIsolatedStorageDemo()
{
    IsolatedStorageFileStream stream =
            new IsolatedStorageFileStream("mydata.txt",
            FileMode.Open);

    StreamReader reader = new StreamReader(stream);
    string data = reader.ReadLine();
    reader.Close();
    stream.Close();

    return data;
}
```

Although the isolated storage is not accessible from the normal file system, you can create directories and access files within the isolated storage using classes from the namespace System.IO.IsolatedStorage. Listing 9-3 shows how you can get file-names from the storage with the method GetUserStoreForDomain with the class IsolatedStorageFile. With this class, you can also create directories and delete files.

Listing 9-3   Returning the Filenames of an Isolated Storage

```
static string[] GetFiles()
{
    IsolatedStorageFile store =
        IsolatedStorageFile.GetUserStoreForDomain();
    string[] filenames = store.GetFileNames("*"))
    store.Close();
    return filenames;
}
```

Active Directory

Active Directory[4] is a useful mechanism if the state does not change often, because it is designed for state that changes rarely, but is often accessed for reading data. You can create custom types for data that should be stored in Active Directory, but installing the custom types can only be done by a domain administrator. The role of a normal system administrator is not good enough. That said, the state that is stored in Active Directory should be of interest to the enterprise, not just a subsidiary. Examples of such state are information about users and information about systems.

Factors to consider when determining whether to store state in the database or in files include the following:

- Storing the state in the database or in files offers durability. The state survives system restarts.

- If the state is changed often, Active Directory is not an option; files and the database might still be a choice. Another option is to split the state into a temporary and a durable version. State that changes often may be accessed from memory, while at certain times it is written to a durable store.

- Accessing state from a file or from the database is not as fast as memory access. An option is to cache the data.

- The lifetime of the state must be controlled manually; it must be deleted explicitly when it should not be used anymore.

- The state is not bound to a single object; it is available to everyone who knows about it and who has the rights to access the data.

- With the size of the state, there is no restriction except the size of the hard disks.

Shared Property Manager

The Shared Property Manager (SPM) is a service offered by Enterprise Services. SPM offers an in-memory state management mechanism that is bound within Enterprise Services applications. You can use SPM to store state that is independent of the object lifetime. It is also possible to share some data among multiple callers.

> **NOTE: Shared Property Manager and COM**
>
> A major issue with the SPM is that it is based on COM, and VARIANTs are used to store the data. To store complete .NET objects, they must be serialized, which can take some time.

Shared properties consist of a **shared property group manager**, **shared property groups**, and **shared properties**, as shown in Figure 9-2. The shared property group

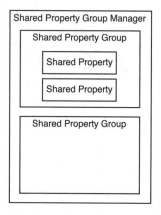

Figure 9-2   Parts of the SPM.

manager is used to create and access shared property groups. Shared property groups are used to manage shared properties. You can use groups to have different properties for every client or to group properties for a specific task.

The classes available with the assembly `System.EnterpriseServices` for shared properties are `SharedPropertyGroupManager`, `SharedPropertyGroup`, and `SharedProperty`.

Shared Property Group Manager

You can use the class `SharedPropertyGroupManager` to create and access shared property groups. The methods of this class are listed in Table 9-1. Besides the methods `CreatePropertyGroup` and `Group`, you can use an enumerator to access all property groups.

When creating a new property group with the method `CreatePropertyGroup`, you must pass a property lock mode and a property release mode. The lock mode is needed for synchronous access, whereas the release mode defines when the property group should be destroyed.

Table 9-1   SharedPropertyGroupManager Class

SharedPropertyGroupManager Members	Description
`CreatePropertyGroup`	The method `CreatePropertyGroup` **creates a new property group or returns an existing group.**
`Group`	`Group` **returns an existing** `SharedProperty-Group` **by passing a group name.**

Property Lock Mode

The **property lock mode** defines how access to a property should be locked. Defining the lock mode is important for concurrent access of the shared property group. The possible values are defined with the enumeration `PropertyLockMode`: `Method` and `SetGet`. With the lock mode `SetGet`, the property is locked only during set and get operations—when the property is accessed. With the lock mode `Method`, all properties of a group are locked for exclusive use of the caller—as long as the method of the serviced component is active.

Property Release Mode

The **property release mode** defines when the property group should be destroyed. The possible values are defined with the enumeration `PropertyReleaseMode`: `Standard` and `Process`.

Setting the value `Standard` defines that the property group is deleted as soon as all clients release the reference to the property group and the garbage collector cleans up. To keep shared properties alive with the standard release mode, it is necessary to keep a reference to the property group in a stateful component.

With the mode `Process`, the property group stays alive until the process of the Enterprise Services application is stopped. Thus, it is not possible to destroy a property group early, and resources might be allocated for longer than necessary.

> **Keeping References**
>
> If you use the standard release mode with shared properties, the properties are released when the garbage collector cleans up. If there seems to be a random behavior with objects that cannot be accessed from a shared property, the problem is likely that all references have been released and the garbage collector did a cleanup. The behavior when the object is released can differ with debug and release builds, and depends on other loads of the system.

Creating a Shared Property Group

The example that follows in the next listings consists of just a simple serviced component `SPMDemo` that does nothing more than get and set state. In this example, you can see how you can use SPM and how you can share information among multiple instances.

Listing 9-4 creates a shared property group in the constructor of a serviced component class implementation. The shared property group manager is accessed by creating a new instance of the class SharedPropertyGroupManager. The call to the method CreatePropertyGroup either creates a new group or returns an existing group, the group being identified by the group name. You can check whether a new group will be created or an existing group will be returned by reading the last argument, existed, of the method CreatePropertyGroup.

The property group release mode is set to PropertyReleaseMode.Process so that the property group stays alive when no object has a reference set.

Listing 9-4 Create a Shared Property Group

```
[EventTrackingEnabled]
public class SPMDemo : ServicedComponent
{
    private SharedPropertyGroup group;

    public SPMDemo()
    {
        // Create a shared property group,
        // or get a reference to an existing group
        bool existed;
        PropertyLockMode lockMode = PropertyLockMode.SetGet;
        PropertyReleaseMode releaseMode =
                PropertyReleaseMode.Process;

        SharedPropertyGroupManager spm =
                new SharedPropertyGroupManager();
        group = spm.CreatePropertyGroup("SPM Demo",
                                        ref lockMode,
                                        ref releaseMode,
                                        out existed);
    }
```

Unique Group Names

If you need a unique name for a group (if you don't want to share this group among multiple components), you can use a GUID for the name. You can create a GUID by calling the static method Guid.NewGuid.

Shared Property Group

The method `CreatePropertyGroup` returns a `SharedPropertyGroup` object. You can use the shared property group to create new properties and to access existing properties. Table 9-2 lists the methods of this class.

Table 9-2   SharedPropertyGroup Class

SharedPropertyGroup Members	Description
CreateProperty Property	The methods `CreateProperty` and `Property` create or return a shared property. With both methods, a property name is used to access the shared property.
CreatePropertyByPosition PropertyByPosition	These methods are similar to `CreateProperty` and `Property`; the difference is that instead of using a property name, an index is used to access the property by its position within the property group.

Shared Property

The methods of the `SharedPropertyGroup` return an object of type `SharedProperty`, which has just one important property, `Value`, enabling you to get and set values. The types that you can use are restricted, and although the type is defined as an object, you can only pass simple data types such as numbers and strings. If you create a struct, as is done in the example in Listing 9-5 with the struct `AttendeeInfo`, the struct may not contain strings or other reference types.

Listing 9-5   AttendeeInfo Structure

```
[Serializable]
public struct AttendeeInfo
{
    public int CurrentAttendeeCount;
    public int MaxAttendees;
}
```

The code in Listing 9-6 demonstrates using the `SharedPropertyGroup` and `SharedProperty` classes. With the method `SetAttendeeInfo`, either a new shared property is created or an existing property is returned by calling the method `CreateProperty`. With the returned object of type `SharedProperty`, the `Value` property is used to set the `AttendeeInfo` that was passed with the method.

With the method `GetAttendeeInfo`, just an existing property is accessed by calling the method `Property`. `Property` returns a `SharedProperty` object, where the `Value` property is used to get the `AttendeeInfo` object back.

Listing 9-6   Using a Shared Property

```
public void SetAttendeeInfo(string courseNumber,
    AttendeeInfo attendeeInfo)
{
   bool exists;
   SharedProperty courseInformation =
        group.CreateProperty(courseNumber, out exists);

   courseInformation.Value = attendeeInfo;
}

public AttendeeInfo GetAttendeeInfo(string courseNumber)
{
   SharedProperty courseInformation =
        group.Property(courseNumber);
   return (AttendeeInfo)courseInformation.Value;
}
```

Client Application

With the client application, one instance of the object `Samples.SPM.SPMDemo` is created to call the method `SetAttendeeInfo` and pass the current attendee count of the course MS-2524 (see Listing 9-7). A second instance of the class `Samples.SPM.SPMDemo` is used to read the values again.

Listing 9-7   Client Application

```
[STAThread]
static void Main(string[] args)
{
   Samples.SPM.AttendeeInfo info;
   info.MaxAttendees = 12;
   info.CurrentAttendeeCount = 8;

   Samples.SPM.SPMDemo obj1 = new Samples.SPM.SPMDemo();
```

```
obj1.SetAttendeeInfo("MS-2524", info);
obj1.Dispose();

Samples.SPM.SPMDemo obj2 = new Samples.SPM.SPMDemo();
info = obj2.GetAttendeeInfo("MS-2524");
Console.WriteLine("MS-2524: Max: {0}, Current: {1}",
     info.MaxAttendees, info.CurrentAttendeeCount);
obj2.Dispose();
}
```

SPM State Characteristics

Factors to consider when determining whether to store state within the SPM include the following:

- State stored within SPM is not durable.

- With simple data types, not a lot of overhead is involved. Storage of complex data types is not supported. The SPM is not designed for a big, scalable solution.

- The state stored within SPM is lost either as soon as the Enterprise Services application is restarted (if the property release mode is set to Process), or if the last reference to it is released (with the property release mode set to Standard).

- SPM state is bound to a single Enterprise Services application; it cannot be accessed from a different application that might be invoked from within the same activity. However, it is possible to share SPM state with different objects in the same application.

- Similar to stateful components, the size is limited within the memory boundaries of a process.

> **TIP: Reality Check: Shared Property Manager**
>
> You should only use the Shared Property Manager to store simple data types. Also, do not use shared properties when high performance is needed. The Shared Property Manager uses a single-threaded apartment, and this can lead to performance problems. With single-threaded apartments and VARIANTs, COM origins cannot be denied with SPM.

ASP.NET State Management

As you learned in Chapter 5, "Networking," you can use ASP.NET Web services to access Enterprise Services applications. ASP.NET offers some great state management technologies that can be accessed directly from serviced components if the Enterprise Services application is configured as a library application. If the serviced component application is configured as a server application, the state can be used to pass the information from the state with the parameters of the methods.

This section covers ASP.NET state management, which is a great way to store state with enterprise applications. If you use ASP.NET for state management, the serviced components can be stateless, and the state information from ASP.NET can be passed to the serviced components as needed.

ASP.NET enables you to store state in the following ways:

- **Session**—With the ASP.NET session state, you can store data that is bound to a client session. The session has a timeout that deactivates the session state after the client is inactive for 20^5 minutes.

- **Application**—Application state is shared among all clients accessing the service. Because of the better features of the cache, cache state should be preferred to the application state.

  The application state is represented in the class `HttpApplicationState`.

- **Cache**—Similar to application state, with the cache the state is shared among all clients accessing the service. As opposed to the application state, the cache can be flexibly configured when it should be deactivated.

  The cache is managed by the class `Cache`.

Application State

Because the features of the cache state surpass (and therefore outdate) the application state, the application state is not discussed in detail in this book. Instead of using the application state, you can always use the cache, which is more flexible. `HttpApplicationState` exists for compatibility with old applications.

Session

The ASP.NET session state is stored in memory, so it can be accessed faster than file-based or database-based state. If you have data that is needed across serviced component method calls, you can put the data into the session.

The class that manages session state is `HttpSessionState` in the namespace `System.Web.SessionState`.

With Web services, you can enable sessions with the named property `Enable-Session` of the attribute class `WebMethodAttribute`, as shown in Listing 9-8. The method `GetCourseMapForAttendee` receives an `Attendee` object from the client to return the courses where the attendee registered. The courses of the attendee are stored in a session variable so that it is not always necessary to query the database for these courses.

`Session` is a property of the `WebService` class that is the base class of `Course-Service`. The `Session` property returns an `HttpSessionState` object that implements an indexer to read and write session variables.

If reading the session value for the item `CourseMap` returns `null`, the course map is read with the help of the `AttendeeControl` class. After the course map is read, it is stored inside the session, using `CourseMap` as the item index.

The indexer of the `HttpSessionState` class always returns an object, so the return value must be cast to the type that was stored inside the session.

Listing 9-8   Web Service Method with Sessions

```
[WebService(Namespace=
    "http://christiannagel.com/2005/CourseManagement")]
public class CourseService : System.Web.Services.WebService
{

    [WebMethod(EnableSession=true)]
    [return: XmlArray("CourseMap")]
    [return: XmlArrayItem("Course")]
    public Course[] GetCourseMapForAttendee(Attendee attendee)
    {
        Course[] courseMap = null;

        object o = Session["CourseMap"];
        if (o == null)
```

```
        {
            AttendeeControl control = new AttendeeControl();
            courseMap = control.GetCourses(attendee);
            Session["CourseMap"] = courseMap;
        }
        else
        {
            courseMap = (Course[])o;
        }
        return courseMap;
    }
}
```

Sessions with ASP.NET use server resources for keeping the session variables in memory; for identification of the client session, a session cookie is used. The HTTP protocol is stateless, so to identify the client that is associated with a session, cookies are sent to the client. The client receives the session cookie with the first request of the Web service, and must pass it with every following request that is sent to the Web service.

Passing cookies to the Web service is supported by the SoapHttpClient-Protocol class, which is the base class of the proxy that is used by the client application. Listing 9-9 shows how cookies can be returned and passed with the Web service proxy. ClientSample.Courses.CourseService is the proxy class that is created by the wsdl.exe[6] utility. If cookies are used with the Web service, as is the case in the example here, a CookieContainer object must be assigned to the Cookie-Container property. With a cookie container assigned, the cookie that is received with the GetCourseMapForAttendee method is remembered in the container and passed again to the Web service with the next method.

Listing 9-9   Client Application Using Cookies for the Session

```
static void Main(string[] args)
{
    Attendee attendee = new Attendee();
    attendee.FirstName = "Arnold";
    attendee.LastName = "Schwarzenegger";

    CourseClient.localhost.Service1 ws = new
            CourseClient.localhost.Service1();
    ws.CookieContainer = new System.Net.CookieContainer();
```

```
Course[] courses = ws.GetCourseMapForAttendee(attendee);

// get the cookies to use them again for the next
// web service method
System.Net.CookieContainer cookies = ws.CookieContainer;

//...
}
```

The session gets automatically deactivated after a timeout. By default, the session is deactivated when the client is inactive for 20 minutes, although you can change the session timeout value in the Web configuration file web.config. The session is configured with the <sessionState> element, as shown in Listing 9-10. The timeout attribute defines the session timeout in minutes. Other than configuring the timeout, you can also configure a session state server, if you are using a Web farm, so that the session state is passed to a session state server or stored inside the database.

Listing 9-10 Session Configuration

```
<sessionState
  mode="InProc"
  stateConnectionString="tcpip=127.0.0.1:42424"
  sqlConnectionString=
    "data source=127.0.0.1;Trusted_Connection=yes"
  cookieless="false"
  timeout="20"
/>
```

Session State in a Web Service Farm

If you are using session state in a Web service farm, the session data must be available to all Web servers. This can be done either by storing the session data in a session state server or by storing the session data in the database.

Part of the ASP.NET runtime is the Windows service ASP.NET state service. This service must be started on one host, and the configuration files of all Web services must reference this service. You can do this by setting the mode attribute (see Listing 9-6) to StateServer and by setting the stateConnectionString to the host of the service.

If you use a database for the session state (this has the advantage that with a database cluster there is no single point of failure), the mode attribute must be set to `SQLServer`, and the `sqlConnectionString` must reference the database. You can create the database by starting the scripts `InstallPersistSqlState.sql` that you can find in the .NET Framework runtime directory <windir>/Microsoft.NET/Framework/<version>.

When the session timeout occurs, the `Session_End` event is raised in the `global.asax` file. In this event procedure, you can write the session state to a permanent store to read it again when the session is started in the `Session_Start` method. The methods are shown in Listing 9-11.

Listing 9-11 Session Start and End Events

```
protected void Session_Start(Object sender, EventArgs e)
{

}

protected void Session_End(Object sender, EventArgs e)
{

}
```

Cache

You can use the ASP.NET cache to store session-independent data in memory. The cache is represented by the class `System.Web.Caching.Cache` class, and is flexible in the way the cache can be invalidated. The dependencies that can be configured with the cache are shown in Table 9-3.

How the cache can be used is shown in Listing 9-12. The Web service method `GetCategories` returns an array of course categories, which are either read from the cache or from a file that is read by the method `ReadCategoriesFromFile`.

Table 9-3   Cache Dependencies[7]

Cache Dependencies	Description
Absolute expiration	With the absolute expiration, you can set a `DateTime` when the cache should be invalidated.
Sliding expiration	Instead of setting an absolute time span, you can define a sliding time when the cache should be invalidated, with a `TimeSpan` value. If the sliding expiration is set, the absolute expiration must be set to `DateTime.MaxValue`. Conversely, if the absolute expiration is set, the sliding expiration must be set to `TimeSpan.Zero`.
Priority	The cache can also be invalidated if the memory is low. If the memory is low, the ASP.NET runtime removes items from the cache depending on their priority setting. Cache objects with lower priorities are removed before cache objects with higher priorities. The priority is set with a value of the enumeration `CacheItemPriority`.
Files	With the cache, you can make a direct dependency on files. The cache automatically gets invalidated when a file changes that is defined with the dependencies. If the state of the cache is read from a file, you can automatically update the cache when the file changes.
Variables	You can also specify variables that are responsible for the invalidation of the cache. As soon as a value of the defined variables changes, the cache is invalidated.

You can access the cache by calling the static property `Current` from the `HttpContext` class. `HttpContext.Current` returns an `HttpContext` instance representing the current HTTP request, and the `HttpContext` class offers the property `Cache` to return a `Cache` object. When using this `Cache` object, a null value is returned if the cache is not filled for the key or the data that is stored with the key.

If the data is not available in the cache, the `Categories` object is inserted into the cache by calling the `Insert` method. The first two parameters of the `Insert` method are the key name and the object that is to be stored in the cache. The third parameter defines a `CacheDependency` object that defines dependency to a file or to variables— in this example, there is no file of variable dependency. Here the cache is just invalidated after a 30-minute timeout, which is defined with `TimeSpan.FromMinutes(30)`.

Listing 9-12   Using the Cache

```
[WebMethod()]
[return: XmlArray("CategoryList")]
[return: XmlArrayItem("Category")]
public Category[] GetCategories()
{
    Category[] categories = null;
    Cache cache = HttpContext.Current.Cache;
    object oCategories = cache["Categories"];
    if (oCategories == null)
    {
        categories = ReadCategoriesFromFile();
        cache.Insert("Categories", categories,
                null, DateTime.MaxValue,
                TimeSpan.FromMinutes(30),
                CacheItemPriority.Normal);
    }
    else
    {
        categories = (Category[])oCategories;
    }
    return categories;
}
```

Accessing ASP.NET State from Within Serviced Components

If the Enterprise Services application is configured as a library application and running on the same host as the Web service, you can access the HTTP context that includes the session and cache directly from the serviced components.

All you must do is reference the assembly `System.Web`, import the namespaces `System.Web` and `System.Web.Caching`, and then you can access the ASP.NET session with the `HttpContext` class, as shown in Listing 9-13. The method `CacheDemo` uses the cache that was created in the Web service; the method `SessionDemo` accesses the session from the Web service.

Listing 9-13   Accessing ASP.NET Cache from the Serviced Component

```
public class StateDemoComponent : ServicedComponent
{
    public void CacheDemo()
```

```
    {
        Cache cache = HttpContext.Current.Cache;
        Categories[] categories =
            (Categories[])cache["Categories"];

        // use the categories
    }

    public void SessionDemo()
    {
        HttpSessionState session = HttpContext.Current.Session;
        AttendeeInfo attendeeInfo =
            (HttpSessionState)session["AttendeeInfo"];

        // use the attendee information
    }
}
```

ASP.NET State Characteristics

With regard to the ASP.NET state characteristics, the different options described earlier must be compared to the session and cache states:

- The ASP.NET state is *not* durable. Session state can survive server restarts if the session is configured to be stored inside the database. The cache is only in-memory data.

- Accessing the cache is very fast, because it is memory based. With the session state, performance differs depending on whether it is configured in-process (which is fastest), with a session-state server, or with the database (the slowest variation).

- The lifetime of the session depends on a session timeout; for the cache, however, you can configure many different lifetime options. The cache can be dependent on variables, files, or just on a time value.

- The session state is bound to a client session, whereas the cache is globally available. If you use the cache with specific client sessions only, you can make its name unique.

- The size of the state is restricted to the size of the virtual memory.

Client State Management

Another option for state is keeping the state on the client and passing it with every method call to the serviced component. You can pass state from the client to the server without defining additional parameters on the method calls. However, you should do so only if the state is not directly related to the method call (for example, logon information). Logon information might be needed in the actions of a method, but it is not directly related to the values of the parameters that are passed.

This section covers two different techniques for passing state. The one that is used depends on the technology used to access the serviced components. If you are using Web services as a façade for the serviced components, you can use SOAP headers to pass information in addition to the method parameters. If you are using .NET remoting to access the serviced components, you can pass remoting call contexts automatically with the method call.

SOAP Headers

With Web services, SOAP requests are sent from the client to the server, and back from the server to the client. A SOAP request is packaged as part of the HTTP request, the headers of which include cookies that are used with the ASP.NET session. The SOAP request that is inside the HTTP package can be described as a SOAP envelope that consists of a SOAP header and a SOAP body, as shown in Figure 9-3.

The SOAP body includes the method calls with the parameters that are passed across the network. The SOAP header is optional, and can include other information that flows with the SOAP request and response messages.

The Web services specifications that extend SOAP requests with security, referral, routing, transactions, and so on make use of the SOAP header to pass the extended information.

With ASP.NET Web services, you can extend the SOAP protocol with a SOAP header. Information to be put into the header is defined with a class that derives from the base class `SoapHeader`, defined within the namespace `System.Web.Services.Protocols`. Listing 9-14 shows the class `AuthenticationInfo` that defines the strings `Username` and `Password` that are sent with the SOAP header.

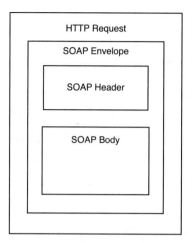

Figure 9-3   SOAP request using HTTP.

With the Web service class, the field authenticationInfo is declared of type AuthenticationInfo. This field must be declared public to be used with the [SoapHeader] attribute. The Web service method UseAuthenticatedUser has the attribute [SoapHeader] with the name of the public field authenticationInfo assigned. Inside the method, username and password can be accessed by querying the values from the field.

Listing 9-14   Defining a Custom SOAP Header

```
public class AuthenticationInfo : SoapHeader
{
   public string Username;
   public string Password;
}

[WebService(Namespace=
      "http://christiannagel.com/2005/CourseManagement")]
public class CourseService : System.Web.Services.WebService
{
   public AuthenticationInfo authenticationInfo;

   [WebMethod]
   [SoapHeader("authenticationInfo")]
```

```
public void UseAuthenticatedUser()
{
    string username = authenticationInfo.Username;
    string password = authenticationInfo.Password;
    //...
}
}
```

How the SOAP header is encompassed in the SOAP request is shown in Listing 9-15. The SOAP envelope with the element `<soap:Envelope>` follows the HTTP header. The `<soap:Envelope>` includes a `<soap:Header>` with the element `<authenticationInfo>` that was specified in Listing 9-14.

Listing 9-15   SOAP Request Passing a SOAP Header

```
POST /StateDemo/Service1.asmx HTTP/1.1
Host: localhost
Content-Type: text/xml; charset=utf-8
Content-Length: length
SOAPAction: "http://christiannagel.com/2005/CourseManagement/DemoAuthenticate-
dUser"

<?xml version="1.0" encoding="utf-8"?>
<soap:Envelope xmlns:xsi="http://www.w3.org/2001/XMLSchema-instance"
xmlns:xsd="http://www.w3.org/2001/XMLSchema" xmlns:soap="http://schemas.xml-
soap.org/soap/envelope/">
  <soap:Header>
    <AuthenticationInfo
        xmlns="http://christiannagel.com/2005/CourseManagement">
      <Username>string</Username>
      <Password>string</Password>
    </AuthenticationInfo>
  </soap:Header>
  <soap:Body>
    <DemoAuthenticatedUser xmlns="http://christiannagel.com/2005/CourseManage-
ment" />
  </soap:Body>
</soap:Envelope>
```

The client application passing the SOAP header to the service is shown in Listing 9-16. An object of the type `AuthenticationInfo` that was defined with the Web service can be created to set the fields `Username` and `Password`. The proxy class that is created for the client application has one additional property, `Authentication-InfoValue`, that is named after the SOAP header. This property enables you to set an

`AuthenticationInfo` object that will be passed with the method `DemoAuthenticateUser` to the Web service.

Listing 9-16   Client Application Passing a Custom SOAP Header

```
CourseService ws = new CourseService();

AuthenticationInfo authenticationInfo =
        new AuthenticationInfo();
authenticationInfo.Username = textUsername.Text;
authenticationInfo.Password = textPassword.Text;

ws.AuthenticationInfoValue = authenticationInfo;
ws.DemoAuthenticateUser();
```

.NET Remoting Call Contexts

If you are using .NET remoting[8] to access the serviced component, you can pass a hidden value with the remote method. In the next example, a username/password pair is passed to the service in a similar way to the Web service example shown previously.

The data that should be passed using a call context must be put into a class that implements the interface `ILogicalThreadAffinative`, as defined in the assembly `System.Runtime.Remoting` within the namespace `System.Runtime.Remoting.Messaging`. Listing 9-17 shows the class `UserInfo` that implements the interface. The interface does not define any methods; it just marks the class that it should be passed with the call context across application domains. Objects that do not implement the interface `ILogicalThreadAffinative` are not propagated across remoting boundaries with a call context. The class `UserInfo` also must be marked with the `[Serializable]` attribute; otherwise, it will not be serialized by the remoting formatter.

Listing 9-17   Serializable Call Context Data

```
[Serializable]
public class UserInfo : ILogicalThreadAffinative
{
    private string username;
    private string password;
```

```
public string Username
{
   get
   {
      return username;
   }
   set
   {
      username = value;
   }
}

public string Password
{
   get
   {
      return password;
   }
   set
   {
      password = value;
   }
}
}
```

Within the method of the serviced component, the call context can be accessed by using the `CallContext` class, as shown in Listing 9-18. The method `GetData` requires a string to identify the value that is passed with the call context, and returns the call context data. The returned object must be cast to the `UserInfo` class that was defined in Listing 9-17.

Listing 9-18 Accessing the Call Context in the Serviced Component

```
public void CallContextDemo()
{
   UserInfo userInfo =
      (UserInfo)CallContext.GetData("authenticationInfo");

   //... Use the user information

}
```

Listing 9-19 shows the assembly attributes that must be defined for the serviced components to be accessed by .NET remoting. With the attribute Application-

ActivationAttribute, the named parameter SoapVRoot must be set, which defines the name of the virtual directory of the ASP.NET Web site that acts as a host for the serviced components.

Listing 9-19   Assembly Attributes for .NET Remoting Access

```
[assembly: ApplicationName("CourseManagement")]
[assembly: ApplicationActivation(ActivationOption.Server,
    SoapVRoot="CallContextDemo")]
[assembly: ApplicationAccessControl(false)]
```

After registering the Enterprise Services application using the command-line utility regsvcs.exe, and after installing the assembly into the global assembly cache, you must manually change the configuration file that was automatically generated by the registration process. You must do so to allow the security to pass the call context data from the client to the server.

Listing 9-20 shows the configuration file web.config that you can find in the directory <windir>system32\com\SOAPVRoots\CallContextDemo. The major part of the configuration file is generated automatically, but starting with .NET 1.1, the call context may not be passed across the channels with the default configuration. For the server providers that are used with the serviced components (by default the HTTP channel has the SOAP formatter associated with it), you must set the attribute typeFilterLevel to the value Full. The providers are used with a channel, so you must add the <channels>, <channel>, <serverProviders>, and <provider> elements accordingly.

Listing 9-20   Web.config File to Allow Passing the Call Context

```
<?xml version="1.0" encoding="utf-8"?>
<configuration>
  <system.runtime.remoting>
    <application>
      <service>
        <wellknown mode="SingleCall"
            type="Samples.Courses.StateDemo, Samples.Courses,
            Version=1.0.1478.40545, Culture=neutral,
            PublicKeyToken=e151efac3427f14b"
            objectUri="Samples.Courses.StateDemo.soap" />
      </service>
      <channels>
```

```
        <channel ref="http">
          <serverProviders>
            <provider ref="wsdl" />
            <provider ref="soap" typeFilterLevel="Full" />
          </serverProviders>
        </channel>
      </channels>
    </application>
  </system.runtime.remoting>
</configuration>
```

After you have configured all of these settings, the client application can create a channel and register the remote object with the .NET remoting runtime to call the method of the serviced component. The call context can be passed by calling the `SetData` method of the `CallContext` class, as shown in Listing 9-21. The first parameter of the method defines the name of the call context data. The call context is passed automatically with the call to the `CallContextDemo` method.

Listing 9-21 Passing the Call Context with the Client Application

```
        HttpChannel channel = new HttpChannel();
        ChannelServices.RegisterChannel(channel);
        RemotingConfiguration.RegisterWellKnownClientType(
                typeof(StateDemo),
                "http://localhost:80/CallContextDemo/" +
                "Samples.Courses.StateDemo.soap");

        StateDemo obj = new StateDemo();
        UserInfo userInfo = new UserInfo();
        userInfo.Username = textUsername.Text;
        userInfo.Password = textPassword.Text;
        CallContext.SetData("authenticationInfo", userInfo);
        obj.CallContextDemo();
        obj.Dispose();
```

Summary

This chapter covered the importance of state management with a distributed solution. Enterprise Services offers a mechanism called Shared Property Manager to deal with state, although you can also put state in the client application and in a Web service, if the Web service is a façade for accessing the serviced components.

You can also put state into the database, into files, or into Active Directory. Active Directory has a specific requirement that the information put into it should mainly be used for read activities, but should not be changed often.

With ASP.NET Web services, you can make use of the features of the ASP.NET runtime to put state into the session or the cache. This chapter also examined accessing the ASP.NET state from within serviced components.

One option not to forget is keeping state in the client application. In this scenario, not only do you have the option to pass this data with arguments of the serviced component methods, but you can also use the SOAP header or the .NET remoting call context.

These topics show that with the design of the solution, you must analyze the data according to durability, volatility, speed, lifetime, affinity, and size requirements so that you can decide where to put the state.

1 Just in time activation is shown in Chapter 2, "Object Activation and Contexts."

2 Accessing serviced components with .NET remoting is discussed in Chapter 5, "Networking."

3 Synchronization is discussed in Chapter 3, "Concurrency."

4 *Professional C#*, 3rd Edition, has a chapter dedicated to the Active Directory (Chapter 24).

5 This is the default timeout value, but it can be configured to a different value.

6 `Wsdl.exe` uses the WSDL documentation of the Web service to create a proxy client class. `Wsdl.exe` is used in Chapter 5.

7 .NET 2.0 and SQL Server also enable you to automatically invalidate the cache when a value in the database changes. With .NET 1.1, such a behavior must be done manually (for example, by creating a trigger in the database).

8 Using .NET remoting with serviced components is discussed in Chapter 5.

10

Queued Components

THE METHOD CALLS USED SO FAR always accessed the serviced component synchronously. Synchronous communication often results in bottlenecks, because when a synchronous method is called, the caller must wait until the method is finished. .NET offers various ways[1] to do asynchronous programming. With asynchronous programming, the method is called by a worker thread, while the calling thread may move its attention to some other work. If you are using asynchronous method calls, both the client and the server must still be active concurrently. This requirement is in contrast to when you are using messaging services. With messaging services, you can do asynchronous calls in a disconnected environment, where the client and the server can have independent lifetimes. The queued components technology is an abstraction of message queuing, which is one of the services offered by Enterprise Services.

This chapter examines the architecture and programming of queued components. Specifically, this chapter covers the following topics:

- Queued components overview
- Product versions
- Message queuing features
- Creating a queued component
- Error handling
- Transactional queues
- Returning data

Overview

Before learning about queued components, you need to understand the foundation of queued components: message queuing. With message queuing, there is a sending and a receiving application, similar to a client and a server implementation as used in all the earlier chapters. As you can see in Figure 10-1, the sender creates messages and puts them into a queue; the receiver gets messages from the queue to read them.

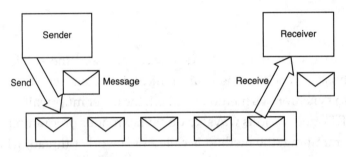

Figure 10-1 Message queuing.

Queued components add one abstraction layer to the message queuing architecture. The abstraction means that with queued components, you no longer have to create messages that are put into the queue; you can invoke method calls of a component instead. You can see a queued components scenario in Figure 10-2. The client application invokes methods in a recorder component. The recorder component looks like the serviced component class as it implements the same interface; however, the method call is converted into a message and put into the message queue instead. On the server side, a listener reads the message from the queue, converts the message into a method call, and uses a player to invoke the method with the serviced component.

In which useful solutions can queued components play an important role?

One scenario is in a completely disconnected environment with a laptop system, as shown in Figure 10-3. A salesperson can be at the customer's site creating an order by entering the order data into the application. If the salesperson commits the order at the customer's site, there is no way that the application can send the order to the server without creating a network connection, perhaps via a mobile phone.

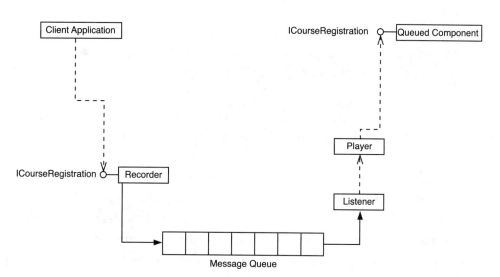

Figure 10-2   Queued components.

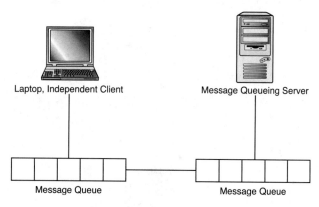

Figure 10-3   Disconnected environment with message queuing.

However, if message queuing is used for the ordering application, the order is finished when the order is sent to the message queue on the laptop system.

When the salesperson is back at the company building and as soon as the laptop is connected to the network, the order message is sent to the target message queue. This transfer happens without interaction of the ordering application, which doesn't need to be running at all.

> **NOTE:** For client systems in a disconnected environment, an independent client is needed. The different types of message queuing products are discussed in the next section.

Message queuing also proves useful if the client and the server are running on the same network. With message queuing, you can distribute the load of the server over time. Consider a book-ordering system in which most orders happen at a specific time—perhaps late in the day when people get home from work and connect to their home networks. During that period of time, the load of the server is high, whereas at night the server is idle. For such a scenario, you could buy a server that survives the highest loads, or you could try to flatten the load over time, something that is easy when using message queuing. Figure 10-4 shows a scenario in which browser clients are accessing a Web site to order books. The Web site uses a message queuing client to send the book orders as messages to the message queue. The message queuing server reads the messages from the message queue as the load allows it and writes the book orders to the database.

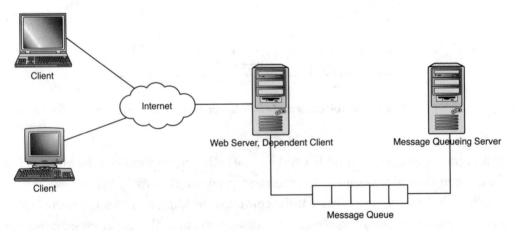

Figure 10-4 Message queuing on the server side.

> **TIP: Reality Check: Message Queuing in a Connected Environment**
>
> In the described scenario, message queuing not only helps to flatten the load on the database server, but it also helps to give faster responses to the client. Message queuing also proves useful in such a scenario when the database server is not fully loaded, because the client will have a faster response when the order is written just to the message queue, instead of being written to the database.

Product Versions

Message queuing is part of the operating system; however, it is not installed by default during Windows setup. You must explicitly select Message Queuing in the Windows Component list of Add Remove Programs in the Control Panel. With the message queuing products, you must differentiate between a client and a server product, as discussed next. You must also consider the message queuing versions that existed before Windows XP and Windows Server 2003, as follows:

- Message Queuing 1.0 (or MSMQ) is part of the Windows NT 4.0 option pack. This version requires SQL Server, where the names of the queues are stored.

- Message Queuing 2.0 is part of Windows 2000. Instead of using SQL Server for the queue names, the queue names are now stored in Active Directory. Without Active Directory, it is only possible to operate message queuing in workgroup mode.

- Message Queuing 3.0 is the version that is delivered with Windows Server 2003 and Windows XP. This version is used in this chapter.

Message Queuing Server

The message queuing server is part of the Windows Server 2003 software distribution. Before installing a message queuing client, you must install a server. To install the server, select Add or Remove Programs, and click Add/Remove Windows Components. When installing the server, you can choose from the options shown in Figure 10-5.

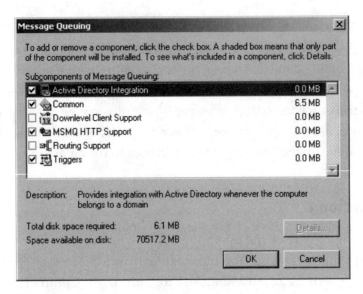

Figure 10-5   Message queuing options.

Your message queuing options include Active Directory Integration, Downlevel Client Support, MSMQ HTTP Support, Routing Support, and Triggers, as follows:

- **Active Directory Integration**—The Active Directory Integration is an optional component. As discussed earlier, without Active Directory, message queuing can only operate in workgroup mode.

- **Downlevel Client Support**—If you have older clients than Windows XP that need to access the message queuing server, you can choose the Downlevel Client Support option.

- **MSMQ HTTP Support**—Message queues not only communicate by using the DCOM protocol; they can also communicate via HTTP.

- **Routing Support**—If the message queuing server should act as an intermediate router that forwards messages from one queue to another, you can choose the Routing Support option.

- **Triggers**—With a trigger, you can configure an application or serviced component that should be invoked when a new message arrives.

Workgroup Mode

Message Queuing 1.0 requires SQL Server to store the queue names. With Message Queuing 2.0, SQL Server is no longer required; instead, queue names are stored in Active Directory. If you do not have Active Directory available, you can operate the message queues in a workgroup mode. With a workgroup mode, you cannot use public names to access the queues, and it is not possible to configure security to allow only specific users to read or write messages.

Message Queuing Client

After installing a message queuing server, you can install the client. The message queuing client is not only available with Windows XP, but also with operating systems such as Windows 98 and Windows CE.

With the client, you must differentiate between two different product installations: the independent and the dependent client. You can select one of the two options during installation of the client:

- **Independent client**—An independent client has its own message store to keep the messages on the local disk before they can be transmitted to the target queue. With a laptop scenario as discussed earlier, you must use an independent client. The messages are stored locally on the disk, and if the network is available again, the messages can be transferred to the server. Because the messages are stored on the disk, messages are not lost if the machine is shut down.

- **Dependent client**—A dependent client always needs a message queuing server to connect to, because a dependent client does not have its own message store. You cannot use a dependent client in a disconnected environment.

Message Queuing Features

From the first part of this chapter, you have gained an overview of message queuing. Although queued components are an abstraction of message queuing, you need to know the concepts behind message queuing itself. To use all the features of queued components, you must understand the message queuing terms and their functionality.

Message Queues

Public and private queues are normally used to send and to receive messages, but there are a lot more queue types available, for many different purposes, including the following:

- A **public queue** is published in Active Directory. Information about these queues is replicated across an Active Directory domain. You can use Active Directory browse and search features to get information about these queues. You can access a public queue without knowing the name of the computer on which it is placed. You can also move such a queue from one system to another without the client knowing it. With a workgroup mode setup, it is not possible to create public queues.

- **Private queues** are not published in Active Directory. These queues can be accessed only by knowing the full path name of the queue. In a workgroup mode, private queues are used to send and to receive messages.

- If you want to keep all messages that are sent or received, you can configure a **journal queue**. You can enable journaling with public or private queues, which automatically create a journal queue.

  With journaling of messages, you must differentiate between source and target journaling. Source journaling means that a journal is kept when the message is sent, whereas target journaling means that a journal is kept when the message is received. You can turn on source journaling with properties of the message to be sent, whereas you configure target journaling with the properties of the message queue.

- If the message does not arrive in the target queue before a specified timeout is reached, the message is stored in a **dead-letter queue**. You can check the dead-letter queue for messages that did not arrive.

  For transactional messages that did not arrive, there is a separate **transactional dead-letter queue**.

- If the message did not arrive, you will get information in the dead-letter queue. However, if the message arrived but you still need some information, you can use acknowledgment messages. Acknowledgment messages are stored in **administration queues**. The sender can specify an administration queue from which it receives notifications as to whether the message was sent successfully or not.

- If you need more than a simple acknowledgment (for example, some return value is needed when a message is sent), you can use a **response queue**. Similar to acknowledgment messages, when sending a message, you can specify a response queue where the receiver of the message should send back a message with some return information.

- To test messages on their route (if you are using the router functionality with a message queue server configuration), you can track messages with the **report queue**.

- **System queues** are private queues that are used by the message queuing system. These queues are used for administrative messages, storing of notification messages, and to guarantee the correct order of transactional messages.

Table 10-1 lists the syntax of queue names depending on the type of the queue.

Table 10-1   Syntax of Queue Names

Queue Type	Syntax
Public queue	ComputerName\QueueName
Private queue	ComputerName\Private$\QueueName
Journal queue	ComputerName\QueueName\Journal$
Machine journal queue	ComputerName\Journal$
Machine dead-letter queue	ComputerName\DeadLetter$
Machine transactional dead-letter queue	ComputerName\XactDeadLetter$

Messages

Messages are sent into message queues and have characteristics of message type, message priority, and delivery mode.

Types

If methods are invoked with queued components, **normal messages** are sent. If the sending application needs information about whether the message was sent or received successfully, an **acknowledge message** is sent. Acknowledge messages can be read from acknowledgment queues. The third message type is a **report message**, which is sent automatically if tracing is turned on. Report messages are sent into report queues.

Priorities

If you are not using transactional queues, you can define a priority with a message. The priority defines the read order of the messages, where messages with higher priorities are read first.

You can define a priority in the range 0 through 7. The default priority value is 3.

With transactional queues, a priority cannot be used, because the transaction guarantees the order of messages.

Delivery

Messages can be sent with an **express** or **recoverable** delivery mode.

With **express delivery**, messages are only stored in memory and, as the name suggests, express delivery is the fastest way to send messages. You cannot use express messages with a disconnected scenario because the client and the server can have different lifetimes. Express mode messages are lost when the system is rebooted.

Recoverable messages use the file system to store messages. For a scenario such as the disconnected laptop one discussed previously, the delivery mode to use is recoverable messages. The directory where the recoverable messages are stored is <windir>\system32\msmq\storage.

Administration Tools

Various tools enable you to administer message queues. With Windows Server 2003 admin tools, you can configure message queues and view and delete messages. The following subsections show you how to configure queues, how to configure access control to queues, and how to manage messages with the admin tools.

Configure Queues

To configure message queues, you can use the Active Directory Users and Computers[2] tool. To see the message queues with this tool, you must turn on these options in the View menu: Users, Groups, and Computers as Containers, and Advanced Features. When these options are turned on, you can see the queues, as shown in Figure 10-6.

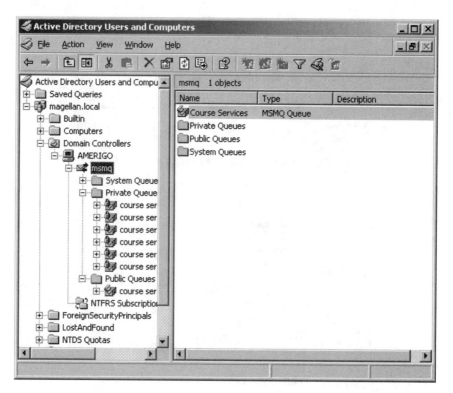

Figure 10-6   Active Directory Users and Computers.

Here you can see the messages in the queues and purge messages from queues if required.

When configuring the properties of a queue, you can configure a queue to enable journaling, to limit the size of the message and journal store, and to require authentication. The dialog box that you will see when configuring the properties of a queue is shown in Figure 10-7.

Another tool that enables you to configure queues and create new ones is the Computer Management[3] tool. If you open Services and Applications in the tree view, you will see the category Message Queuing. Below this entry, you can see the message queues and the messages inside the queues. You can also create new queues, as shown in Figure 10-8.

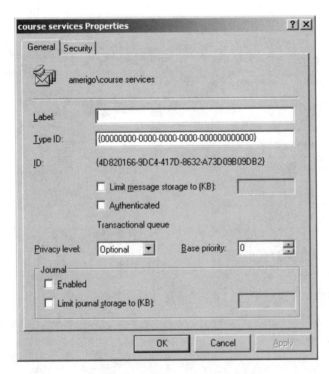

Figure 10-7   Configuring a message queue.

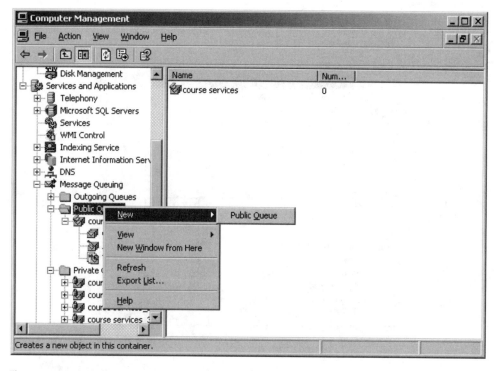

Figure 10-8   Creating new queues with the Computer Management tool.

Configure Access Control

If the option Authenticated is turned on (see Figure 10-7), you can use the options on the Security tab to configure access control to the message queue. You can define which users or user groups are allowed to send, to receive, and to peek at messages, and who is allowed to change queue properties (see Figure 10-9). The dialog box is very similar to that used to set the access control to normal files; you just have other permissions that can be set with queues.

Manage Messages

Messages can be managed with both Computer Management and Active Directory Users and Computers. As long as messages are not read from the queue, you can see the messages with the label (if one was set), priority, size, and message identifier, as

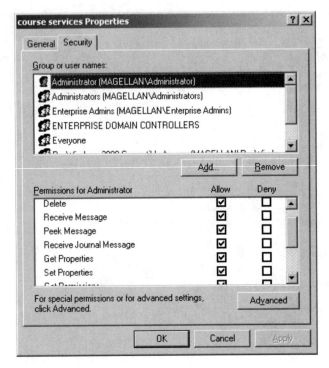

Figure 10-9   Access control configuration.

shown in Figure 10-10. If you turn on journaling (see the option in Figure 10-7), a copy of the messages is made, which enables you to read the copy after the message has been read from the normal queue.

If you select a single message to view its properties, you can see the time the message was sent and when it arrived, the sender of the message, and the first 240 bytes of the message.

Creating a Queued Component

Now you know quite a lot about message queuing, and you can start creating a queued component. To create an Enterprise Services application with queued components, you must do the following:

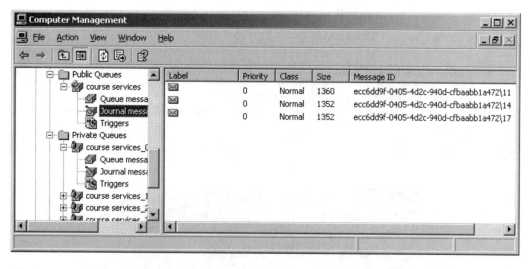

Figure 10-10   Manage messages.

- Apply assembly attributes for queued component applications.
- Define an interface that can be used with queued components.
- Register the Enterprise Services application as was already done in previous chapters.

Assembly Attributes

The Enterprise Services-specific assembly attributes are shown in Listing 10-1. You must set the [ApplicationActivation] attribute to ActivationOption.Server; the listener cannot run in the process of the client application. Specific to queued components, you must define the attribute [ApplicationQueuing]. Applying this attribute sets the Queued property after the application is configured, as shown in Figure 10-11, in the Component Services Explorer. With the optional property QueueListenerEnabled, you can specify whether a component should be auto-matically instantiated when a message arrives in the queue, so that the player can invoke the messages with the queued component. The listener reads messages from the queue and creates a component instance. The player then invokes the methods that are defined by the message with the component. If you have a high message load, you can specify a maximum number of concurrent players with the named property `MaxListenerThreads`.

Listing 10-1 Assembly Attributes

```
[assembly: ApplicationName("Course Services")]
[assembly: ApplicationActivation(ActivationOption.Server)]
[assembly: ApplicationAccessControl(false)]
[assembly: ApplicationQueuing(Enabled=true, QueueListenerEnabled=true)]
```

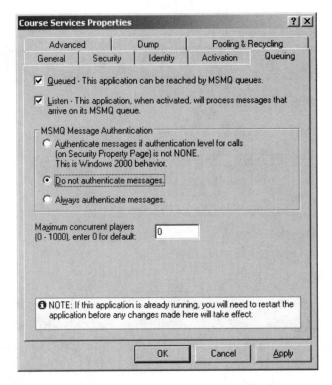

Figure 10-11   Application properties for queued applications.

Interface Definition

To define the methods that should be accessed by message queuing, you should declare an interface.[4] The attribute `[InterfaceQueuing]` defines that the methods of this interface should be accessible by the queued component functionality.

Interfaces that have this attribute applied show up in the Component Services Explorer with the property Queued selected, as shown in Figure 10-12.

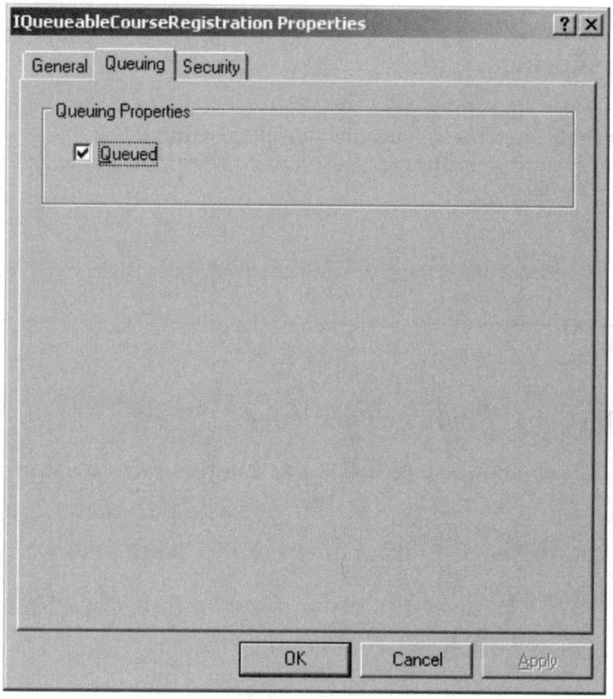

Figure 10-12   Queuing properties of the interface.

Listing 10-2 shows the interface `IQueueableCourseRegistration` with the attribute `[InterfaceQueuing]`. Methods of such an interface might only have input parameters, and they might not have a return type. The reason for this is that the component cannot send return values directly to the client when it is accessed in a disconnected form.

Another issue with queued interfaces that does not pop up immediately is that such interfaces only support simple data types. You cannot define a custom class as parameter of such an interface method. Applying the `[Serializable]` attribute with such classes does not help here, because queued components are based on COM features. As you will see when creating the client application, the recorder that writes the message into the message queue is a COM object, which allows serialization of COM components, but not .NET objects. A requirement for a component to be serialized to a message queue using queued components[5] is to implement the COM interface IPersistStream. Instead of implementing this interface, you can define a string parameter, as demonstrated here, and pass an XML representation of the component.

Listing 10-2   Queuable Interface IQueueableCourseRegistration

```
[InterfaceQueuing]
public interface IQueueableCourseRegistration
{
    void RegisterCourse(string xmlCourseRegistration);
}
```

NOTE: Queuable Interface Parameters

You cannot use custom classes as parameters with methods of queuable interfaces. Using XML strings as a parameter is a good way to avoid the need to implement the COM interface IPersistStream.

The CourseControl Class

The serviced component class has no specific requirements for queued components. Listing 10-3 shows the class CourseControl that implements the interface IQueueableCourseRegistration. In the method RegisterCourse, the received XML string is used to create a .NET object using the .NET XML serialization mechanism. With the class XmlSerializer, a .NET object can be serialized into and deserialized from an XML stream. The XmlSerializer class is defined in the namespace System.Xml.Serialization.

Next, this object is passed to the RegisterCourse method of the CourseDataControl serviced component. The CourseDataControl component writes the course registration information to the database.[6]

Listing 10-3   The CourseControl Class

```
public class CourseControl : ServicedComponent,
                             IQueueableCourseRegistration
{

    public void RegisterCourse(string xmlCourseRegistration)
    {
        StringReader reader =
            new StringReader(xmlCourseRegistration);
        XmlSerializer ser =
            new XmlSerializer(typeof(CourseRegistration));
        CourseRegistration courseRegistration =
            (CourseRegistration)ser.Deserialize(reader);
        reader.Close();

        CourseDataControl courseData = new CourseDataControl();
        courseData.RegisterCourse(courseRegistration);

    }
}
```

XML Serialization

With the .NET XML serialization mechanism, you can convert a .NET object into XML, and XML streams into .NET objects. The main class of this feature is the XmlSerializer. With the method Serialize, you can serialize a .NET object into an XML stream, where all public fields and properties are serialized. The method Deserialize uses an XML stream to return a .NET object.

With .NET runtime serialization, you must declare the [Serializable] attribute with the serializable classes, an attribute that is not used with XML serialization. Another big difference is that .NET runtime serialization serializes private fields, whereas XML serialization only accesses public fields and properties.

You can control XML serialization with attributes defined in the System.Xml.Serialization namespace. For example, the attribute

XmlElementAttribute enables you to define the name of an XML element, XmlAttributeAttribute allows definition of XML attributes, and XmlIgnoreAttribute ensures that the public property is not serialized within the XML.

Registration

After the .NET Enterprise Services application has been built, you can configure it in the same way as the applications in the previous chapters using the regsvcs.exe utility. What is new here is that with the registration, message queues are created automatically.

The message queues have the same name as the Enterprise Services application that is defined with the [ApplicationName] attribute. Opening the admin tools, you can see that one public queue, five private queues, and one dead-letter queue are created. Multiple queues are used for retry scenarios.

Multiple Queues for Sending Retries

If the message is received in the queue, a lot can still go wrong (for example, a problem invoking the method in the queued component). In such a case, automatic failover happens. At first, the message is sent to the public queue. If it cannot be delivered successfully, the message is moved to the first private queue. From this queue, the player tries again to invoke the methods according to the message. With each queue, multiple retries are done, before the message is moved to the next private queue. If the message cannot be delivered successfully at all, it is moved to the dead-letter queue.[7]

In addition to the registration of the serviced component application, you should install the assembly into the global assembly cache.

Client

When using queued components, the client application cannot just instantiate the serviced component as was done in the earlier chapters. Instead, the client application must use a moniker to instantiate a recorder. The recorder implements the same interface as the queued component to accept method calls that are converted to messages, and the messages are put into the message queue.

Monikers

A *moniker* is a term from COM technologies. The first moniker introduced was in the days of OLE.[8] For example, with a link to a document (for example, an Excel document), a file moniker is stored in the containing document (for example, a Word document). A moniker knows how to instantiate a COM object and how to initialize it with data. If a link to an Excel sheet is placed into a Word document, the created file moniker stores the CLSID of Excel and the filename of the Excel sheet. Instantiating the linked Excel sheet activates the moniker, which in turn activates the Excel application component by using the CLSID and initializes the component by passing the filename.

A moniker is a COM object that knows how to instantiate and initialize a COM object (or a .NET object).

Using .NET, you can use the method `BindToMoniker` of the `Marshal` class (in the namespace `System.Runtime.InteropServices`) to instantiate a moniker.

With queued components, the new moniker and the queue moniker are needed. The new moniker allows you to create a COM object by passing the progid or CLSID of the component. The new moniker calls the Windows API function `CoCreate-InstanceEx`[9] to instantiate the component. If the new moniker is prefixed with the queue moniker, the new moniker passes the CLSID of the component to the queue moniker.

The code here shows how the new moniker can be used to instantiate a .NET serviced component:

```
string progid = "Samples.Courses.Services.CourseControl";
ICourseRegistration qc =
        (ICourseRegistration)Marshal.BindToMoniker(
        "new:" + progid);
```

To create a recorder component, the new moniker must be prefixed with the queue moniker. Here, `queue:` represents the queue moniker.

```
string progid = "Samples.Courses.Services.CourseControl";
IQueueableCourseRegistration qc =
        (IQueueableCourseRegistration)Marshal.BindToMoniker(
        "queue:/new:" + progid);
```

You can find the new and queue monikers in the registry with the progids new and queue. Both components are implemented in the COM DLL `comsvcs.dll`.

With the queue moniker, a recorder is instantiated that records the method calls. The client code using the queue and new monikers to send a message to the earlier created queued component is shown in Listing 10-4. The method `RegisterCourse` accepts a `CourseRegistration` object, which is serialized using the `XmlSerializer` class. After you have invoked the method `RegisterCourse` in the recorder, you must release the recorder. Because the recorder is an old COM object, you must release it by calling the method `Marshal.ReleaseComObject`. The `Marshal` class is defined in the namespace `System.Runtime.InteropServices`. If you fail to release the recorder, the message might not be written to the message queue at all. The recorder uses an optimization technique so that it doesn't have to write every method call as a single message to the message queue, so that multiple method calls can be packed into the same message instead. The final sending of the message is done when the recorder is released.

Listing 10-4 Client Application Instantiating a Recorder

```
        private void RegisterCourse(
                CourseRegistration courseRegistration)
    {
        try
        {
            StringWriter writer = new StringWriter();
```

```
        XmlSerializer ser =
            new XmlSerializer(typeof(CourseRegistration));

        ser.Serialize(writer, courseRegistration);

        string progid = "Samples.Courses.Services.CourseControl";
        ICourseRegistration cc = (ICourseRegistration)
            Marshal.BindToMoniker("queue:/new:" + progid);

        cc.RegisterCourse(writer.ToString());

        Marshal.ReleaseComObject(cc);
    }
    catch (Exception ex)
    {
        MessageBox.Show(ex.Message);
    }
}
```

With this client code, the default settings of the queue, and the new moniker, the message queue that is configured with the Enterprise Services application of the serviced components is used to send messages in a default way. However, you can influence which queue the messages are sent to and how the messages should be configured. Table 10-2 shows the parameters that you can use to influence sending of messages with the queue moniker.

Table 10-2 Queue Moniker Parameters

Parameter	Description
ComputerName	If you have multiple systems where the Enterprise Services application is running, you can specify the system with the target queue using the ComputerName parameter. If you do not specify this parameter, the DCOM client configuration[10] of the serviced component defines the system name of the target queue.
QueueName	If the message should be sent to a specific queue, you can specify the name of the queue with the QueueName parameter. The complete name of the queue is constructed from the ComputerName and QueueName parameters: ComputerName\QueueName.

Table 10-2 **(continued)**

Parameter	Description
PathName	Instead of specifying the computer name and the queue name, you can set the PathName parameter. With the PathName parameter, the complete name of the queue must be set. You can see the syntax of the path name in Table 10-1.
FormatName	Instead of using a path name to specify a queue, message queuing enable you to specify a format name. With a format name, you don't have to set the computer name. With public queues, the target system is found automatically by getting the computer name from Active Directory. With a public queue, the FormatName can be specified with FormatName:PUBLIC=UUID, where UUID is the unique identifier of the queue. You can also specify a private queue with the FormatName parameter using this syntax: FormatName:PRIVATE=MachineGUID\QueueNumber. With the DIRECT syntax of the FormatName, you can define what protocol, machine name, and queue name should be used to access the target queue. The syntax of the DIRECT format name is this: FormatName:DIRECT=Protocol:ComputerName\QueueName. The protocol TCP is supported with all message queuing versions, and the HTTP protocol is supported with Message Queuing 3.0, but it must be installed separately. If you want to specify protocol with the DIRECT format, you can set the protocol name to OS.
AppSpecific	With the AppSpecific parameter, you can set application-specific information that is attached to the message.
AuthLevel	The authentication level can be set to 0 (MQMSG_AUTH_LEVEL_NONE) or 1 (MQMSG_AUTH_LEVEL_ALWAYS). With authenticated messages, the sender needs a certificate so that the message is digitally signed.
Delivery	Delivery enables you to determine how messages are stored and delivered. Possible values are 0 (MQMSG_DELIVERY_EXPRESS) and 1 (MQMSG_DELIVERY_RECOVERABLE).
EncryptAlgorithm	If you do not want the message to be read on the way to the target queue, you can encrypt it. With the parameter EncryptAlgorithm, you can specify the algorithm that should be used to encrypt the message.

Table 10-2 (continued)

Parameter	Description
HashAlgorithm	If you want to ensure that the message cannot be tampered with, you can create a checksum by specifying a hash algorithm with the HashAlgorithm parameter.
Journal	If a source journal should be used to copy sent messages, you can send the Journal parameter to the value 2, (MQMSG_JOURNAL). A value of 1 (MQMSG_DEADLETTER) means that the message is sent to the dead-letter queue if it cannot be sent to the target queue after a timeout occurs.
Label	If you specify a label, it is attached to the message.
MaxTimeToReachQueue MaxTimeToReceive	With the parameters MaxTimeToReachQueue and Max-TimeToReceive, you can specify timeout values. MaxTime-ToReachQueue defines the maximum number of seconds until the message must be written to the target queue, whereas MaxTimeToReceive defines the maximum number of seconds until the message is read from the queue. Instead of setting the number of seconds with these two parameters, you can set the values INFINITE or LONG_LIVED.
Priority	With the Priority parameter, you can set a value in the range 0 (MQ_MIN_PRIORITY) to 7 (MQ_MAX_PRIORITY) that is used to read the message with the highest priority first. The default value is 3 (MQ_DEFAULT_PRIORITY). With transactional queues, setting the priority is not possible.
PrivLevel	The privacy level defines how much of the message should be encrypted using the encryption algorithm that is defined with the EncryptAlgorithm parameter. With the values BODY_ENHANCED, BODY, or NONE, you can define whether the complete message, only the body, or nothing should be encrypted.
Trace	If you turn tracing on with the value 1 (MQMSG_SEND_ROUTE_TO_REPORT_QUEUE), a trace of the route is written to the report queue. By default, tracing is set to 0 (MQMSG_TRACE_NONE).

Error Handling

With queued components, you cannot get errors directly by calling the method of the queued component, because the method will only be recorded and will play at a later time. Errors can occur when the message is sent into the queue, or when the message is received from the queue.

You have already learned in this chapter about the dead-letter queue, which receives messages either when the message cannot be sent, or when the message cannot be received after a timeout.

Queued components have an automatic mechanism to deal with errors on both the client and the server side. You can create a custom **error component** that implements the interface `IPlaybackControl`, which you can find in the namespace `System.EnterpriseServices`.

The error component itself is a serviced component that can be installed on both the client and the server systems. The interface `IPlaybackControl` defines different methods for dealing with errors on the client and on the server: `FinalClientRetry` and `FinalServerRetry`.

The method `FinalClientRetry` is called with client-side errors, when the message cannot be delivered to the target queue before the timeout is reached. If the message cannot be delivered to the target queue, the message is put into the dead-letter queue of the client system, and the method `FinalClientRetry` is called.

For a server-side error, if calling the methods of the queued components failed (for example, because of incorrect parameters, or because of erroneous data access), the method `FinalServerRetry` is invoked.

`FinalClientRetry` and `FinalServerRetry` are not the only methods where you can do the recovery; in fact, with these methods, there is not a lot you can do at all. The real error recovery can be done in the methods that are called after the methods of the `IPlaybackControl` interface, as the error recovery mechanism invokes the same methods in the error component that were called with the erroneous component. The error component must therefore implement the same interface as the serviced component that is doing the normal work, although the implementation can differ. Here you can do some recovery actions, or create an e-mail that is sent to the system administrator.

If the methods of the error component succeed, the message is removed from the dead-letter queue.

A sample implementation of the error component is shown in Listing 10-5. The class `ErrorHandlerCourseControl` implements the interfaces `IPlaybackControl` and `IQueueableCourseRegistration`. This error component just writes the failing information to a log file; the name of the file is defined with the construction string of the serviced component class.[11]

In the `IPlaybackControl` methods `FinalServerRetry` and `FinalClient-Retry`, an entry is just written to the Windows event log.

What is more important with the error component is that it implements the interface `IQueueableCourseRegistration`—the same interface that was implemented by the normal serviced component class `CourseControl` (Listing 10-3). Of course, here the implementation of this method is different. Instead of writing the course registration information to the database, it is written to a simple file. With the information in the file and the event log entry (you could also create an e-mail), the system administration can take any necessary actions.

Listing 10-5   Implementation of an Error Component

```
[ConstructionEnabled(true, Default="d:/demos/MessageLog.txt")]
public class ErrorHandlerCourseControl: ServicedComponent,
    IPlaybackControl, IQueueableCourseRegistration
{
    private string errorFileName;
    protected override void Construct(string s)
    {
        errorFileName = s;
    }

    public void FinalServerRetry()
    {
        System.Diagnostics.EventLog.WriteEntry(
            "Course Services",
            "Server error with queued component; logfile: " +
            errorFileName);
    }

    public void FinalClientRetry()
    {
        System.Diagnostics.EventLog.WriteEntry(
            "Course Services",
```

```
            "Client error sending message to the queue; logfile: " +
            errorFileName);
    }

    public void RegisterCourse(string xmlCourseRegistration)
    {
        StreamWriter writer = File.AppendText(errorFileName);
        writer.WriteLine(xmlCourseRegistration);
        writer.WriteLine("-------");
        writer.Close();
    }
}
```

The error component must be associated with the queued component class. This is done by using the attribute [ExceptionClass]. The name of this attribute is somewhat misleading, however, because the class defined with this attribute is not a .NET exception class (that is, it does not inherit from System.Exception). However, if this class is instantiated, it is an exception outside of the normal program flow.

Listing 10-6 shows the attribute [ExceptionClass] applied to the class CourseControl that was created earlier. The constructor of this attribute class defines the progid of the error handler class. The default-generated progid of the error component is the name of the class, including the namespace.

Listing 10-6   Using the [ExceptionClass] Attribute

```
[ExceptionClass("Samples.Courses.Services." +
                "ErrorHandlerCourseControl")]
public class CourseControl: ServicedComponent,
                            IQueueableCourseRegistration
{
    //...
```

After you have registered the serviced component with the attribute [Exception-Class], you can see the error class in the Component Services Explorer, as shown in Figure 10-13.

To test the error component, you can modify the code of the RegisterCourse method to create an exception. You can also stop the database or do something else to make the serviced component fail. On doing this, you can see the message moving from one queue to another with the Computer Management tool. Remember to refresh the queues in this tool so that you can see the actual messages. Be aware that

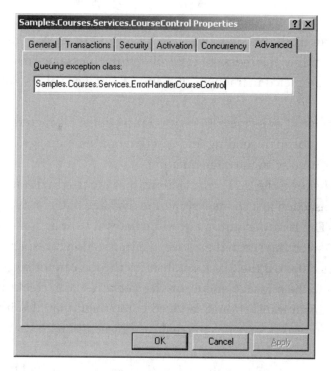

Figure 10-13   Exception class for queued components.

the error recovery takes a while and that before the error component is invoked, the message is moved from one private queue to the other. Within every active private message queue, the message is retried several times, and the time between the retries increases.

Transactional Queues

In Chapter 7, "Transaction Services," and in Chapter 8, "Compensating Resource Management," transactions were discussed. Queued components can participate in the same transaction as a normal transactional serviced component. With queued components, transactional queues are automatically created, as shown earlier in Figure 10-7, where a label is set to Transactional Queue.

Queued components seem to contradict the characteristics of transactions because transactions should only be active for a short time. With message queuing, the time from sending the message to receiving the message can take a while. The transfer can be completed in fractions of a second, but it can also span minutes, days, or weeks.

Such a behavior of messaging fits with transactional characteristics, because the transaction does not span sending and receiving of the message. Instead, multiple transactions are used with message queuing.

Figure 10-14 shows the three transactions that are used with message queuing.

The first transaction just spans writing the message to the message queue on the client system. The recorder automatically creates a transaction—if one does not already exist. As you can see in the figure, the transaction can span another component that writes data to a file[12] or a database. If the file cannot be created, the message is not sent to the message queue, or vice versa. You can create a transaction for the client by using a transactional serviced component that also invokes methods with the queue moniker, or you can create a transaction with the services without component technology.

The second transaction is created when the message is moved from the source to the target queue. As soon as the target queue can be reached, a transaction is created. This way, if the message cannot be moved to the target queue, the message is not lost.

The third transaction happens when the message is read from the target queue to invoke the method with the queued component. The player automatically enlists a transaction in the DTC. If the queued component is also marked with a transactional setting such as `TransactionOption.Required`, reading the message and writing to the database will be enlisted in the same transaction. If writing to the database fails, the message is rolled back to the queue.

Returning Data

With queued components, you cannot get return values immediately when calling the methods of the queued component. You must use different techniques if you need some data returned from the queued component.

If you need some information when the message cannot be delivered successfully, you can use error components to deal with this issue. If error handling is not enough,

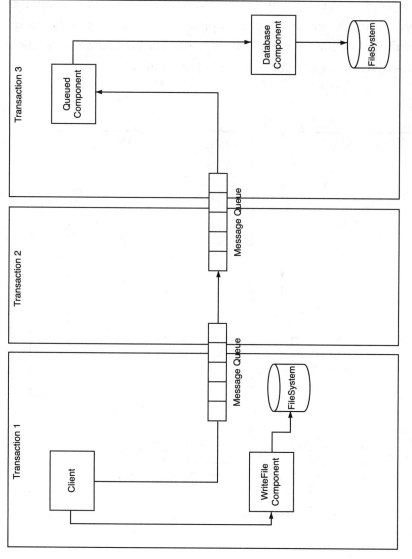

Figure 10-14 Transactions with queued components.

but you need some information from the serviced component returned, you can implement a queued component on both the client and the server system. Figure 10-15 shows such a scenario.

If you use queued components on the client and on the server, you must pass the queued component from the client application to the server application so that the server application can do a callback to the queued component of the client application. As the client application invokes the queued component by using a queue moniker, the server application similarly needs information for the queue moniker to invoke the serviced component in the client application. You can pass the information needed for the queue moniker (that must include the host name of the client system) with a parameter of the queued component method call.

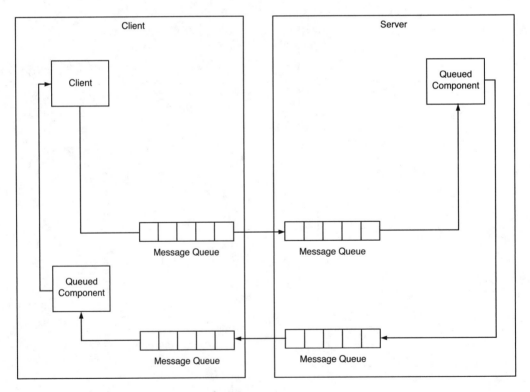

Figure 10-15　Queued components on the client and server system.

> **NOTE: Returning Data with Loosely Coupled Events**
>
> You have one more option to get information from the server system back to the client application. You can use loosely coupled events together with queued components. This is the most flexible option, and is discussed in Chapter 11, "Loosely Coupled Events."

Summary

This chapter covered the architecture of message queuing and how to implement queued components. With queued components, you can increase the overall scalability of your solution and give independent lifetimes to client and server applications.

When applying the attribute `[InterfaceQueuing]`, you can create message queues automatically. With the client application, it is obvious that queued components are based on COM technology, because a COM queued moniker is needed to instantiate the recorder.

When using queued components, error handling must be implemented differently from other applications, because the client and the server might not be running concurrently. Functionality for this issue is built in to the technology with error components.

1 With Web services, the `wsdl.exe` utility creates a class that offers both synchronous and asynchronous methods. Many other classes that do network or data access also offer both synchronous and asynchronous methods. You can also use delegates to invoke any method in an asynchronous way.

2 On a domain controller, this tool is available with Administrative Tools.

3 The Computer Management tool is in the Administrative Tools list.

4 There is no strict requirement that interfaces must be declared, because the attribute `[InterfaceQueuing]` can also be applied to classes. However, as discussed in Chapter 1, "Introducing .NET Enterprise Services," the use of interfaces is preferred.

5 If you use the classes from the namespace `System.Messaging` to write messages to the message queue, serializable classes are supported. With these classes, you do not have to implement the COM interface `IPersistStream`.

6 Writing data to the database was discussed in Chapter 6, "Data Access."

7 You can read more about error handling later in this chapter.

8 Object linking and embedding.

9 `CoCreateInstance` and `CoCreateInstanceEx` are Win32 API calls to instantiate COM objects.

10 See Chapter 5, "Networking," for the DCOM client configuration.

11 Construction strings are shown in Chapter 2, "Object Activation and Contexts."

12 You can create transactional file access with the compensating resource manager discussed in Chapter 8, "Compensating Resource Management."

11

Loosely Coupled Events

W ITH SERVICED COMPONENTS, SOMETIMES YOU NOT only want to invoke methods, but you also have the serviced component call back into the calling component. With Enterprise Services applications, you can do this with the help of loosely coupled events (LCEs).

With LCEs, the client is not called directly by the serviced component, but the serviced component publishes events to the COM+ facility instead. The COM+ facility forwards the event to clients.

Specifically, this chapter covers the following topics:

- The architecture of LCEs
- Programming LCEs
- Using LCEs across the network
- LCEs and queued components

LCE Overview

With both COM and .NET remoting, the component that is running on the server can invoke methods in the client application. With both of these technologies, the events are invoked directly from the component in the client application.

You can see the architecture of COM events in Figure 11-1. The client application must query for the interface IConnectionPointContainer and invoke the method FindConnectionPoint to get a reference to the IConnectionPoint interface returned. Using the IConnectionPoint interface, the client can pass a reference to

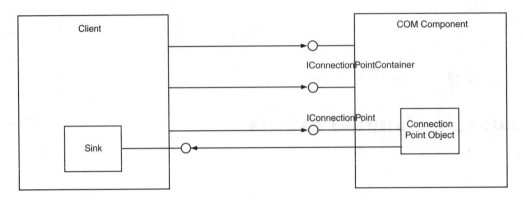

Figure 11-1   COM events.

the sink object to the server by calling the `Advise` method. The sink object is a COM object that is implemented in the client application. After these steps to build up the connection from the server to the client, the server component can invoke methods in the sink object. This is not only possible on the local system; with DCOM, it can also be done across the network.

With a distributed .NET solution, .NET events can be sent across the network, with the network functionality for events being handled by .NET remoting.[1] When you use events with .NET remoting, the remoting server declares an event that the client uses to register a method that has the same signature as defined with the type of the event. The type of an event is a delegate.[2] The delegate defines the parameter and return types of the handler method that must be implemented by the client application. The client application implements a handler method and registers this method with the event of the remote object. After the setup is done, the remote object can call back into the client application by calling the `Invoke` method of the event.

In a comparison of .NET remoting events to COM events, the .NET remoting architecture is simpler. The reason is that COM events are fully based on interfaces, whereas .NET remoting events allow you to define simple methods.

With both COM and .NET events, the server and client are connected directly, the same event can be delivered to multiple clients, and one client can register to receive events from multiple servers (see Figure 11-2). If multiple clients are connected to one server object, the server object must deal with multiple connections

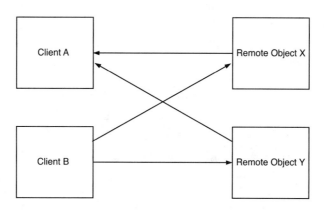

Figure 11-2   Events with multiple systems.

and invoke the handler method with every connection. Dealing with these connections becomes extremely important, because the server object has direct connections. If a connection to one client fails, the handler method should be invoked with the other client applications that have working connections. This does not happen automatically; you must add fail-safe code to invoke the methods in the client yourself.

LCEs add infrastructure support between the server that is publishing events and the client where the events are invoked. Figure 11-3 provides an overview of LCEs. With LCEs, an event class is registered in the COM+ catalog. The event class forwards events that are fired by the publisher to all subscribers. There is no need for the publisher to deal with direct connections to the subscribers, because the connection management is done by the event class. The event class is automatically generated by the LCE runtime.

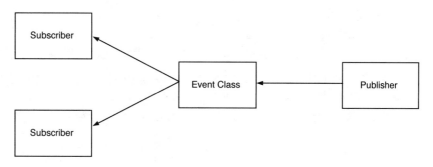

Figure 11-3   LCE architecture.

The following sections cover the main parts of the LCE architecture to provide more information about the event class, publishers, subscribers, and filters.

Event Class

The event is defined with an event interface and an event class. You need not implement the methods of the event class, because the implementation is done automatically. For the automatic generation of this class, just the metadata is needed, so that the automatic generated event class can invoke methods in subscribers that implement the same interface.

Publishers

The publisher is an application that instantiates event classes and fires events by calling methods of the event class. Publishers do not need to be implemented as serviced components; a publisher can be any application type that only has the job to call a serviced component. It is often useful for the publisher to be a serviced component (for example, when the publisher also acts as a normal server-side component that is called by a client application).

Subscribers

LCEs define two different types of subscribers: persistent and transient.

A **persistent subscriber** is a serviced component. A persistent subscription is registered within the Enterprise Services configuration. This configuration is used to start the subscriber when an event occurs.

The persistent subscriber may be configured within the same application as the publisher, but usually this is not done.

A **transient subscriber** can be implemented with any application type (for example, a transient subscriber can be a Windows Forms application). The transient subscriber must subscribe to the event when it is running; there is no way the transient subscriber can be started automatically when the event occurs.

Figure 11-4 shows LCEs with transient and persistent subscribers.

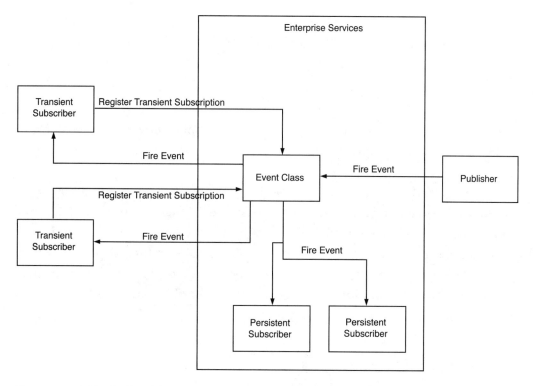

Figure 11-4 LCE solution with transient and persistent subscribers.

Filters

Events can be filtered before they are delivered to the client application. You can see the position of a filter in the call flow in Figure 11-5. When the publisher fires an event that has a filter assigned, the event is not directly sent to the subscriber by the event class; instead, the event is filtered before it is forwarded to the subscriber. The filter can define that the event is not forwarded to all subscribers, and can also define the order that is used to call back into the subscribers.

You must differentiate between two filter types: a subscriber filter and a publisher filter.

A **subscriber filter** is defined by the subscriber application. With this type of filter, the subscriber defines interest for an event depending on values of the

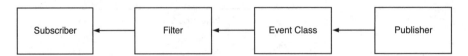

Figure 11-5   Filter in the LCE event flow.

parameters of the event method (for example, the client is only interested when the parameter `ActualStockCount` of the method `StockChanged` has a value lower than 5).

A **publisher filter** is defined by the publishing component. If multiple clients are subscribed to a single event, by default there is no guarantee of the order that is used to invoke methods in the client application. If you need a specific order to invoke methods in the client application, you can create a publisher filter. A publisher filter can also be used to define that not all subscribed clients should be called. If the publishing component should influence the way the subscribers are called, a publisher filter is the way to go.

Programming LCEs

To implement LCEs, you must define an event class and create a publisher and a subscriber. The event class defines the methods that are invoked by the publisher and implemented by the subscriber.

Figure 11-6 shows an overview of the example that will be completed in this section. The event class `CourseOrderEvent` implements the interface `ICourse-OrderEvent` with a single method `CourseOrder`.

The class `CourseControl` with the method `RegisterCourse` was already shown in the preceding chapter. Here this class is extended to take the role as a publisher. When the method `RegisterCourse` is invoked, a `CourseOrderEvent` is generated.

The event is handled by the subscriber class `CourseInformation`, which implements the same interface as the event class, `ICourseOrderEvent`.

Event Class

It is useful to define the event class with its interface in a separate assembly from the publisher because this interface is used by both the publisher and the subscriber.

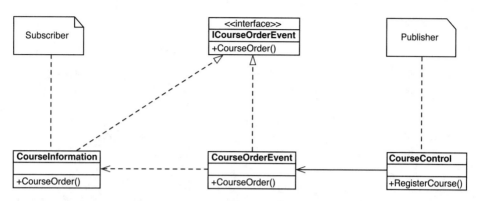

Figure 11-6   Loosely coupled events sample.

With the sample application, the assembly for the event class is `Samples.Courses.Services.Event`.

The event class must be marked with the attribute `[EventClass]`. With this class, just the declaration and information about the methods are needed; the class defines all methods that are called by the publisher and implemented by the client. You do not need to implement the methods in the event class because this class is only needed for registration information. The COM+ infrastructure implements these methods automatically to invoke the same methods in the client application.

Listing 11-1 shows an event class for `CourseOrderEvent`. There is no need to implement the method `NewCourseOrder` because this method will be generated automatically by the COM+ runtime. Both the interface and the class have predefined IDs that are assigned with the `[Guid]` attribute. Assigning predefined identifiers is useful with the event class so that you know these identifiers with the subscriber applications and do not have to check for automatically generated identifiers. The `GuidAttribute` class is defined in the namespace `System.Runtime.InteropServices`. You can create unique identifiers with the tools `guidgen.exe` and `uuidgen.exe`.[3]

Listing 11-1   Event Class

```
[Guid("FC08D776-B9F2-4ccc-8EA3-1CD86F42A586")]
public interface ICourseOrderEvent
{
```

```
        void NewCourseOrder(string courseNumber,
                            Attendee[] attendees);
}


[EventClass]
[Guid("1644EDB0-9E10-4368-943B-5193AA47E0C7")]
public class CourseOrderEvent : ServicedComponent,
                                ICourseOrderEvent
{
    public CourseOrderEvent ()
    {
    }

    public void NewCourseOrder(string courseNumber,
                               Attendee[] attendees)
    {
    }
}
```

> **NOTE: Defining a Class for an Event Class**
>
> The event class is implemented automatically by the COM+ run-time, and the class you create is just an empty class without an implementation. You might ask why you cannot define just an interface rather than a class when no implementation is needed. The answer is that what is needed for the automatic creation of the event class is not only a COM type library that defines the interfaces and methods, but also the class ID. The easiest way to do this is to create a serviced component class.

Table 11-1 shows the optional named properties that you can use with the class EventClassAttribute. You can use these properties to define behavior of the event class implementation that is automatically created by the Enterprise Services infrastructure.

After an event class is registered, the event configurations show up in the Component Services Explorer on the Advanced tab of the component properties, as shown in Figure 11-7. With all other classes, the LCE settings do not show up. The settings Fire in Parallel and Allow In-Process Subscribers are defined with the class EventClassAttribute properties that were shown in Table 11-1.

Table 11-1   EventClassAttribute Properties

Property	Description
AllowInprocSubscribers	By default, subscribers can run in the same process as the publisher. If you set the named property AllowInproc-Subscribers to false, the subscriber cannot be activated in the same process as the publisher.
FireInParallel	When the COM+ infrastructure invokes methods in the client applications, by default the methods are invoked one after the other in a serial order. If subscribers should be invoked concurrently using multiple threads, you must set the property FireInParallel to true.
PublisherFilter	With the property PublisherFilter, you can define a class that implements a publisher filter. With a publisher filter, the filter can define what subscribers should be called in what order. Publisher filters are discussed later in this chapter.

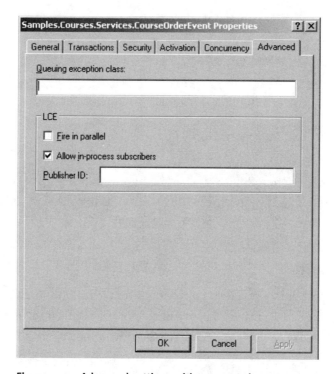

Figure 11-7   Advanced settings with an event class.

Publisher

The publisher is just a serviced component that instantiates the event class and invokes methods of this class. Here the serviced component from that accepts course orders is extended.

Listing 11-2 shows the method `RegisterCourse` from the class `CourseControl`. After the course registration is written to the database, the method `NewCourseOrder` of the event class `CourseOrderEvent` is invoked to inform all subscribers of the course order.

Listing 11-2   Publisher Component Firing Events

```
public void RegisterCourse(
    CourseRegistration courseRegistration)
{

    using (CourseDataControl courseData = new CourseDataControl())
    using (CourseOrderEvent eventObj = new CourseOrderEvent())
    {
        courseData.RegisterCourse(courseRegistration);
        eventObj.NewCourseOrder(
            courseRegistration.CourseData.Course.Number,
            courseRegistration.GetAttendees());
    }
}
```

> **NOTE: Publisher Application Type**
>
> It is not necessary to implement the publisher as a serviced component. The publisher can be any application type; the only requirements are to instantiate the event class and to invoke methods.

Persistent Subscriber

A persistent subscriber is a serviced component that implements the interface of the event class. Listing 11-3 shows the serviced component class of the subscriber. The subscriber class `CourseInformation` implements the event interface

`ICourseOrderEvent`. The method `NewCourseOrder` is called from the COM+ infra-structure when an event occurs.

In the implementation of the method `NewCourseOrder`, a message box pops up. The class `CourseInformationForm` is a custom forms dialog class that derives from the base class `System.Windows.Forms.Form`. This class is implemented in a separate assembly that defines custom classes for the user interface. The form `Course-InformationClass` just shows the course name and lists the attendee names.

Listing 11-3 Subscriber Component

```
public class CourseInformation : ServicedComponent,
                                 ICourseOrderEvent
{
    public CourseInformation()
    {
    }

    public void NewCourseOrder(string courseNumber,
                               Attendee[] attendees)
    {
        using (CourseInformationForm form =
            new CourseInformationForm())
        {
            form.Init(courseNumber, attendees);
            form.ShowDialog();
        }
    }
}
```

After the component is registered, the subscription must be added. No assembly attributes cause this to happen automatically. You can add a subscription either manually by using the Component Services Explorer, or programmatically by using COM+ admin components.[4]

When configuring the subscription manually, you can select the component in the Component Services Explorer and click Subscriptions. To start the Subscription Wizard, just choose Action | New | Subscription. Some of the steps of this wizard are shown in Figures 11-8 through 11-10. Figure 11-8 shows all the interfaces that are implemented by the subscriber component; you can either select the event interface, or you can select a single method that the subscription component should subscribe to. The dialog box that opens when you click the Next button asks for the event class

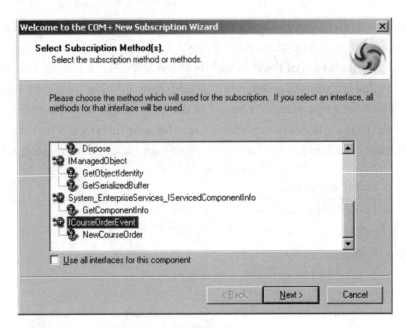

Figure 11-8   Select the subscription method or interface.

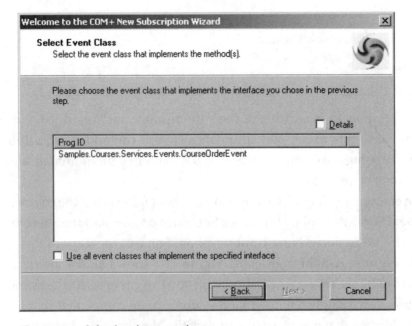

Figure 11-9   Selecting the event class.

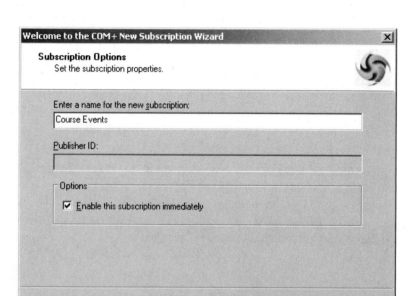

Figure 11-10   Enabling the subscription.

that you want to subscribe to. If multiple event classes implement the same interface, you can select one of many (see Figure 11-8). The last questions asked are shown in Figure 11-10; you can enter a name for the subscription and select whether the subscription should be active immediately.

After setting up the configuration for the subscription, you can start the client application to generate a new course order. The new course order automatically starts up the subscriber application to invoke the method `NewCourseOrder` (see Listing 11-3).

Transient Subscriber

Contrary to the persistent subscriber, the transient subscriber can be any application type and will not be started automatically. Here a transient subscriber in the form of a Windows application is created.

Figure 11-11 shows the main classes of the Windows Forms client application. The class `TransientSubscriberForm` is the main UI form class of this application that derives from the base class `System.Windows.Forms.Form`. The class `Course-RegistrationInformation` implements the event interface `ICourseOrderEvent`

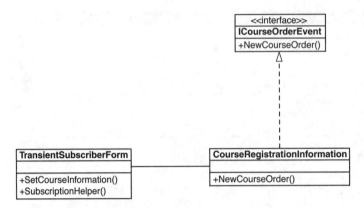

Figure 11-11   Transient subscriber sample classes.

to receive events from the COM+ infrastructure. CourseRegistrationInforma-tion changes UI elements in the forms class with information about events received.

Listing 11-4 shows some methods of the class TransientSubscriberForm that change the UI element values when an event is received. The method SetCourse-InformationHelper is a helper method that changes values in the list box list-Attendees and in the text box textCourseName.

One important fact with Windows controls that you must be aware of is that Windows controls are bound to a thread. Methods of these controls may not be invoked from any other thread than the creator thread. The same applies for the Windows Forms controls that just wrap the Windows controls. Because the events might arrive on a different thread from the main thread, you must change the thread to the creator thread before setting properties or invoking methods of the Windows Forms controls.

For changing the thread, every Windows Forms control offers an Invoke method. The Invoke method is thread independent and forwards the request to the creator thread.

In the method SetCourseInformation that will be called from the sink class CourseRegistrationInformation, the method Invoke of the Form class is called to turn the control to the creator thread of the form. The Invoke method accepts a delegate as a parameter, so the delegate SetCourseInformationDelegate with the parameters needed is defined.

Listing 11-4 Helper Methods to Change UI Element Values

```
private delegate void SetCourseInformationDelegate(
    string courseName, Attendee[] attendees);

public void SetCourseInformation(string courseName,
    Attendee[] attendees)
{
    object[] args = new object[2];
    args[0] = courseName;
    args[1] = attendees;
    Invoke(new Form1.SetCourseInformationDelegate(
        SetCourseInformationHelper), args);
}

private void SetCourseInformationHelper(string courseName,
    Attendee[] attendees)
{
    textCourseName.Text = courseName;
    listAttendees.DataSource = attendees;
}
```

> **NOTE: Threading and Windows Forms Applications**
>
> Do not invoke methods of Windows Forms controls from a thread that did not create the controls. Windows controls are bound to a thread, so you use the `Invoke` method to turn the control to the creator thread.

The transient subscriber application must define a class that implements the interface that is defined with the event class. The event interface `ICourseOrderEvent` was defined in Listing 11-1. The class `CourseRegistrationInformation` takes the role of the subscriber to implement this interface. Listing 11-5 shows the implementation of this class.

The methods of this class will be invoked by the COM+ infrastructure when events occur. Often such a class is called a **sink class**.

In the example application, this class is named `CourseRegistrationInformation` and is shown in Listing 11-5. This class implements the interface `ICourseOrderEvent` and just invokes the method `SetCourseInformation` defined earlier.

The implementation of the methods `Activate` and `GetEventInformation` is shown later. These methods are used to create the subscription.

Listing 11-5   **Sink Class for the Transient Subscriber Application**

```
public class CourseRegistrationInformation : ICourseOrderEvent
{
   private TransientSubscriberForm form;

   public CourseRegistrationInformation(
         TransientSubscriberForm form)
   {
      this.form = form;
   }

   public void NewCourseOrder(string courseNumber,
         Attendee[] attendees)
   {
      form.SetCourseInformation(courseNumber, attendees);
   }

   public static void GetEventInformation(out eventCLSID,
         out eventIID)
   {
      // TBD
   }

   public static void Activate(string subscriptionName,
         string eventCLSID, string eventIID, object sink)
   {
      // TBD
   }
}
```

The most important aspect with the transient subscriber is the subscriber registration. The subscriber application has to register subscribing information in the COM+ configuration, which can only be done programmatically.

For the subscription, the IDs of the event class and interface are needed, and there are various ways to get to this information. One option is to read the COM+ catalog and query for the event class. Another option is to read the ID from the assembly using the `System.Type` class; the property `Guid` returns the associated identifier that is defined with the class or interface. Reading the ID from the assembly is only possible if you've applied the `[Guid]` attribute to the class, as was done earlier in

Listing 11-1. The option that is used here is to get the identifiers from a configuration file. The method `GetEventInformation` is shown in Listing 11-6. The class `ConfigurationSettings`, defined in the `System.Configurations` namespace, is used to read the `EventCLSID` and `EventIID` configuration values.

Listing 11-6   Reading Event Information from a Configuration File

```
public static void GetEventInformation(out string eventCLSID,
        out string eventIID)
{
    eventCLSID = ConfigurationSettings.AppSettings.Get(
        "EventCLSID");
    eventIID = ConfigurationSettings.AppSettings.Get(
        "EventIID");
}
```

Listing 11-7 shows the application configuration file that defines the identifiers needed for the subscription. The IDs are the same as defined with the event class.

Listing 11-7   Application Configuration File

```
<?xml version="1.0" encoding="utf-8" ?>
<configuration>
  <appSettings>
    <add key="EventIID"
        value="{FC08D776-B9F2-4ccc-8EA3-1CD86F42A586}" />
    <add key="EventCLSID"
        value="{1644EDB0-9E10-4368-943B-5193AA47E0C7}" />
  </appSettings>
</configuration>
```

There is no .NET support to create a transient subscription; you must use COM interop to use the `COMAdminCatalog` component. With Visual Studio, you can create a .NET wrapper to the COM object by selecting Project | Add Reference | COM, and by selecting COM+ 1.0 Admin Type Library.[5] The generated wrapper interface `COMAdminCatalog`[6] is in the namespace `COMAdmin`.

Listing 11-8 shows the implementation of the method `Activate` from the class `CourseRegistrationInformation` that registers a transient subscription. To register a transient subscription, you must add an entry to the `TransientSubscriptions` collection of the COM+ catalog. Invoking the method `GetCollection` with the parameter "TransientSubscriptions" returns an `ICatalogCollection` object, the Add method of which adds a new entry to the collection. With this entry, the parameters Name, Enabled, EventCLSID, InterfaceID, and Subscriber-Interface must be set. With the Name parameter, you can specify any subscription name; EventCLSID and InterfaceID define the identifiers of the event class. These IDs were defined with the event class so that the subscriber registers to the correct event. The SubscriberInterface parameter requires the subscriber object to be set so that this object can be called from the COM+ infrastructure. Finally, coll.SaveChanges writes the configuration to the catalog.

Listing 11-8   Creating a Transient Subscription

```
public static void Activate(string subscriptionName,
    string eventCLSID, string eventIID, object sink)
{
try
    {
    COMAdminCatalog catalog = new COMAdminCatalog();
    ICatalogCollection coll;

    coll = catalog.GetCollection("TransientSubscriptions")
            as ICatalogCollection;

    ICatalogObject subscription =
            (ICatalogObject)coll.Add();

    if (subscription == null)
    {
        throw new Exception("Subscription Exception");
    }

    string eventCLSID;
    string eventIID;
    GetEventInformation(out eventCLSID, out eventIID);

    subscription.set_Value("Name", "CourseInfo");
    subscription.set_Value("Enabled", true);
    subscription.set_Value("EventCLSID", eventCLSID);
    subscription.set_Value("InterfaceID", eventIID);
    subscription.set_Value("SubscriberInterface", sink);

    coll.SaveChanges();

    Marshal.ReleaseComObject(catalog);
    }
```

```
        catch (Exception ex)
        {
            MessageBox.Show(ex.Message);
        }
    }
```

The subscription is initiated by a handler in the `TransientSubscriberForm` class, as shown in Listing 11-9. Here a sink object is initiated, and this sink object is passed to the method `CourseRegistrationInformation.Activate`, where the subscription is done.

Listing 11-9   Starting the Subscription

```
    private void button1_Click(object sender, System.EventArgs e)
    {
        CourseRegistrationInformation sink =
            new CourseRegistrationInformation(this);

        string eventCLSID;
        string eventIID;
        CourseRegistrationInformation.GetEventInformation(
            out eventCLSID, out eventIID);

        CourseRegistrationInformation.Activate("CourseEvents",
            eventCLSID, eventIID, sink);
    }
```

Now you can start the subscriber application and wait for events to arrive.

Filters

As discussed in the "LCE Overview" section of this chapter, you can filter events by both the subscriber and the publisher, as demonstrated here.

Subscriber Filters

With a subscriber filter, a subscriber can define which events should arrive on the subscriber site. Every subscriber defines its own subscription filter, as shown in Figure 11-12.

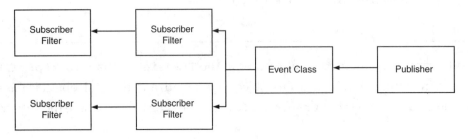

Figure 11-12 Subscriber filters.

You can define filter criteria for the subscriber filter in the COM+ catalog information. Figure 11-13 shows a parameter filter with the criteria `AttendeeCount > 8`. Here the event is only delivered to the subscriber if the parameter `AttendeeCount` of the event method has a value higher than 8. In the Component Services Explorer, you can set the parameter filter with the properties of the subscription.

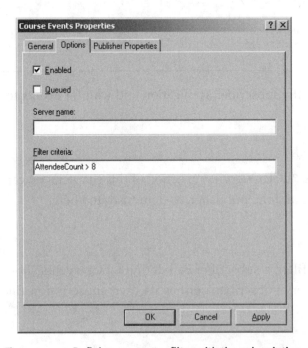

Figure 11-13 Defining parameter filter with the subscription.

A subscriber filter can also be defined programmatically. With transient subscribers, this is the only way to define subscriber filters.

With the subscriber filter, you can define the filter with simple data types such as numbers and strings. For the filter criteria, you can use relational operators such as =, ==, !, !=, ~, ~=, and <> for comparing values. The operators = and == are the same with the filter criteria; likewise, ! and <> can be used interchangeably. To combine multiple parameters, you can use the logical keywords AND, OR, and NOT.

Publisher Filters

A publisher filter is completely different from a parameter filter. Figure 11-14 shows the call flow with a publisher filter. The publisher filter is invoked from the event class when an event occurs and has the responsibility to forward the events. In contrast to subscriber filters, just one publisher filter deals with all subscribers. The publisher filter decides when and how the events should be forwarded to the subscribers, which is possible because the publisher filter gets a subscriber collection so that the filter can control event forwarding.

A publisher filter is a component that implements the COM interface `IMulti-InterfacePublisherFilter` with the methods `Initialize` and `PrepareToFire`.

The method `Initialize` associates an event class with the publisher filter. When this method is called, the publisher filter receives a reference to the interface `IMultiInterfaceEventControl` that can be used to get the list of registered subscribers. This reference should be remembered in the publisher filter so that an actual subscriber list can be accessed when needed.

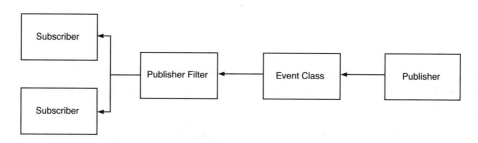

Figure 11-14   Publisher filter.

The method `PrepareToFire` is called immediately when the event class fires an event. The event class passes the event interface and the method that is fired, in addition to a reference to the interface `IFiringControl`. With the `IFiringControl` interface, you can fire the event to the subscriber that should receive the event. `IFiringControl` has just a single method, `FireSubscription`, that requires an `IEventSubscription` passed. You can get references to the `IEventSubscription` interface from the list of subscribers. Here you can decide what subscriber should get the event, and the order of firing the events.

Creating Publisher Filters with .NET

With .NET, there is no support to implement a publisher filter. If you want to create a publisher filter with C#, you must redefine all the required COM interfaces. However, you do have another option: You can create a publisher filter using C++. Such a publisher filter works great in cooperation with an event class defined in C#.

Using LCEs Across the Network

The easy scenario using LCEs is on a single system, where the event class and the subscriber must reside on a single system. If you want to use LCEs distributed across multiple systems, you have a couple of options, as follows:

- LCE routing
- Event class proxies

LCE Routing

With the configuration of a persistent subscriber, you can define a server name with the subscription options, as shown in Figure 11-15. Do not be confused by the term *server name* used here; you specify the computer name of the subscriber system (which acts as a server when the event is distributed, but is a client in another role).

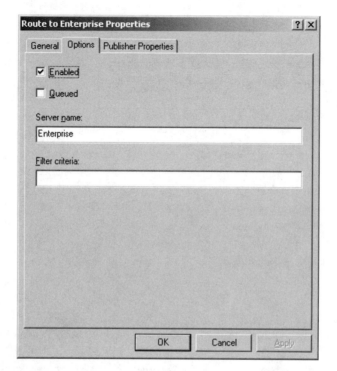

Figure 11-15   Configuring a server name with the subscription.

When a subscriber is instantiated, the event service looks for the server name in the subscription configuration. If a server name is defined, the event is forwarded to the subscriber on the configured system.

The subscriber must be installed on both the routing and the target system. Using COM+ routing, you can add multiple routes to different systems so that the event can be easily distributed in the network. Figure 11-16 shows an LCE routing configuration in a distributed solution. The publisher fires events to the event class. In this scenario, three subscriptions are configured. One subscriber is on the same system as the publisher, whereas two subscribers have other routes configured. One route references the system Enterprise (see Figure 11-15), whereas another subscription is configured to reference the system Andromeda. The subscriber router forwards events to these subscribers.

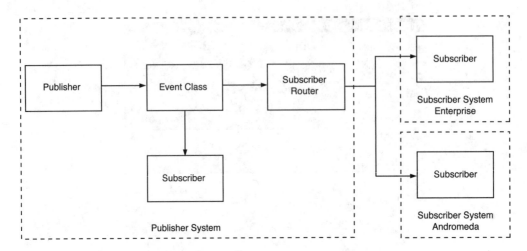

Figure 11-16　LCE scenario with routing.

> **NOTE: COM+ Routing Subscribers**
>
> The disadvantage with COM+ routing is that this option is possible only with persistent subscribers. All routing subscribers are serviced components.

Event Class Proxies

You can also use networking from the publisher to the event class. Because the event class is a serviced component, you can create an application proxy[7] that connects to the event class.

Figure 11-17 shows a scenario with a publisher on a different system from the event class. The publisher uses the application proxy to access the event class. The event class fires the event to the subscriber.

Of course, you can combine LCE routing with event class proxies so that at least three systems interact: the system of the publisher, the LCE router system, and the subscriber system.

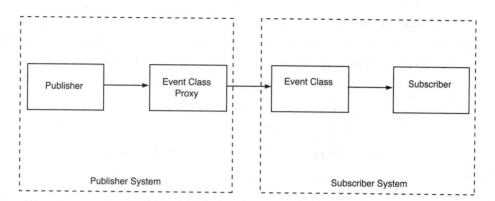

Figure 11-17   Using event class proxies.

> **Distributed LCE Rule**
>
> With LCEs, the event class and the subscriber must always reside on the same system. To enable LCEs across the network, the publisher can run on a different system from the event class. It is also possible to use subscriber routers that forward requests to subscribers on other systems. You can combine both scenarios in one solution.

LCE and Queued Components

Another scenario that adds more complexity but great functionality to LCEs is using LCEs in conjunction with queued components.[8] With queued components, you can make the call from the publisher to the subscriber asynchronous and disconnected.

With queued components, the recorder is used that records the method calls invoked to pass them as messages to a message queue, and the player reads the messages from the message queue to invoke the methods in the serviced component.

You can place a player and recorder between the publisher and the event class and between the event class and the subscriber. In both cases, you must mark the interface of the event class with the [InterfaceQueuing] attribute, as shown here:

```
[InterfaceQueuing]
[Guid("FC08D776-B9F2-4ccc-8EA3-1CD86F42A586")]
public interface ICourseOrderEvent
{
    void NewCourseOrder(string courseNumber, string attendeeName);
}
```

Of course, if you mark an interface as queuable, the interface methods must be defined according to the restrictions of queuable interfaces: You may only use input parameters, and you can only use simple data types because the recorder requires an implementation of the COM interface IPersistStream.

Now consider two ways to use LCEs with queued components:

- Event classes as queued components
- Subscribers as queued components

Event Classes as Queued Components

With the first queued component scenario, the player and recorder are placed in between the publisher and the event class. This way the lifetime of the publisher and the event system can be independent. Figure 11-18 shows such a scenario where the publisher fires the event by using a recorder that writes messages to the message queue. On the target system, the message is read and the player invokes the methods in the event class. The event class in turn fires the event to the subscriber.

To make this scenario happen, the event class must be registered as a listener, which can be done with the attribute class ApplicationQueuingAttribute. The publisher must use a queue moniker to send the event calls to the message queue.

Subscribers as Queued Components

If you want disconnected behavior between the event class and the subscriber, the subscriber must be defined as a queued component. Such a scenario is shown in Figure 11-19.

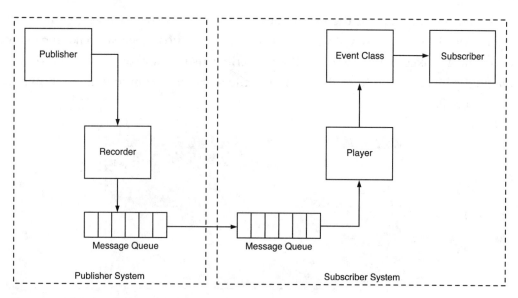

Figure 11-18   Using the event class as a queued component.

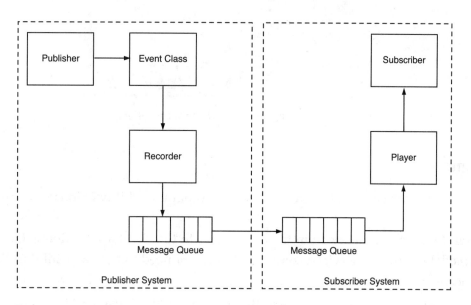

Figure 11-19   Using the subscriber as a queued component.

When the interface of the event class is queueable, you must set the attribute [ApplicationQueuing] with the application of the subscriber. To make the event class that invokes the methods of the subscriber use a moniker, you must set the Queued property with the subscription of the subscriber component, as shown in Figure 11-20.

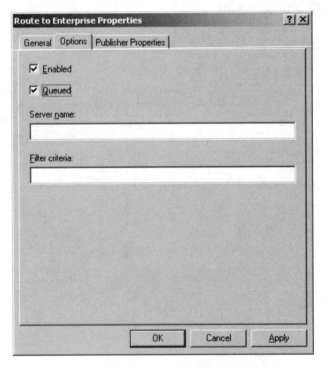

Figure 11-20 Enabling queuing with the subscription.

Summary

This chapter has covered the architecture and programmability of loosely coupled events.

With LCE, the callback from the component to the client application is loosely coupled, because the serviced component does not need to deal with all the client connections. The client application acts as a subscriber to define the events of interest for the client application, whereas the server component acts as a publisher that fires the events to the event subsystem.

With this, you can define loose coupling filters with the event subsystem where the subscriber can define not to receive all events.

Loosely coupled events can also be combined with queued components. If the client application is using a disconnected environment to invoke serviced components, the same is possible on the way back from the server to the client by combining queued components with loosely coupled events.

1 .NET remoting was discussed in Chapter 5, "Networking."

2 A delegate is an object-oriented type-safe pointer to a method.

3 The use of these utilities is covered in Chapter 4, "COM Interop."

4 Later in this chapter, the COM+ admin components are used to configure transient subscriptions. You can read more about the configuration using these components and the .NET classes in Chapter 13, "Deployment and Configuration."

5 If you are using the command line, `tlbimp.exe` is the tool to create a .NET wrapper from a COM component.

6 You can read more about this COM component in Chapter 13.

7 Creating application proxies is discussed in Chapter 5.

8 Queued components are discussed in Chapter 10, "Queued Components."

12
Security

SECURITY IS A VERY IMPORTANT ASPECT with distributed solutions. When thinking about how to implement security in your solution, you must define where security is important. Who is allowed to access the database, and do they need read or write access? Where is secure data transfer needed across the network? What data must be secured with the transfer? Which user groups are allowed to use which business components?

Authentication, authorization, impersonation, and confidentiality are important facets regarding security. This chapter covers these facets not only with Enterprise Services applications, but also with technologies that play an important part with distributed business solutions.

Specifically, this chapter covers the following topics:

- Security overview
- Identity
- Access checks
- Authentication levels and impersonation
- Using ASP.NET Web services as façade
- Enterprise Services and .NET remoting

Security Overview

Before delving into the details of handling security with business solutions, you need to understand three important terms: *authentication*, *authorization*, and *confidentiality*.

When a user accesses a component, he must be identified, a mechanism known as **authentication**. With authentication, different mechanisms can be used, such as the username/password with Windows authentication, or basic authentication or certificates.

After verifying the user, the next question arises: Is the user allowed to access the requested resources? This verification is known as **authorization**. Enterprise Services uses a role-based mechanism so that there is no need to deal with Windows users and groups while developing the solution. The system administrator can map users and groups to corresponding roles.

The third major part regarding security is **confidentiality**. With distributed solutions, data is sent across the network, and the transfer of data in clear text makes it possible for hackers to sniff the network to get confidential data. You have various options available to help secure network data. You can use a checksum so that no one can change the data, or you can encrypt the data that is transferred so that no one can sniff the network to read your data.

With a distributed solution, you not only use Enterprise Services technologies, but also other technologies of similar importance that interact with serviced components. With many technologies, security options are similar; with many others, however, they are quite different.

Consider, for example, the technologies that may interact in a distributed solution. Clients of Enterprise Services applications can be Web services, ASP.NET Web Forms, or Windows Forms; protocols to be used are DCOM, .NET remoting, and SOAP. SQL Server is used as the data store. This section covers all these technologies with regard to security.

Figure 12-1 shows the technologies that can play a part in your distributed solution. Consider first the client side. You can use a Windows Forms application that directly accesses the serviced components using DCOM, or using .NET remoting.[1] If you use .NET remoting, Internet Information Server (IIS) acts as a host for the serviced component.

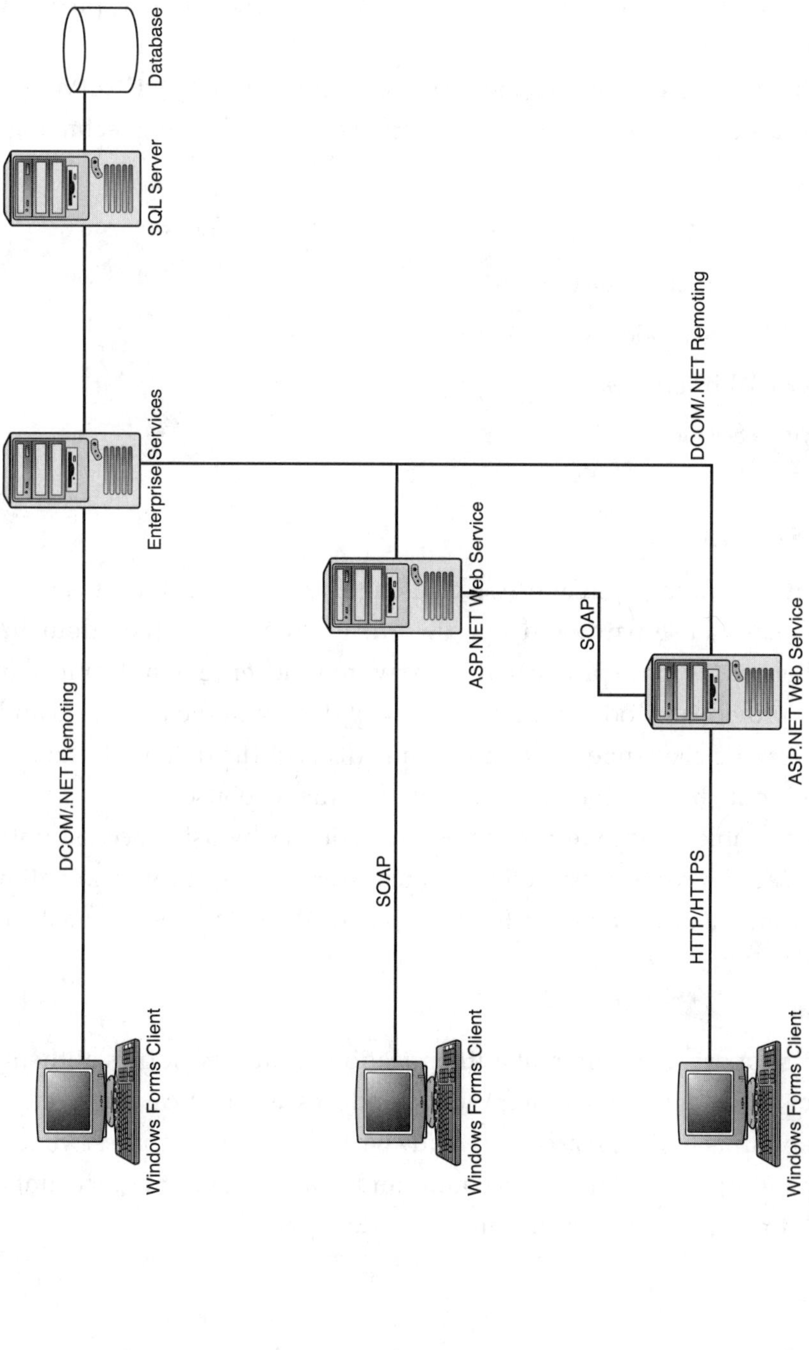

Figure 12-1 Technologies in a distributed solution.

A different scenario arises when accessing the Enterprise Services application via a Web service as façade. Here a Windows Forms client accesses the Web service using the SOAP protocol. A different client of the Web service could be an ASP.NET Web application that itself is accessed by a browser-based client. Here the protocol HTTP or HTTPS is used.

The Web service itself accesses the serviced component using DCOM.

Now it is time to consider the security aspects of the following technologies:

- Windows security
- SQL Server
- Internet Information Server
- ASP.NET Web applications
- ASP.NET Web services
- Enterprise Services

Windows Security

The Windows operating system uses a challenge/response protocol to authenticate users. Users have a username and a password, and they know their domain name. With a challenge/response protocol, the password is never sent in clear text. Instead, the security provider encodes a random block of data with the password and sends it to the caller (the challenge). The caller must decrypt the data with the password and send this data back to the security provider (the response).

Windows enables you to restrict access to resources by using access control lists (ACLs). The access control list defines which users or user groups are allowed to access the resource in which way (for example, read, write, modify, create, delete).

SQL Server

SQL Server supports two different authentication modes: Windows authentication and Mixed Mode authentication. With Windows authentication, you can use Windows accounts to define access to read/write/modify databases. Mixed Mode authentication supports Windows accounts and SQL accounts. SQL accounts can be configured directly in SQL Server Enterprise Manager.

Using Windows accounts with SQL Server has the advantage that the accounts have all the features of Windows accounts. You can manage these accounts with the Users and Computers tool, you can configure the Windows privileges needed, the password can be configured with Windows administration tools, and access to these accounts is monitored with the Windows security event logging.

If you use SQL Server authentication instead of Windows authentication, the username and password must be set with the connection string, which can be a security leak. You should never write the connection string directly to the code. A connection string in the code would not allow administrator changes when the server changes; in addition, if the connection string contains username/password, it is possible to read this information from the assembly. Instead, the connection string can be written to a configuration file or to the construction string of the serviced component. A security issue still exists, however, because every user with read access to the configuration file knows the username and password to access the database. With .NET 1.1, you can avoid such a security leak by writing encrypted identity information to the registry, as shown in the note "Storing Secrets" later in this chapter.

Accounts and Connection Pools

Sometimes end-user access checks must happen at the database level. Although this is possible, you must be aware that connection pooling works only if the same connection string with the same user context is used. If you use different Windows accounts that open connections, different connection pools for every user are used.

It is important that you remember another security aspect with regard to SQL Server: SQL injection attacks, which you can avoid by using parameter objects instead of using string concatenation when building the SQL commands.

Using stored procedures instead of accessing the tables and views directly makes a more granular access control possible. Both of these issues are discussed in Chapter 6, "Data Access."

Storing Secrets

With .NET 1.1, you can store secrets (such as the password in a connection string) by using the utility `aspnet_setreg.exe`,[2] which enables you to encrypt a username and password and to store it in the registry.

This command writes encrypted values for the username and password to the registry key `HKEY_LOCAL_MACHINE\Software\CourseManagement\identity`. You must change the registry key to allow read permission for the account that will read the username and password (for example, the account of the ASP.NET runtime that accesses the user information).

```
aspnet_setreg -k:SOFTWARE\CourseManagement\identity
-u:"username" -p:"password"
```

In the ASP.NET configuration file, you can define a connection string using Windows authentication:

```
<configuration>
    <add key="connectionString" value="server=servername,
        database=database, trusted_connection=true" />
</configuration>
```

The username and password from the registry are used if you specify that the user should be impersonated with the `<identity>` element. Setting the `userName` and `password` attributes to a value that starts with `registry` ensures that the identity information is taken from the registry.[3]

```
<identity impersonate="true"
userName="registry:HKLM\Software\CourseManagement\ASPNET_SETREG,
    userName"
password="registry:HKLM\Software\CourseManagement\ASPNET_SETREG,
    password" />
```

This account will be impersonated when the ASP.NET page is accessed, so this account will be used to open the database connection. This account must have access to the database and read access to the registry key.

Internet Information Server

With business applications, Internet Information Server (IIS) plays a role with ASP.NET Web applications, ASP.NET Web services, and as a host for .NET remoting. With regard to IIS, this discussion covers authentication and secure data transfer.

Authentication

With IIS, you can configure authentication as shown in Figure 12-2. To configure authentication, select a Web site in the Internet Information Services Manager,[4] and then open the Directory Security tab after selecting Action | Properties.

When anonymous access is enabled, the user accessing the Web site does not need to supply a username because the credentials that are used with anonymous users are defined with a Windows user account with the configuration setting. By default, an account called IUSR_<hostname>[5] is used; for resources that should be accessed by anonymous users, this is the account you used to define ACLs.

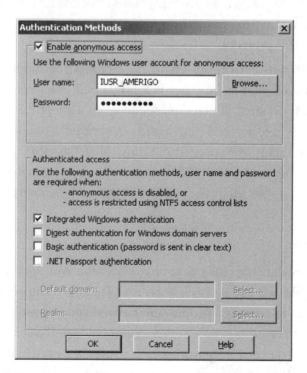

Figure 12-2   Configure IIS authentication.

If you allow only authenticated users to access the Web site, you can deselect the option Enable Anonymous Access. You can define authentication with these options:

- **Integrated Windows authentication**—With Windows authentication, exchange of the logon information is passed in a secure form. This authentication mechanism uses either NTML or Kerberos. You can use integrated Windows authentication only if the user who accesses the Web site is using Internet Explorer and a firewall is not in the way from the client to the Web server.

- **Digest authentication**—Digest authentication is preferred to basic authentication because the password is not sent in clear text. The disadvantage of digest authentication is that it is only possible with Active Directory accounts—you cannot use local Windows accounts on the Web server— and the client must be Internet Explorer 5.0 or higher.

- **Basic authentication**—Basic authentication is an unsecure authentication mechanism. Here passwords are transmitted in clear text. If you use basic authentication, you can secure the exchange of username and password by using the HTTPS protocol.

- **.NET Passport authentication**—With .NET Passport authentication, the user has the advantage that he only needs a single pair of username/password to access all Passport sites. When the user accesses a site, he is redirected to the Passport site, where account information is verified. Then he is redirected to the Web site if logon was successful. Using .NET Passport, you still have to manage a custom user profile, because the only user information from the Passport site is a user identifier called PUID (.NET Passport unique ID).

Secure Data Transfer

For secure data transfer from the client browser to the Web server, you can use the HTTPS protocol. HTTPS is a secure HyperText Transfer Protocol that uses Secure Sockets Layer (SSL) to encrypt the data sent between computers. HTTPS requires a secure server, and to set up a secure server you must install a server certificate.

You can get a server certificate from a certification authority such as Verisign.[6] If you use IIS only within an intranet, you can also install certificate services that are available with Windows Server 2003. Figure 12-3 shows the installation of the certificate services selected from the Control Panel option Add Remove Programs | Windows Components.

To install a server certificate with IIS, you can open the IIS manager and select a Web site in the tree view. Then select Action | Properties on the menu and open the Directory Security tab to install a server certificate (see Figure 12-4). Clicking the button Server Certificate starts the Web Server Certificate Wizard, which automatically requests a certificate from the certification authority.

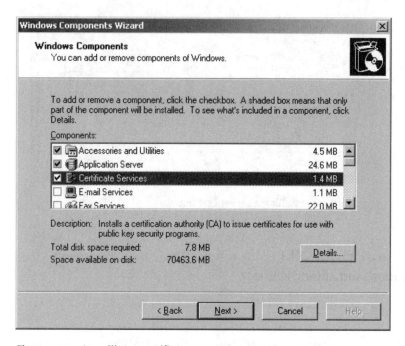

Figure 12-3   Installing a certificate server.

ASP.NET Web Applications

ASP.NET security plays an important role with ASP.NET Web applications and ASP.NET Web services. ASP.NET is often the front end of Enterprise Services, so here the authentication is done before serviced components get a chance to verify the user. Therefore, a very important aspect is the user identity of the user to run the ASP.NET process.

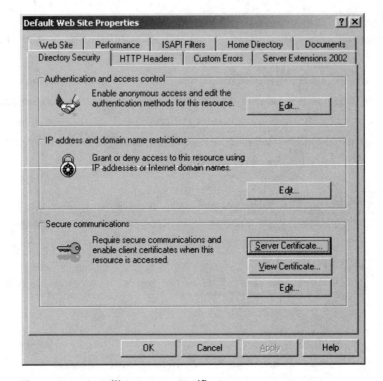

Figure 12-4   Installing a server certificate.

With regard to ASP.NET Web applications, this discussion covers identity, authentication, and authorization.

Identity

With IIS 5, you can define the identity of the ASP.NET runtime process with the <processModel> element in the .NET configuration file machine.config:

```
<processModel enable="true" userName="machine"
   password="AutoGenerate"
   . . .
/>
```

By default, the username is set to machine, which defines that the unprivileged account ASP.NET is used. The value SYSTEM defines that the highly privileged account System is used. You can configure any other account to be used with the ASP.NET runtime.

With IIS 6, the identity configuration for ASP.NET is different, because IIS 6 integrates ASP.NET functionality in the management tools. Instead of configuring the account with the .NET machine configuration file, you configure the identity with IIS 6 application pools. You can create and configure application pools and define the identity of the application pool in IIS Manager (see Figure 12-5). By default, the account used is Network Service, although you can also configure any Windows account you need.

The application pool to be used for a Web application is defined with the Web application configuration. Figure 12-6 shows how you can define which application pool should be used with a specific Web application.

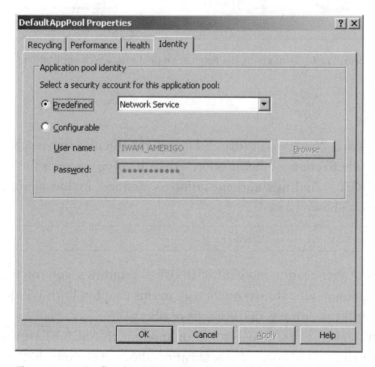

Figure 12-5   Configuring IIS 6 application pool identity.

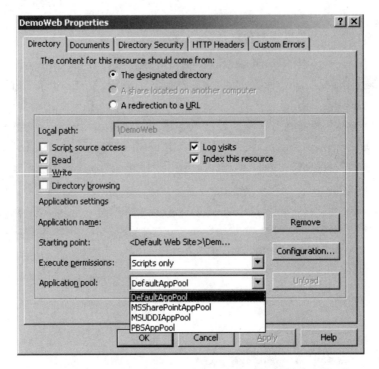

Figure 12-6   Configuring the application pool with a Web application.

Authentication

ASP.NET supports Windows, Forms, and Passport authentication mechanisms. With **Windows authentication**, authentication is the job of IIS, acting as the security front end of ASP.NET. Windows authentication is defined in the configuration file web.config, as shown here:

```
<authentication mode="Windows" />
```

If you set the authentication mode of ASP.NET to Windows, you can use any of the IIS authentication modes shown previously in this chapter. With Windows authentication, the authentication is in the hands of IIS.

The most frequently used authentication mode with ASP.NET Web applications is **Forms authentication**. Forms authentication allows a custom check of username and password where you can store the logon information in the database, simple files, or wherever you want. Forms authentication is configured as follows:

```
<authentication mode="Forms">
  <forms name=".ASPXAUTH" loginUrl="login.aspx"
    protection="All" />
</authentication>
```

The Forms authentication mechanism uses a cookie[7] to verify that a client is already logged on. The name of the cookie is defined with the `name` attribute of the `forms` tag. The attribute `protection="All"` specifies that the cookie is protected with encryption and validation. If the user is not logged on (no cookie is passed from the client to the server), the request is redirected to the page defined by the `loginUrl` attribute.

In the login page, the user can be asked for a username and a password. The code sample here gets the username and password from two `TextBox` controls: `textUsername` and `textPassword`. If the password is not stored in clear text, the method `FormsAuthentication.HashPasswordForStoringInConfigFile` can be used, which uses a hash algorithm (here MD5) to hash the password. The `Authenticate` method is a custom method to verify username/password; you can write an implementation to verify the logon information with data from the database or from an XML file. If the `Authenticate` method returns true, `FormsAuthentication.RedirectFromLoginPage` is used to redirect the request to the page that was first requested. The first parameter of this method sets the username that can be accessed within other pages (using `HttpContext.User.Identity.Name`). The second parameter defines whether the cookie that is sent to the client should be stored permanently, or whether a temporary cookie should be used. Passing `false` returns a temporary cookie that is removed when the browser is closed.

If the `Authenticate` method returns false, an error message is shown:

```
void OnLogin(Object sender, EventArgs e)
{
    string username = textUsername.Text;
    string password =
```

```
FormsAuthentication.HashPasswordForStoringInConfigFile(
    textPassword.Text, "md5");

if (Authenticate(username, password))
{
    FormsAuthentication.RedirectFromLoginPage(username,
        false);
}
else
{
    labelError.Text = "Login failed";
}
}
```

Authorization

Who is allowed to access pages is defined in the `<authorization>` section. To allow only authenticated users, you must set the `<deny>` element with the attribute `users="?"`:

```
<authorization>
    <deny users="?" />
</authorization>
```

With ASP.NET authorization, you can define different settings for every file or directory by specifying a `<location>` element around the `<system.web>` configuration:

```
<location path="Info.aspx">
    <system.web>
        <authorization>
            <allow users="*"/>
        </authorization>
    </system.web>
</location>
```

You can specify authorization for users or groups of users. In the `<allow>` and `<deny>` sections, the `users` attribute specifies users who are allowed or denied access to the resource, whereas user groups are defined with the `roles` attribute. If Windows authentication is used, Windows groups map directly to ASP.NET roles; however, you can also add custom roles to ASP.NET roles.

ASP.NET Web Services

ASP.NET Web services use the same base technology as ASP.NET Web applications, so the Windows authentication mechanism is available, too. You cannot use Forms authentication because it is not possible to present a user interface for the client application.

Whereas XML Web services are platform independent, this cannot be said for Windows authentication. For platform-independent authentication, you can use a SOAP header, either creating this yourself, or by using Web Services Enhancement (WSE)[8] from Microsoft. In this section, both techniques are discussed.

Authentication with ASP.NET Web Services and SOAP Headers

A SOAP header is passed with the SOAP request. ASP.NET enables you to define a custom SOAP header by creating a class that derives from `SoapHeader` and applying the attribute `[SoapHeader]` to a Web method. In the following example, the username and password will be sent inside a SOAP header.

Listing 12-1 shows the class `AuthenticationInfo` that derives from `SoapHeader`. With such a class, you just have to define the data that is sent in the SOAP header; here the class has two public fields: `Username` and `Password`.

Listing 12-1   A Custom SOAP Header Class AuthenticationInfo

```
public class AuthenticationInfo : SoapHeader
{
   public string Username;
   public string Password;
}
```

To make the SOAP header available and required with the Web method, the attribute `[SoapHeader]` is applied to the method `GetCourses` in Listing 12-2. The `[Soap-Header]` attribute requires a string in the constructor that defines the name of a public field; here the public field is named `authInfo` and is of type `Authentica-tionInfo`. If you set this attribute, the members from the `AuthenticationInfo` class are passed with the SOAP request and can be read inside the Web method by using the public field.

Listing 12-2   Using the [SoapHeader] Attribute

```
[WebService(Namespace="http://christiannagel.com/demoservices/2004")]
public class CourseService
{
    public AuthenticationInfo authInfo;

    [WebMethod]
    [return: XmlArray("Courses")]
    [return: XmlArrayItem("Course")]
    [SoapHeader("authInfo")]
    public Course[] GetCourses()
    {
        //... read user information in authInfo

        if (!User.Identity.IsAuthenticated)
        {
            XmlQualifiedName name = new
                XmlQualifiedName("AuthenticationError");
            SoapException ex = new SoapException(
                "Request denied", name);
            throw ex;
        }
        //...
    }
}
```

Listing 12-3 shows the SOAP request that must be sent from the client to the service. Inside the envelope, you can see the element `<soap:Header>` with authentication information.

Listing 12-3   SOAP Request with a SOAP Header

```
<soap:Envelope xmlns:xsi="http://www.w3.org/2001/XMLSchema-instance"
xmlns:xsd="http://www.w3.org/2001/XMLSchema" xmlns:soap="http://schemas.xml-
soap.org/soap/envelope/">
  <soap:Header>
    <AuthenticationInfo
       xmlns="http://christiannagel.com/Demos/CourseServices/2004">
      <Username>string</Username>
      <Password>string</Password>
    </AuthenticationInfo>
  </soap:Header>
  <soap:Body>
```

```
<GetCourses
    xmlns="http://christiannagel.com/Demos/CourseServices/2004" />
</soap:Body>
</soap:Envelope>
```

When you create a Web services proxy for the client application, the class `Authentication Info` is created. As you can see in Listing 12-4, you can create an instance of the `AuthenticationInfo` class and set the property `AuthenticationInfo-Value` of the proxy class to define the user identity information to be passed to the service.

Listing 12-4   Client Application

```
CourseManagement.AuthenticationInfo authInfo =
    new CourseManagement.AuthenticationInfo(
    "username", "password");

CourseManagement.CourseService ws =
    new CourseManagement.CourseService();
ws.AuthenticationInfoValue = authInfo;
Course[] courses = ws.GetCourses();
```

For the Web service user authentication, you can create a handler that deals with checking the user. A handler is a class that implements the interface `IHttpModule`. In the handler, you can access the SOAP header to read and verify (for example, by checking a database) the user information.

Authentication with Web Services Enhancement

As an alternative to using a custom SOAP header, you can use the SOAP header information that is defined with the WS-Security specification. One part of the WS-Security specification is a `<UsernameToken>` element that is used for authentication. The content of this element looks very similar to the `<AuthenticationInfo>` element shown previously in this chapter.

For ASP.NET 1.1, you can get an implementation of WS-Security by downloading Web Services Enhancement (WSE) 2.0[9] from Microsoft. WSE is a toolkit consisting of assemblies for ASP.NET Web services and .NET clients. The toolkit implements some of the Web services proposed standards, such as securing Web services, routing SOAP messages between servers, and sending attachments that cannot be serialized as XML.

To use WSE, you must configure the `Microsoft.Web.Services` configuration handler and add a SOAP extension type in the configuration file `web.config`, as shown in Listing 12-5.

Listing 12-5   Configuration of WSE in Web.config

```
<configSections>
  <section name="microsoft.web.services"
type="Microsoft.Web.Services.Configuration.WebServicesConfiguration,
Microsoft.Web.Services, Version=2.0.0.0, Culture=neutral,
PublicKeyToken=31bf3856ad364e35" />
</configSections>

<system.web>
  <webServices>
    <soapExtensionTypes>
      <add type="Microsoft.Web.Services.WebServicesExtension,
        Microsoft.Web.Services,Version=2.0.0.0, Culture=neutral,
        PublicKeyToken=31bf3856ad364e35"
        priority="1" group="0"/>
    </soapExtensionTypes>
  </webServices>
```

Listing 12-6 shows how you can access authentication information with WSE. When using the WSE classes, you must import the namespaces `Microsoft.Web.Services` and `Microsoft.Web.Services.Security`. Within the Web method, you can access the SOAP context with the `Current` property of the `RequestSoapContext` class. The method `GetUsernameToken` is a custom helper method that extracts the user token from the context.

Listing 12-6   Accessing the SoapContext

```
[WebMethod]
[return: XmlArray("Courses")]
[return: XmlArrayItem("Course")]
public Course[] GetCourses()
{
    SoapContext requestContext = RequestSoapContext.Current;
    if (requestContext == null)
    {
```

```
        // throw SOAP error - non-SOAP request or WSE not installed
    }

    UsernameToken theToken = GetUsernameToken(requestContext);
    string username = theToken.Username;
    string password = theToken.Password;

    //...
}
```

Listing 12-7 shows how you can extract the UsernameToken from the SOAP context. The SoapContext contains information from the client request, such as security information referrals, or attachments. You can access the security information from the Security property; Security.Elements returns a collection of objects that implement the ISecurityElement interface. One type of ISecurityElement is a signature, and that is what we are interested in here. The signature contains security tokens (for example, the UsernameToken that is fetched from the SecurityToken property).

Listing 12-7   Extracting the UsernameToken

```
private UsernameToken GetUsernameToken(
    SoapContext requestContext)
{
    UsernameToken token = null;
    foreach (ISecurityElement securityElement in
        requestContext.Security.Elements)
    {
        Signature sig = securityElement as Signature;
        if (sig != null)
        {
            if ((sig.SignatureOptions &
                SignatureOptions.IncludeSoapBody) != 0)
            {
                SecurityToken securityToken = sig.SecurityToken;
                if (securityToken is UsernameToken)
                {
                    token = (UsernameToken) securityToken;
                }
            }
        }
    }
    return token;
}
```

The authentication used to verify that the username and password are valid can be done with the help of a custom token manager class. The configuration for WSE is shown in Listing 12-8, using the element `<microsoft.web.services>` in the configuration file `web.config`. You must define a username token manager within the `<security>` element, with the help of the `<SecurityTokenManager>` element. The type attribute specifies the name of the class and the assembly.

Listing 12-8   Configuration of a Custom Token Manager

```
<microsoft.web.services>
  <security>
    <SecurityTokenManager qname="wsse:UsernameToken" type=
      "Demos.CustomUsernameTokenProvider, CustomTokenProvider"
    />
  </security>
</microsoft.web.services>
```

The username token manager class is shown in Listing 12-9. For custom authentication based on username and password, you must create a class that derives from the base class `UsernameTokenManager`, where you can do the username and password verification in the overridden method `AuthenticateToken`. With this method, a `UsernameToken` object is received that you can use to verify the username and password, perhaps with data from a database.

Listing 12-9   A Custom Username Token Manager

```
public class CustomUsernameTokenManager : UsernameTokenManager
{
    protected override string AuthenticateToken(
        UsernameToken token)
    {
        if (token == null)
            return new ArgumentNullException(
                "No username token received");

        // TBD: verify username/password
        // e.g., with entries in a database

        return token.Username;
    }
}
```

Enterprise Services

The security with Enterprise Services is discussed next, covering the following different aspects:

- You can configure the identity of the process that the serviced components run in.
- With role-based security, you can define an authorization mechanism to decide who is allowed to use components, interfaces, and methods.
- Impersonation and delegation define whether access to resources is allowed with the same identity.
- Using authentication levels, you can define whether data that is sent across the network should be readable by network sniffers.

All this is explained with more detail next.

Identity

If the Enterprise Services application is configured as a server application, you can configure the identity setting to indicate which user should be used for the process to run the application. For debugging purposes, Interactive User is the best configuration to use. With a production system, configuring Interactive User proves useful only if the application is running on the client system. You should never use this setting on a server system, because this means if no user is logged on to the system, the application will not run.

With an application that should run on the server, you must configure a user as shown in Figure 12-7. For the application, you must create a specific Windows account that has the user right Logon as a Batch Job. For the account you configure here, you also have to assign access permissions to the resources that the serviced components access (for example, to the message queue or files).

> **NOTE: Identities and Library Applications**
>
> With library applications, you cannot configure the identity because the application runs in the process of the client application, so the identity of the client process is used.

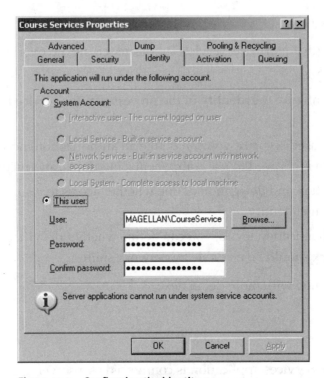

Figure 12-7　Configuring the identity.

If the Enterprise Services application is configured as a Windows service, you can also set the identity to local service, network service, or local system.

The **local system** account is a special built-in account that has full access to the local system. On the local system, this account has more privileges than a system administrator. If the local system account is on a domain controller, the account can access the Active Directory.

The **local service** account is another special built-in account. This account has fewer permissions compared to the local system account, and it has the same access level as members of the Users group, so this account can help you protect resources.

If the serviced component needs access to network resources, you can use the **network service** account instead. This account is similar to the local service account; however, it is allowed to access the network.

> **Interactive User**
>
> The interactive user should only be used if the application is running on the client system, and should be used only when the user is logged on, and for debugging purposes.
>
> For Enterprise Services applications that run on the server system, you must use a different user account.

Authorization

Enterprise Services uses a role-based authorization check. The programmer defines the roles, whereas the system administrator assigns users and groups as members of roles.

Roles are defined using simple strings that are valid only within an Enterprise Services application. Strings make it easy to verify whether a user accessing the component is a member of a specific role.

> **Separation of Roles and Users/Groups**
>
> The separation of roles and Windows users/groups allows the roles to be defined by the programmer, whereas the system administrator adds users and groups to the roles when maintaining the application.

Enabling Access Checks

With a COM+ application, you can define which users or user groups are allowed to use applications, components, interfaces, and methods. To enable access checks with the application, you must enable the option Enforce Access Checks for This Application, as shown in Figure 12-8. By setting the security level, you can define whether access check should be done on the process or component level. If you set this option to the component level, you can define different access for components, interfaces, and methods.

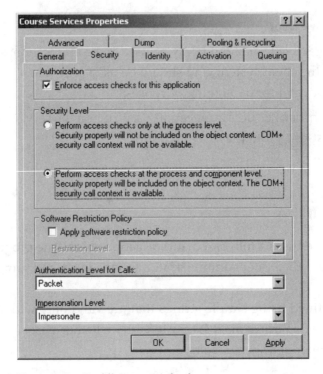

Figure 12-8   Enabling access checks.

You can configure access checks using the assembly attribute [Application-AccessControl]. With the named property AccessChecksLevel, you can define whether the access check should only happen with the application (AccessChecks-LevelOption.Application) or with the application and components (Access-ChecksLevelOption.ApplicationComponent).

```
[assembly: ApplicationAccessControl(true,
    AccessChecksLevel=AccessChecksLevelOption.ApplicationComponent)]
```

Defining Roles

To configure access checks, you must define roles using simple strings, so there is no need to deal with checking ACLs. You can define roles by selecting the item Role in the tree view of the Component Services Explorer and then selecting Action | New | Role.

Figure 12-9 shows the roles Assistant, Attendee, and Curriculum Manager. The new role Admin is being created. In this figure, the roles are shown as hats; the hats demonstrate that one user can have multiple roles—he or she can wear multiple hats.

You can define roles in the assembly with the attribute class `SecurityRole-Attribute`. This is a good way to define the roles because they are defined by the programmer and not by the system administrator.

Listing 12-10 uses the attribute `[SecurityRole]` to define the roles Attendee, Assistant, and Curriculum Manager. If you use the constructor with two arguments and assign the second argument a `true` value, the property `SetEveryoneAccess` is set to `true`. This optional value defines that the Everyone group should automatically be added to the role. For all other roles, the system manager must define the users and groups that should act as the specific role.

Listing 12-10   Defining Roles

```
[assembly: SecurityRole("Attendee", true)]
[assembly: SecurityRole("Assistant")]
[assembly: SecurityRole("Curriculum Manager")]
```

Figure 12-9   Defining roles.

Defining Role Access

After roles are defined, you can determine which roles are allowed to use the application, components, interfaces, and methods. You can find the option Enforce Component Level Access Checks on the Security tab of the component properties (see Figure 12-10). Enabling this option defines that access is checked at the component level; after you set this, you can define which roles are allowed to use the component. If you allow roles to use the component, these roles are allowed to use every interface and every method of the component. If you want a stricter granularity, you can define access checks at the interface and method level.

As you configure the security options of an interface, you can define which roles are allowed to use the interface (see Figure 12-11). The roles that are already allowed to use the component are also allowed to use the interface and cannot be deselected. The allowed roles are shown as Roles Inherited by Selected Item(s). In the figure, the inherited role is Curriculum Manager.

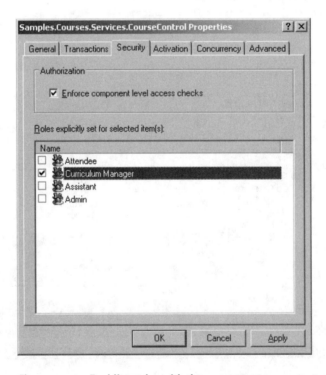

Figure 12-10 Enabling roles with the component.

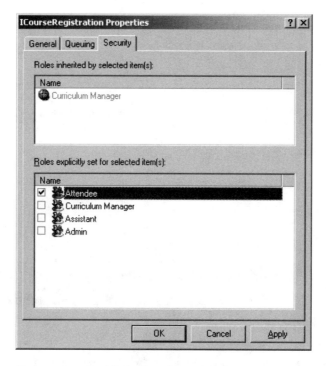

Figure 12-11   Enabling roles with an interface.

In the code, you can define the roles that are allowed to use components/interfaces/methods by applying the attribute [SecurityRole]. Listing 12-11 shows the roles Attendee and Assistant applied to the interface ICourseRegistration. The class CourseControl has the role Curriculum Manager applied to it. With this configuration, curriculum managers are allowed to use all methods of the component, whereas attendees and assistants are allowed to use all methods of the interface ICourseRegistration.

The attribute [SecureMethod] applied to the method RegisterCourse defines that the method can only be used through interfaces. Without this attribute, it would be possible to bypass the security check by calling the method directly on the class. The attribute [SecureMethod] can be applied to the method and class level. Applying this attribute to a method means that the method must be called by using an interface. Applying the attribute to the class means that all methods of the class can be called only by using an interface.

Listing 12-11   Applying Roles to Components

```
[SecurityRole("Attendee")]
[SecurityRole("Assistant")]
public interface ICourseRegistration
{
    [SecureMethod()]
    void RegisterCourse(CourseRegistration courseRegistration);
}

[SecurityRole("Curriculum Manager")]
[Transaction(TransactionOption.Required)]
public class CourseControl : ServicedComponent, ICourseRegistration
{
    //...
```

NOTE: SecurityRole Attribute Behaviors

The attribute [SecurityRole] has two different behaviors. If the attribute is applied as an assembly attribute, a new role with the defined name is created. If the attribute is applied to a class, an interface, or a method, the role is added to the list of roles allowed to use the component/interface/method.

When all the roles are defined, the system administrator can assign users and groups to the roles. Just open the Users element in the tree view of the Component Services Explorer and select Action | New | User. In Figure 12-12, the group Curriculum Managers is added to the role Curriculum Manager.

NOTE: Adding Groups to the List of Users

To add groups to the list of users, you must change the object types by clicking the Object Types button and selecting the Groups option. By default, groups are not shown.

To manage the users and groups that are allowed to use the serviced component application, you can offer a different management tool than the Component Services Explorer. A custom tool can be adapted to the requirements of your application,

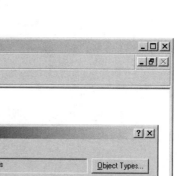

Figure 12-12 Assigning users and groups to roles.

instead of offering all the options to change the behavior of the application. To create a custom tool to manage groups and users, you can use the COMAdmin[10] COM component.

Checking Roles Within Methods

If you want a greater granularity of access check—not only with the method level, but also inside a method—you can check for roles programmatically. This proves useful if you want to allow different users to use the methods depending on the value of parameter(s) that are passed.

An example of such a scenario is when a customer should be given some higher allowance that can only be done by a supervisor. To check for the supervisor role programmatically, you can use the class method `IsCallerInRole` from the class `ContextUtil`.[11] This method needs a string parameter that is the role to check for and returns true if the caller is in the requested role and false if it is not.

```
public void SetAllowance(Customer customer, float allowance)
{
   if (allowance > maxNormalAllowance)
   {
       if (!ContextUtil.IsCallerInRole("Supervisor"))
           throw new UnauthorizedAccessException(
               "You are not allowed to give that much " +
               "allowance. Contact the supervisor");
   }
}
```

Authentication Levels and Impersonation

With the application configuration of Enterprise Services, you can configure the authentication level for calls and impersonation levels. Figure 12-13 shows the Security tab of the Component Services Explorer, where you can change the options. Of course, you can also define these options with attributes.

Authentication Levels

The authentication levels define how the user is identified and how secure the data is when sent across the network. The authentication level can be defined with the attribute class ApplicationAccessControlAttribute, applying the property Authentication to a value of the AuthenticationOption enumeration:

```
[assembly: ApplicationAccessControl(true,
    Authentication=AuthenticationOption.Privacy)]
```

The possible values of the AuthenticationOption enumeration and their meanings are shown in Table 12-1.

> **NOTE: Authentication Levels with Clients and Servers**
> If the caller (client) and callee (server) define different authentication levels, the most secure authentication level is negotiated automatically.

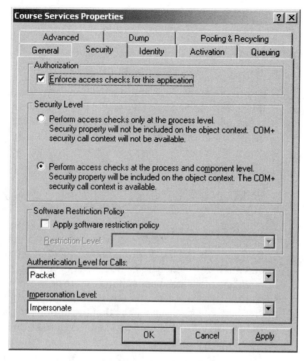

Figure 12-13 Configuring authentication and impersonation levels.

Table 12-1 AuthenticationOption Enumeration

AuthenticationOption	Description
None	If the `AuthenticationOption` is set to `None`, authentication is not done. With this option, the callers are trusted that they are who they say they are. Clearly, you should avoid this option.
Connect	The option `Connect` means that authentication only happens when the client connects to the object. With every method call that is done after the connection happens, no authentication occurs. The security problem that can occur with this option is if the network is sniffed by a malicious user, the malicious user can wait for a legitimate caller and make calls in place of the legitimate caller.
Call	Setting the option to `Call` means that the authentication happens with every method that is called. Regarding security, this is a better choice than the `Connect` option.

Table 12-1   (continued)

AuthenticationOption	Description
Packet	If a single method call requires multiple packets to be transferred across the network, the authentication can happen at different times. It is only done once for all packets in a method call if the `Call` option is used, but with the `Packet` option, authentication is done with every packet that is sent across the network.
Integrity	All the other options shown so far only deal with checking the caller. A malicious user can still change the data in packets sent across the network (for example, change some parameter values). With the option `Integrity`, a checksum is used to verify that the packets are not changed.
Privacy	`Privacy` is the most secure option. In addition to the other options, all data that is sent across the network is encrypted, so it cannot be read by a malicious user sniffing on the network.
Default	The `Default` option means that the option that is defined with the computer settings should be used. The default value is defined with the `DefaultAuthenticationLevel` property in the `LocalComputer` collection settings.[12] The default value of a system is `Packet`.

Impersonation

Usually the client and server applications run with different identities. If you must access resources under the identity of the client, impersonation is needed.

Figure 12-14 shows a distributed solution with a Windows Forms application that is accessing serviced components on a middle-tier server and the serviced component in turn accessing another server. The Windows Forms application is running under the identity of the user John because this user interactively logged on to the system. If the same user account must be used to access the resources on the middle-tier server, the user must be impersonated. In turn, if the same user identity must be used to access the resources on the next server, the user identity must be delegated to the next server.

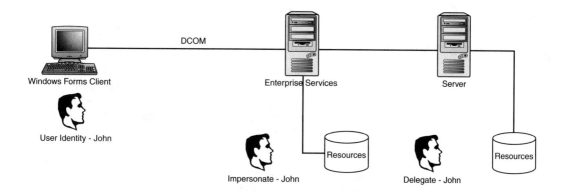

Figure 12-14 Impersonation and delegation.

Impersonation defines a level of trust. Contrary to the other configuration settings that are related with the server part of the Enterprise Services application, the impersonation configuration defines the behavior of the application as a client. Setting the impersonation level with the serviced component defines whether the application that is called by the serviced component is allowed to impersonate the client.

You can define the trust that you give to the server by setting the named property `ImpersonationLevel` with the attribute class `ApplicationAccessControl-Attribute`:

```
[assembly: ApplicationAccessControl(true,
    ImpersonationLevel=ImpersonationLevelOption.Identify)]
```

Table 12-2 lists the different values that you can configure with the `ImpersonationLevelOption` enumeration.

To impersonate the caller identity in the serviced component, you must invoke the Win32 API method `CoImpersonateClient`; to set the identity of the thread back, `CoRevertToSelf` must be called. Listing 12-12 shows a helper class `COMSecurity` that wraps the COM methods. The class `COMSecurity` defines the methods `ImpersonateClient` and `RevertToSelf`. The native methods that are invoked with the Platform Invoke mechanism are defined with the attribute `[DllImport]`.

Table 12-2 ImpersonationLevelOption Enumeration

ImpersonationLevelOption	Description
Anonymous	With the option Anonymous, the client is anonymous to the server. The server cannot get information about the user.
Identify	The impersonation option Identify allows the server to identify the caller. Impersonation can be done to do ACL checks only.
Impersonate	With the Impersonate option, the server is allowed to impersonate the caller identity. This way the server can access local resources acting as the client identity.
Delegate	The Delegate option is the most trusted level. With this level, the server can access resources on other computers as the client identity. Setting this option only works with the Kerberos authentication mechanism.
Default	The Default option means that the option that is defined with the computer settings should be used. The default value is defined with the DefaultImpersonationLevel property in the LocalComputer collection settings. The default value of a system is Identify.

Listing 12-12 Wrapping COM API Calls

```
class COMSecurity
{
    [DllImport("OLE32.DLL", EntryPoint="CoImpersonateClient"
            CharSet=CharSet.Auto)]
    public static extern uint ImpersonateClient();

    [DllImport("OLE32.DLL", EntryPoint="CoRevertToSelf"
            CharSet=CharSet.Auto)]
    public static extern uint RevertToSelf();
}
```

To impersonate the identity of the caller, you can use the COMSecurity class as shown in the method ImpersonationDemo. Using the try/finally section guarantees that the identity is set back if a failure occurs. You cannot keep the impersonated identity across multiple method calls, because the identity is associated with a thread and the thread that is used to deal with a single client can change.

```
public void ImpersonationDemo()
{
   COMSecurity.ImpersonateClient();
   try
   {
      //...
   }
   finally
   {
      COMSecurity.RevertToSelf();
   }
}
```

Reading the Identity of the Caller

To get information about the callers of the serviced component, you can access the security call context by using the class SecurityCallContext. Table 12-3 shows the members of this class.

Table 12-3   SecurityCallContext Class

SecurityCallContext Member	Description
CurrentCall	CurrentCall is a static property that returns an instance of the SecurityCallContext class.
IsSecurityEnabled	IsSecurityEnabled returns true if security is enabled.
NumCallers	NumCallers returns the number of callers that are in the call chain to the serviced component.
DirectCaller	The DirectCaller property returns a Security-Identity object that represents the direct caller of the serviced component.
OriginalCaller	The property OriginalCaller returns a Security-Identity object of the user identity that was the first in the call chain to instantiate a method that finally arrived with the security context of the current serviced component.

Table 12-3   (continued)

SecurityCallContext Member	Description
`Callers`	The `Callers` property returns an instance of the class `SecurityCallers`. `SecurityCallers` is a collection class that contains all `SecurityIdentity` objects that are used in the call chain. The `Callers` property includes the original and direct callers and all identities that are in between the original and direct callers.
`MinAuthenticationLevel`	The `MinAuthenticationLevel` property returns the authentication level that is defined with the security call context. The possible authentication levels were shown earlier in this chapter.
`IsCallerInRole`	The method `IsCallerInRole` requires a string parameter to pass a role. `IsCallerInRole` returns true if the direct caller user identity is in the role that is passed with this method. `SecurityCall-Context.Current-Call.IsCallerInRole("role")` can be used rather than `ContextUtil.IsCaller-InRole("role")`.
`IsUserInRole`	With the method `IsUserInRole`, you can pass any username to check whether this user is in the defined role.

Enterprise Services and .NET Remoting

When you use .NET Enterprise Services in conjunction with .NET remoting[13] and Windows Server 2003, the full COM+ security is available.

Before installing the Enterprise Services application with .NET remoting, you must install a certificate with IIS,[14] because security with .NET remoting is only possible with the HTTPS protocol.

You can enable .NET remoting with the Enterprise Services application by using the `SoapVRoot` property with the class `ApplicationActivationAttribute`:

```
[assembly: ApplicationActivation(ActivationOption.Server,
    SoapVRoot="SecurityDemo")]
```

Registering the Enterprise Services application with the SOAP option[15] creates a virtual Web site. With the security option enabled, the Web site is configured to use HTTPS. You can verify this by starting the IIS Manager, selecting Properties with the new Web site in the tree view, opening the Directory Security tab, and then clicking the button Edit in the section Secure Communication. Figure 12-15 shows the dialog box to enable secure communication with IIS Manager.

By default, anonymous access is disabled.

Now you can create an application proxy to be installed on the client systems. The application proxy automatically uses the HTTPS protocol to access the serviced component.

Figure 12-15 Enabling secure communication with IIS.

Summary

This chapter covered several security aspects. In this chapter, you have seen that you cannot deal with security aspects of serviced components without security configuration of surrounding technologies.

With ASP.NET Web applications, you have seen Windows- and Forms-based authentication mechanisms. Because Web services do not offer a user interface for the client, authentication via SOAP headers was discussed.

With the Enterprise Services application, you have seen how to configure a role-based security that allows defining different access to components, interfaces, and methods. Impersonation and delegation allow accessing resources with the same identity of the caller. The authentication level settings make it possible to encrypt the data that is sent across the network.

1 DCOM and .NET remoting are discussed in Chapter 5, "Networking."

2 You can download this utility from the MSDN Web site at
   `http://support.microsoft.com/default.aspx?scid=KB;en-us;329290`.

3 For this feature, you must install the hotfix 329250:
   `http://support.microsoft.com/default.aspx?scid=KB;en-us;329250`.

4 This tool is available with the Administrative Tools.

5 In the screenshot, this is the account IUSR_AMERIGO.

6 The Web site of Verisign is `http://www.verisign.com`.

7 .NET 2.0 allows for cookieless Forms authentication.

8 The book examples are based on WSE 2.0, a technology that supports Web services specifications. This technology will be replaced by a new communications architecture (codename Indigo) sometime before the release of the Windows operating system codenamed Longhorn. Indigo is discussed in Chapter 14, "The Future of Distributed Applications."

9 You can download this toolkit from `http://msdn.microsoft.com/webservices`.

10 The COMAdmin COM component is discussed in Chapter 13, "Deployment and Configuration."

11 The class `ContextUtil` is discussed in Chapter 2, "Object Activation and Contexts."

12 Changing these settings is shown in Chapter 13.

13 Read Chapter 5 for more information about .NET remoting.

14 Installing certificates with IIS is discussed earlier in this chapter.

15 Serviced components that use .NET remoting must also be installed in the global assembly cache.

13
Deployment and Configuration

I N ALL PREVIOUS CHAPTERS, THE ENTERPRISE Services applications have either been installed by using automatic deployment or by using the utility `regsvcs`. The configuration has been done by using attributes or by changing the configuration with the Component Services Explorer. All this is fine on a developer and testing system.

To install the Enterprise Services application on the production system, however, you usually want to create an installation package and offer custom programs that can be used by the system administrator to configure the application.

This chapter explains how you can manage deployment and configuration with Enterprise Services applications. Specifically, this chapter covers the following topics:

- Deployment
- Attributes
- Admin components

Deployment

You can configure Enterprise Services applications with automatic or manual deployment. Before delving into the options in detail, you should familiarize yourself with the basic concepts in the following subsections.

Automatic Deployment

This form of deployment is done automatically when a .NET client application creates a serviced component instance. This is a great feature during development because you do not have to configure the application manually with every new test. However, for the production system, such a deployment scenario is not really usable.

Automatic deployment is not usable with production systems for many reasons, including the following:

- It is not possible to do automatic deployment across the network.
- Administrator privileges are required by the client application. If the client of the serviced component is ASP.NET, the ASP.NET identity does not have administrator privileges.
- The client application must be a .NET application.

Manual Deployment

The Enterprise Services application can be deployed manually with the help of the regsvcs utility. This utility is part of the .NET runtime, so you have it available on all systems where .NET is installed.

With regsvcs, you can set several options that influence registration and configuration of new or existing Enterprise Services applications. Table 13-1 lists the regsvcs options.

Besides configuring the assembly with regsvcs, you should not forget to install the assembly into the global assembly cache.[1] Some services require the assembly in the global assembly cache.

Creating a Custom Installer

The utility regsvcs.exe is a .NET program that uses the classes RegistrationConfig and RegistrationHelper to register the assembly. The automatic registration process uses the same classes to configure the components, although you can use these classes yourself if you're creating a custom registration program.

Table 13-1 Regsvcs Options

Regsvcs Options	Description

`/fc`
`/c`
`/exapp`
	The options `/fc`, `/c`, and `/exapp` influence creation of a new application. The option `/fc` is set by default and ensures that a new application is created if one does not exist. If the application already exists, the existing one is used. If you supply the `/c` option rather than `/fc`, an error occurs if the application already exists. With the option `/exapp`, only an existing application is used; an error occurs if one does not exist.

`/tlb:<tlbfile>` `/extlb`	The `/tlb` and `/extlb` options are for type libraries. The `/tlb` option allows definition of a filename for the exported type library. With the `/extlb` option, you can use an existing type library.
`/appname:<name>` `/parname:<name>`	With the `/appname` option, you can define a name that will be used for the newly created application, overriding the value that is defined with the attribute class `ApplicationNameAttribute`. You can set a partition name with the `/parname` option.
`/reconfig` `/noreconfig`	If an application already exists, the `/reconfig` option indicates that the configuration values should be changed according to the values that are defined with attributes in the assembly. If you set the option `/noreconfig`, the attributes of the assembly are ignored. By default, the option `/reconfig` is set, so that all changes you have done with the Component Services Explorer are returned to the values of the assembly.
`/nologo` `/quiet`	The `/nologo` option suppresses output of the logo. The `/quiet` option suppresses not only the logo, but also any other output. This option is helpful if you use `regsvcs` in an installation script.
`/componly`	The `/componly` option defines that interfaces and methods should not be registered, just components and applications.
`/appdir:<path>`	The `/appdir` option defines the root directory of the application. You should use this option to set the directory where you place files to be read using a relative path.
`/u`	The `/u` option enables you to uninstall the application.

Table 13-2 shows the properties of the `RegistrationConfig` class, which defines the configuration options used by the `RegistrationHelper` class. The properties of this class have similar meanings to the options of the `regsvcs` utility.

Installation flags that can be set with the `RegistrationConfig` enumeration are shown in Table 13-3.

Table 13-4 shows the methods of the class `RegistrationHelper`.

Table 13-2 RegistrationConfig Class

RegistrationConfig Properties	Description
Application	The `Application` property defines the name of the application. This property is used by the `regsvcs` utility with the `/appname` option in Table 13-1.
ApplicationRootDirectory	The `ApplicationRootDirectory` property defines the root directory of the application. See the `/appdir` option in Table 13-1.
AssemblyFile	The `AssemblyFile` property defines the filename of the assembly that should be installed.
Partition	The `Partition` property defines the partition name. See the `/parname` option in Table 13-1.
TypeLibrary	The `TypeLibrary` property defines the name of the type library that is created during the installation and configuration. See the `/tlb` option in Table 13-1.
InstallationFlags	The `InstallationFlags` property enables you to specify how the registration should behave if the application already exists. The values that you can set with the `InstallationFlags` are defined by an enumeration. This enumeration is shown in Table 13-3.

Table 13-3 InstallationFlags Enumeration

InstallationFlags Enumeration Values	Description
Default	With the value of `Default`, it is assumed that the application already exists and is registered and configured.

Table 13-3 (continued)

InstallationFlags Enumeration Values	Description
CreateTargetApplication	A new application is created. See the /c option in Table 13-1.
FindOrCreateTargetApplication	Either a new application is created, or an existing application is used. See the /fc option in Table 13-1.
ReconfigureExistingApplication	An existing application is newly configured. See the /exapp option in Table 13-1.
ExpectExistingTypeLib	The type library. See the /extlb option in Table 13-1.
ConfigureComponentsOnly	See the /Componly option in Table 13-1.
ReportWarningsToConsole	Setting this value writes warnings to the console. With the regsvcs utility, warnings are reported by default. The /quiet option suppresses warnings.
Install Register Configure	The enumeration values Configure, Install, and Register should *not* be used anymore.

Table 13-4 RegistrationHelper Class

RegistrationHelper Methods	Description
InstallAssembly	The method InstallAssembly enables you to pass an assembly file with parameters to define the application name, type library, and installation flags.
InstallAssemblyFromConfig	The method InstallAssemblyFromConfig requires a RegistrationConfig parameter that defines the configuration settings.
UninstallAssembly UninstallAssemblyFromConfig	The methods UninstallAssembly and UninstallAssemblyFromConfig allow uninstallation of the serviced component, either with single parameters or with a RegistrationConfig parameter.

In addition to the `RegistrationHelper` class, you can use a `Registration-HelperTx` class. `RegistrationHelperTx` offers the same methods to install the components, but this class supports transactions. `RegistrationHelperTx` is a serviced component because it derives from the base class `ServicedComponent` and is marked with transactional attributes. You can see this component in the Component Services Explorer with the application .NET Utilities.

Listing 13-1 shows how you can use the `RegistrationHelper` class. First an instance of the `RegistrationConfig` class is created, where the properties are set to define the application name, the assembly, and the installation flags. The registration configuration is passed to the method `InstallAssemblyFromConfig`. If an exception is raised (for example, the application is already existing, or the assembly cannot be loaded), the exception of type `RegistrationException` is caught. A registration exception contains error information with a collection of type `RegistrationErrorInfo`.

Listing 13-1   Using the RegistrationHelper Class

```
static void Main()
{
    RegistrationConfig config = new RegistrationConfig();
    config.Application = "Demo Application";
    config.AssemblyFile = "c:/demoapplications/demoapp.dll";
    config.InstallationFlags =
        InstallationFlags.CreateTargetApplication |
        InstallationFlags.ReportWarningsToConsole;

    try
    {
        RegistrationHelper helper = new RegistrationHelper();
        helper.InstallAssemblyFromConfig(ref config);
    }
    catch (RegistrationException ex)
    {
        if (ex.ErrorInfo != null)
        {
            foreach (RegistrationErrorInfo info in ex.ErrorInfo)
            {
                Console.WriteLine("error: {0}, {1}",
                    info.ErrorCode, info.ErrorString);
            }
        }
    }
}
```

```
catch (COMException ex)
{
   Console.WriteLine("COM Error: {0} {1}",
      ex.ErrorCode, ex.Message);
}
}
```

NOTE: Error Information

In case of errors, do not forget to check the event log. The errors logged here are often much more descriptive than the errors you get from the exceptions.

Event Logging

To write event log messages, you can use the EventLog class from the namespace System.Diagnostics.

This class is simple to use: You just have to invoke the static method WriteEntry as shown here to write a message to the event log. The first argument specifies the event source, which can be the name of the application that generates the event. With the second argument, you can set a text to describe the event. The third argument specifies the type of the event. With the type, you can define whether the message is just for informational purposes, a warning, or an error.

```
EventLog.WriteEntry("Sample Application", "Error Message",
   EventLogEntryType.Error);
```

The static method WriteEntry adds a log entry to the application log, as you can verify with the admin tool Event View. You can start the Event View from the Administrative Tools.

If you want to create a separate log for your application, you can do this with the static method CreateEventSource. In the short code sample, a new event source with the name Sample Application in the log SamplesLog is created if it does not already exist. Next, an EventLog object is instantiated. With an EventLog object, you can set the Log and Source properties to define where the log entries should be written.

```
if (!EventLog.Exists("SamplesLog"))
    EventLog.CreateEventSource("Sample Application", "SamplesLog");

EventLog log = new EventLog();
log.Log = "SamplesLog";
log.Source = "Sample Application";
log.WriteEntry("Error Message", EventLogEntryType.Warning);
```

Creating an Installation Package

For easy distribution, you can create Microsoft Installer packages directly with the COM+ Application Export Wizard. You can create separate packages for a server installation and for a proxy installation on the client system.

Figure 13-1 shows the dialog box you get when you choose Action | Export in the Component Services Explorer. You must have an application selected to see this menu.

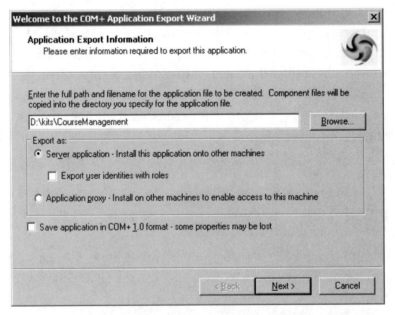

Figure 13-1   Creating an MSI package with the COM+ Application Export Wizard.

Selecting the option Server Application creates an MSI package that can be installed on other server systems. This package includes all components with all their settings. If you select the option Export User Identities with Roles, the users who are assigned to the roles[2] are stored in the package. This option is only useful if the installation of the package is done in the same Active Directory domain where the package is created, because the security identifiers that are stored with the roles are not available in a different domain.

With the option Application Proxy, an MSI package is created that contains proxy components that can be installed on the client systems.

The option Save Application in COM+ 1.0 Format proves useful if the package should be installed on Windows 2000 systems. However, because COM+ 1.0 has fewer features than COM+ 1.5, the configuration of the new features is lost.

With the installation of the MSI package, the application proxy gets installed and configured. The installation of the assemblies and type libraries is in the directory <program files>\ComPlus Applications\<application identifier>. You can see the application identifier on the General screen of the application properties.

The assemblies of the application are not only installed in the Program Files directory, but also in the global assembly cache. There is no need to install the assemblies into the global assembly cache manually.

The application proxy is shown with a different notation in the Component Services Explorer. You can see information about all components in the Explorer, but you cannot change any of these values because these configurations do not apply to client proxies; they only apply to server components. The only option you can change is the remote server name[3] in the Activation settings of the application.

Assembly Installation in the Global Assembly Cache

The assemblies of the serviced components are automatically installed into the global assembly cache. However, all dependent assemblies are not automatically installed. You must install the dependent assemblies manually, or even better, create a custom Installer package for installation of the dependent assemblies.

Attributes

You can define nearly all options to configure Enterprise Services applications by using attributes. In all the previous chapters, many different attributes have been used to configure applications, components, and interfaces. The attributes of the namespace `System.EnterpriseServices` are summarized in Table 13-5.

Table 13-5　Attributes

Attribute	Target	Description
ApplicationName	Assembly	Defines the name of the application.
ApplicationID	Assembly	Defines the application identifier, which is very useful if you need a known identifier. Otherwise, the identifier is automatically created.
Description	Assembly Class Interface Method	Defines descriptive text that shows up in the Serviced Components Explorer.
ApplicationActivation	Assembly	Defines whether the application should run as library or server application.
ConstructionEnabled	Class	Defines a construction string that is used to initialize the component.
EventTrackingEnabled	Class	With this attribute, the component can be monitored in the Component Services Explorer.
MustRunInClientContext	Class	Defines that the component must run in the same context as the caller.
ObjectPooling	Class	With this attribute, you can create an object pool where objects are instantiated before they are needed by clients.
PrivateComponent	Class	A component marked with this attribute can only be used within an application, but not with a caller from outside the application.

Table 13-5 (continued)

Attribute	Target	Description
Synchronization	Class	Defines the synchronization requirements of the component.
JustInTimeActivation	Class	Defines that the component is activated when the client invokes a method and deactivated when the method is finished.
Transaction	Class	Defines the transaction requirements of the component.
AutoComplete	Method	This attribute can be assigned to a method. It defines the automatic outcome of the method and deactivates the component when the method finishes.
LoadBalancingSupported	Class	If load balancing is installed on the server, this attribute defines that the component supports load balancing.
ApplicationQueuing	Assembly	Defines that the application reads messages from a message queue.
InterfaceQueuing	Class Interface	Defines that the interface can be called with a queue moniker.
ExceptionClass	Class	Defines an error class for queued components. This class is instantiated when the message arriving in the message queue cannot be processed.
EventClass	Class	Marks a class as an event class. This class is automatically created by the Enterprise Services runtime.
ApplicationAccessControl	Assembly	Defines whether authentication is enabled with the application and whether the components, interfaces, and methods should have different authentication rules. This attribute also defines impersonation, delegation, and secure data transfer.
ComponentAccessControl	Class	Enables authentication on the component level.

Table 13-5 (continued)

Attribute	Target	Description
SecureMethod	Class Method	Defines that the caller can only use interfaces to access the method(s).
SecurityRole	Assembly Class Interface Method	This attribute defines which roles are needed to access the classes, interfaces, and methods. If this attribute is used on an assembly scope, new roles are created.

Admin Components

Nearly all options to configure the Enterprise Services application can be set by using attributes. However, many configurations will either need to be configured manually or by use of the admin components.[4]

To use the admin components, you need to know how to use the catalog collections and items, and you must know the structure of the catalog. There are hundreds of methods and properties of the COM interfaces and catalog objects, and it is impossible to describe them all here. If you know how to deal with one of these items, you will understand how to deal with the other ones. Knowledge of these components enables you to create an application for the system administrator to install, or to configure the Enterprise Services application.

The admin components are COM components that you can use from within .NET applications by using COM interop. Referencing the COM+ 1.0 admin type library from Visual Studio[5] creates a runtime callable wrapper[6] that you can use from within a .NET application.

Listing 13-2 shows a small example of how you can work with the COM admin components. To start, you always have to create a new instance of the COMAdmin-Catalog. This component offers the interfaces ICOMAdminCatalog and ICOM-AdminCatalog2. ICOMAdminCatalog2 derives from ICOMAdminCatalog, so it offers the same methods as the base interface and adds some more. ICOMAdmin-Catalog was defined with COM+ 1.0, whereas ICOMAdminCatalog2 was defined with COM+ 1.5, so all new features can be accessed only from the newer interface. In the example, the interface ICOMAdminCatalog2 is used.

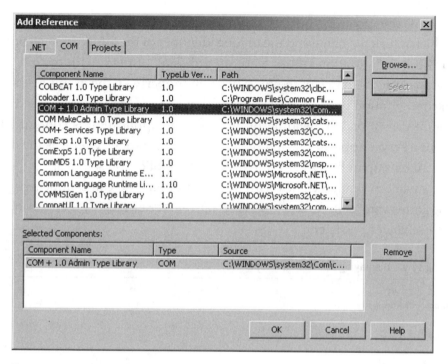

Figure 13-2   Referencing the COM+ 1.0 admin components.

With the returned interface, you can access the top-level collections such as the applications with the `GetCollection` method. This method requires the name of a top-level collection to return the objects. Allowed top-level collections are (among others) `Applications`, `ComputerList`, `DCOMProtocols`, `EventClassesForIID`, `InprocServers`, and `TransientSubscriptions`.

Calling the method `GetCollection` with the argument `Applications` returns a COM object that implements the interface `ICatalogCollection`, enabling you to cast to this interface. The items of this collection are not filled after the method `GetCollection` returns, because you might not need all application objects, so you call the method `Populate` to fill the collection. In addition to using the `Populate` method, you can use `PopulateByKey` and `PopulateByQuery`, which enable you to define a key or a query so that only a subset of the applications is filled into the collection.

To access the values of the application objects, you use the properties Name and Key, which return the name and the unique identifier of the application respectively. If you want configuration values, you can access all of them with the get_Value method, passing the name of the configuration property. In the example, the application configuration properties Activation and Description are fetched. Activation returns 0 or 1 depending on whether the application is configured as a library or a server application, and the Description property returns the description that shows up in the Description field in the application settings.

If you want to change values with the application, you can call the set_Value method, afterward calling SaveChanges on the ICatalogCollection object to make the changes persistent.

Listing 13-2   Displaying Application Properties

```
using System;
using COMAdmin;

class Test
{
    [STAThread]
    static void Main()
    {
        ICOMAdminCatalog2 catalog = new COMAdminCatalog();

        ICatalogCollection applications =
            (ICatalogCollection)catalog.GetCollection("Applications");
        applications.Populate();

        foreach (ICatalogObject application in applications)
        {
            Console.WriteLine("{0}: {1}", application.Name,
                application.Key);
            Console.WriteLine("- {0} {1}",
                application.get_Value("Activation"),
                application.get_Value("Description"));
        }
    }
}
```

Populate and SaveChanges

Remember, when reading collection items with `GetCollection`, you must call `Populate` to fill the items. When writing configuration values to the catalog items with `set_Value`, you must call `SaveChanges` on the `ICatalogCollection` object to write the changes to the catalog.

In Figure 13-3, you can see the structure of catalog and how you can navigate from the `Applications` collection to other items in the catalog. Application objects inside the `Applications` collection contain `Components`, `LegacyComponent`, and `Roles`. Stepping into the hierarchy, every role in the `Roles` collection contains the collection `UsersInRole`. A component in the `Components` collection contains `InterfacesForComponent`, `RolesForComponent`, and `SubscriptionsForComponent` collections.

Listing 13-3 shows how you can get to the components that are configured in this application from an application object. The `Applications` object is accessed via the interface `ICatalogCollection`, which has the `GetCollection` method. This method requires a string parameter that defines the collection that should be accessed—here it is the `Components` collection. Figure 13-3 shows that `Components` is a valid collection name for application objects. The identifier of the application is passed as the second parameter of the `GetCollection`. Again, the `Populate` method must be called to fill all component objects, and then the properties of the component objects can be queried with the `get_Value` method. Here the property values for `ConstructorString` and `DLL` are shown.

Listing 13-3 Iterating Components in an Application Collection

```
ICatalogCollection applications =
    (ICatalogCollection)catalog.GetCollection("Applications");
applications.Populate();

foreach (ICatalogObject application in applications)
{
    Console.WriteLine("{0}: {1}", application.Name,
        application.Key);
    Console.WriteLine("- {0} {1}",
```

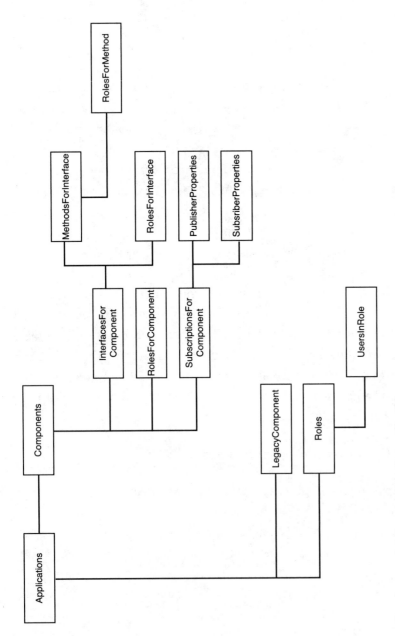

Figure 13-3   Catalog structure for applications.

```
        application.get_Value("Activation"),
        application.get_Value("Description");

    ICatalogCollection components =
        (ICatalogCollection)applications.GetCollection(
            "Components", application.Key);
    components.Populate();

    foreach (ICatalogObject component in components)
    {
        Console.WriteLine("- {0}: {1}", component.Name,
            component.Key);
        Console.WriteLine("- {0}",
            component.get_Value("ConstructorString"));
        Console.WriteLine("- {0}",
            component.get_Value("DLL"));
    }
}
```

Configuring the Application as a Service

COM+ 1.5 has a new feature that allows Enterprise Service applications to be offered as a Windows service. With .NET 1.1, you cannot define a Windows service for the application using attributes, but you can use the admin components to make a Windows service from an existing application.

With Windows services, you have the advantage that the application can start immediately when the system starts. Another advantage is that you send service control requests to the service, which the service reacts to in a custom way.

Listing 13-4 shows how you can create a Windows service. First you must instantiate the COMAdminCatalog component to get access to the ICOMAdminCatalog2 interface. This COM interface offers the method CreateServiceForApplication, which configures the application as a Windows service. The first parameter is the identifier of the application, the second parameter the name of the service. You then specify the start type of the services, error control, dependencies, username, password, and whether the service is allowed to interact with the desktop. For the start type of the service, you can define whether the service should start automatically when the system starts (value SERVICE_AUTO_START) or whether you want to start it manually (value SERVICE_DEMAND_START). For the dependencies, you can set whether other services must be started before this service can start.

Listing 13-4 **Creating a Windows Service**

```
ICOMAdminCatalog2 catalog = new COMAdminCatalog();
catalog.CreateServiceForApplication(
    "{27B91DB8-E9F8-4BF5-88D2-22143DBAC978}", "DemoService",
    "SERVICE_DEMAND_START", "SERVICE_ERROR_NORMAL",
    "", "username", "password", false);
```

Summary

You have several different options when deploying Enterprise Services applications. The easiest option—automatic deployment—has its use only in a development environment. To install the application with a production server, you need to create a Windows Installer package.

You can use .NET attributes to define how the Installer package is configured. You can also use .NET classes to register the application, in particular the class RegistrationHelperTx, allowing custom programs to configure applications.

Despite all the .NET attributes, there are still some options left that you cannot do with .NET, but you can use COM interop for these scenarios. To get access to the complete catalog information from .NET applications, you can use an RCW to access the COM component COMAdminCatalog.

1 Use the utility gacutil to install the assembly into the global assembly cache. The global assembly cache is discussed in Chapter 2, "Object Activation and Contexts."

2 Role-based security is discussed in Chapter 12, "Security."

3 Configuration of the server is discussed in Chapter 5, "Networking."

4 In Chapter 11, "Loosely Coupled Events," admin components are used to create transient subscriptions with loosely coupled events.

5 You can also use the command-line utility tlbimp.exe to reference the COM DLL comadmin.dll in the directory <windows>\<system32>\com.

6 Runtime callable wrappers (RCWs) are discussed in Chapter 4, "COM Interop."

14

The Future of Distributed Applications

NOW THAT YOU HAVE READ CHAPTERS 1 through 13, you know about the existing services that are offered by .NET Enterprise Services. It is time to take a look into the future. This chapter examines upcoming technologies and how you can prepare your current application architectures for a smooth migration.

So far in this book, XML Web services have been used as a front end to Enterprise Services. Web services primarily are based on messages, whereas Enterprise Services is founded on object orientation. Of course, these two technology aspects fit together well, but you have also seen some issues where the root of Enterprise Services—COM technology—comes up. One example is queued components, where a COM moniker must be used to write messages to the message queue. The successor of Enterprise Services is not based on COM, but integrates Web services.

Indigo is the codename of a new communication technology of Microsoft that will be delivered after the release of .NET 2.0. Indigo will integrate the features from ASP.NET Web services, .NET remoting, and .NET Enterprise Services within one product.

Specifically, this chapter covers the following topics:

- Web services specifications
- Indigo overview
- Moving from Enterprise Services to Indigo

Web Services Specifications

Before dealing with Indigo, this discussion first reviews specifications for Web services. Some of these specifications are in a draft stage, and some changes can still be expected. A few of these specifications are already implemented with the Web Services Enhancement (WSE) 2.0 toolkit.[1]

For now, let's look at the main blocks of the specifications and see where these specifications map to Enterprise Services technologies. Figure 14-1 shows the main parts of the Web services specifications and their interrelations: messaging, transactions, reliable messaging, and security.

The following subsections examine these technologies from an Enterprise Services point of view.

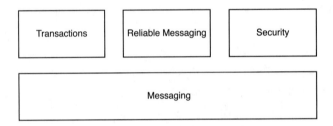

Figure 14-1　Main parts of Web services specifications.

Network Communication

With Enterprise Services, you can use DCOM and .NET remoting[2] as application-level protocols. DCOM is a Microsoft proprietary protocol that has its origin with COM and adds object features to the DCE-RPC[3] protocol. .NET remoting is an application-level protocol that enables you to use different transports and formatters. .NET remoting can be intercepted by using sink providers.

SOAP

Whereas both DCOM and .NET remoting are based on objects (methods of objects are invoked across the network), Web services use a message-based approach. Messages are sent between the client and the server.

A message is constructed by using the SOAP protocol, a lightweight protocol for exchanging structured information.

The content that is sent with a message is a SOAP envelope, which consists of a SOAP header and a SOAP body. The SOAP body includes the methods and parameters that are invoked, whereas the SOAP header includes additional metadata that is sent with the message. With the header, information such as authentication information to identify the caller, routing information to route the message to different servers, and transaction identifiers can be passed. Examples of different SOAP header information are explained in the upcoming sections.

SOAP Document and RPC Styles

For a better understanding of the difference between the object-based method approach and the newer message approach, it is best to look at the different outcomes of SOAP message styles. In its first incarnation, SOAP was defined to invoke methods on a remote object, using an object-oriented approach. At that time, the **RPC style** of the SOAP message was born. Later the **document style** message was invented, which is a more flexible variant that uses a message-based approach. With a message-based approach, documents are sent across the network. In addition to the document and RPC styles, you must differentiate how the parameters are transferred. You define the parameter transfer with the binding style, which can be defined either as **encoded** or **literal**. Normally, the RPC style is used in conjunction with encoding of parameters, whereas the document style is used with literal parameters.

Let's compare the outcomes of the RPC encoding and the document literal styles. The example uses the method `AddCustomer` with a `Customer` parameter:

```
public string AddCustomer(Customer c);
```

The `Customer` class is a simple class that contains `Firstname`, `Lastname`, and an embedded `Address`. The `Address` class contains `City` and `Country` fields:

```
public class Customer
{
    public string Firstname;
    public string Lastname;
```

```
    public Address Address;
}

public class Address
{
    public string City;
    public string Country;
}
```

Listing 14-1 shows how this method is invoked by using a SOAP message with RPC encoding style. The method to be called is defined with the AddCustomer element. This method has a single parameter: c of type Customer. Because of the encoded format, every type is defined within the SOAP message. Every type that is defined within the types namespace has a type associated with the xsi:type attribute. This is very similar to normal method calls that have parameters of specific types.

Listing 14-1   SOAP Message with RPC Encoding Style

```
<soap:Envelope xmlns:xsi="http://www.w3.org/2001/XMLSchema-instance"
  xmlns:xsd="http://www.w3.org/2001/XMLSchema"
  xmlns:soapenc="http://schemas.xmlsoap.org/soap/encoding/"
  xmlns:cn="http://christiannagel.com/2005/demos/"
  xmlns:types="http://christiannagel.com/2005/demos/encodedTypes"
  xmlns:soap="http://schemas.xmlsoap.org/soap/envelope/">
  <soap:Body
    soap:encodingStyle="http://schemas.xmlsoap.org/soap/encoding/">
    <cn:AddCustomer>
      <c href="#id1" />
    </cn:AddCustomer>
    <types:Customer id="id1" xsi:type="types:Customer">
      <Firstname xsi:type="xsd:string">Arnold</Firstname>
      <Lastname xsi:type="xsd:string">Schwarzenegger</Lastname>
      <Address href="#id2" />
    </types:Customer>
    <types:Address id="id2" xsi:type="types:Address">
      <City xsi:type="xsd:string">Los Angeles</City>
      <Country xsi:type="xsd:string">USA</Country>
    </types:Address>
  </soap:Body>
</soap:Envelope>
```

Now compare this to the SOAP message with document literal style in Listing 14-2. Here a message containing AddCustomer is sent with Firstname, Lastname, and

Address elements. Address again contains City and Country elements. You cannot see the types in the SOAP message. Instead, the document that is passed from the client to the server conforms to an XML schema that acts as a contract between the client and server. The XML schema is defined with the WSDL document.

Listing 14-2   SOAP Message with Document Literal Style

```
<soap:Envelope xmlns:xsi="http://www.w3.org/2001/XMLSchema-instance"
xmlns:xsd="http://www.w3.org/2001/XMLSchema"
xmlns:soap="http://schemas.xmlsoap.org/soap/envelope/">
  <soap:Body>
    <AddCustomer xmlns="http://christiannagel.com/2005/demos/">
      <c>
        <Firstname>Arnold</Firstname>
        <Lastname>Schwarzenegger</Lastname>
        <Address>
          <City>Los Angeles</City>
          <Country>USA</Country>
        </Address>
      </c>
    </AddCustomer>
  </soap:Body>
</soap:Envelope>
```

One of the big advantages of the message-based approach using documents is its version independence, if the XML schema is carefully designed. If you add parameters with the RPC method, you can make the caller bound to a specific version of the service. This is different when documents are sent. You can define XML schemas in a way that future versions can be compatible with existing versions, so that older clients do not have problems invoking newer versions of the Web service methods even though the XML schema was extended.

SOAP Header

A big advantage of SOAP is that it can be easily extended. With the SOAP header,[4] you can extend the SOAP message with custom information that is passed independent of the document that is sent in the body of the SOAP message. This extensibility is used with all the other Web services specifications. Contrary to SOAP, the DCOM protocol does not have a documented way to extend it, and with .NET remoting extensions can be added by using sink providers.[5]

SOAP is independent of the protocol beneath it. Nowadays, most Web services make use of the HTTP protocol, but this is not a requirement. One example of a different protocol is shown in the SOAP specification[6] that lists e-mail binding as one option.

One important change with SOAP 1.2 is that SOAP has been rewritten in terms of an **XML information set** (XML infoset) rather than the XML serialization required by SOAP 1.1. The XML infoset is a definition of the information in an XML document and describes the behavior of tools operating on the XML content. With this change, the wire format can be different from the `<?xml ..?>` notation (for example, by using a binary format), so the data sent across the network call can be smaller.

Web Services Addressing

The **WS-Addressing** specification defines a way to address Web services in a protocol-independent format. Listing 14-3 shows an example in which the destination is addressed with the `wsa:To` element and the server knows where the response should be sent with the `wsa:ReplyTo` element.

This addressing mechanism enables you to send messages across firewalls and gateways. This feature cannot be compared with DCOM, because DCOM relies on the underlying protocol for this mechanism, and you must open DCOM ports at firewalls or create network tunnels.

Listing 14-3 WS-Addressing Example

```
<S:Envelope xmlns:S="http://www.w3.org/2003/05/soap-envelope"
    xmlns:wsa="http://schemas.xmlsoap.org/ws/2004/08/addressing">
  <S:Header>
    <wsa:MessageId>
      uuid:F457FDEB-C334-4a50-8D3F-EFCF7C8E0424
    </wsa:MessageId>
    <wsa:ReplyTo>
      <wsa:Address>http://client.com/client1</wsa:Address>
    </wsa:ReplyTo>
    <wsa:To>http://server.com/CourseManagement</wsa:To>
    <wsa:Action>http://server.com/AddCourse<wsa:Action>
  </S:Header>
  <S:Body>
    ...
  </S:Body>
</S:Envelope>
```

Web Services Eventing

WS-Eventing is a Web services specification that can be compared with a higher-level service functionality of Enterprise Services: loosely coupled events[7] (LCEs).

WS-Eventing defines how a SOAP message looks when sent from a client to create a subscription, so that the publisher can call back into the client.

As you can see in the subscription example in Listing 14-4, WS-Eventing is largely based on the WS-Addressing specification. All elements that start with the `wsa` namespace belong to the WS-Addressing specification. In the SOAP header, the server is addressed with the `To` element, and the client is defined with the `ReplyTo` element.

The subscription is done in the SOAP body with the `Subscribe` and `NotifyTo` elements, giving the publisher the link of the Web service that should be called when the `CourseMonitor` event occurs.

With the subscription message, a timeout and a filter can also be defined. The filter has similar functionality to LCEs, which enable the client to define an expression under which case the event should be returned.

Listing 14-4 WS-Eventing Subscription Example

```
<S:Envelope xmlns:S="http://www.w3.org/2003/05/soap-envelope"
    xmlns:wsa="http://schemas.xmlsoap.org/ws/2004/08/addressing"
    xmlns:wse="http://schemas.xmlsoap.org/ws/2004/08/eventing">
  <S:Header>
    <wsa:Action>
      http://schemas.xmlsoap.org/ws/2004/08/eventing/Subscribe
    </wsa:Action>
    <wsa:MessageID>
      uuid:6388E7FF-90D0-4e28-9832-7D1E84D23ACD
    </wsa:MessageID>
    <wsa:ReplyTo>
      <wsa:Address>http://myclient.com/myeventsink</wsa:Address>
    </wsa:ReplyTo>
    <wsa:To>http://server.com/CourseMonitor/EventSource</wsa:To>
  </S:Header>
  <S:Body>
    <wse:Subscribe>
      <wse:Delivery>
        <wse:NotifyTo>
          <wsa:Address>
```

```
          http://myclient.com/myeventsink/MaxCourseAttendeesReached
        </wsa:Address>
        <wsa:ReferenceProperties>
          <ew:MySubscription>4711</ew:MySubscription>
        </wsa:ReferenceProperties>
      </wse:NotifyTo>
    </wse:Delivery>
  </wse:Subscribe>
 </S:Body>
</S:Envelope>
```

Besides defining a subscription message, WS-Eventing defines renew and unsubscribe messages. With a renew message, the subscriber can renew the subscription before it expires. The unsubscribe message is used by a subscriber if there is no more interest in the events.

WS-Eventing Compared to LCE

It might look like WS-Eventing should be compared to .NET remoting events or COM connection points rather than LCE. WS-Eventing does not define an intermediary, which is used with LCE. However, there is a good reason that an intermediary is not defined with the WS-Eventing specification: Such behavior can be part of the implementation.

Using the WS-Addressing specification in conjunction with WS-Eventing, you can achieve an intermediary functionality with a specific implementation.

Reliable Messaging

With business applications, reliable transfer of messages is needed, but the HTTP protocol does not guarantee reliable messaging. The problems that can occur are that messages can be received multiple times or not at all. To provide reliable messaging, the specification WS-ReliableMessaging is defined.

WS-ReliableMessaging uses the following mechanisms to guarantee reliable message transfers:

- **Sequences**—When messages are sent from the source to the destination, a unique identifier is used to define a sequence of messages. Several messages can belong to one sequence.

- **Message numbers**—Within a sequence, the messages are numbered. Every message has a unique number within the sequence. With the message, the last message number is also sent so that the receiver knows when all messages have been received.

- **Acknowledgments**—Acknowledgments are sent to indicate the successful receipt of the message. To increase performance, acknowledgments are sent with acknowledgment ranges (for example, messages 1 through 5 have been received successfully). To increase performance, the receiver can also send a negative acknowledgment (Nack) to indicate that a message must be sent again.

Figure 14-2 shows a sender and a receiver using WS-ReliableMessaging. The application source sends a message to the reliable messaging (RM) source facility. This facility is responsible for transmitting the message several times until it is received by the RM destination. The RM destination receives all messages of a sequence and must put them in the correct order according to the message numbers before the messages are delivered to the application destination.

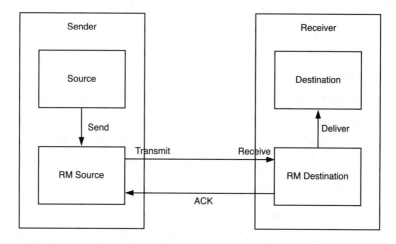

Figure 14-2   Reliable messaging.

Listing 14-5 shows an example of a reliable message that is sent within a SOAP header. The sequence consists of an identifier, a message number, and the last message number. The identifier is created from the destination with a unique ID. In addition to the message number and the last message number, the sequence can contain an expiration time when the message should time out.

Listing 14-5   WS-ReliableMessaging Sequence Example

```
<wsrm:Sequence>
  <wsu:Identifier>http://andromeda.com/sequence/4711</wsu:Identifier>
  <wsrm:MessageNumber>4</wsrm:MessageNumber>
  <wsrm:LastMessage>8</wsrm:LastMessage>
</wsrm:Sequence>
```

Reliable Messaging and Message Queuing[8]

A technology such as message queuing is not defined in the specification WS-ReliableMessaging. Storing messages before they are sent does not affect the wire protocol, so it is not defined within the specification. However, the specification explicitly states that an implementation of WS-ReliableMessaging typically provides (at least as an option) message persistence.

Therefore, with a specific implementation of WS-ReliableMessaging, you can replace the functionality of queued components.

Transactions

As discussed in Chapter 7, "Transaction Services," with transactions the result is all or nothing; either all actions occurred, or nothing happened. Transactions require contexts[9] to identify the objects that participate in the same transaction.

The structure and functionality of .NET Enterprise Services is somewhat similar to Web services specifications. WS-Coordination is a specification similar to the COM+ and .NET remoting contexts. The specification WS-AtomicTransaction is an extension of WS-Coordination to support transactions across Web services. The functionality of WS-AtomicTransaction is somewhat similar to the transaction services.

WS-BusinessActivity is another specification that is an extension of WS-Coordination. This specification deals with long-running transactions.

The following subsections examine these three specifications.

Web Services Coordination

The **WS-Coordination** specification defines a framework to coordinate the actions of distributed applications. This specification enables coordination of multiple Web services (for example, coordination for transaction processing and workflow management that spans different Web services).

The architecture of WS-Coordination defines a **coordination service** and a **coordination context**. Comparing this to serviced components, you can compare the coordination service with the distributed transaction coordinator (DTC) and the coordination context to the transaction context.[10] Similar to the DTC, multiple coordination services interoperate to coordinate different services. The coordination context is used like the transaction context to identify the calls that should be coordinated.

The coordination service is an aggregation of an activation service, a registration service, and a set of coordination protocols:

- **Activation service**—With help of the activation service, a coordination context is created. The activation service offers the method `CreateCoordinationContext`, which returns a `CoordinationContext`.

- **Registration service**—The registration service defines a `Register` method that is used by all participants to register for a coordination protocol.

- **Coordination protocols**—WS-Coordination cannot be used on its own; another coordination specification is needed that defines the coordination type, such as WS-AtomicTransaction or WS-BusinessActivity.

Figure 14-3 helps explain WS-Coordination. In summary, when two applications use their own coordinators, the following steps are taken:

1. Application A sends a `CreateCoordinationContext` message to its activation service for a coordination type. With the `CreateCoordinationContext` message, a coordination type[11] is requested. The activation service returns a

context that contains the activity identifier, the coordination type, and an endpoint reference to the registration service RS1.

2. Now application A can send a message to application B. This message contains the context in the SOAP header.

3. Application B uses a different coordinator, coordinator 2. Application B sends the `CreateCoordinationContext` message to the activation service AS2 with the coordination context from the message that was received. The activation service creates a new coordination context that contains the same activity identifier and coordination type, but a reference to the registration service RS2.

4. Now Application B can register for a coordination protocol that is supported by the coordination type.

5. The registration is forwarded from RS2 to RS1 so that the coordinators can now interact.

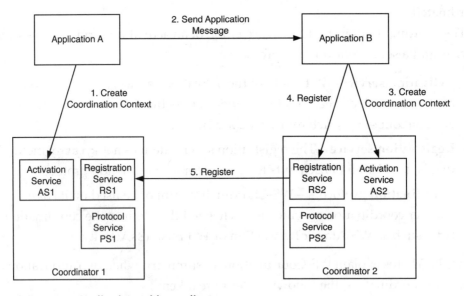

Figure 14-3 Applications with coordinators.

Listing 14-6 shows an example of a coordination context that is passed within the SOAP header to the Web service that participates in the coordination. With the coordination context, the participants know the coordination type and the registration service.

As you can see in Listing 14-6, the coordination context is inside the `<wscoor:CoordinationContext>` element. Inside this element, the `<wscoor:Coorination-Type>` defines the type of the coordination; here the type is defined by `http://schemas.xmlsoap.org/ws/2003/09/wstx`, which is the type definition of WS-AtomicTransaction. The `<wsu:Identifier>` element defines a unique identifier that is used with all messages that will be coordinated (here with all messages that belong to the same transaction). This identifier is created by the activation service; this service returns a new identifier for every new transaction. The element `<wscoor:RegistrationService>` is the information for the participant about how the coordinator can be accessed.

Listing 14-6 Coordination Context Example

```
<S:Envelope
    xmlns:soap="http://www.w3.org/2003/05/soap-envelope">
  <S:Header>
  ...
    <wscoor:CoordinationContext
        xmlns:wscoor="http://schemas.xmlsoap.org/ws/2004/10/wscoor"
        xmlns:tt="http://thinktecture.com/2005/Demos"
        soap:mustUnderstand="true">
      <wscoor:Expires>
        2006-03-24T13:20:00.000-05:00
      </wscoor:Expires>
      <wsu:Identifier>
        http://server.com/CourseServices/3456
      </wsu:Identifier>
      <wscoor:CoordinationType>
        http://schemas.xmlsoap.org/ws/2004/10/wsat
      </wscoor:CoordinationType>
      <wscoor:RegistrationService>
        <wsa:Address>
          http://coordinationserver/coordinationservice/registration
        </wsa:Address>
        <wsa:ReferenceProperties>
          <tt:BetaCode>...</tt:BetaCode>
          <tt:SomeMark>...</tt:SomeMark>
        </wsa:ReferenceProperties>
      </wscoor:RegistrationService>
      <tt:IsolationLevel>
```

```
      RepeatableRead
    </tt:IsolationLevel>
  <wscoor:CoordinationContext>
  ...
  </S:Header>
```

WS-AtomicTransaction

The WS-AtomicTransaction specification is based on the WS-Coordination specification and defines three protocols with all-or-nothing semantics. Those three semantics are completion, volatile two-phase commit, and durable two-phase commit.

This specification is meant to be used for Web services inside the enterprise; it is not meant to have distributed transactions across different companies, because the transaction mechanism means locking of resources. You would not want to lock your database because of a different company interacting with your services. WS-BusinessActivity, which is discussed later in this chapter, is better suited for this kind of interaction.

Like the other transactions that have been shown with Enterprise Services, WS-AtomicTransaction exhibits an all-or-nothing behavior that characterizes these transactions.

The following subsections cover the different protocols supported by WS-AtomicTransaction.

Completion Protocol

The completion protocol is a simple protocol whereby the application sends commit or rollback messages to the coordinator and the coordinator commits or aborts the transaction. When the application sends a commit, the coordinator still can abort the transaction; with a rollback message, the transaction must be aborted.

Two-Phase Commit (2PC) Protocol

With a two-phase commit protocol, the first phase is the preparation of the transaction, whereas the second phase is the commit or abort phase.

Figure 14-4 shows an example of a successful transaction with the 2PC protocol. First the coordinator must send a `Prepare` message to all participants, and the participants return a `Prepared` message if they can fulfill the transaction on their part. When all participants agree to the transactional outcome, the coordinator sends a `Commit` message to all participants, and they return with a `Committed` message after the work has been completed.

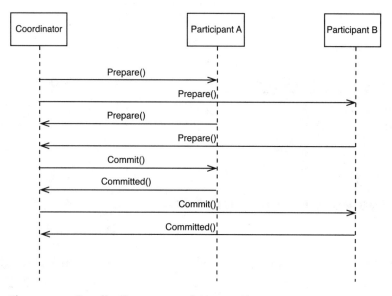

Figure 14-4 Coordinating a successful transaction.

When the participant has agreed to the transaction with a `Prepared` message, there is no way that he can abort the transaction afterward; after the participant has agreed to a successful preparation, it cannot be undone. If the participant has a temporary problem after the preparation, he can send a `Reply` message to the coordinator to get the last message sent by the coordinator again.

Figure 14-5 shows a scenario of a failing transaction. Here participant B returns an `Aborted` message to the coordinator in the prepare phase. Because of this, the coordinator sends a `Rollback` message to all remaining participants so that they can undo their preparation.

A participant has one more option during the prepare phase: If the participant does not want to take part in phase 2, but he also does not want to abort the transaction, he can send a `ReadOnly` message to the coordinator. With this message, the participant is ignored in the outcome of the transaction.

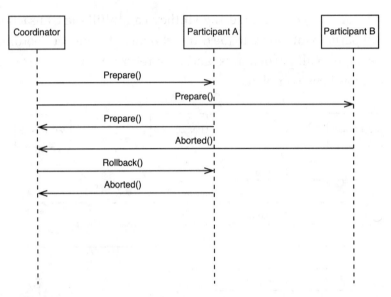

Figure 14-5　Coordinating a failing transaction.

The 2PC protocol comes in two variants: **volatile** and **durable**. The volatile 2PC can be used for volatile resources, such as a cache, whereas the durable 2PC is used for permanent storage, such as databases.

WS-BusinessActivity

Although the WS-AtomicTransaction specification is meant for short-lived transactions that might lock resources, WS-BusinessActivity is meant for long-lived transactions that are known by the name *business activities*. Here no resources should be locked; business activities may span a long time. With a business activity, human interaction, such as manufacturing of some product, might be necessary.

With transactions, a bank account example is often used where money is moved from account A to account B. In reality, this is not a good example of an atomic transaction, because the bank from which the money is moved does not trust the bank to which the money is moved, and the resources are not locked while the money is moved. The bank example is a really good example of a business activity instead. Moving the money from one account to another one can take some time; of course, the bank uses this time to increase its own value. Moving the money from one account to another first reduces the amount from account A, and after a while the amount is added to account B. If the transfer to account B fails, compensation starts, in which the money is moved back to account A. Of course, this compensation may reduce the amount returned because of potential bank charges subtracted. Instead of letting the database do the work to undo the actions, a compensating process can undo the actions.

WS-BusinessActivity defines two protocols: BusinessAgreementWithParticipantCompletion and BusinessAgreementWithCoordinatorCompletion. With the BusinessAgreementWithParticipantCompletion protocol, the participant knows when he has completed all work for the activity; with the BusinessAgreementWith-CoordinatorCompletion protocol, however, the coordinator tells the participant that no more work will be asked of it.

Figure 14-6 shows a successful sequence of a business activity with completion initiated from the coordinator. The coordinator sends the `Complete` message to all participants. With a successful completion, when all work is done for the participant, the participants return the `Completed` message. After all participants return the `Completed` message, the coordinator sends a `Close` message. Upon receipt of the

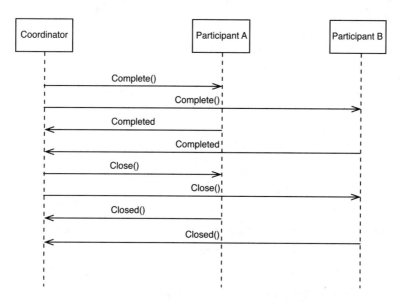

Figure 14-6 Successful BusinessAgreementWithCoordinatorCompletion.

Close message, the participant knows that the complete business activity was successful and that it must return a Closed message.

If the business activity uses the protocol BusinessAgreementWithParticipant-Completion, the result is very similar. The only difference is that the completion process is not initiated with the Complete message from the coordinator, but with the Completed message from the participant.

Figure 14-7 shows a sequence with one participant returning a failure. As in the sequence before, the coordinator initiates the completion sequence with the Complete message that is sent to the participants. Participant B answers with the Fault message rather than the Completed message. The fault is accepted by the Faulted message from the coordinator. The participant that successfully answered with the Completed message now receives the Compensate message from the coordinator. Participant A can now undo the actions done earlier and sends the Compensated message after the undo action is completed.

> ### Comparing Business Activities with Atomic Transactions
>
> An atomic transaction must be completed in a short time span, because with atomic transactions, resources are locked. With business activities, individual tasks can be seen from the outside, because resources are not locked. You begin the process of undoing a business activity action by starting a compensation action.
>
> One activity inside a business activity may be implemented by using atomic transactions.

Security

Security with Web services must cover all the aspects of security discussed thus far with regard to Enterprise Services.[12] Because distributed solutions are accessing services across different organizations more frequently, security with Web services must cover an even broader range of security issues.

Figure 14-8 shows a typical scenario in which a client (requester) invokes a Web service through an intermediary. The intermediary service forwards the request to the target Web service. If you compare the security requirements of this scenario with

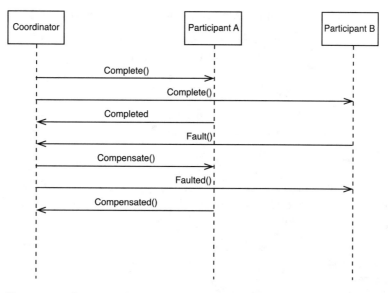

Figure 14-7   Compensating BusinessAgreementWithCoordinatorCompletion.

impersonation and delegation (as shown in Chapter 12, "Security"), this is only one of the issues with the intermediary. The intermediary can do some preprocessing before the request is forwarded, and the intermediary can be hosted by a different organization than the target Web service. This can make it necessary for part of the message that is sent by the requester to be read by the intermediary, whereas the intermediary is not allowed to read the part of the message that is directed to the target Web service. Security must not only be possible with direct connections from the requester to the intermediary and the intermediary to the target Web service, but it must also span the way from the requester to the target Web service.

The base of all security issues is defined with the SOAP Message Security specification, which is in the hands of OASIS.[13] This security specification defines how

Figure 14-8   Using intermediaries.

security token formats (username, X.509 certificates, Kerberos tickets), signature formats, and encryption technologies can be specified with a SOAP message. Listing 14-7 shows an example of how a username can be passed in a SOAP header.

Listing 14-7 Passing a Username in the SOAP Header

```
<soap:Envelope
    xmlns:soap="http://www.w3.org/2001/12/soap-envelope"
    xmlns:wsse="http://schemas.xmlsoap.org/ws/2003/06/secext">
  <soap:Header>
  ...
    <wsse:Security soap:role="" soap:mustUnderstand="true">
      <wsse:UsernameToken>
        <wsse:Username>Ebony</wsse:Username>
      </wsse:UsernameToken>
      ...
    </wsse:Security>
  </soap:Header>
<soap:Envelope>
```

The Enterprise Services features such as authentication, authorization, and secure data transfer are covered by the SOAP Message Security specification for Web services.

Other Web service security specifications extend the specification from OASIS. Here are a few of them:

- **Web Services Trust Language (WS-Trust)**—For a secure communication between two parties, the parties must exchange security credentials. How this is done is defined in the base specification. However, these two parties must trust the security credentials of the other party. Within this specification, it is defined how security tokens can be issued and exchanged and how trust relationships can be established.

- **Web Services Secure Conversation Language (WS-SecureConversation)**—The WS-SecureConversation specification defines how security contexts can be established and how keys can be passed between parties. WS-Secure-Conversation makes use of WS-Trust if a security token service is used.

- **Web Services Federation Language (WS-Federation)**—Federation is about security with different organizations. It is not a good idea for the client system and the Web service system, which are located in different organizations, to be directly responsible for the security between the two parties. Instead, the security should be defined by the two organizations, independent of the systems that take place in the conversation.

Federation servers build up a trust between different organizations that interact. Federation defines terms, keys, and auditing requirements; how the identity can be shared; and how security token exchange occurs.

The specification also defines how attributes between organizations can be shared (for example, by using a UDDI service as an attribute store).

With federation, not every application has to deal with these issues itself.

All these Web service specifications are not useful without an implementation. WSE[14] implements just a few of these specifications; Indigo will implement all the features defined by these specifications.

Indigo

Indigo[15] is an upcoming flexible architecture that replaces technologies such as .NET remoting, ASP.NET Web services, .NET Enterprise Services, DCOM, and WSE. It is planned that this technology will be released in Windows XP and Windows Server 2003 and the upcoming operating system codenamed Longhorn. As of this writing, the plan is to release Indigo a while after .NET 2.0, so this technology is still some ways off in the future. However, it is always good to know what is coming so that you can prepare. After reading this section, you will understand that working with Enterprise Services today will put you in a good position to move to Indigo in the future.

Figure 14-9 shows the main parts of the Indigo architecture: hosting environments, connector, service model, system services, and messaging services.

Hosting Environments

When running a service, you need a host that runs the service. As you can see in Figure 14-9, Indigo is flexible with the hosting environment. Contrary to ASP.NET Web services, which require the ASP.NET runtime for the services, Indigo can run services in ASP.NET, a container, a custom executable, an NT service, or the DllHost process that is used with serviced components.

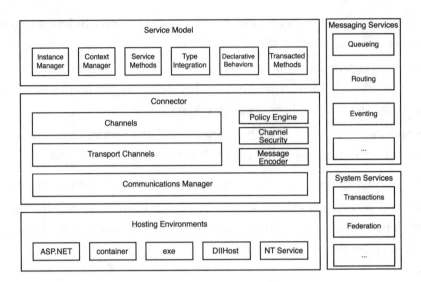

Figure 14-9   Indigo architecture.

The ASP.NET runtime can be used if Web applications take an important role in the solution. The container is a new concept to be introduced with the Longhorn operating system. NT services can be used on systems where IIS is not needed, but the service should be started automatically when the system starts. Custom executables can be used in a peer-to-peer solution. When Windows applications interact directly, they can be a host for Indigo services. Another option is DllHost; this is the process that runs the Enterprise Services application. In the following sections, you will read a lot more about Indigo support for Enterprise Services.

This flexibility is similar to .NET remoting, in that .NET remoting services can run in the same types of applications.

System Services

System services is a block that makes use of .NET 2.0 Framework core features, examples of which are transactions and federation.

System.Transactions[16] is a new namespace with .NET 2.0, with classes you can use to create transactions programmatically. The transactions have automatic support with local, DTC, and WS-AtomicTransaction transactions.

The federation services are used to build up a trust between different organizations so that applications can interact without having to deal with trust issues themselves. This service is an implementation of the specification WS-Federation discussed previously in this chapter.

Connector

The connector represents the core messaging framework of Indigo. Figure 14-10 shows the main parts of the connector: messages, ports, channels, and services.

A **message** is a SOAP envelope that is sent from service to service. The SOAP envelope consists of a SOAP header and a SOAP body, as described earlier. A **service** offers some functionality because it is the target of a message. A service can be accessed via a named entry point: the **port**. Within the port, the message is dispatched through a **channel**.

Examples of protocols that are offered by transport channels are HTTP, TCP, IPC, and SMTP. The channel also defines a specific message exchange pattern, such as request messages that are followed by a reply, or datagram messages that require no reply. Another message exchange pattern is the **dialog channel**. With the dialog channel, reliable delivery can be guaranteed (for example, that the message is received exactly once or that messages are sent in the correct order). Compare this behavior to the Web service specification WS-ReliableMessaging discussed previously in this chapter. The dialog channel is an implementation of this specification.

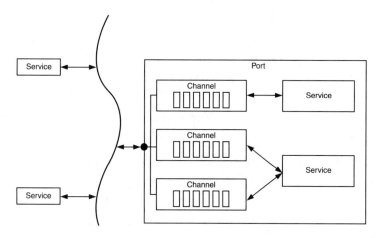

Figure 14-10   Ports, channels, services, and messages.

A channel may add additional processing code (for example, to deal with security and transactions).

Service Model

Applications can make direct use of ports, channels, services, and messages. However, there is one abstraction layer that typically will be the programming interface for service-based applications: the service model (see Figure 14-9). With the service model, a connection between the object-oriented architecture and the service-oriented architecture is made.

With the service model, you get a unification of .NET remoting, ASP.NET Web services, and .NET Enterprise Services. All these technologies put their advantages into the Indigo world.

Indigo gets the services-based approach, interoperability with other platforms through SOAP, and simple configuration from ASP.NET Web services. .NET remoting makes it possible to use features of the Common Language Runtime (CLR) such as stateful objects, events, and a distributed lifetime mechanism across different application domains. The same is possible with Indigo. With .NET Enterprise Services, services that ship with the operating system can easily be used from .NET components by applying attributes. In the code examples to follow, you will see that you can program Indigo in a similar way to .NET Enterprise Services, so the migration should be smooth.

Messaging Services

Figure 14-9 also shows the Messaging Services block that is offered with Indigo. Queuing, routing, and eventing are implementations of Web service specifications discussed previously.

The queuing implementation of Indigo will not replace the full-featured message queuing service; instead, message queuing services will be accessible by Web services, and for some lighter requirements, message queuing services will not be necessary.

The routing implementation will not replace the TCP/IP-level routing for which Cisco routers play a role; instead, routing functionality is added to the application level to define routes in the SOAP header (that is, where the message should go).

Eventing is an implementation of the WS-Eventing specification, which adds a subscription mechanism to Web services. As time continues, other services will be added to this list.

Moving from Enterprise Services to Indigo

In the following examples, you can see how the code will change when you migrate your applications to the Indigo technology.

Listing 14-8 shows the class CourseManagement that derives from Serviced-Component. This class has the attributes [ComponentAccessControl], [Secure-Method], and [Transaction]. This is nothing different from how you have created serviced components so far; the classes and attributes are the same. The only difference you might have already discovered is a new namespace: System.Service-Model.Compat. Using this namespace is the easiest way to move your applications to Indigo.

Listing 14-8   Using Indigo with the Compatibility Mode

```
using System.ServiceModel.Compat;

[ComponentAccessControl]
[SecureMethod]
[Transaction(TransactionOption.Required)]
public class CourseManagement : ServicedComponent
{
    public void CreateCourse(Course course)
    {
        //...
    }
}
```

Going the direct route instead of using the compatibility mode is shown in Listings 14-9 and 14-10.

In Listing 14-9, you can see a contract of a service that is defined with the interface ICourseManagement. The services you need from Indigo are declared using attributes, as you already know from Enterprise Services. The [ServiceContract] attribute marks the interface ICourseManagement as a contract of a service-oriented application. The attribute [OperationBehavior] that is associated with the method

CreateCourse defines transactional requirements with the properties Auto-CompleteTransaction and AutoEnlistTransaction. This is very similar to the transactional attributes used with Enterprise Services.

Listing 14-9   Indigo Service Contracts

```
using System.ServiceModel;

[ServiceContract(Namespace="http://www.thinktecture.com/demos")]
public interface ICourseManagement
{
   [OperationBehavior(
      AutoCompleteTransaction=true,
      AutoEnlistTransaction = true)]
   void CreateCourse(Course course);
}
```

Listing 14-10 shows the implementation of the interface ICourseManagement with the class CourseManagement. The attribute [BindingRequirements] defines what features must be supported by interceptors. In the listing, the properties are set to require transactions and to disallow message queuing. The attribute [Service-Behavior] defines execution behavior. With the property InstanceMode, it can be set if the object should be newly instantiated for every method call (Instance-Mode.PerCall), if the object should be stateful for a client (InstanceMode.PrivateSession), or if the object state should be shared (InstanceMode.Singleton). Concurrency and transaction behavior is defined with the properties Concurrency-Mode and AllowConcurrentTransactions.

Listing 14-10   Indigo Service Class

```
using System.ServiceModel;

[BindingRequirements(
   TransactionFlowRequirements = RequirementsMode.Require,
   QueuedDeliveryRequirements = RequirementsMode.Disallow,
   RequireOrderedDelivery = true
)]
[ServiceBehavior(
   InstanceMode = InstanceMode.PrivateSession,
   ConcurrencyMode = ConcurrencyMode.Single,
   AllowConcurrentTransactions = true
)]
```

```
public class CourseManagement : ICourseManagement
{
    public void CreateCourse(Course course)
    {
        //...
    }
}
```

As you can see from these examples, you get a real unification of .NET remoting, ASP.NET Web services, and .NET Enterprise Services. Of course, you do not have to re-implement your applications at all, because .NET Enterprise Services, .NET remoting, and ASP.NET Web services will still be functional on the upcoming operating system versions. You might also be able to integrate existing applications with new Indigo applications, because Indigo will have a DCOM channel to interact with serviced components directly.

Summary

This chapter examined how Web services technologies map to the technologies that are available with .NET Enterprise Services. Here is a summary of those mappings:

- **Contexts**—WS-Coordination
- **Transactions**—WS-AtomicTransactions
- **Loosely coupled events**—WS-Eventing
- **Queued components**—WS-ReliableMessaging

The concepts of Enterprise Services map to Web services specifications. However, you do not need to worry about building Enterprise Services applications today. As you have seen in the examples in this chapter, programming with Indigo for these services is very similar to Enterprise Services programming, so your migration should be smooth. You might also be able to interact with serviced components directly, because the DCOM protocol will be a supported Indigo channel.

1 The use of this toolkit is covered in Chapter 12.

2 These protocols are discussed in Chapter 5, "Networking."

3 DCE-RPC is the short name for Distributed Computing Environment – Remote Procedure Calls. DCE-RPC was defined by the Open Software Foundation, which was founded as cooperation between different UNIX vendors.

4 In Chapter 12, an example demonstrates how you can use the SOAP header to pass authentication information.

5 You can read about .NET remoting sink providers in the Apress book *Advanced .NET Remoting*.

6 `http://www.w3.org/TR/2002/NOTE-soap12-email-20020626`.

7 Chapter 11, "Loosely Coupled Events," is about loosely coupled events.

8 Message queuing and queued components are discussed in Chapter 10, " Queued Components."

9 COM+ and .NET remoting contexts are discussed in Chapter 2, "Object Activation and Contexts."

10 The DTC and transaction contexts are discussed in Chapter 7.

11 One example is a coordination type that is defined with the specification WS-AtomicTransaction.

12 Security with Enterprise Services is discussed in Chapter 12.

13 OASIS is an international consortium that drives development, convergence, and adoption of e-business standards. See `http://www.oasis-open.org`.

14 WSE is discussed in Chapter 12.

15 The code examples shown in this chapter are based on a preview edition and will change with release of the products. You can download updated samples from `http://www.christiannagel.com/enterpriseservices`.

16 Classes from this namespace are discussed in Chapter 7.

15
Case Study

THE LAST CHAPTER OF THIS BOOK gives an example of a distributed solution with many aspects that have been shown in Chapters 1 through 14. In this chapter, you learn how you can use Enterprise Services in collaboration with Windows and Web applications and Web services (that is, how to put it all together).

This chapter shows portions of a solution[1] that demonstrates how to implement and how to interact with serviced components.

The application that is demonstrated is a course management and a course registration solution for two virtual companies.

Specifically, this chapter covers the following topics:

- Use case—course management
- Sample projects
- CourseManagement.Entities—entity classes
- The `CourseManagement` database
- `CourseManagement.Data`—data access
- `CourseManagement.Control`—serviced components
- `CourseManager`—Windows Forms client
- `CourseRegistrationService`—Web services
- `CourseRegistrationWeb`—Web application
- `CourseRegistration`—queued components

Use Case—Course Management

The example application is a course management application for the virtual company Cool Training. This company offers training for .NET programming in addition to Windows and UNIX and Cisco administration, all in different locations. With the sample application, courses and course dates can be maintained; the sample application also enables customers to register for courses. A Web service is offered that can be accessed by the partners of Cool Training to order course places.

The major use cases for this application are shown in the use case diagram in Figure 15-1. The actors in this solution are the curriculum manager, course admin, sales, customer, and partner. The curriculum manager creates new courses and their descriptions, including the title, prerequisites, topics, and so on. Course admin adds course dates to the course information; that information also includes the price, location, and maximum attendee count.

Customers and partners can place orders for courses by writing attendees to specific course dates. Because some customers still place their order by phone or fax, the same use cases are used by the sales actor, which reacts to phone calls and enters the information into the application.

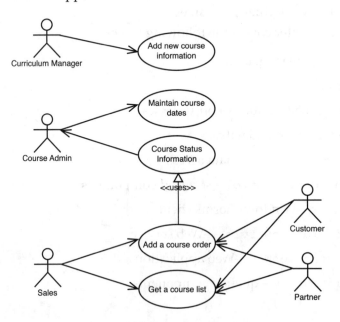

Figure 15-1   Use case diagram.

Figure 15-2 shows the deployment scenario of the course management solution. The Cool Training solution stores the course data in SQL Server, and a business server reads and writes data to the SQL Server. The serviced components running in the business server are accessed from a Windows Forms application on the desk of the sales and the course admin actors.

Partners such as the companies Best Training Offers and Neverland Training have their own Web sites and just include the Cool Training catalog with their offers. For this functionality, a Web service is available that is invoked by the Best Training Offers Web application.

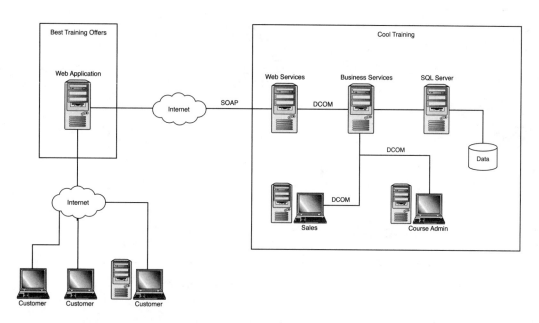

Figure 15-2 Deployment of the course management solution.

Sample Projects

For this solution, different projects have been created. When you download the zip file from the Web, you can extract all the project files and restore the sample database. All the projects for the sample are included with the solution.

Figure 15-3 shows the projects and their dependencies. The projects and their purpose are as follows:

- **CourseManagement.Entities**—CourseManagement.Entities is a component library that contains the entity classes within the course management solution. This library is referenced from many other projects.

- **CourseManagement.Data**—CourseManagement.Data is a component library that contains classes that access the database. This library is used from serviced components.

- **CourseManagement.Control**—CourseManagement.Control is the component library that contains serviced components. Here components are defined that make use of automatic transactions.

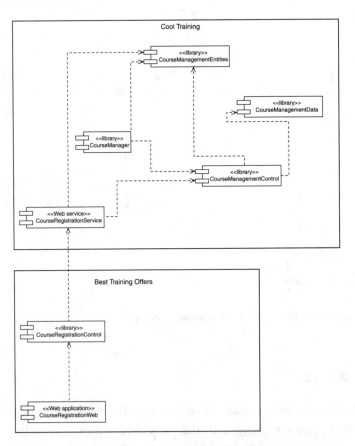

Figure 15-3 Projects (assemblies) with the sample solution.

- **CoursesManager**—CoursesManager is a Windows Forms application that is used by the Cool Training company to manage courses. This executable directly makes use of the Enterprise Services application `CourseManagement.Control`.

- **CourseRegistrationService**—CourseRegistrationService is a Web service that is offered for the partners of Cool Training that makes it possible to register attendees for courses.

- **CourseRegistrationWeb**—The Web application CourseRegistrationWeb is the user interface to make it possible to register for courses. This application is part of the solution of the partner company Best Training Offers.

- **CourseRegistration.Control**—The Web application does not directly access the Web service to register course attendees. Instead, it uses queued components that are implemented in the Enterprise Services application `CourseRegistration.Control`. Thus, the registration succeeds even if the Web service is not available.

After you have extracted the zip file, you must restore the SQL Server sample database from the backup file and create Web applications for the projects `CourseRegistrationWeb` and `CourseRegistrationService`. Then you can open the solution file with Visual Studio.

With the projects, a post-build command is set, so that all binaries are copied to the directory binaries. In this directory, you can also see a `build.bat` file that installs all assemblies in the global assembly cache and registers the Enterprise Services applications.

CourseManagement.Entities — Entity Classes

In the following scenarios, you can see how you can define entity classes. Figure 15-4 shows the major entity classes of the solution. The class `Course` holds the data of a course; the description of the course is in the class `CourseDescription`. For every date for which a course is planned, the `CourseDate` class holds relevant data such as the start date of the course, the location, the maximum attendee count (which depends on the room), the number of days, and the price.

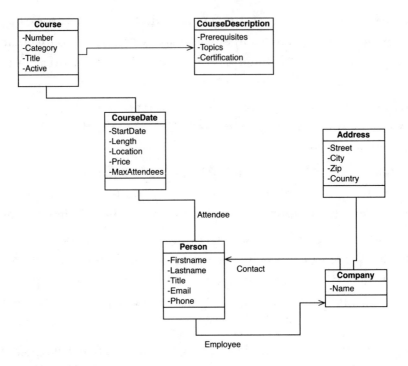

Figure 15-4 Entity classes.

The class `Person` has different roles according to the associations. Persons associated with the `CourseDate` class are attendees of the course. With the `Company` class, a person can be the main contact for the company or just an employee.

Some data is needed for all entity classes. The common information is contained in the base class `Entity` that is shown in Listing 15-1. Common to all entity classes is a GUID, which is used for identification when storing the data in the database, and a timestamp.[2]

The `Entity` class has two constructors. The constructor is declared with the `internal` access modifier and is used when objects are created that are filled with data read from the database; the default constructor with the protected access modifier is used for instantiating new objects that should be written to the database. The internal access modifier only allows instantiating objects from within the same assembly. This restriction prevents developers from using this constructor unintentionally when writing the client application (which is a different assembly).

When storing the entity classes, it proves useful to know whether the data changed, so the Entity class has the properties IsNew and IsModified. The isNew field is set to true when a new entity object is created that was not previously stored in the database. The isModified field is set to true when an object state that must be stored is changed. With the internal constructor, both the isNew and isModified fields are set to false, because the object already exists and is created with data from the database. The protected constructor of the Entity class is used to instantiate new objects, so the isNew field is set to true.

Listing 15-1 Entity Class

```
using System;

namespace CourseManagement.Entities
{
    [Serializable]
    public class Entity
    {
        protected Entity()
        {
            id = Guid.NewGuid();
            timestamp = null;
            isModified = false;
            isNew = true;
        }

        internal Entity(Guid id, byte[] timestamp)
        {
            this.id = id;
            this.timestamp = timestamp;
            isNew = false;
            isModified = false;
        }

        private readonly Guid id;
        public Guid Id
        {
            get
            {
                return id;
            }
        }
    }
```

```csharp
        private readonly byte[] timestamp;
        public byte[] Timestamp
        {
            get
            {
                return timestamp;
            }
        }

        protected bool isModified;
        public bool IsModified
        {
            get
            {
                return isModified;
            }
        }

        protected bool isNew;
        public bool IsNew
        {
            get
            {
                return isNew;
            }
        }
    }
}
```

The Course class is shown in Listing 15-2. This class derives from the base class Entity. Similar to the base class, the constructor with the internal access modifier is used with objects that are created when data is read from the database. The method ToString is overridden from the base class Object, because the string that is returned here is used with data binding to get a default representation of the Course objects. Data binding is used later with the user interface, to display the string representation of the course in the user dialog boxes.

The Course class has properties that represent a course: the course number, title, and category. Because the company Cool Training offers training with different categories, the property Category helps to map a course to a category.

Courses are never deleted when they are no longer in use; instead, the course is set to an inactive state, hence the Active property.

Specific dates of courses can be accessed by using the `CourseDates` property, which returns an `ArrayList` collection of `CourseDate` objects.

Listing 15-2   Course Class

```
using System;
using System.Collections;

namespace CourseManagement.Entities
{
    [Serializable]
    public class Course : Entity
    {
        public Course(Category category)
        {
            this.category = category;
        }

        internal Course(Category category, string number,
                        string title, int length, Guid courseId,
                        byte[] timestamp)
            : base(courseId, timestamp)
        {
            this.category = category;
            this.number = number;
            this.title = title;
            this.defaultLength = length;
        }

        public Course(string number, string title, int length)
        {
            this.number = number;
            this.title = title;
            this.defaultLength = length;
            this.active = true;
        }

        public override string ToString()
        {
            return number + " " + title;
        }


        private string number;
        public string Number
        {
```

```
    get
    {
        return number;
    }
    set
    {
        number = value;
        isModified = true;
    }
}

private string title;
public string Title
{
    get
    {
        return title;
    }
    set
    {
        title = value;
        isModified = true;
    }
}

private bool active;
public bool Active
{
    get
    {
        return active;
    }
    set
    {
        active = value;
        isModified = true;
    }
}

private int defaultLength;
public int DefaultLength
{
    get
    {
        return defaultLength;
    }
```

```
      set
      {
         defaultLength = value;
         isModified = true;
      }
   }

   readonly private Category category;
   public Category Category
   {
      get
      {
         return category;
      }
   }

   private bool isCourseDateAdded = false;
   public bool IsCourseDateAdded()
   {
      return isCourseDateAdded;
   }

   private ArrayList courseDates;
   public ArrayList CourseDates
   {
      get
      {
         return courseDates;
      }
      set
      {
         courseDates = value;
      }
   }

   public void AddCourseDate(CourseDate courseDate)
   {
      courseDates.Add(courseDate);
      isCourseDateAdded = true;
   }
   }
}
```

The other entity classes such as Company, Person, and CourseDate are very similar, so they are not listed here.

Data access classes that are in the assembly CourseManagement.Data instantiate entity objects with the help of the utility class EntityCreator. Here the **factory pattern** is used. The EntityCreator class acts as a factory that instantiates entity objects, and it only has static methods. To make it impossible to create instances of this class, the constructor has the access modifier private.[3]

The static methods CreateCourse and CreateCourseDate make use of the internal constructor of the Course and CourseDate classes to instantiate entity objects. The EntityCreator class is in the same assembly as the Course and CourseDate classes, so the internal constructors can be used.

Listing 15-3 EntityCreator Class

```
using System;

namespace CourseManagement.Entities
{
   public class EntityCreator
   {
      private EntityCreator()
      {
      }

      public static Course CreateCourse(Category category,
            string number, string title, int length,
            Guid courseId, byte[] timestamp)
      {
         return new Course(category, number, title, length,
            courseId, timestamp);
      }

      public static CourseDate CreateCourseDate(Course course,
            DateTime startDate, int length, string location,
            decimal price, int maxAttendees, Guid courseDateId,
            byte[] timestamp)
      {
         return new CourseDate(course, startDate, length,
            location, price, maxAttendees, courseDateId,
            timestamp);
      }
   }
}
```

The CourseManagement Database

The solution uses the database CourseManagement with SQL Server, the tables of which are shown in Figure 15-5. A GUID is used as an identifier for most tables; and for updating data, it is only necessary to compare with the timestamp column to see whether data has changed between the read and the update.

With the database, stored procedures are used to access the data, two of which are shown here. Listing 15-4 is the stored procedure that returns all courses of a specific category. Only the active courses are returned; the inactive courses are useful only for history reports.

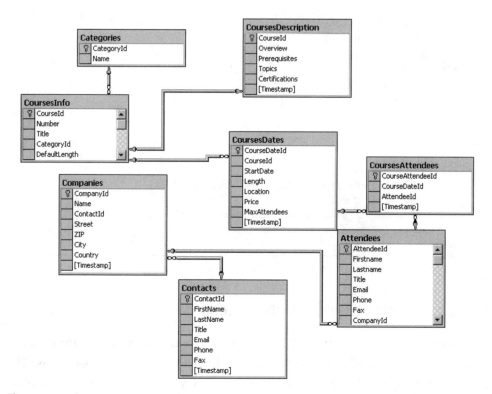

Figure 15-5   CourseManagement database.

Listing 15-4　Stored Procedure GetActiveCoursesByCategory

```
CREATE PROCEDURE GetActiveCoursesByCategory
    (
        @CategoryId char(6)
    )
AS
    SELECT CourseId, Number, Title, DefaultLength, [Timestamp]
    FROM CoursesInfo
    WHERE (Active = 1 and CategoryId = @CategoryId)
    RETURN
```

Listing 15-5 shows the stored procedure `InsertAttendee`, which is used to add a new course attendee to the database.

Listing 15-5　Stored Procedure InsertAttendee

```
CREATE PROCEDURE InsertAttendee
    (
        @AttendeeId UniqueIdentifier,
        @FirstName nvarchar(50),
        @LastName nvarchar(50),
        @Title nchar(10),
        @Email nvarchar(50),
        @Phone nvarchar(50),
        @Fax nvarchar(50),
        @CompanyId UniqueIdentifier
    )
AS
    INSERT INTO Attendees
          (AttendeeId, FirstName, LastName, Title, Email,
           Phone, Fax, CompanyId)
    VALUES (@AttendeeId, @FirstName, @LastName, @Title,
            @Email, @Phone, @Fax, @CompanyId)
    RETURN
```

CourseManagement.Data—Data Access

The classes of the assembly `CourseManagement.Data` are shown in Figure 15-6. For every category of data that is queried or updated in the database, a class exists: The class `CourseData` is used to read and write data from the `Courses` table; the class `CompanyData` reads and writes data from the `Company` table. When reading data

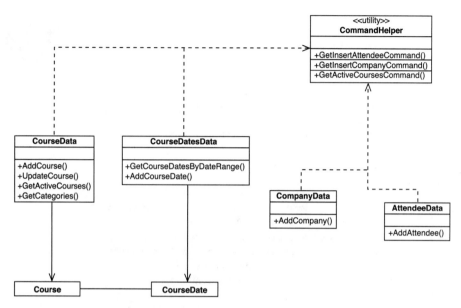

Figure 15-6 Data access classes.

from the database, an entity object is created and returned; when writing data to the database, an entity object is stored. The relationship to the entity objects is shown with the `CourseData` and the `Course` classes.

To maintain the `SqlCommand` objects and their parameters, which are used to invoke the stored procedures, the `CommandHelper` utility class creates and stores the commands.

Listing 15-6 shows an extract of the `CommandHelper` class, a utility class (private constructor) that is only used within the `CourseManagement.Data` assembly (internal access modifier). On the first call of `GetInsertCourseCommand`, the `insertCourseCommand` object is instantiated, and the `SqlCommand` object and parameters that are needed for the stored procedure are defined.

Listing 15-6 CommandHelper Class

```
using System;
using System.Data;
using System.Data.SqlClient;

namespace CourseManagement.Data
{
```

```
internal class CommandHelper
{
    private CommandHelper()
    {
    }

    static private SqlCommand insertCourseCommand;

    static internal SqlCommand GetInsertCourseCommand()
    {
        if (insertCourseCommand == null)
        {
            insertCourseCommand = new SqlCommand();
            insertCourseCommand.CommandText = "AddCourseInfo";
            insertCourseCommand.CommandType =
                    CommandType.StoredProcedure;
            insertCourseCommand.Parameters.Add("@CourseId",
                SqlDbType.UniqueIdentifier);
            insertCourseCommand.Parameters.Add("@Number",
                SqlDbType.NChar, 10);
            insertCourseCommand.Parameters.Add("@Title",
                SqlDbType.NVarChar, 50);
            insertCourseCommand.Parameters.Add("@DefaultLength",
                SqlDbType.Int);
          insertCourseCommand.Parameters.Add("@Active",
                SqlDbType.Bit);
        }
        return insertCourseCommand;
    }

    //...
}
}
```

Listing 15-7 shows a class that reads and writes to the database: `CourseData`. The methods shown here are `AddCourse` and `GetActiveCourses`. `AddCourse` writes a new course to the database; `GetActiveCourses` returns an `ArrayList` of `Course` objects.

A connection string is passed to the constructor of `CourseData` so that it can be used for other method calls on the class. The connection string is passed from the serviced components that define the connection string as a construction string.

For the `AddCourse` method, the utility class `CommandHelper` is used to create the `SqlCommand` object to access the database. `GetInsertCourseCommand` returns a

`SqlCommand` object that has the defined parameters to invoke the respective stored procedure. Now only the parameter values must be filled with the values from the `Course` object. `command.ExecuteNonQuery` invokes the stored procedure.

The implementation of the method `GetActiveCourses` is very similar to the method `AddCourse`; this is just an example to return data read from the database. The `SqlCommand` object that is returned from `CommandHelper.GetActiveCourses-Command` just needs one parameter, but returns records. To read the records, `command.ExecuteReader` is invoked, which returns a `SqlDataReader` used to read record by record in a while loop. The `GetXX` methods return the values of specific columns; these values are used to create a new instance of the `Course` class. The `EntityCreator.CreateCourse` method allows creation of `Course` objects, instantiated with the unique identifier and the timestamp. The new `Course` object is added to an `ArrayList` collection, and finally the complete `ArrayList` containing all `Course` objects is returned from `GetActiveCourses`.

Listing 15-7   CourseData Class

```
using System;
using System.Collections;
using System.Data;
using System.Data.SqlClient;
using CourseManagement.Entities;

namespace CourseManagement.Data
{

    public class CourseData
    {
        private string connectionString;

        public CourseData(string connectionString)
        {
            this.connectionString = connectionString;
        }

        public void AddCourse(Course course)
        {
            SqlConnection connection =
                    new SqlConnection(connectionString);
```

```
    SqlCommand command =
        CommandHelper.GetInsertCourseCommand();

    command.Connection = connection;
    command.Parameters["@CourseId"].Value = course.Id;
    command.Parameters["@Number"].Value = course.Number;
    command.Parameters["@Title"].Value = course.Title;
    command.Parameters["@DefaultLength"].Value =
        course.DefaultLength;
    command.Parameters["@Active"].Value = course.Active;

    connection.Open();
    try
    {
        command.ExecuteNonQuery();
    }
    finally
    {
        connection.Close();
    }
}

public ArrayList GetActiveCourses(Category category)
{
    SqlConnection connection =
        new SqlConnection(connectionString);

    SqlCommand command =
        CommandHelper.GetActiveCoursesCommand();

    command.Connection = connection;
    command.Parameters["@CategoryId"].Value = category.Id;

    connection.Open();
    ArrayList courses = new ArrayList();
    SqlDataReader reader = command.ExecuteReader(
        CommandBehavior.CloseConnection);

    try
    {
        while (reader.Read())
        {
            Guid id = reader.GetGuid(0);
            string number = reader.GetString(1);
            string title = reader.GetString(2);
            int length = reader.GetInt32(3);
            byte[] timestamp = (byte[])reader[4];
            Course c = EntityCreator.CreateCourse(
```

```
                category, number, title, length, id,
                    timestamp);
                courses.Add(c);
            }
        }
        finally
        {
            reader.Close();
        }
        return courses;
    }

    //...
    }
}
```

> **Data Access Application Blocks**
>
> Instead of directly using ADO.NET, you can use the Data Access
> Application Block,[4] which helps reduce your code.

CourseManagement.Control—Serviced Components

This section examines the next project, CourseManagement.Control. This project
contains the serviced components of the Cool Training solution. Figure 15-7 shows
a few of the serviced components: QueryCourseControl, UpdateCourseControl,
and UpdateCourseDateControl. Reading and writing course data is separated into
two different components (QueryCoursecontrol and UpdateCourseControl)
because there are different transactional requirements.[5] Both of these classes, however, make use of the same class CourseData[6] to read and write courses from the
database.

As you can see in the figure, all the serviced component classes implement their
specific interface. UpdateCourseControl also makes use of the serviced component
UpdateCourseDataControl, because it might be necessary to add or update course
dates along with Course objects.

The implementation of UpdateCourseControl is shown in Listing 15-8. The
class UpdateCourseControl implements the interface IUpdateCourse, which

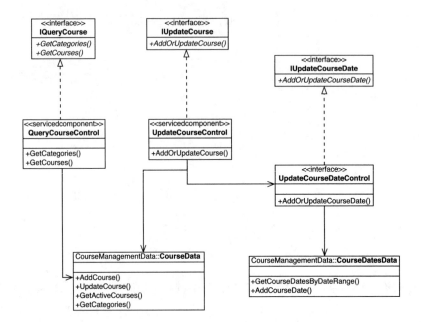

Figure 15-7   Serviced component classes.

defines a single method `AddOrUpdateCourse` that is used to insert or modify a course in the database.

The attributes that are assigned to the class define the transactional behavior of the class (`TransactionOption.Required`), the connection string to the database (`ConstructionEnabled`), and how it is allowed to invoke the methods of the serviced component.

The role `Course Admin` is allowed to add new courses and modify existing ones, whereas the role `Course Assistant` is only allowed to modify courses. Because adding new courses and modifying existing ones is done in the same method, both roles are assigned to the class; inside the implementation, roles other than `Course Admin` are denied access by checking the role with `ContextUtil.Is-CallerIn-Role`. An `UnauthorizedAccessException` is thrown if this is not the case.

The properties `IsNew` and `IsModified` are used to check whether the courses must be added anew or whether existing courses should be modified. This decides whether `courseData.AddCourse` or `courseData.UpdateCourse` is called.

For every course date associated with the course, the serviced component
`UpdateCourseDateControl` does the insert or update of the course date.

Listing 15-8   UpdateCourseControl Class

```
using System;
using System.Collections;
using System.EnterpriseServices;
using CourseManagement.Data;
using CourseManagement.Entities;

namespace CourseManagement.Control
{
    public interface IUpdateCourse
    {
        void AddOrUpdateCourse(Course course);
    }

    [Transaction(TransactionOption.Required)]
    [ConstructionEnabled(true, Default=
        "server=localhost;database=CourseManagement;" +
        "trusted_connection=true")]
    [SecurityRole("Course Admin")]
    [SecurityRole("Course Assistant")]
    [SecureMethod]
    public class UpdateCourseControl : ServicedComponent,
            IUpdateCourse
    {
        private string connectionString;

        protected override void Construct(string s)
        {
            connectionString = s;
        }

        [AutoComplete]
        public void AddOrUpdateCourse(Course course)
        {
            if (course.IsNew)
            {
                if (!ContextUtil.IsCallerInRole("Course Admin"))
                {
                    throw new UnauthorizedAccessException(
                        "You are not allowed to add new courses");
                }
```

```
            CourseData courseData = new CourseData(connectionString);
            courseData.AddCourse(course);
        }
        else if (course.IsModified)
        {
            CourseData courseData = new CourseData(connectionString);
            courseData.UpdateCourse(course);
        }

        if (course.IsCourseDateAdded())
        {
            foreach (CourseDate courseDate in course.CourseDates)
            {
                if (courseDate.IsNew || courseDate.IsModified)
                {
                    using (UpdateCourseDateControl comp =
                        new UpdateCourseDateControl())
                    {
                        comp.AddOrUpdateCourseDate(courseDate);
                    }
                }
            }
        }
    }
}
```

Now take a look at another serviced component class: QueryCourseControl. This class implements the interface IQueryCourse with the methods GetCategories and GetCourses, both of which return an ArrayList object. With GetCategories, the collection returned contains a list of all different course categories; the GetCourses method returns a collection of all courses where the courseSelection can be applied. CourseSelection is a helper class that allows defining with the query what data should be returned (for example, whether courses only for a specific collection should be returned and what date range should be used if the course dates should be returned).

In the implementation of GetCourses, all active courses for the category courseSelection.Category are queried using the data class CourseData. If the course dates should be returned, which is defined with the courseSelection.Get-Dates Boolean property, they are added to each course with the help of the Course-DatesData class.

Listing 15-9   QueryCourseControl Class

```
using System;
using System.Collections;
using System.EnterpriseServices;
using CourseManagement.Data;
using CourseManagement.Entities;

namespace CourseManagement.Control
{
    public interface IQueryCourse
    {
        ArrayList GetCategories();
        ArrayList GetCourses(CourseSelection courseSelection);
    }

    [Transaction(TransactionOption.Supported)]
    [ConstructionEnabled(true, Default=
        "server=localhost;database=CourseManagement;" +
        "trusted_connection=true")]
    [SecurityRole("Course Admin")]
    [SecurityRole("Course Assistant")]
    [SecureMethod]
    public class QueryCourseControl : ServicedComponent, IQueryCourse
    {
        public QueryCourseControl()
        {
        }

        private string connectionString;

        protected override void Construct(string s)
        {
            connectionString = s;
        }

        [AutoComplete]
        public ArrayList GetCategories()
        {
            CourseData data = new CourseData(connectionString);
            return data.GetCategories();
        }

        [AutoComplete]
        public ArrayList GetCourses(CourseSelection courseSelection)
        {
```

```
CourseData courseData = new CourseData(connectionString);
ArrayList courses = courseData.GetActiveCourses(
    courseSelection.Category);

if ((courses.Count >= 1) && (courseSelection.GetDates))
{
    CourseDatesData courseDatesData = new
        CourseDatesData(connectionString);

    foreach (Course course in courses)
    {
        ArrayList courseDates =
            courseDatesData.GetCourseDatesByDateRange(
            course, courseSelection.BeginDate,
            courseSelection.EndDate);
        course.CourseDates = courseDates;
    }
}

return courses;
    }
  }
}
```

Listing 15-10 shows the assembly attributes from the file `assemblyinfo.cs`. The name of the application is set with the attribute class `ApplicationNameAttribute`; the application is configured as a server application with the option `Activation-Option.Server`. With the attribute `[SecurityRole]`, the roles that are created with the application are defined.

Listing 15-10   Assembly Attributes

```
[assembly: AssemblyDelaySign(false)]
[assembly: AssemblyKeyFile("../../../../coursekey.snk")]
[assembly: AssemblyKeyName("")]

[assembly: ApplicationName("Course Management")]
[assembly: Description("Sample Application")]
[assembly: ApplicationActivation(ActivationOption.Server)]

[assembly: SecurityRole("Partner", true)]
[assembly: SecurityRole("Course Admin")]
[assembly: SecurityRole("Course Assistant")]
```

```
[assembly: SecurityRole("Sales")]
[assembly: ApplicationAccessControl(true, AccessChecksLevel=
        AccessChecksLevelOption.ApplicationComponent)]
```

CourseManager—Windows Forms Client

The Windows Forms application that deals with adding new course dates is shown in Figure 15-8. The user interface is just a simple one to demonstrate the task and not to distract from the relevant code.

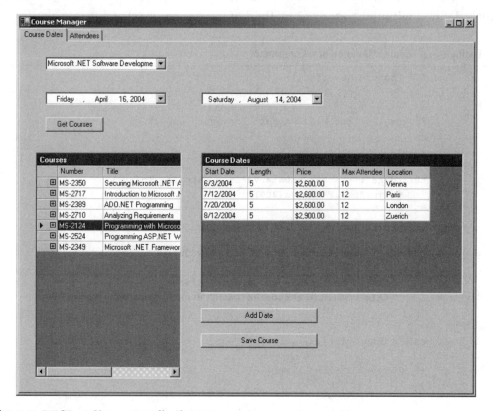

Figure 15-8   CourseManager application.

At the top in the user interface, you can see a ComboBox control where a course category can be selected. Two DateTimePicker controls set a date range for the course dates to be shown. In Listing 15-11, you can see that the second DateTimePicker control by default is set to a day 200 days from now. The default value of the first DateTimePicker control is set to today.

Two DataGrid controls are used to show the courses and course dates. The form also has three buttons to query for the courses (Get Courses), to add course dates (Add Date), and to save a course and its dates (Save Course).

When the application is started, the course categories are returned from the QueryCourseControl serviced component (see Listing 15-11). The returned course categories are assigned to the DataSource property of the ComboBox comboBox-Categories, so the combo box lists all categories. What is shown inside the combo box is defined with the ToString method of the Category struct.

Listing 15-11   CourseManagerForm Constructor

```
public CourseManagerForm()
{
    //
    // Required for Windows Form Designer support
    //
    InitializeComponent();

    this.dateTimePickerEndDate.Value = DateTime.Today +
        TimeSpan.FromDays(200);

    try
    {
        using (QueryCourseControl cc = new QueryCourseControl())
        {
            this.categories = cc.GetCategories();
            this.comboBoxCategories.DataSource = this.categories;
        }
    }
    catch (Exception ex)
    {
        MessageBox.Show(ex.Message);
    }
}
```

The method `OnGetCourses` (Listing 15-12) is the `Click` event handler for the Get Courses button. First the selected course category is needed, which is read from the combo box with `comboBoxCategories.SelectedItem`. The property `Selected-Item` returns the object from the collection that is associated with the selected item; in this case, the object is of type `Category`.

The returned category is used with the `QueryCourseControl` class to get all courses for this category within the date range set with the `DateTimePicker` controls. The returned array is set to the `DataSource` property of the datagrid `data-GridCourses`.

To define which columns should be shown in the datagrid, you can use the `TableStyles` collection of the `DataGrid` to define the mapping between the columns to the properties of the classes.

Datagrid Mapping to Array Lists

To assign the table mapping style—using datasets—set the `MappingName` of the `DataGridTableStyle` to the table inside the dataset. This is different with other sources of data. To use the `TableStyles` mapping with an array list, the `MappingName` must to be set to the type name `ArrayList`.

To map the columns of the datagrid to custom objects in the array list, set the `MappingName` of the `GridColumnStyle` to the name of the property of the class (for example, `Title` or `Number` for the `Course` class).

Listing 15-12   Get Courses

```
private void OnGetCourses(object sender, System.EventArgs e)
{
    Category category =
        (Category)this.comboBoxCategories.SelectedItem;

    using (QueryCourseControl cc = new QueryCourseControl())
    {
        courses = cc.GetCourses(
```

```
        CourseSelection.ByCategoryAndDates(category,
            dateTimePickerStartDate.Value,
            dateTimePickerEndDate.Value));

    this.dataGridCourses.DataSource = courses;
}
}
```

Listing 15-13 shows the OnSelectCourse method that is the handler of the Click event from the datagrid dataGridCourses. When a course is selected, this method is called to display all course dates associated with the course.

The selected course is calculated with the row index of the datagrid, and then the CourseDates property of this course is set to the DataSource of the second datagrid dataGridCourseDates, so that all dates are shown. The mapping with the second datagrid is done in a similar way to the mapping of the first datagrid.

Listing 15-13   Selection of a Course

```
private void OnSelectCourse(object sender, System.EventArgs e)
{
    string courseNumber = (string)this.dataGridCourses[
        this.dataGridCourses.CurrentRowIndex, 0];
    Course selectedCourse = (Course)courses[
        this.dataGridCourses.CurrentRowIndex];
    this.dataGridCourseDates.DataSource =
        selectedCourse.CourseDates;
}
```

The user of the application can add course dates by clicking the button Add Date, the Click event handler of which is shown in Listing 15-14, OnAddDate. Similar to Listing 15-13, the current selected course is selected from the datagrid dataGrid-Courses. A new form AddDateForm is shown to the user, enabling him to enter the data for the new data, such as the start date, the location, the maximum attendee count, and so on. When the user clicks the OK button, the course date is added to the course via the AddCourseDate method.

Listing 15-14   Adding a Course Date

```
private void OnAddDate(object sender, System.EventArgs e)
{
```

```
    Course selectedCourse =
        (Course)courses[this.dataGridCourses.CurrentRowIndex];

    AddDateForm form = new AddDateForm(selectedCourse);
    if (form.ShowDialog() == DialogResult.OK)
    {
        selectedCourse.AddCourseDate(form.CourseDate);
        this.dataGridCourseDates.DataSource = null;
        this.dataGridCourseDates.DataSource =
            selectedCourse.CourseDates;
    }
}
```

Listing 15-15 shows the handler for the `Click` event from the Save Course button: `OnSaveCourses` (see Listing 15-8). Here the serviced component `UpdateCourseControl` is used to save the course changes (including the added dates) to the database.

Listing 15-15   Saving Courses and Dates

```
private void OnSaveCourses(object sender, System.EventArgs e)
{
    Course selectedCourse =
        (Course)courses[this.dataGridCourses.CurrentRowIndex];
    using (UpdateCourseControl cc = new UpdateCourseControl())
    {
        cc.AddOrUpdateCourse(selectedCourse);
    }
}
```

CourseRegistrationService—Web Services

For the partner companies, such as Best Training Offers and Neverland Training, a Web service is offered. The Web service does not have methods that deal with adding courses and course dates because this is not a service for the partners. Instead, the Web service has methods that deal with course queries and adding of attendees.

The project type for the Web service is an ASP.NET Web service.

Listing 15-16 shows the types that are defined for the Web service. These types differ from the entity classes defined in Listing 15-2 because the data offered for the partners differs from the data contained in the entity classes. With the data types for the Web service, only the XML representation is needed, so it is okay to have all fields defined with the `public` access modifier.

The types `Course` and `CourseDate` are used for the method `GetCourses`, and the types `CourseRegistration`, `Company`, and `Person` are used for the method `RegisterCourse`.

Listing 15-16   Defined Types for the Web Service

```
[XmlType(Namespace=
    "http://christiannagel.com/2005/04/CourseManagement/Types")]
public class Course
{
    public string Number;
    public string Title;
    public CourseDate[] CourseDates;
}

[XmlType(Namespace=
    "http://christiannagel.com/2005/04/CourseManagement/Types")]
public class CourseDate
{
    public Guid CourseDateId;
    public int Length;
    public string Location;
    public decimal Price;
    public DateTime StartDate;
}

[XmlType(Namespace=
    "http://christiannagel.com/2005/04/CourseManagement/Types")]
public class CourseRegistration
{
    public Guid CourseDateId;
    public Person[] Attendees;
    public Company Company;
    public Person Contact;
}

[XmlType(Namespace=
```

```
      "http://christiannagel.com/2005/04/CourseManagement/Types")]
public class Company
{
    public string Name;
    public string Street;
    public string ZIP;
    public string City;
    public string Country;
}

[XmlType(Namespace=
    "http://christiannagel.com/2005/04/CourseManagement/Types")]
public class Person
{
    public string FirstName;
    public string LastName;
    public string Title;
    public string Email;
    public string Phone;
    public string Fax;
}
```

The Web service method `GetCourses` is shown in Listing 15-17. This method returns a `Course` array and requires a string for the category ID as an argument. The attribute `[XmlElement("Category")]` is applied to the argument so that in the XML representation, the argument shows up as `Category`.

With the `Course` array, `CourseDate` types are included. The attribute `[XmlInclude]` is used to allow the SOAP request to include the `Course` and `CourseDate` data types.

With the implementation of the Web service method, the serviced component `QueryCourseControl` is used to get an `ArrayList` of all courses returned. The helper method `GetCourseArray` converts the `ArrayList` object to a simple `Course` array type that is returned from the Web service.

Listing 15-17   Web Service Method GetCourses

```
[WebMethod]
[XmlInclude(typeof(Course))]
[XmlInclude(typeof(CourseDate))]
[return: XmlArrayItem("Course")]
[return: XmlArray("CoursesList")]
```

```
public Course[] GetCourses([XmlElement("Category")]
    string categoryId)
{
  ArrayList coursesCollection = null;
  DateTime beginDate = DateTime.Today;
  DateTime endDate = DateTime.Today + TimeSpan.FromDays(200);

  using (QueryCourseControl queryControl =
      new QueryCourseControl())
  {
    Entities.Category category = new Entities.Category();
    category.Id = categoryId;
    coursesCollection = queryControl.GetCourses(
        CourseSelection.ByCategoryAndDates(
        category, beginDate, endDate));
  }

  return GetCourseArray(coursesCollection);
}
```

NOTE: Creating an Alias with the Using Directive

With the Web service implementation, the `Course` class from the `CourseManagement.Entities` namespace is used in addition to the `Course` class from the `CourseManagement.Registration-Service` namespace. To avoid compiler errors that might result from an ambiguity (that is, it is not clear which class to use), you can add the namespace.

To avoid writing the long namespace name, you can create an alias for the namespace with the `using` directive:

`using Entities = CourseManagement.Entities;`

Now the `Course` class from the namespace `Course-Management.Entities` can be used as `Entities.Course`.

Listing 15-18 shows the Web service method `RegisterCourse`, which receives a `CourseRegistration` parameter and invokes the serviced component `Register-CourseControl`. The helper method `GetCourseRegistrationInformation` converts the types received from the Web service to the entity classes.

Listing 15-18   Web Service Method RegisterCourse

```
[WebMethod]
[XmlInclude(typeof(CourseRegistration))]
[XmlInclude(typeof(Company))]
[XmlInclude(typeof(Person))]
public void RegisterCourse(CourseRegistration
      courseRegistration)
{
   Entities.Company company;
   Entities.Person[] attendees;
   GetCourseRegistrationInformation(courseRegistration,
         out company, out attendees);

   using (RegisterCourseControl registerCourse =
         new RegisterCourseControl())
   {
      registerCourse.AddCourseRegistration(company,
            attendees);
   }
}
```

CourseRegistrationWeb—Web Application

The partners Web site uses a simple ASP.NET Web application. In the sample projects, this project has the name CourseRegistrationWeb.

This Web application has two pages: CourseList.aspx and Register-Course.aspx. With the page CourseList.aspx, all courses for the category .NET Software Development and their dates are listed. After a course date is selected, the page RegisterCourse.aspx displays.

Figure 15-9 shows the first page, CourseList.aspx, which is implemented with two DataGrid controls.

Similar to Windows Forms applications, the datagrid with Web Forms can be bound to a normal array. By using a custom binding expression, you can bind the elements in template columns to the properties of the classes contained in the array. With Visual Studio, you can enter the binding expression by selecting the label in the Template Editor and then selecting the DataBindings property in the Property Editor. The binding expression to bind the Number property of the Course class is shown here:

```
((CourseRegistrationWeb.CourseServices.Course)
       Container.DataItem).Number
```

Listing 15-19 shows the helper class `CacheControl`. The method `GetCourses` uses the Web service to get all courses for the category `SWNET`. Because the course list does not change often and it is needed for the complete Web application, it is stored in the ASP.NET cache object.[7] Therefore, if the course list is already stored in the cache object, it is returned from the cache. If it is not stored in the cache object, the Web service `RegistrationService` is accessed to get the course list; the course list is written to the cache and returned from the method.

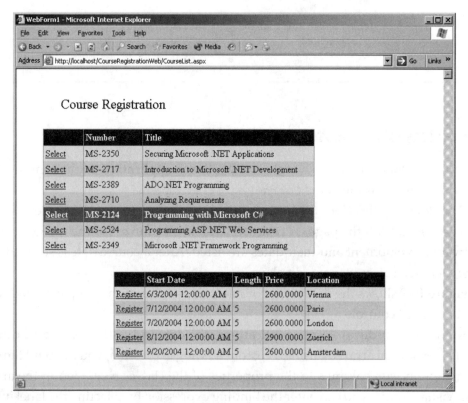

Figure 15-9   Course registration Web application.

Listing 15-19   Helper Class CacheControl

```
public class CacheControl
{
    private CacheControl()
    {
    }

    public static Course[] GetCourses()
    {
        Course[] courses = null;
        object oCourses = HttpContext.Current.Cache["Courses"];
        if (oCourses == null)
        {
            RegistrationService ws = new RegistrationService();
            courses = ws.GetCourses("SWNET");
            HttpContext.Current.Cache.Add("Courses", courses,
                null, DateTime.MaxValue, TimeSpan.FromMinutes(360),
                System.Web.Caching.CacheItemPriority.Normal,
                null);

            HttpContext.Current.Trace.Write("CourseManagement",
                "Read courses from Web");
        }
        else
        {
            courses = (Course[])oCourses;
            HttpContext.Current.Trace.Write("CourseManagement",
                "Read courses from Cache");
        }
        return courses;
    }
}
```

Listing 15-20 shows the Page_Load handler method of the Web page
CourseList.aspx. Here the courses are read with help of the class CacheControl.
The method GetCourses returns an array of Course objects that are used as a
DataSource of the datagrid dataGridCourses and the DataBind method called to
initiate binding.

Listing 15-20   CourseList.aspx—Page_Load

```
private void Page_Load(object sender, System.EventArgs e)
{
    courses = CacheControl.GetCourses();

    this.dataGridCourses.DataSource = courses;
    this.dataGridCourses.DataBind();
}
```

The datagrid `dataGridCourses` has the method `OnSelectCourse` registered for the `SelectedIndexChanged` event, as shown in Listing 15-21. When a course is selected in the first datagrid, the second datagrid is bound to the course dates of the course. Compare the implementation of this method to the Windows Forms method that was shown in Listing 15-13.

Listing 15-21   CourseList.aspx—OnSelectCourse

```
private void OnSelectCourse(object sender, System.EventArgs e)
{
    Course selectedCourse = (Course)courses[
        this.dataGridCourses.SelectedIndex];
    this.dataGridCourseDates.DataSource =
        selectedCourse.CourseDates;
    this.dataGridCourseDates.DataBind();
}
```

The second datagrid, `dataGridCourseDates`, has the method `OnRegisterCourse` (see Listing 15-22) registered for the `SelectedIndexChanged` event. This method does a server-side transfer to the second page, `RegisterCourse.aspx`. The second page needs some information from the first page, so this information is passed inside the HTTP context by storing context items `SelectedCourse` and `Selected-CourseDates`. The method `Server.Transfer` immediately transfers the request to the new page without going back to the client.

Listing 15-22   CourseList.aspx—OnRegisterCourse

```
private void OnRegisterCourse(object sender, System.EventArgs e)
{
    // Get selected course and course dates
    Course selectedCourse = (Course)courses[
        this.dataGridCourses.SelectedIndex];
```

```
CourseDate selectedCourseDate = (CourseDate)
    selectedCourse.CourseDates[
        this.dataGridCourseDates.SelectedIndex];

// Store context information for the next page
HttpContext.Current.Items.Add("SelectedCourse",
    selectedCourse);
HttpContext.Current.Items.Add("SelectedCourseDate",
    selectedCourseDate);

// do a server side transfer to the page RegisterCourse.aspx
Server.Transfer("RegisterCourse.aspx");
}
```

In the page RegisterCourse.aspx, the user can enter information about the company, the contact person, and a course attendee. The registration request is started with the OnRegister method shown in Listing 15-23. In this method, objects are created that are initialized with the data from the Web page; all this information is contained in the CourseRegistration[6] object. Then the course registration request is sent.

Because the Web application should be available in cases when the Web service cannot be reached and when we do not want to wait until the Web service method has completed, queued components[9] are used. The implementation of the queued component is shown in the next section; calling the queued component is shown here.

The queued component requires the complete registration information as an XML string, which is created with StringWriter and XmlSerializer. For these two classes, the namespaces System.IO and System.Xml.Serialization must be imported.

With the queue moniker that is instantiated using Marshal.BindToMoniker, the recorder is instantiated to send the data of the method call RegisterCourse to the message queue.

Listing 15-23   RegisterCourse.aspx—OnRegister Method

```
private void OnRegister(object sender, System.EventArgs e)
{
    // create objects for serialization
    Company company = new Company();
```

```csharp
company.Name = textCompany.Text;
company.Country = textCountry.Text;
company.City = textCity.Text;
company.Street = textStreet.Text;

Person contact = new Person();
contact.FirstName = textContactFirstName.Text;
contact.LastName = textContactLastName.Text;
contact.Title = textContactTitle.Text;
contact.Email = textContactEmail.Text;
contact.Phone = textContactPhone.Text;
contact.Fax = textContactFax.Text;

Person attendee = new Person();
attendee.FirstName = textAttendeeFirstName.Text;
attendee.LastName = textAttendeeLastName.Text;
attendee.Title = textAttendeeTitle.Text;
attendee.Email = textAttendeeEmail.Text;

CourseRegistration courseRegistration =
     new CourseRegistration();
courseRegistration.Company = company;
courseRegistration.Contact = contact;
Guid selectedCourseId =
     new Guid((string)ViewState["selectedCourseId"]);
courseRegistration.CourseDateId = selectedCourseId;
courseRegistration.Attendees = new Person[1];
courseRegistration.Attendees[0] = attendee;

// serialize the course registration to an XML string
StringWriter writer = new StringWriter();
XmlSerializer ser =
     new XmlSerializer(typeof(CourseRegistration));
ser.Serialize(writer, courseRegistration);
string xmlCourseRegistration = writer.ToString();

// submit course registration using a QC moniker
string progid =
     "Registration.Control.CourseRegistrationControl";
IQueueableCourseRegistration qc =
     (IQueueableCourseRegistration)
     Marshal.BindToMoniker("queue:/new:" + progid);

qc.RegisterCourse(xmlCourseRegistration);

Marshal.ReleaseComObject(qc);
}
```

CourseRegistration—Queued Component

The Web application of Best Training Offers is a queued component used to invoke the Web service from Cool Training. The implementation of the queued component is shown in Listing 15-24.

The interface `IQueueableCourseRegistration` is marked with the attribute `[InterfaceQueuing]`. The method `RegisterCourse` has a string parameter that is queuable.

The class `CourseRegistrationControl` implements the interface `IQueueable-CourseRegistration`. In the implementation of `RegisterCourse`, the XML string contained in the `xmlCourseRegistration` parameter is converted to a `Course-Registration` object by using XML deserialization. The `CourseRegistration` object is then used to invoke the method `RegisterCourse` of the Web service. If an exception is thrown, retries are done automatically via the queuing mechanism.

Listing 15-24   CourseRegistrationControl

```
using System;
using System.IO;
using System.Xml;
using System.Xml.Serialization;
using System.EnterpriseServices;
using Registration.Control.CourseServices;

namespace Registration.Control
{
    [InterfaceQueuing]
    public interface IQueueableCourseRegistration
    {
        void RegisterCourse(string xmlCourseRegistration);
    }


    [JustInTimeActivation(true)]
    public class CourseRegistrationControl : ServicedComponent,
        IQueueableCourseRegistration
    {
        public CourseRegistrationControl()
        {
        }

        [AutoComplete]
```

```
public void RegisterCourse(string xmlCourseRegistration)
{
    // deserialize the course registration information,
    // and invoke the Web service to register the course

    StringReader reader = new StringReader(xmlCourseRegistration);
    XmlSerializer ser =
        new XmlSerializer(typeof(CourseRegistration));
    CourseRegistration courseRegistration =
        (CourseRegistration)ser.Deserialize(reader);
    reader.Close();

    RegistrationService ws = new RegistrationService();
    ws.RegisterCourse(courseRegistration);
}
}
}
```

Listing 15-25 shows the attributes for the application of the queued component. To read messages from the queue, the attribute [ApplicationQueuing] is set.

Listing 15-25   Application Attributes for the CourseRegistration.Control Application

```
[assembly: ApplicationName("Course Registration")]
[assembly: Description("Best Training Offer - Course Registration")]
[assembly: ApplicationActivation(ActivationOption.Server)]
[assembly: ApplicationAccessControl(false)]
[assembly: ApplicationQueuing(Enabled=true, QueueListenerEnabled=true)]
```

Summary

In this chapter, you have seen a sample application covering component libraries accessing SQL Server stored procedures, serviced components with transactional attributes, a Windows Forms application that accesses the serviced components, a Web service that is used as an entry door for the partners, a Web application that makes use of the Web service, and a second Enterprise Services application with queued components that is used to access the Web service in a disconnected manner.

You can consider the sample application in more detail, but this chapter has covered most of the important issues. The sample application is not complete. The user interfaces could be improved, and more methods could be implemented with the components. However, such fine-tuning does not differ much from what you learned in this chapter; you just have to do it.

You can also think about extending the application with more features (for example, creating history reports for course attendees, login functionality for the Web application, registration for multiple courses, and so on).

Final Thoughts

I hope you enjoyed the journey through the technologies discussed in this book, and enjoyed and learned from the various tasks herein.

Throughout this book, you have learned how to develop and use serviced components by maximizing the functionality of .NET Enterprise Services and related technologies. .NET Enterprise Services technologies have a long history in the IT world and a promising future. As you learned in the last part of this book, the technology will soon evolve into a technology known as Indigo (and you will be prepared because of your in-depth understanding of Enterprise Services).

To get more information and updated examples for this book, visit my Web site at `http://www.christiannagel.com/EnterpriseServices`. Feedback is welcome!

1 You can download the complete solution from the Web site `http://www.christiannagel.com/enterpriseservices`.

2 As discussed in Chapter 6, "Data Access," GUIDs and timestamps help with disconnected scenarios.

3 With .NET 2.0, you can use the `static` keyword as a class modifier to define a utility class that cannot be instantiated. The compiler checks that there are no instance methods with this class.

4 You can download the Data Access Application Block from the MSDN Web site: `http://msdn.microsoft.com/library/default.asp?url=/library/en-us/dnbda/html/daab-rm.asp`.

5 When using services without components, you can define transactional requirements within the method level, as discussed in Chapter 7, "Transaction Services."

6 The class `CourseData` was discussed in the previous section, because this class is in the assembly `CourseManagement.Data`.

7   The ASP.NET cache is discussed in Chapter 9, "State Management."

8   The `CourseRegistration` class is shown in Listing 15-15.

9   Queued components are covered in Chapter 10, "Queued Components."

Further Reading

NOW THAT YOU HAVE COMPLETED this book and have been introduced to all the technologies and functionalities discussed herein, you might want to expand on your understanding of some of the concepts covered in this book. Although many worthy books on related topics are on the market, you certainly cannot go wrong with the following titles (some of which you might be familiar with from footnotes within this book):

- *Professional C#*, 4th Edition, by Christian Nagel et al. (Wrox Press, 2005).

- *.NET Web Services: Architecture and Implementation*, by Keith Ballinger (Addison-Wesley, 2003).

- *Advanced .NET Remoting*, 2nd Edition, by Ingo Rammer and Mario Szpuszta (Apress, 2005).

- *Essential ASP.NET with Examples in C#*, by Fritz Onion (Addison-Wesley, 2003).

- *Pro .NET 1.1 Network Programming*, 2nd Edition, by Christian Nagel et al. (Apress, 2004).

- *Essential .NET Volume 1: The Common Language Runtime*, by Don Box with Chris Sells (Addison-Wesley, 2003).

- *Windows Forms Programming in C#*, by Chris Sells (Addison-Wesley, 2004).

- *Pragmatic ADO.NET: Data Access for the Internet World*, by Shawn Wildermuth (Addison-Wesley, 2003).

- *Transactional COM+: Building Scalable Communications*, by Tim Ewald (Addison-Wesley, 2001).

- *Patterns of Enterprise Application Architecture*, by Martin Fowler (Addison-Wesley, 2003).

- *Essential ADO.NET*, by Bob Beauchemin (Addison-Wesley, 2002).

- *.NET and COM: The Complete Interoperability Guide*, by Adam Nathan (Sams, 2002).

- *Building Secure Microsoft ASP.NET Applications: Authentication, Authorization, and Secure Communication* (Microsoft Press, 2003).

- *Writing Secure Code*, 2nd Edition, by Michael Howard and David LeBlanc (Microsoft Press, 2003).

Index

Symbols

2PC (two-phase commit) protocol,
456-458

A

abort bit (transactions), 250
abstraction, 10
access checks, 45
  enabling, 407-408
access control
  defining roles (authorization), 410-413
  for message queues, configuring, 333
access control lists (ACLs), 388
access speed of state, 291
accessing. *See also* **data access**
  ASP.NET state from serviced
    components, 310-311
  serviced components
    DCOM, 162-171
    SOAP services (.NET remoting),
      172-190
    Web services, 192-199
ACID (atomicity, consistency,
  isolation, durability), 238
acknowledge messages, 330
  WS-ReliableMessaging, 451
ACLs (access control lists), 388
Activate method, overriding, 66
activation service, 453

Active Directory, state management,
  296-297
Active Directory Integration option
  (message queuing server
  installation), 326
Active Template Library (ATL), 156
activities, 17, 38, 96-98
  selecting synchronization options, 108
  services without components, 109
    Activity class, 110
    example, 112-116
    ServiceConfig class, 110
    ServiceDomain class, 109
    winin serviced components, 116
  stateful components, 109
  synchronization domain, 97
Activity class, 110
  methods, 112
admin components, 436-441
administration
  Component Services tool, 23
  queues, 329
  tools for message queuing, 331-334
ADO.NET
  datasets, 222
    filling, 224-228
    tables in, 224
    updating, 228-233
  overview, 203-206
affinity of state, 291

THIS BOOK IS SAFARI ENABLED

INCLUDES FREE 45-DAY ACCESS TO THE ONLINE EDITION

The Safari® Enabled icon on the cover of your favorite technology book means the book is available through Safari Bookshelf. When you buy this book, you get free access to the online edition for 45 days.

Safari Bookshelf is an electronic reference library that lets you easily search thousands of technical books, find code samples, download chapters, and access technical information whenever and wherever you need it.

TO GAIN 45-DAY SAFARI ENABLED ACCESS TO THIS BOOK:

- Go to **http://www.awprofessional.com/safarienabled**
- Complete the brief registration form
- Enter the coupon code found in the front of this book on the "Copyright" page

If you have difficulty registering on Safari Bookshelf or accessing the online edition, please e-mail customer-service@safaribooksonline.com.